PENGUIN REFERENCE BOOKS

The Penguin Dictionary of
LANGUAGE

David Crystal was born in 1941 and spent the early years of his life in Holyhead, North Wales. He went to St Mary's College, Liverpool, and University College London, where he read English and obtained his Ph.D. in 1966. He became lecturer in linguistics at University College, Bangor, and from 1965 to 1985 was at the University of Reading, where he was Professor of Linguistic Science for several years. He is currently Honorary Professor of Linguistics at the University of Wales, Bangor. His research interests are mainly in English language studies, and he has been much involved with the clinical and remedial applications of linguistics in the study of language handicap.

David Crystal has published numerous articles and reviews, and his books include *Linguistics* (Penguin 1971, second edition 1985), *Child Language Learning and Linguistics, Introduction to Language Pathology, A Dictionary of Linguistics and Phonetics, Clinical Linguistics, Profiling Linguistic Disability, Who Cares About English Usage?* (Penguin 1984), *Listen To Your Child* (Penguin 1986), *Rediscover Grammar, The English Language* (Penguin 1988), *The Cambridge Encyclopedia of Language, Pilgrimage, The Cambridge Encyclopedia of the English Language, English as a Global Language* and *Language Play* (Penguin 1998). He is also the editor of the Cambridge family of general encyclopedias.

David Crystal now lives in Holyhead, where he works as a writer, lecturer and consultant on language and linguistics, and a reference books editor. He is also a frequent radio broadcaster. In June 1995 he was awarded the OBE.

The Penguin Dictionary of
LANGUAGE

David Crystal

SECOND EDITION

PENGUIN BOOKS

PENGUIN BOOKS

Published by the Penguin Group
Penguin Books Ltd, 27 Wrights Lane, London W8 5TZ, England
Penguin Putnam Inc., 375 Hudson Street, New York, New York 10014, USA
Penguin Books Australia Ltd, Ringwood, Victoria, Australia
Penguin Books Canada Ltd, 10 Alcorn Avenue, Toronto, Ontario, Canada M4V 3B2
Penguin Books (NZ) Ltd, Private Bag 102902, NSMC, Auckland, New Zealand

Penguin Books Ltd, Registered Offices: Harmondsworth, Middlesex, England

First published as *An Encyclopedic Dictionary of Language and Languages* by Blackwell 1992
Published in Penguin Books 1994
Second edition published under the present title 1999
4

Set in 7.5/10.5 pt ITC Stone Serif
Typeset by Rowland Phototypesetting Ltd, Bury St Edmunds, Suffolk
Printed in England by Clays Ltd, St Ives plc

PREFACE

The motivation for this book came from my sense of an increasing gap between the questions about language which people routinely ask and the availability of information in existing reference books on the subject. Typical of these questions are 'How many people speak Spanish?', 'What language do they speak in Ukraine?', and 'How do you pronounce Xhosa?'. In preparing the first edition, in 1991–2, I recall being asked about the meaning of such terms as Nostratic, LINC, dyslexia, glossolalia, and creole. Looking for a convenient one-stop source which would quickly give a basic answer to such questions, I was surprised to find nothing. A good dictionary might provide a basic definition, but usually in a highly compressed manner, and without the amplification which many of these terms need if one is to be sure of their use. An encyclopedia, on the other hand, tends to exclude terminology.

My own previous writing in this domain was not much help. My *Cambridge Encyclopedia of Language* covered the right domain, but its thematic structure meant that information on a particular topic (such as Polish) was spread in various places, and pronunciations were not given. My *Dictionary of Linguistics and Phonetics* was alphabetical, but focused exclusively on the more specialized vocabulary found in those subjects. It explicitly excluded the linguistic terminology of such areas as language teaching and learning, speech therapy, stylistics, desk-top publishing, philology, traditional grammar, writing systems, language names, and the many everyday notions which relate to the use of language.

The present book tries to combine the convenience of the alphabetical dictionary with the general range of the thematic encyclopedia. It focuses on the more popular and relevant concepts to do with language, but I have taken into account the more systematic kinds of enquiry which are likely to accompany the contemporary increased focus on language, in such areas as the British National Curriculum. I have also introduced an 'interface' with linguistics, including several basic theoretical notions, the names of a number of linguistic branches, models, and theories, and the essential descriptive terms in phonetics.

For the second edition, I have completely revised the geolinguistic data in the book, updating the population statistics on individual countries to the mid-1990s, and taking into account the results of the latest surveys about numbers of speakers. Several entries have had to be fundamentally revised, in the light of the political changes of the early 1990s – notably the countries and languages which were previously grouped under Yugoslavia and Czechoslovakia, and those countries which have adopted new constitutions affecting language (as in South Africa) or new names (such as the Democratic Republic of Congo, formerly Zaire). Several new entries deal with issues which have come to prominence in the 1990s, such as Ebonics, Estuary English, and New Englishes, and I have included a number of entries to do with the critical issues of ecolinguistics, endangered languages, and human linguistic rights. I have also increased the number of cross-references between entries, and added an index of all language names included in the book.

I am most grateful to the many readers who have written to me, over the past few years, drawing my attention to various infelicities and gaps in the first edition – and also, I am glad to say, confirming my original intuition that this kind of hybrid reference book has a useful role to play. I hope that if readers find anything in this new edition which is not as it should be, they will continue to let me know, in the interests of improving coverage and treatment for future editions.

David Crystal
Holyhead, Anglesey LL65 1PB
March 1998

CONVENTIONS

The alphabetical arrangement of the entries is letter-by-letter, as in a dictionary.

Many entries are followed by cross-reference (➤) to other entries, separated by semicolons and listed in alphabetical order. If several cross-references have a word in common, they are grouped together in the following way:

> language delay/pathology; (= language delay; language pathology;)
> clinical/educational linguistics; (= clinical linguistics; educational
> linguistics;)

I had two criteria in mind when choosing cross-references: to refer to notions on which the sense of an entry depends (the clarification factor), and to provide an opportunity to follow up notions of related interest (the browsing factor). It is important to appreciate that other terms used in an entry may still have their own entries in the book, even though they are not listed in the cross-references.

A phonemic transcription (Received Pronunciation) is given for those headwords which might present an uncertainty of pronunciation to the general reader. When boldface items appear in the body of an entry, in most cases the pronunciation of those items is given, if necessary, after the headword in its alphabetical place in the book. Foreign pronunciations are also given, in a few entries, using the symbols of the International Phonetic Alphabet.

Pronunciation key

iː	*see*	ʊ	*put*	aʊ	*out*	k	*coo*	s	*so*	l	*lie*
ɪ	*him*	uː	*do*	ɪə	*here*	g	*go*	z	*zoo*	r	*row*
e	*get*	ɜː	*bird*	ɛə	*care*	tʃ	*chew*	ʃ	*shoe*	w	*way*
a	*sat*	ə	*about*	ʊə	*poor*	ʤ	*jaw*	ʒ	*bei**ge***	j	*you*
ʌ	*sun*	eɪ	*ape*	p	*pie*	f	*fee*	h	*hi*		
ɑː	*calm*	aɪ	*time*	b	*by*	v	*view*	m	*my*		
ɒ	*dog*	ɔɪ	*boy*	t	*tie*	θ	*thin*	n	*no*		
ɔː	*saw*	əʊ	*so*	d	*die*	ð	*the*	ŋ	*sing*		

A

A An abbreviation of **adjective**, **adverb**, or **adverbial**.

AAVE ➤African-American Vernacular English.

abbreviation A reduced version of a word, phrase, or sentence. There are many types of word abbreviation, such as acronyms (*EEC*), blends (*brunch*), and shortened forms (*ad*). Sentence abbreviation is usually studied under the heading of **ellipsis**: *I phoned Fred and asked him to dinner* (where there has been ellipsis of *I* before *asked*). ➤➤acronym; blending; clipping; ellipsis.

Abkhaz /ˈabkaz/ A member of the Abkhazo-Adyghian group of Caucasian languages, spoken by *c*.100,000 people in the north-west Caucasus, mainly in the Abkhaz region of Georgia (where it has official status) and in parts of Turkey. It is written in the Cyrillic alphabet. ➤➤Abkhazo-Adyghian.

Abkhazo-Adyghian /abˈkazəʊ əˈdɪdʒɪən/ A group of Caucasian languages found in the north-west of the Caucasus region; also known as **Northwest Caucasian**. The languages are noted for their large number of consonants (over 80, in the case of Ubykh) and small number of vowels (as few as two, according to some analyses). ➤➤Abkhaz; Adygey; Caucasian; Kabardian.

ablative case /ˈablətɪv/ One of the ways in which some inflected languages make a word change its form, in order to show a grammatical relationship with other parts of the sentence. The ablative mainly affects nouns, along with any related words (such as adjectives or pronouns). It signals a range of locational or instrumental meanings which in English would be expressed by certain prepositions – for instance, the ablative of Latin *amicus* 'friend' is *amico*, which would usually be translated as 'by', 'with', or 'from a friend'. ➤➤case; inflection 1.

ablaut /ˈablaʊt/ A change of vowel which causes a word to take on a different grammatical function. For example, in the forms of the verb *drink*, one change of vowel produces a past tense, *drank*, and another produces the past participle, *drunk*. This kind of relationship between vowels is also called **vowel gradation**. It is very common in Indo-European languages. ➤➤Indo-European; vowel.

aboriginal languages ➤Australian.

absolute construction A constituent of a sentence which is separate or disconnected from the rest of the sentence. A famous example is the Latin **ablative absolute** construction, such as *hoc facto* ('this having been done'), which can be used without influencing the grammatical form of the other words in the sentence. In English, adjectives and adverbs can often be used within a sentence in an absolute way, as in *Angry*, *he left the room* or *Nevertheless*, *the meal was cold.* ➤ablative case; sentence.

absolute universal ➤universal.

abstract 1. A summary of a piece of writing, often placed at the beginning or end of a printed text, such as an article or report. The term is also used in the study of narrative, for an optional element which summarizes the whole of a story. ➤narrative. **2**. ➤concrete 1.

abuse ➤vocal abuse.

Académie française /akadə'mi: frɑ'sɛːz/ The French Academy, instituted in France in 1635 by Cardinal Richelieu, which set the pattern for many subsequent bodies in other countries. Its statutes define as its principal function 'to labour with all possible care and diligence to give definite rules to our language, and to render it pure, eloquent, and capable of treating the arts and sciences'. The 40 academicians were drawn from the ranks of the church, nobility, and military. The Academy continues to speak out against what it sees as regrettable change in the language (such as the widespread use of English loan words), has produced many notable publications (its first dictionary appeared in 1694), and has considerable influence in French society; but it has had little real effect in altering the way the French language has developed. ➤academy; French.

academy In the context of language, an institution which tries to protect a language from what it considers to be undesirable influences, to maintain excellence in its use, and to define its rules through the writing of grammars, dictionaries, and other manuals. Academies date from the 16th century, the most influential being the French Academy. Spain, Sweden, Hungary, and several other countries have academies, but the concept has never attracted much enthusiasm in the main English-speaking nations (though there is a body with such a name in South Africa), largely on the grounds that any attempt to control the development of a language by putting it in the charge of a small number of people is futile. ➤Académie française; codification; prescriptivism; purism.

Accadian ➤Akkadian.

accent 1. In phonetics, those features of pronunciation which signal a person's regional or social identity (e.g. an 'educated accent', a 'northern accent'). The term is often contrasted with **dialect**, which includes features of grammar and vocabulary. ➤dialect; phonetics; received pronunciation. **2**. In phonology, a type of perceived prominence heard on a spoken word or syllable; the word *dictionary*, for example, has its first syllable strongly accented. Syllables which lack this prominence are said to be **unaccented**. The pattern of relative prominence in a sequence of syllables is called **accentuation**, and the study of accentuation is sometimes called **accentology**. ➤phonology; stress. **3**. In graphology, a mark placed above a letter, showing how that letter is to be pronounced. French accents, for example, include a grave *è*, similar to the sound of *e* in English *set*, and an acute *é*, similar to the *ay* of English *say*. Consonants too may have an accent, as in Serbo-Croatian *ć*. ➤acute accent; circumflex; diacritic; grave accent.

accentuation ➤accent 2.

acceptable Descriptive of any usage which native speakers feel is possible or normal in a language. Acceptable utterances are contrasted with **unacceptable** ones (such as, in standard English, **It may shall go* or **I should of done it*) and with such **marginally acceptable** cases as *?That baby's cross and crying*. Asterisks and question marks are used to identify the problem cases. ➤grammatical; semi-sentence; usage.

accidence One of the main divisions within the field of grammar, according to older approaches to language study. It refers to the ways in which a word changes its form in order to carry out different grammatical functions in a sentence. Examples include the contrast between singular and plural (*horse/horses*) or that between present and past tense (*walk/walked*). In linguistics, the subject-matter of accidence is subsumed under morphology. ➤inflection 1; morphology.

accommodation Adjustments which people make unconsciously to their speech, influenced by the speech of those they are talking to. It is quite a common experience to hear people accommodating to the speech of those around them, and some find themselves especially prone to it. Both **convergence** (moving closer together) and **divergence** (moving further apart) are found, reflecting respectively the rapport or lack of rapport between the speakers. In the case of convergence, an accent may change quite noticeably, and cause the listener to enquire about the speaker's origins. The situation can be embarrassing, if the listener discovers that the accent is not a genuine one! ➤accent 1; convergence 1.

accusative case One of the ways in which inflected languages make a word change its form, in order to show a grammatical relationship with other parts of the sentence. The accusative usually marks a word (typically a noun or pronoun) as being the object of a verb. In German, for example, when the phrase 'the good lad' is the subject of a sentence, it is *der gute Junge*; when it is object (as in 'I see the good lad'), it is *(Ich sehe) den guten Jungen*. When the noun changes, the associated words change with it – in this instance, both 'the' and 'good' are also marked with an accusative ending. In English there is no accusative case ending for nouns. The difference between subject and object of a clause can be seen only from the word order: compare the headlines *Cat eats mouse* and *Mouse eats cat*. Only with certain pronouns is there any sign of an accusative case, as in the change from *he* to *him* or *she* to *her*. The term **objective** is often used instead of accusative, therefore, to describe such instances. ➤case; inflection 1; object; word order.

Achehnese ►Achinese.

achievement test In language studies, a test which measures how much of a language someone has learned after following a particular course of instruction. Such tests are commonly used at the end of school terms, and enable teachers to evaluate the success of their teaching as well as to identify weaknesses in their students. A distinction is often drawn between this kind of test and a **proficiency test**, which measures how much of a language someone knows, regardless of how this knowledge has been acquired. ►►language learning.

Achinese /atʃɪˈniːz/ A Malayic (Austronesian) language spoken by *c*.3 million people in the northern part of Sumatra, Indonesia; also called **Achehnese**, and earlier spelled **Atjehnese**. It is written in the Roman alphabet. ►►Austronesian.

Acholi /əˈtʃəʊliː/ A Nilotic language spoken by over 750,000 speakers in north Uganda and south Sudan, closely related to Lango; also spelled **Akoli**. It is written in the Roman alphabet. ►Lango; Nilotic.

acoustic cues Features of the acoustic signal which enable listeners to distinguish speech sounds. For example, the first two formants prove crucial to the identification of vowels, and voice onset time is crucial to the discrimination of voiced and voiceless consonants. ►►formant; voice onset time; voicing.

acoustic nerve The eighth (VIII) cranial nerve, running from the cochlea to the brain; also called the **auditory nerve**. It is used for the transmission of (speech) sound. ►►see auditory phonetics.

acoustic phonetics The branch of phonetics which studies the physical properties of speech sounds. It uses instrumental techniques of investigation to provide an objective account of speech patterns, which can then be related to the way sounds are produced and heard. ►►burst; experimental phonetics; filtered speech; formant; phonetics.

acquired language disorder A language disorder which results from injury or disease, and not from an abnormal course of early child development; contrasts with a **developmental** language problem. Examples include the various disorders which can arise from damage to the language centres of the brain, such as aphasia. An example of a developmental problem would be language delay. ►►aphasia; dysarthria; dyspraxia; language delay/pathology.

acquisition The process or result of learning a particular aspect of language, or the language as a whole. The term is used with reference both to the learning of a first language by children (**child language acquisition**) and to the learning of further languages or varieties (**second language** or **foreign language acquisition**). It may also be used in more restricted senses, within particular theories of language learning and use. ►►CHILDES; critical period; generalization; innateness hypothesis;

internalization; language learning; mean length of utterance; monitor model; motherese; open 3; overextension; proto- 2; psycholinguistics.

acrolect ➤creole.

acronym /'akrənɪm/ A word made up out of the initial letters of other words. Some are pronounced letter by letter (*BBC*, *EEC*); some are pronounced as whole words (*NATO*, *UNESCO*). Lower-case letters may also be used (*e.g.*, *i.e.*). In some cases, the letters may represent different parts of the same word (*ID*). Some acronyms have become so well known as words that what their constituent letters stand for may be forgotten (*AIDS, laser*). In some approaches, the term is restricted to only those items which can be pronounced as whole words; items which have to be spelled out as a sequence of letters are then given a separate classification as **initialisms**. ➤➤abbreviation.

acrostic /ə'krɒstɪk/ A poem or other text in which certain letters in each line make up a name or message. In Old English, for example, there are texts in which the author has put the letters of his name into the lines, and poetic riddles in which the lines contain the letters which make up the answer to the question. An acrostic based on the last letters of words or lines is a **telestich** /tə'lestɪk/. ➤➤riddle.

active knowledge The knowledge of a language which a user actively employs in speaking or writing; usually contrasted with **passive knowledge**, which is what a person understands in the speech or writing of others. Native speakers' passive knowledge of vocabulary is invariably much greater than their active knowledge: people know far more words than they ever use. ➤➤competence; vocabulary.

active voice ➤voice 1.

actor–action–goal The usual order of elements in an English clause. The actor (the grammatical subject) is followed by the action (the verb), which is followed by the goal of the action (the object), as in *Mary left the house*. Many languages use this order, but other orders are to be found, such as action–actor–goal in Welsh. ➤➤clause; goal; word order.

acute accent The accent ´, used to distinguish the sound values of letters in several languages, such as French, Spanish, and Polish. It may be used both on vowels (e.g. *é, á*) and on consonants (e.g. *ś, ń*). In English it may be seen on such words as *cliché* or *résumé*. ➤➤accent 3.

Adamawa-Ubangi /adə'mɑːwə/ A group of *c*.175 languages found in the northern part of central Africa, from eastern Nigeria into southwestern Sudan, belonging to the Niger-Congo family; formerly known as **Adamawa-Eastern**. Its main members (in the Ubangi group) are Banda, Gbaya, Ngbaka, and Zande. Several pidgin languages, notably Sango, are used throughout the area. ➤➤Niger-Congo; pidgin; Sango.

address, forms of The linguistic means by which people express their personal and social orientation towards those with whom they are communicating. Examples include the use of familiar and polite pronouns (such as *tu* vs. *vous* in French), terms of endearment (*darling*, *mate*), and the choice between first names, surnames, titles, nicknames, and other forms. ➤endearment, terms of; T/V forms.

adjacency pair In the analysis of conversation, a single sequence of utterances by different speakers, in which the first utterance constrains the second in some way. For example, a question generally elicits an answer, and a suggestion leads to an acceptance or rejection. ➤conversation analysis; turn.

adjective (adj., A) A type of word whose main function is to modify a noun, expressing a characteristic quality or attribute. Adjectives typically occur within noun phrases, when they are referred to as **attributive adjectives** (*a happy occasion*), but they may occur in other parts of a sentence, such as after a verb (*It's red*), when they are referred to as **predicative adjectives**. They may also function as the head of an **adjective** (or **adjectival**) **phrase** (*very sad*). In many languages, adjectives show contrasts of degree (*happier, happiest*). ➤degree; epithet; gradability; modification 1; noun; predicate; word class; *cartoon below*.

adjunct A less important or optional element in a grammatical construction, whose removal does not affect the structural identity of the construction. For example, in the sentence *John, it's time we left*, the removal of the vocative element *John* has no effect on the identity of the following construction. Adjectives and adverbs are also typically used as adjuncts. ➤adjective; adverb; vocative case.

'Goodness! How satisfying it must be to form one's own adjectives.'

adverb (adv., A) A type of word whose chief function is to specify the mode of action of a verb, such as *quickly* in *They walked quickly*. However, several other kinds of word have been grouped under the heading of adverb by grammarians, and the result is a word class which is heterogeneous. Among these items are intensifying words (*very, quite*), negative particles (*not*), and sentence connectors (*however, moreover*). A phrase with an adverb as its head is an **adverb phrase** (*very quickly*), but this term is also sometimes used to include any phrases which are like adverbs in function (*in the garden*). A clause which functions like an adverb is an **adverb clause** (also called an **adverbial clause**). ➤➤adverbial; clause; phrase; word class.

adverbial (A) An element of clause structure which functions like an adverb. It may be a single adverb (*soon*), an **adverbial phrase** (*very soon, in the morning*), or an **adverbial clause** (*when it was dark* . . .). Adverbials are often classified on the basis of the kind of meaning they express, such as time (answering the question 'When?'), place ('Where?'), and manner ('How'). ➤➤adverb; clause.

adversative A grammatical ending, word, or construction which expresses the notion of contrast. Examples in English include *but, however*, and *although* (as in *She wore a coat, although it was quite warm*). ➤➤conjunction.

Adygey, also **Adyge** or **Adyghe** /'adəgeɪ/ A member of the Abkhazo-Adyghian group of Caucasian languages, spoken by *c.*300,000 people in the north-west Caucasus, mainly in the Adygey region of Russia (where it has official status) and in Turkey, by other groups in Jordan, Syria, and Iraq, and by small numbers of immigrants in Israel, Europe, and the USA; also called **Circassian**. It is written in the Cyrillic alphabet. ➤➤Abkhazo-Adyghian.

aerometry /ɛəˈrɒmətriː/ The measurement of air flow during speech; also called **electroaerometry**. Several instruments, such as the electroaerometer, have been designed to provide air-flow data, using a special face mask which allows separate measures of air flow to be made from mouth and nose. ➤➤experimental phonetics; pneumotachograph.

affected ➤recipient.

affective meaning The emotional meaning of an utterance; often referred to simply as **affect**. It includes the expression of moods, attitudes, dispositions, and other feelings, and is encountered especially in the use of tones of voice and emotive vocabulary. Other terms for this dimension of meaning include **expressive, emotive**, and **attitudinal meaning**. ➤➤connotation; meaning.

affirmative Descriptive of a sentence or verb which has no marker of negation, as in *The paint is on the shelf*; also called **positive**. The primary function of affirmative sentences is to express an assertion. ➤➤negation.

affix A meaningful element which is attached to a word root, in order to make a more complex word. Examples of **affixation** may be found before the root (a

prefix), in the middle of a root (an **infix**), and after a root (a **suffix**). English has many prefixes (*de-, un-, pre-*) and suffixes (*-ed, -tion, -ly*), and **infixes** (inserted within the root) can be found in Latin, Arabic, and many other languages. Languages which express grammatical relationships primarily through the use of affixes are known as **affixing languages** (e.g. Bantu languages). ➤➤morphology; root 1.

affricate /'afrɪkət/ A type of consonant consisting of a stop released as a fricative, at the same place of articulation. Examples in English include the first and last sounds in *church* and *judge*. ➤➤fricative; stop.

Afghan ➤Pashto.

Afghanistan (population in 1995 estimated at 21,017,000) About 50 languages are spoken in the country, over half the population using Pashto, which is an official language along with Dari (the local name for Persian). Dari in particular is important as a lingua franca, and English is increasingly being used for international trade. Other languages include Tadzhik, Uzbek, Turkmen, Baluchi, Brahui, and Pashayi. ➤➤Pashto; Persian.

Africa A vast and complex linguistic area, containing more languages than any other continent. No one knows just how many languages there are: low estimates suggest *c.*1000; high estimates suggest *c.*3000. It is often difficult to tell where one language ends and the next begins, or to decide whether varieties are dialects of the same language or are different languages. Many of the languages have never been recorded or written down. Sometimes, only their name is known. Very few of the languages are spoken by large numbers of people. As a consequence, Africa is a continent of lingua francas, both within and between nations. English and French are most commonly used, and certain African languages have an important international role – Swahili, for example, is used throughout much of East Africa (in an area comparable in size to most of Europe). In an important classification proposed in the 1960s, four main families of African languages were recognized. However, it must be appreciated that such classifications are extremely tentative, based on the comparison of a small number of features from those languages which have so far been analysed. It is a massive step to move from here to hypotheses about the historical relationship of these languages to each other. Nor is it easy to find character-istics which unite all African languages – though certain features are typical of certain areas (such as click and implosive consonants, not commonly encountered outside Africa). ➤➤Afro-Asiatic; family of languages; Khoisan; Niger-Congo; Nilo-Saharan.

African-American Vernacular English (AAVE) The nonstandard English spoken by lower-class black people in American urban communities; also known as **Black English Vernacular (BEV)**, **Afro-American English**, **Black English**, and a variety of other labels with varying degrees of acceptability. Among its distinc-tive features are the lack of a final *-s* in the 3rd person singular present tense (e.g. *she walk*), no use of forms of *be* when used as a linking verb (e.g. *They real fine*), and the use of *be* to mark habitual meaning (e.g. *Sometime they be walking round here*). The linguistic origins of AAVE are controversial. According to one view, AAVE originates in the creole English used by the first blacks in America, now much influenced by contact with standard English. An alternative view argues that AAVE features can also be found in white dialects (especially those in the south), suggesting an origin in white English; the variety then became distinctive when blacks moved north to the cities, and found their southern features perceived as a marker of ethnic identity. ➤ creole; dialect; Ebonics; standard.

Afrikaans A West Germanic language, a derivative of Dutch, spoken by *c*.6.4 million people in the Republic of South Africa (*c*.6 million), Namibia, Malawi, Zambia, and Zimbabwe, with some through immigration in a few other countries (e.g. Australia, Canada); also sometimes called **Cape Dutch**. It is a derivative of the language which was brought by settlers in the 17th century, and now shows many differences from European Dutch, especially as a result of its contact with local African languages. Afrikaans is now the first language of *c*.60% of the White population and *c*.90% of the Coloured (mixed race) population. It has been an official language in South Africa, along with English, since 1925, and there is a developing Afrikaans literature. It is written in the Roman alphabet. ➤ Dutch; Germanic; South Africa.

Afro-American English ➤ African-American Vernacular English.

Afro-Asiatic The major language family to be found in northern Africa, the eastern horn of Africa, and south-western Asia, containing over 200 languages spoken by over 200 million people. There are six major divisions which are thought to have derived from a parent language that existed around the 7th millennium BC. By far the largest and most widespread subgroup is Semitic. ➤ Berber; Chadic; Cushitic; Egyptian; Omotic; Semitic.

agent An element of a clause which typically expresses the person (or animate being) responsible for a particular action. For example, *cat* is the agent in such sentences as *The cat chased the mouse* or *The mouse was chased by the cat*. Parts of a word may also have an agentive function, as with the *-er* suffix of *farmer* ('one who farms'). ➤ affix; clause; impersonal.

agglutinative language ➤ typology of language.

agnosia /agˈnəʊzɪə/ The lack of ability to interpret sensory information. In the case of **auditory agnosia** (or, more specifically, **auditory verbal agnosia**), the disability affects the recognition of speech sounds. **Visual verbal agnosia** is the corresponding problem for the written language. ➤ language pathology.

agrammatism /eɪˈgramətɪzm/ A language disorder characterized by the omission of the elements which express grammatical relationships (such as inflectional endings, articles, and prepositions); also called **agrammatic speech**. It is especially found in people suffering from expressive aphasia (as seen in this extract: *go ambulance . . .*

hospital . . . go hospital tomorrow . . .). The term is used only in clinical description. ➤►aphasia; paragrammatism; telegrammatic speech.

agraphia ➤dyslexia.

agreement ➤concord.

Ainu /'aɪnuː/ An isolated language spoken by an uncertain number of people (thought to be as few as 15 in 1996) in Hokkaido, Japan, and in the Sakhalin and Kuril Islands. The language and culture lost much ground to Japanese during the first half of the 20th century. The ethnic group numbers over 30,000. ➤►isolate; Japanese.

airstream The source of energy for speech sound production; also called an **airstream mechanism**. Most speech is produced using air from the lungs (pulmonic air), but other types of airstream can be found. ➤►glottalic; phonetics; pulmonic; velaric.

Akan /'akan/ A Kwa language spoken by *c.*7 million people, mainly in Ghana, also in the Côte d'Ivoire, with some speakers in Togo. The name is commonly used for a closely related group of languages, such as Ashante, Fante, and Twi, which are often mutually intelligible but considered as separate languages because of their different cultural and literary traditions. Akan is a major lingua franca in Ghana. It is written in the Roman alphabet. ➤►Kwa; lingua franca.

Akkadian /ə'keɪdɪən/ A Semitic language spoken in Mesopotamia from *c.*2300 BC to *c.*500 BC; also spelled **Accadian** and sometimes called **Assyro-Babylonian**, from the names of its two major dialects (Assyrian and Babylonian). It replaced Sumerian as the everyday language of the region. The Babylonian dialect was being widely used as a lingua franca by the beginning of the 1st millennium BC, but within a few centuries it was supplanted by Aramaic – though Babylonian continued in use as a language of scholarship until the 1st century AD. Akkadian was written in cuneiform script, and was deciphered in the 19th century. ➤►Aramaic; cuneiform; Semitic; Sumerian.

Akoli ➤Acholi.

Albania (population in 1995 estimated at 3,549,000) The official language is Albanian; in addition there are minorities speaking Greek, Macedonian, Romanian, and Romani. There is growing use of English for international trade. ➤►Albanian.

Albanian An Indo-European language, the official language of Albania, spoken by about 5 million people in the following areas: Albania (over 3.2 million), the Kosovo area of Yugoslavia (*c.*1.5 million), and parts of Greece, Italy, and Bulgaria. Its chief linguistic interest is that it is the only member of a separate branch of the Indo-European family. It is divided into two main dialect areas, known as Gheg (in the north) and Tosk (in the south), each consisting of many further dialect divisions, and not always mutually intelligible. The language has been much influenced by its contacts with nearby languages, especially in vocabulary. There are few early written remains, dating only from the 15th century. A Latin alphabet was introduced in 1909, and since 1950 the standard language has been based on the Tosk dialect. ➤Albania; Indo-European.

Aleut ➤Eskimo-Aleut.

alexandrine /alɪg'zɑːndrɪn/ A poetic line of twelve syllables, the standard metre of French poetry since the 16th century. Its length makes it unpopular in English – a feature captured in the *Essay on Criticism* by Pope: *A needless Alexandrine ends the song, / That, like a wounded snake, drags its slow length along.* ➤metrics.

alexia ➤dyslexia.

Algeria (population in 1995 estimated at 28,513,000) The official language is Arabic, spoken by over 80% of the population. Other languages include Kabyle, spoken by over 2.5 million, Tamashek, and about a dozen other languages. French is important for international trade and tourism; but in 1996 English replaced French as the chief foreign language taught in schools. ➤Arabic; Kabyle.

Algonkian or **Algonquian** /al'gɒŋkɪən/ A family of over 30 Amerindian languages, covering a broad area across central and eastern Canada, and down through central and southern USA. Many well-known tribes are represented, such as Arapaho, Blackfoot, Cheyenne, Cree, Fox, Micmac, Mohican, Ojibwa, and Shawnee, though only Cree (*c.*60,000) and Ojibwa (*c.*45,000) have large numbers of speakers. The spelling **Algonkin** refers to a dialect of Ojibwa. Several other languages spoken mainly in south-eastern USA have now been grouped along with Algonkian into a **Macro-Algonkian** family, notably the Muskogean group, which includes Choctaw and Muskogee. All these languages use the Roman alphabet when written down. ➤Amerindian.

alias A name adopted by people who wish their real identity to be unknown. The context is frequently a criminal one, but there are several innocent circumstances where an alias might be used, such as an immigrant who uses an alias to avoid people having to pronounce an exotic original name. ➤onomastics.

allegro ➤lento.

alliteration A sequence of words (or of stressed syllables within words) beginning with the same sound. The effect is particularly evident in poetry, but may be found in any genre or style, such as advertising or newspaper headlines. A well-known literary example is the repeated *p* and *w* sounds in Gray's *The ploughman homeward plods his weary way* ('Elegy in a Country Churchyard'). ➤assonance; rhyme.

allo- A prefix referring to a variant form of a linguistic unit, where the variation does not alter the unit's basic identity in the language. The notion is most commonly encountered with reference to variants of phonemes (**allophones**) and morphemes (**allomorphs**), but is also used with reference to other areas of linguistics and semiotics, such as the variant forms of a grapheme (**allographs**). For example, *a*, *A*, and A are allographs of the grapheme {a}; despite the variations, they are all recognizably forms of the same basic unit. ➤free variation; grapheme; morpheme; phoneme.

allomorph, allophone ➤allot-.

allonym /'alənɪm/ A name assumed by an author which belongs to someone else. It is not a common practice, because of legal sanctions. The reasons for adopting a false name range from literary playfulness to outright deception. ➤pseudonym.

allophonic transcription ➤transcription.

alphabet A type of writing system in which a set of symbols (letters) represents the important sounds (phonemes) of a language. Most Western languages derive their alphabets from the Latin alphabet, which in turn derives from Greek, and ultimately from the North Semitic alphabet which developed *c*.1700 BC in Palestine and Syria. This alphabet consisted of 22 consonant letters; letters representing vowels were added much later, by the Greeks. Most modern alphabets contain between 20 and 30 symbols, but the exact size depends on the complexity of the sound system, and alphabets are known with over 70 letters (e.g. Khmer). Languages also vary greatly in the regularity with which they represent the relationship between sounds and letters. Some alphabets are used in a very regular way (Spanish and Finnish are examples); others are used in a highly irregular way (such as Gaelic and, to a lesser extent, English). ➤Arabic; Brahmi; Cyrillic; Devanagari; graphology 1; International Phonetic Alphabet; i.t.a; letter; majuscule; ogham; Roman alphabet; rune; writing.

alphabetism A word made up out of the initial letters of other words, each being separately pronounced, such as *VIP* and *EEC*. These forms are often classed as a type of acronym. ➤acronym.

Alsatian ➤France.

Altaic /al'teɪɪk/ A family of about 60 languages spoken by *c*.115 million people over a vast area from the Balkan peninsula to the north-east of Asia. They are classified into Turkic, Mongolian, and Manchu-Tungus groups, though the hypothesis of common ancestry is not universally agreed. There is little written evidence of early development: some Turkic material dates from the 8th century, but there is nothing known of Mongolian before the 13th century, and Manchu records are found only from the 17th century. In the 20th, there was considerable effort to modernize the languages. Several new literary varieties emerged, based on local languages

Opposite Alphabetic systems: the development of the early alphabet, and the relationship between several modern alphabets.

A comparison table of alphabets and scripts. Columns (left to right): Phoenician, Old Hebrew, Early Greek, Classical Greek, Etruscan, Early Latin, Modern Roman, Greek (form / name), Cyrillic, Hebrew (form / name), Arabic (form / name). The letterform columns contain script glyphs; the readable name and Roman/Cyrillic columns are given below.

Modern Roman	Greek name	Cyrillic	Hebrew name	Arabic name
Aa	alpha	Аа	aleph, 'alef	'alif
Bb	beta	Бб	bēth	bā
Cc	gamma	Вв	gimel	tā
Dd	delta	Гг	dāleth	thā
Ee	epsilon	Дд	hē	jim
Ff	zēta	Ее	vav, waw	hā
Gg	ēta	Ёё	zayin	khā
Hh	thēta	Жж	heth	dāl
Ii	iota	Зз	teth	dhāl
Jj	kappa	Ии Йй	yod, yodh	rā
Kk	lambda	Кк	kāph	zāy
Ll	mu	Лл	lāmedh	sin
Mm	nu	Мм	mēm	shin
Nn	xi	Нн	nūn	sād
Oo	omicron	Оо	samekh	dād
Pp	pi	Пп	'ayin	tā
Qq	rho	Рр	pē	zā
Rr	sigma	Сс	sade, sadhe?	'ayn
Ss	tau	Тт	qōph	ghayn
Tt	upsilon	Уу	rēsh	fā
Uu	phi	Фф	sin	qāf
Vv	chi, khi	Хх	shin	kāf
Ww	psi	Цц	tāv, tāw	lām
Xx	omega	Чч		mim
Yy		Шш		nun
Zz		Щщ		hā
		Ъъ		wāw
		Ьь		yā
		Ыы		
		Ээ		
		Юю		
		Яя		

Greek forms: Αα Ββ Γγ Δδ Εε Ζζ Ηη Θθ Ιι Κκ Λλ Μμ Νν Ξξ Οο Ππ Ρϱ Σσς Ττ Υυ Φφ Χχ Ψψ Ωω (e.g. Uzbek), and some of the older written languages were reformed (e.g. Turkish). ➤Manchu-Tungus; Mongolian; Turkic.

alternation The relationship between the different forms of a linguistic unit, usually symbolized by the swung dash (~). For example, the relationship between singular and plural forms of the noun *house* can be shown thus: *house* ~ *houses*. ➤morpheme.

alternative communication system A type of replacement communication system devised to help disabled people who cannot communicate in the normal way. An example would be a board or screen of pictorial symbols, to which the disabled person points by using a part of the body (e.g. arm, mouth, eyebrow) to operate a signalling device. Other forms of communication system, designed to supplement rather than replace normal language use, are called **augmentative systems**. A common example is braille. ➤Blissymbolics; braille; communication board/disorder; language pathology.

alveolar /alviːˈəʊlə, alˈvɪələ/ Descriptive of a consonant sound made by the tongue tip or blade against the bony prominence immediately behind the upper teeth (the **alveolar ridge**). Examples include [t] as in *two* and [d] as in *do*. Sounds articulated just behind the alveolar ridge are called **postalveolar**. ➤consonant.

alveo-palatal /ˈalviːəʊˈpalətl/ Descriptive of a sound made by the front of the tongue a little in advance of the palatal articulatory area; also called **alveolo-palatal**. An example is Polish *ś*. ➤palate.

ambiguous Descriptive of a word or sentence which expresses more than one meaning. Ambiguity within the word (**lexical ambiguity**) is seen in *chip*, which can be the product of a computer or a potato. Ambiguity of sentence structure (**grammatical** or **structural ambiguity**, also called **constructional homonymity**) is seen in *Visiting uncles can be boring* – which can mean both 'When we visit uncles . . .' and 'When uncles visit us . . .' To show the alternative meanings in a sentence is to **disambiguate** it. ➤meaning.

ambilingualism The ability to speak two languages with equal facility. The notion is usually included within the more general concept of bilingualism. ➤bilingualism.

amelioration A change of meaning in which a word loses an earlier unpleasant sense. An example is *mischievous*, which formerly had a strong sense of 'disastrous', but now has the milder sense of 'playfully annoying'. ➤pejoration.

American Samoa (population in 1995 estimated at 43,000) The official language is English. About 90% of the people speak Samoan. There are also some speakers of Tongan and Tokelau. ➤English.

American Sign Language (ASL) A sign language used as a first language by deaf people in the USA; also called **Ameslan**. It makes use of a large number of signs (at least 4000), and has a structure and functional range of comparable complexity to that encountered in spoken or written language. Several varieties of ASL exist, ranging from those which show no influence of the spoken medium to those which have been markedly shaped by properties of English (e.g. its word order). Many countries have a natural sign language with comparable properties (though they are not mutually intelligible), and labelled accordingly – British Sign Language (BSL), Danish Sign Language, etc. ➤➤deafness; sign language; Washoe.

Amer-Ind /'amərɪnd/ A type of sign language devised for language-handicapped people by an American speech pathologist, Madge Skelly (1903–). It is an adaptation of the signing used by American Indian tribes. More a gestural code than a language, it contains a limited number of signs which have been chosen on the grounds of their immediate recognizability, regardless of the language background of the user. ➤➤Amerindian; sign language.

Amerindian /amə'rɪndɪən/ A group of nearly 1000 languages spoken by the indigenous peoples of North, Central, and South America; also called **American Indian**. The group comprises a wide range of language families whose origins and inter-relationships are unclear. They are usually described with reference to the main geographical areas involved, but certain families cut across the areal divisions, such as Penutian and Hokan. **North American** languages comprise at least 50 families, which are often classified into four main types: **Eskimo-Aleut**, **Na-Dene**, **Algonkian**, and **Macro-Siouan**. There are also c.30 isolated languages. Few of the indigenous languages have been able to hold their own in the face of the arrival of English and other European languages, and the total number of Amerindian first-language speakers is only c.22 million. The **Meso-American** (or **Middle American**) area contains languages belonging to both North and South American families, as well as to the **Oto-Manguean** family, which is restricted to the Central region. **South American** languages contain possibly over 100 families, often grouped at a very general level into three main types: **Macro-Chibchan, Gê-Pano-Carib**, and **Andean-Equatorial**. In former times as many as 2000 languages may have been spoken in this continent, but fewer than 600 of these have been attested, and many remain to be fully described. The arrival of Western civilization led to Spanish or (in Brazil) Portuguese becoming the dominant languages throughout the area. South America none the less remains one of the most linguistically diversified areas in the world. In a new but controversial classification presented in 1985 by American linguist Joseph Greenberg (1915–), all the New World languages are brought together, and grouped into three main families: Na-Dene, Eskimo-Aleut, and Amerind. Eskimo-Aleut is seen as part of a 'Euroasiatic' super-family, whose other members include Indo-European, Altaic, Japanese, Korean, and several others. Amerind in particular is conceived as a vast family, consisting of over 200 groups of languages covering the whole of North, Central, and South America. ➤➤Algonkian; Andean-Equatorial; Eskimo-Aleut; Gê-Pano-Carib; isolate; Macro-Chibchan; Macro-Siouan; Na-Dene; Nostratic; Oto-Manguean; Penutian.

Ameslan /'ameslan/ ➤American Sign Language.

Amharic /amˈharɪk/ A Semitic language, spoken by *c*. 15 million as a first language in Ethiopia (where it has official status), a further 5 million in nearby regions, and by several million more as a second language throughout Ethiopia and in Sudan. Its written records date from the 14th century. It is written in the Amharic alphabet, which has 33 basic consonant characters each of which is in seven forms, depending on the accompanying vowel. A revised system has been proposed, and there is a movement towards standardizing the language. ➤Ethiopia; Semitic; standard.

Amorite /'amərait/ A Semitic language spoken in the area of modern north Syria from *c*.2000 to *c*.1500 BC. Little is known about it, because the evidence for its existence comes only from lists of proper names and a few glosses in inscriptions. ➤Semitic.

anacoluthon /anəkəˈluːθn/ An unexpected break in the syntax of a sentence. For example, a speaker might leave a sentence incomplete, or suddenly change direction, as in *What I really – what I should have done was leave.* ➤syntax.

anacusis /anəˈkjuːsɪs/ ➤deafness.

anagram A word or phrase formed by changing the order of letters of another word or phrase. They are commonplace as clues for crossword puzzles, and several ingenious anagrams have been worked out: *total abstainers*, for example, is an anagram of *sit not at ale bars*. ➤word game.

analects A selection of passages taken from an author. The word is from Latin *analecta*, 'things gathered, picked up'.

analogy 1. A parallel or similar instance, referred to because it helps the process of explanation. For example, people often draw an analogy between the human brain and a computer, or between the heart and a pump. **2**. A change which affects a language when regular forms begin to influence less regular forms. Young children, for example, alter irregular nouns and verbs to make them conform to the regular pattern, saying such things as *mans* and *wented*. Analogy can also be seen operating over long periods of time, causing permanent change in a language. An example is the verb *helpan* 'help' in Old English, which had *healp* as a past tense and *holpen* as a past participle; by the 14th century, this verb had become regular, using the normal *-ed* ending. ➤language change.

analytic language ➤typology of language.

analytic sentence ➤tautology.

ananym /'anənɪm/ A name which has been written backwards. The concept is not as pointless as it may seem at first sight: the word **AMBULANCE**, for example, may sometimes be seen reversed on the vehicle, so that drivers can read the name more efficiently in their rear-view mirror. ➤onomastics; p. 17.

Ananyms.

anap(a)est /ˈanəpiːst/ ➤foot.

anaphora /əˈnafərə/ A grammatical relationship in which a linguistic unit takes its interpretation from some other part of the sentence, typically from something previously expressed. The third person pronoun *she*, for example, has an **anaphoric** relationship to the noun phrase *the lady* in *The lady came in. She sat down.* Some scholars restrict the notion to backwards reference, and distinguish cases of forwards reference as **cataphora**, or **cataphoric reference** (as in *Look at him, the tall waiter*). ➤antecedent; endophora; reference 2.

anaptyxis /anəpˈtɪksɪs/ ➤epenthesis.

anarthria /anˈɑːθrɪə/ ➤dysarthria.

Anatolian /anəˈtəʊlɪən/ A group of Indo-European languages, now extinct, spoken from *c.*2000 BC in parts of present-day Turkey and Syria. The main language is Hittite, extant in tablets of cuneiform writing dating from the 17th century BC. The earliest forms ('Old Hittite') are the oldest Indo-European texts so far discovered. Other languages of the group include Palaic, Lydian, Lycian, and Luwian. The term is also used in a broader sense, to include all the languages spoken in the region of Anatolia (Asia Minor), including several (such as Hurrian and Urartian) which are not members of the Indo-European family, or (as in the case of Phrygian) whose relationship to Indo-European is uncertain. ➤➤Indo-European; p. 156.

Andamanese /ˈandəməˈniːz/ ➤Indo-Pacific.

Andean-Equatorial A major group of *c*.250 Amerindian languages spoken in many parts of South America, divided into Andean and Equatorial groups, each of which contains several families. The most important languages include the Arawakan family, which once extended into North America, and which is still widespread, being spoken from Central America to southern Brazil. Goajiro (*c*.120,000) is its main member. The Quechumaran group is pre-eminent in the Andes highlands between Colombia and Argentina, with Quechua and Aymará important members. In the south, in and around Paraguay, Guaraní is the major member of the Tupian family. These languages all use the Roman alphabet when written down. ➤➤Amerindian; Aymará; Guaraní; Quechua.

Andorra (population in 1995 estimated at 68,000) The official languages are Catalan (spoken by *c*.60% of the population) and French. Castilian Spanish is also widely used for international trade and in tourism. ➤➤Catalan; French; Spanish.

angle brackets ➤brackets.

Anglo-Frisian ➤Germanic.

Anglo-Saxon ➤English.

Angola (population in 1995 estimated at 11,539,000) The official language is Portuguese, but over 40 other languages are spoken, notably Umbundu (*c*.4 million – an important lingua franca), Mbundu (*c*.3 million), and Kongo (*c*.1.1 million). English is also increasingly used for international trade and tourism. ➤➤Portuguese.

Anguilla (population in 1995 estimated at 7100) The official language is English. Most of the population use an English-based creole which is widespread in the Lesser Antilles. ➤➤creole; English.

animal communication ➤zoösemiotics.

animate Descriptive of words which refer to living things, and not to objects or concepts, which are **inanimate**. The notion is particularly used in the classification of nouns. ➤➤gender; noun.

Annamite /ˈanəmaɪt/ ➤Vietnamese.

anomia /eɪˈnəʊmɪə/ A language disorder in which the primary symptom is a word-finding difficulty, especially difficulty in remembering the names of people, places, and things. It is common in all forms of aphasia, and may be the primary form of language deficit (**anomic** or **nominal aphasia**). In less severe form, it is sometimes called **dysnomia**. ➤➤aphasia; language pathology.

antecedent That part of a sentence to which some other part (typically a pronoun) grammatically refers. The antecedent is usually a noun or noun phrase, and generally appears earlier in the sentence or discourse than the item which refers to it. For example, in *The car in the garage has had its paint scratched*, the antecedent of *its* is *the car.* ➤➤anaphora.

anthropological linguistics A branch of linguistics which has focused on the study of non-Western languages – especially those of the Americas – in relation to social or cultural patterns and beliefs. It particularly looks at the classification of these languages into types, at the way they are distributed in geographical areas, and at what happens when they come into contact with each other. A contrast is sometimes drawn with **linguistic anthropology**, a branch of anthropology which explores the place of language in the life of human communities. ➤➤areal linguistics; ethnolinguistics; language contact; typology of language.

anthroponymy /anθrə'pɒnəmi:/ ➤onomastics.

anthropophonics /anθrəpə'fɒnɪks/ The study of the potential which human beings have to make vocal sound. It includes such matters as the physical dimensions of the vocal tract, and how these change with age and between sexes and races. ➤➤vocal tract.

Antigua and Barbuda (population in 1995 estimated at 63,900) The official language is English. Most of the population use an English-based creole which is widespread in the Lesser Antilles. ➤➤creole; English.

antonymy /an'tɒnəmi:/ A type of sense relation expressing the meaning of oppositeness; for example, the contrast between *hot* and *cold*. A distinction is sometimes drawn between **gradable antonyms**, where it is possible to express degrees of the difference (as with *hot and cold*), and **ungradable antonyms**, where there is an either/or contrast (as with *single* and *married*). This distinction can be illustrated by the acceptable forms *hotter* and *hottest*, and the unacceptable forms **more single* and **most single.* ➤➤complementarity; gradability; sense; synonymy.

aorist /'ɛərɪst/ A form of the verb in some inflecting languages, referring especially to an action which lacks any particular completion, duration, or repetition. The form occurs in Classical Greek; modern examples include Turkish and some Slavic languages. ➤➤aspect; tense 1.

Apache /ə'patʃi:/ ➤Na-Dene.

apex ➤apical; tongue.

aphasia /ə'feɪʒə/ A disorder caused by damage to one or more of the language centres in the brain of a previously normal speaker. It is sometimes distinguished from **dysphasia**, when this is conceived as a less severe or developmental condition (as in the case of **developmental dysphasia**, often used for the study of language learning difficulties in children); but many scholars and clinicians use the two terms synonymously. The primary symptoms are disability in producing or understanding grammatical and semantic structure. If the disability relates primarily to language production, the aphasia is **expressive**; if it relates primarily to comprehension, it is **receptive**; and if both domains are severely affected, it is **global**. The study of aphasia is called **aphasiology**. ►►agrammatism; Broca's aphasia; clinical linguistics; language areas/delay; neurolinguistics; Wernicke's aphasia.

aphasic children ►language delay.

aphonia /eɪ'fəʊnɪə/ ►dysphonia.

aphorism A succinct statement expressing a general truth. Examples of aphoristic utterances include many proverbs (*Least said, soonest mended*) as well as everyday observations (*So far, so good*). They often have a distinctive rhythmical structure. Books of quotations provide hundreds of examples of longer aphorisms, such as Dr Johnson's *Patriotism is the last refuge of a scoundrel*. ►►proverb.

apical /'eɪpɪkl, 'apɪkl/ Descriptive of a consonant sound made by the tongue tip (**apex**) at or near the upper incisor teeth or teeth ridge. An example is the trilled [r] often heard in Welsh and Scottish varieties of English. ►►tongue.

apico- Descriptive of any sound made using the tip of the tongue. A consonant made by the tongue tip against the top teeth is an example of one such sound – an **apico-dental** consonant, as in the common Irish pronunciation of [t]. ►►apical; tongue.

apocope /ə'pɒkəpiː/ The deletion of the final element in a word, as when *of* is reduced to a vowel in such phrases as *cup of tea*. The omission may involve a single sound or letter, or a whole syllable. The process is common in historical sound change; for example, unstressed final sounds were generally lost between Old English and Middle English. ►►elision; sound change; syncope.

apostrophe 1. A punctuation mark which signals the omission of letters or numbers (*she'll, n't, o'clock, the '80s*) or expresses a grammatical contrast (chiefly, in English, the genitive construction, as in *the boy's car* vs. *the boys' car*). There is considerable uncertainty surrounding certain uses of the apostrophe, in modern English, with forms such as *the 1860s* and *the 1860's* or *St Pauls* and *St Paul's* being used variously by publishing houses and other institutions. The contemporary trend is towards simplification, with the apostrophe tending to be omitted when it is optional. There is some evidence to suggest that incorrect usage is increasing – both in errors of omission (when it should be present, as in *The girls hat*) and in errors of addition (when it should be absent, as in *I saw the cat's*) – and expressions of popular concern have increased correspondingly. However, it should be noted that the rules governing the use of the apostrophe are of relatively recent origin, having been largely devised by grammarians and printers only in the mid-19th century. The validity of some of these rules was disputed not long after their formulation, and it is not too surprising, therefore, that we should be left a century later with a legacy of unease, and that many adults as well as children should find the use of the form difficult. ➤➤genitive case; punctuation. **2**. A figurative expression in which an idea or inanimate object is directly addressed, or an absent person is addressed as if present. Examples include the literary (*Come, civil night . . .* , from *Romeo and Juliet*) and the everyday (*Where are you, Tom?*, said while waiting for (late) Tom's arrival). ➤➤figurative language.

appellative /əˈpelətɪv/ ➤eponym.

applied linguistics The use of linguistic theories, methods, and findings in elucidating and solving problems to do with language which have arisen in other areas of experience. The domain of applied linguistics is extremely wide, and includes foreign language learning and teaching, language disorders, translation and interpreting, lexicography, style, forensic speech analysis, and the teaching of reading. ➤➤clinical/educational/forensic linguistics; language learning/planning/teaching; lexicography; linguistics; reading; stylistics; translatology.

applied pragmatics ➤pragmatics.

apposition A sequence of adjacent nouns or noun phrases which have the same reference and grammatical role in the sentence. An example is *Mrs Smith, the optician, was able to see me*, where the noun phrases *Mrs Smith* and *the optician* are in apposition (Mrs Smith *is* the optician). ➤➤noun.

approach ➤method.

appropriateness The suitability of a linguistic form or variety to a particular social situation. For example, contracted forms of the verb (*won't, I'm*) are generally felt to be more appropriate when used in informal conversational speech than in formal writing. The notion is widely used in linguistics as an alternative to the prescriptive approach to usage variation, in which alternatives are described as 'correct' vs. 'incorrect'. ➤➤correctness; prescriptivism.

approximant A class of consonant sounds, defined in terms of their manner of articulation: the sounds are made with a minimum degree of constriction, similar to that of vowels. Examples include [w] as in *wet* and [j] as in *yes*. ➤➤manner of articulation; obstruent; semivowel.

apraxia /eɪˈpraksɪə/ The loss of ability to carry out purposeful movements on request, as a result of damage to specific areas of the brain, but in the absence of any basic deficits of a motor or sensory kind; also called **dyspraxia**. In the linguistic context, it is often referred to as **articulatory** or **verbal apraxia**, and is characterized by laboured and distorted speech production. ➤➤language pathology.

aptitude test ➤language aptitude.

aptronym /ˈaptrənɪm/ A name which derives from a person's nature or occupation, such as the surnames *Smith* or *Barber*. The name may be used humorously or ironically, as with *Mr Clever*. ➤➤onomastics.

Arabic The chief member of the Semitic family of languages, spoken by over 200 million people as a first language in many countries of northern Africa and south-eastern Asia. An uncertain further number use it as a second language, chiefly in Islamic countries, and it is also widely distributed through immigration, especially in France. The largest numbers of speakers are in Algeria, Egypt, Iraq, Morocco, Saudi Arabia, Sudan, Syria, Tunisia, and Yemen. An eastern and a western dialect grouping can be recognized. **Classical** (or **Literary**) **Arabic** is the language of the Koran, and the sacred language of Islam, and thus known to Muslims worldwide (*c.* 1,100 million in 1996). There is a standard spoken Arabic closely based on the Classical form, and this is used in formal writing and as a lingua franca among the various dialects, several of which are mutually unintelligible. The 28-letter Arabic alphabet, written from right to left, is second only to the Roman alphabet in its use worldwide. There is evidence of written Arabic from pre-3rd century AD inscriptions. A golden age of literature followed the arival of Islam in the 7th century, and there was a literary renaissance in the 19th century, much influenced by contact with Western forms. Socio-linguistically, Arabic is noted for its diglossic situation, and phonetically for the use of sounds which involve the pharynx (notably the pharyngeal consonants). ➤➤diglossia; pharyngeal; Semitic.

Aramaic /arə'meɪ̯k/ A Semitic language spoken by *c.*200,000 people in Iran and Iraq, with many more in other parts of the Middle East. Classical Aramaic (along with its alphabet) was widely used as a lingua franca in the Middle East from around the 6th century BC, and later replaced Hebrew as the spoken language of the Jews. A western dialect was the language used by Jesus Christ and his apostles, and a descendant of this can still be heard in a few villages of Lebanon and Syria. Around the 7th century AD Aramaic was supplanted by Arabic. A western dialect, Syriac, is the language of the Syrian Catholic Church. The 22-letter alphabet, written from right to left, is of linguistic importance as the ancestor of the Hebrew, Arabic, and several other alphabets. ➤➤alphabet; lingua franca; Semitic; Syriac.

Araucanian or **Araukan** /arə'keɪnɪən, ə'rɔːkn/ ➤Penutian.

Arawakan /arə'wakn/ ➤Andean-Equatorial.

arbitrariness The absence of any physical correspondence between linguistic signals (such as words) and the entities in the world to which they refer. There is nothing in the way the word *table* is pronounced or written which physically resembles the thing 'table'. The opposite view is sometimes maintained, with evidence adduced from onomatopoeic and other symbolic uses of sound. ➤➤nominalism; onomatopoeia; sound symbolism.

archaism An old word or phrase no longer in general spoken or written use, but found for example in poetry, nursery rhymes, historical novels, biblical translations, and place names. Archaic vocabulary in English includes *damsel*, *hither*, *oft*, and *yonder*. Archaic grammar includes the verb endings *-est* and *-eth* (*goest*, *goeth*), and such forms as *'tis* and *spake*. Archaic spellings can be seen in *Ye olde tea shoppe*. ➤➤language change; obsolescence 1.

areal linguistics The study of geographical regions which are characterized by shared linguistic properties. A **linguistic area**, also sometimes called a **Sprachbund**, contains languages belonging to more than one family, but displays common traits that are not found in the other members of at least one of the families. Click sounds, for example, are associated with several different language families in the area of southern Africa. ➤➤click; geographical linguistics.

Argentina (population in 1995 estimated at 34,513,000) The official language is Spanish. Over 20 other languages are spoken in the country, including several Amerindian languages (e.g. Guaraní, Araucanian, Mataco, Quechua) and a number of immigrant languages (e.g. Italian, German). English is increasingly used for international trade and tourism, alongside Spanish. ➤➤Spanish.

argot /ˈɑːɡət, ˈɑːɡəʊ/ Special vocabulary used by a secretive social group, to protect its members from outside interference; also known as **cant** or **speech disguise**. Such groups include criminals, confidence tricksters, terrorists, ghetto groups, and street gangs. A gun, for example, might be known as a typewriter, a stick of rock, or a flute. An invented set of names might be used for numbers, days, and dates. ➤➤slang.

Armenia (population in 1995 estimated at 3,671,000) The official languages are

Areal linguistics. A linguistic area – the distribution of front-rounded vowels in Europe. These vowels (e.g. French *soeur* 'sister', German *müde* 'tired') are found along a diagonal axis across northern Europe, and are heard in French, Dutch, German, Danish, Norwegian, Swedish and Finnish. This feature cannot be explained on historical grounds.

Armenian (spoken by c.90% of the population) and Russian. There are also speakers of Azerbaijani and Kurdish. ➤➤Armenian; Russian.

Armenian An Indo-European language spoken by nearly 7 million people chiefly in the Republic of Armenia (c.3.6 million) and Turkish Armenia, and through emigration in many parts of Europe, the USA, and the Middle East. Classical Armenian (**Grabar**) is the language of the older literature, which dates from the 5th century AD, and is the liturgical language of the modern Armenian Church. It is written in a 38-letter alphabet devised by St Mesrop. The modern language exists in two main varieties: Eastern (based on the dialect of the Yerevan region, and used in the Republic of Armenia) and Western (based on the dialect of the Istanbul area, and used in Turkey). ➤➤Armenia; Indo-European.

article A type of word which specifies whether a noun is definite or indefinite, as illustrated by English *the* vs. *a*. Articles were considered a separate part of speech in Greek, though current approaches are more likely to include them within the class of determiners. ➤➤definiteness; determiner.

articulation The use of the vocal organs above the larynx to produce the sounds of speech. The chief **articulators** are the tongue and lips, which actively make contact with such areas as the teeth and hard palate. The study of articulation is carried on by **articulatory phonetics**, also called **physiological phonetics**. ➤➤manner of articulation; phonetics; place of articulation; rate of speech; secondary articulation; vocal organs.

articulation disorder The omission or incorrect production of speech sounds, due to interference with the normal processes of articulation by the vocal organs; the extent of the problem can be assessed using an **articulation test**. In the case of a **functional articulation disorder**, the errors appear in the absence of any evident physical reason for the problem. This is particularly noticeable, with varying levels of severity, in the immature speech of young schoolchildren. ➤➤articulation; phonology.

articulatory apraxia ➤apraxia.

articulatory phonetics ➤articulation.

articulatory setting ➤setting.

artificial language A language which has been invented to serve some particular purpose. Several have been devised in an attempt to foster international communication, and thus solve the 'problem of Babel'. These, such as Esperanto and Novial, are often called **auxiliary languages** or **universal languages**. Artificial languages and systems of communication have also been devised in order to program computers (e.g. BASIC), communicate with robots, and help people with learning difficulties (e.g. Blissymbolics). ➤➤alternative communication system; auxiliary language; Esperanto; Glosa; Ido; Interglossa; Interlingua; Novial; Volapük.

artificial larynx A portable device which provides a source of vibration for speech, used by many people whose larynx has been removed following an operation (usually for throat cancer). The speaker places the device against the neck, near where the larynx would normally be, presses a button to cause a buzzing noise, then mouths the sounds of speech. The voice quality is often somewhat harsh, but users have some degree of control over volume and tone, and their former accent is preserved. ➤laryngectomy; larynx.

artificial speech The speech which is produced by a speech synthesizer, or 'artificial talker'. Early devices produced speech of very poor, robotic quality. Modern devices are capable of producing utterances indistinguishable from natural speech. ➤speech synthesis.

Aryan /ˈarɪən/ ➤Indo-Aryan.

ascender That part of a letter which extends above the height of the lower-case letter *x*, in the line of print (as seen in *t, h, l*). The part which descends below the depth of the *x* (i.e. below the line) is called the **descender** (as seen in *g, p, y*). ➤lower case; typography.

ASL An abbreviation of **American Sign Language**.

aspect A grammatical category which marks the duration or type of temporal activity denoted by the verb. A contrast might be drawn, for example, between the completion of an action and its lack of completion. Slavic languages make great use of aspectual contrasts. In English, these contrasts are less clear-cut, but are certainly involved in the distinction between simple and progressive (*I run* vs. *I am running*) and present vs. perfect (*I see* vs. *I have seen*) – features which would be placed under the heading of 'tense' in traditional grammars. ➤perfect; progressive; tense 1; verb.

aspiration Audible breath which accompanies the articulation of certain types of sound. For example, when [p], [t], and other voiceless plosive sounds are released, it is possible to feel the aspiration by placing the hand in front of the mouth. Sounds which make prominent use of aspiration (especially [h]) are sometimes called **aspirates**. ➤plosive; voicing.

Assamese /asəˈmiːz/ A member of the eastern group of Indo-Aryan languages, spoken by over 14.5 million people chiefly in the state of Assam, north-east India, with some speakers in nearby Bhutan and Bangladesh. It is written in the Bengali alphabet, and is closely related to Bengali. ➤Indo-Aryan.

assimilation The influence exercised by one sound upon the articulation of another, so that the sounds become more alike, or identical; the notion contrasts with **dissimilation**, where the sounds become less alike. The process is especially common in the study of sound change; for example, Latin *noctem* 'night' became Italian *notte*, with the /k/ becoming /t/. In contemporary English usage, the /n/ in the phrase *ten mugs* will in normal (i.e. reasonably fast) speech become /m/, because of the influence of the following sound. Several types of assimilation can be recognized in the analysis of everyday conversation. Purists sometimes insist that people should speak slowly and carefully, so as to avoid assimilations; but speech production of this kind would sound highly unnatural, and no one (not even purist critics) can avoid assimilating some of the time. ➤➤coalescence; coarticulation; dissimilation; elision; fusion; harmony; purism; sound change.

assonance The repeated use of vowels or vowel-like sounds to achieve a particular effect. The notion is especially found in the analysis of poetry, heard to acclaimed effect in such lines as *the wailing warning from the approaching headland / Are all sea voices, and the heaving groaner / Rounded homewards* . . . (T.S. Eliot, 'The Dry Salvages'). ➤➤alliteration; rhyme; vowel.

Assyrian /ə'sɪrɪən/ ➤Akkadian.

Assyro-Babylonian /'asɪrəʊ babɪ'ləʊnɪən/ ➤Akkadian.

asterisk A symbol used in linguistics in two main ways. **1**. It shows that a usage in a given language is unacceptable or ungrammatical; for example, **He are ready.* ➤➤acceptable; grammatical. **2**. In historical linguistics, it shows that a form has been reconstructed by a process of philological reasoning, and has not been found in any written records; for example, the word for 'five' in Indo-European would be written **penkʷe*. An asterisked form is also sometimes called a **starred form**. ➤➤Indo-European; philology.

asyndeton ➤syndeton.

atelic verb /ə'telɪk/ ➤telic verb.

Athabaskan /aθə'baskn/ ➤Na-Dene.

Atjehnese /atʃə'niːz/ ➤Achinese.

atlas, linguistic ➤dialect atlas.

attested form A linguistic form for which there is clear evidence of present or past use. The notion contrasts with the reconstructed forms of historical linguistics, or an analyst's intuitive impressions about usage. ➤➤asterisk; reconstruction.

attribute 1. In phonetics, an identifiable feature of sound sensation, such as pitch or loudness. ➤➤auditory phonetics. **2**. In syntax, an item (typically an adjective or noun) which is used to modify the head of a noun phrase (*red* car, *garden* chair). The function of the item is then said to be **attributive**, contrasting with the **predicative** function which some of these items also display (*the car is red*). ➤➤head; noun phrase; predicate.

attributive ➤adjective; attribute 2.

audiogram A graph used to record a person's ability to hear pure tones, routinely employed in the investigation of deafness. The audiogram can display the ability to hear sound both through the air and through the bones of the skull, and different symbols are used to distinguish the performance of left and right ears. ➤➤audiology; p. 28.

audiolingual method A language-teaching method based on the use of drills and dialogues for speaking and listening; also called the **aural-oral** or **mim-mem method** (the latter an abbreviation of 'mimicry + memorization'). The method is widely used commercially, in the provision of tapes and other materials for private use. ➤➤language laboratory/teaching; method.

audiology The study of hearing and hearing disorders, especially their diagnosis, assessment, and treatment. Its practitioners are **audiologists**. The measurement of hearing is the concern of **audiometry**, and the chief instrument used in this task is an **audiometer**, which registers hearing loss in decibels. ➤➤audiogram; deafness; decibel; p. 28.

audiometry ➤audiology.

auditory acuity The ability to detect and discriminate sound. The term is also used to refer to the sharpness or clarity with which sounds can be distinguished. ➤➤auditory phonetics.

auditory agnosia ➤agnosia.

auditory discrimination The process of distinguishing between sounds. In the context of language, an auditory discrimination test would present listeners with contrasts between speech sounds (e.g. [p] vs. [b]) to see whether they can detect a difference. The technique is widely used by speech therapists when working with children who have language-learning problems. ➤➤auditory phonetics; speech therapy.

auditory nerve ➤acoustic nerve.

auditory phonetics A branch of phonetics which studies the way people perceive sound, as mediated by the ear, auditory nerve, and brain. It includes such specific areas as the perception of pitch and loudness, and the way in which individual speech sounds are analysed and identified. It also includes issues to do with the transcription of speech, and ways of training the ability to distinguish speech sounds. ➤➤auditory acuity/discrimination; dichotic listening; ear training; phonetics; speech perception.

augmentative ➤diminutive.

augmentative communication ➤alternative communication system.

aural-oral ➤audiolingual method.

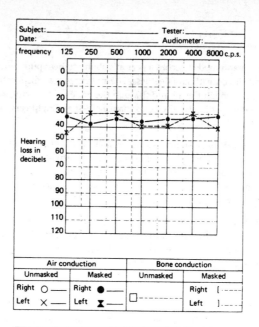

(a)

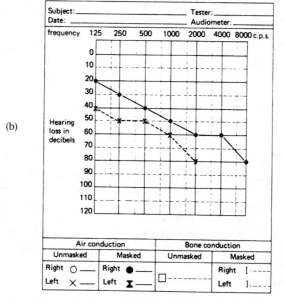

(b)

Audiograms of two types of hearing loss: (a) conductive deafness; (b) sensorineural deafness.

Australia (population in 1995 estimated at 19,089,000) English is the official language, spoken by *c*.95% of the population. It is the home language of 82.6% of the population, according to the 1991 census. There are now over 100 immigrant language minorities (e.g. Italian, Chinese, Arabic, Greek, German, Vietnamese), with numbers significantly increasing in recent years, especially from East Asian countries. Less than 1% of the population speak any of the various aboriginal languages. ➤➤Australian; English.

Australian A group of *c*.230 aboriginal languages spoken in Australia by an uncertain number of people, probably less than 30,000. The languages have been grouped into 28 families, all of which are thought to be related. All but one of these families are found in the northern parts of Western Australia, Northern Territory, and Queensland, in an area comprising no more than an eighth of the continent. By contrast, a single family, Pama-Nyungan, covers the remainder of the continent, with *c*.50 living languages. The languages with the largest number of speakers are Tiwi, Warlpiri, Aranda, Mabuyag, and Western Desert; most have speakers numbering in the low hundreds or less. The number of living languages has halved since the 18th century, and many of those remaining are nearly extinct. The future of aboriginal languages is thus uncertain, but they have become a focus of attention since the 1960s, following the movement to improve the rights of the people. Several now have a written form (using the Roman alphabet), and bilingual school programmes have been devised. ➤➤Australia.

Austria (population in 1995 estimated at 8,097,000) The official language is German, with many using Bavarian German dialects. Slovene is an official regional language in the south-west, in southern Carinthia, spoken by *c*.30,000. Other language minorities include Czech, Hungarian, Romani, varieties of Serbo-Croatian, and Sorbian. English is increasingly used for international trade and tourism, along with German. ➤➤German; Slovene.

Austro-Asiatic A family of over 170 languages spoken throughout south-east Asia by *c*.75 million people, chiefly in countries between China and Indonesia, with a few further west in northern India and the Nicobar Islands. The three main branches of the family are Mon-Khmer, which contains by far the largest group of languages, and Munda and Nicobarese, which are spoken well to the west of the Mon-Khmer area. Linguistic classification is difficult, however, as few of the languages have written records, and the relationship of the family as a whole to other families is uncertain. ➤➤Mon-Khmer; Munda; Nicobarese.

Austronesian A family of *c*.1200 languages, spoken by *c*.270 million people in a large geographical area from Madagascar to Easter Island, and from Taiwan and Hawaii to New Zealand; also called **Malayo-Polynesian**. It is one of the largest families, the uncertainty in the number of languages resulting from difficulties in deciding whether two varieties are different languages or dialects of the same language, and from the existence of many 'mixed' languages which have grown up as a result of trade contacts. The family is usually divided into three groups. The **Western Austronesian** group contains *c.*500 languages spoken in Madagascar, Malaysia, the Indonesian Islands, the Philippines, Taiwan, parts of Vietnam and Cambodia, and the western end of New Guinea. Two languages of Micronesia (Chamorro and Palauan) are also included. The **Eastern Austronesian** group, usually referred to as **Oceanic**, contains *c.*500 languages spoken over most of New Guinea, and throughout the 10,000 or so islands of Melanesia, Micronesia, and Polynesia, but with only *c.*2.5 million speakers. The **Central Austronesian** group contains *c.*150 languages spoken by *c.*4.5 million people in the central islands of Indonesia. ➤➤Achinese; Balinese; Batak; Buginese; Cebuano; Fijian; Ilocano; Javanese; Madurese; Malagasy; Malay; Maori; Motu; Pilipino; Samoan; Sundanese; Tahitian; Tongan.

automatic speech recognition ➤speech recognition.

automatic translation ➤machine translation.

autonomous speech ➤idioglossia.

aux. An abbreviation of **auxiliary verb**.

auxiliary language A language which has been adopted by a speech community for such purposes as international communication, trade, or education, though only a minority of the community may use it as a mother tongue. English is the most widely used auxiliary language; others include French, Spanish, Portuguese, German, Swahili, and Arabic. ➤➤artificial language; lingua franca; pidgin.

auxiliary verb A verb which is subordinate to the chief lexical verb in a verb phrase, helping to express such grammatical distinctions as tense, mood, and aspect. English auxiliary verbs include the various forms of *be*, *do*, and *have*, as well as the **modal auxiliaries** – *may*, *might*, *will*, *can*, and several others – used singly or in certain combinations, e.g. *was running*, *may go*, and *has been hurt*. Some approaches recognize **semi-auxiliaries**, which display only some of the properties of the auxiliary class (e.g. *dare*). ➤➤aspect; lexical verb; mood; tense 1; verb.

Avar /ˈavɑː/ A member of the Dagestanian group of Caucasian languages, spoken by *c.*600,000 people in the north-east Caucasus, mainly in the Dagestan region of Russia and in Azerbaijan. It is written in the Cyrillic alphabet, and is used as a lingua franca by several ethnic groups in the area, including the Andi and Dido. ➤➤lingua franca; Nakho-Dagestanian.

Avestan /əˈvestn/ ➤Iranian.

avoidance languages Languages which permit communication between a person and others with whom there is a social taboo; sometimes loosely called **mother-in-law languages**. The concept specifically relates to Australian aboriginal languages, where there may be strict taboos between certain relatives, such as a man and his wife's mother and maternal uncles. In Dyirbal, for example, the everyday language is known as Guwal, and the avoidance language as Dyalnguy, which would be used whenever a taboo relative was within earshot. ➤➤Australian; taboo language.

Aymará /aɪməˈrɑ:/ A member of the Quechumaran group of Andean-Equatorial languages, spoken by over 2.2 million people chiefly in Bolivia (c.1.8 million) and Peru, and part of nearby Argentina. It is written in the Roman alphabet. It was once a major language throughout the central Andes, forming part of the Inca Empire. ➤➤Amerindian; Andean-Equatorial.

Azerbaijan (population in 1995 estimated at 7,500,000) The official languages are Azerbaijani (spoken by c.75% of the population) and Russian (c.6%). There are c.12 other languages, including Armenian and Avar. ➤➤Azerbaijani; Russian.

Azerbaijani /azəbəˈdʒɑ:ni:/ A member of the Turkic branch of the Altaic family of languages, spoken by c.14 million people in Azerbaijan (where it is an official language) and Iran, and in Turkey, Syria, and Afghanistan; also called **Azeri**. It generally uses the Cyrillic alphabet in Azerbaijan and the Arabic alphabet in Iran. It is usually distinguished on linguistic grounds, as Southern Azerbaijani, from Northern Azerbaijani, spoken by c.7 million people. ➤➤Azerbaijan; Turkic.

Azeri /əˈzeri:/ ➤Azerbaijani.

Azores (population in 1995 estimated at 240,000) The official language is Portuguese. English is increasingly used as a language of tourism. ➤➤Portuguese.

Aztec /ˈaztek/ ➤Nahuatl.

Aztec-Tanoan /ˈaztek təˈnəʊən/ A group of c.30 languages spoken in parts of western and south-western USA and western Mexico, most with very few speakers. The group includes Comanche, Paiute, Shoshone, and Hopi. Three Mexican languages are still widely spoken: Nahuatl (also called Aztec, many varieties c.1.4 million), Tarahumar (c.40,000), and Papago-Pima (c.12,000). All these languages use the Roman alphabet when written down. ➤➤Amerindian; Nahuatl.

B

Baba Malay /ˈbɑːbə məˈleɪ/ ➤Malay.

babbling A type of infant sound production characteristic of the period immediately before the onset of language – typically, in the second half of the first year. It often involves repeated syllable patterns of the [bababa] type, which the term reflects. Babbling patterns are not random, but relate to features of the linguistic environment in which the child is learning. ➤➤acquisition; cooing.

Babylonian /babəˈləʊnɪən/ ➤Akkadian.

baby talk 1. A simplified speech style used by adults to young children, typically involving special words or word endings (*doggie, choo-choo*), short sentences, repeated utterances, and exaggerated speech melody, loudness, and rhythm. This kind of language is also heard when people talk to animals and (to a lesser extent) when people who are on intimate terms tease each other. ➤➤motherese. **2**. An immature form of speech, used by children. At around age 18 months, for example, English children can be heard to say such things as *Man go* or *Kick ball*, usually with immature pronunciation. This is often loosely referred to as 'baby talk', but this term has no precise meaning when used in studies of child language acquisition. ➤➤telegrammatic speech.

back formation An abnormal type of word formation where a shorter word is derived by removing an affix from a longer word. *Burglar* was in the language first, then people derived *burgle* from it; similarly, *televise* was derived from *television*. This process is abnormal because usually people make up new words by adding affixes to them. ➤➤affix; word formation.

back slang A secret language in which words are said backwards, usually based on the reversed spelling. Examples from English include [tekram] for *market*, [ekilop] for *police*, and [tenip] for *pint*. Back slang is quite common among children, but has been observed in adult use, too – such as by soldiers, barrow boys, shopkeepers, and thieves. It is probably used in a jocular way by most people, from time to time. ➤➤slang; word game.

back sound ➤front sound.

back translation A means of testing the quality of a translation. One translator turns language A into language B. A second translator turns B back into A, and the resulting A text is then compared with the original A text. If the texts are virtually identical, it is strong evidence that the original translation was of high quality. ➤➤translation.

Bahamas (population in 1995 estimated at 274,000) The official language is English, with over 85% of the population using an English-based creole (Bahamas Creole). ➤➤creole; English.

Bahasa Indonesia /bə'hɑːsə/ ➤Malay.

Bahrain (population in 1995 estimated at 555,000) The official language is Arabic. There are minority populations speaking Farsi (c.48,000), Urdu (c.20,000), and various languages of the Philippines (c. 20,000). English is increasingly used for international trade and tourism. ➤➤Arabic.

Balinese A member of the Austronesian family of languages, spoken by c.3.8 million people on the island of Bali, Indonesia. It is written in both the Balinese and Roman alphabets. ➤➤Austronesian.

Balochi ➤Baluchi.

Baltic A branch of the Balto-Slavic family of languages, spoken by c.5 million people along the Baltic coast, with a further million abroad (mainly through emigration to the USA). The chief languages are Latvian and Lithuanian. There are also a few written remains of Old Prussian. Other languages of the family are now extinct. ➤➤Balto-Slavic; Latvian; Lithuanian.

Balto-Slavic A grouping of Baltic and Slavic languages, placed together as a single branch of Indo-European, spoken by c.300 million people, over half of whom speak Russian. There is some dispute as to whether the evident similarities are the result of a common origin or a consequence of more recent mutual linguistic influence. ➤➤Baltic; Slavic.

Baluchi or **Balochi** /bəluːtʃiː/ A member of the Iranian group of languages, spoken by c.5 million people chiefly in Pakistan (in Baluchistan, the country's westernmost province, c.4 million) and Iran, with some in Afghanistan, Bahrain, and India. It is written in the Arabic alphabet. There is a Baluchi Academy. ➤➤Iranian.

Bamana /bə'mɑːnə/ ➤Bambara.

Bambara /bam'bɑːrə/ A Mande language spoken by c.3 million people, mainly in Mali, with some speakers in adjoining areas to the south and west; also called **Bamana** (Bambara is also the name of the people). It is written in the Roman alphabet. ➤➤Mande.

Bamileke /ba'mɪleke/ A group of Benue-Congo languages, spoken by c.1.2 million people in Cameroon; sometimes considered varieties of one language. They are non-Bantu languages, spoken by many tribes in the region, and written in the Roman alphabet. ➤➤Benue-Congo.

Bangladesh (population in 1995 census, 117,372,000) The official language is Bengali, spoken by over 98% of the population. Over 30 other languages are spoken, the largest numbers using Arakan, Burmese, Chakma, and Santali. Assamese and Sylhet are sometimes distinguished as separate languages. English is increasingly used for international trade and tourism. ➤Bengali.

Bank of English An international English language project established in 1991 with the aim of compiling a database of 220 million words of contemporary speech and writing. It was set up by COBUILD at the University of Birmingham, under the editorship of John Sinclair and Gwyneth Fox. ➤COBUILD; corpus.

Bantu /ban'tu:/ A large group of languages (estimates vary between 300 and 500) spoken by Bantu peoples throughout central and southern Africa; *c*.100 million speakers. Bantu languages have often been treated as a separate language family, but nowadays they are usually classified as part of the Benue-Congo group of Niger-Congo languages. They include such prominent languages as Swahili, Rwanda, and Zulu. ➤Bamileke; Benue-Congo; Kongo; Makua; Nyanja; Rwanda 2; Swahili; Xhosa; Zulu.

Barbados (population in 1995 estimated at 261,000) The official language is English. The local dialect (Bajan) shows the increasing influence of US English, as well as some features of West Indian creoles. ➤English.

bare infinitive ➤infinitive.

Bari /'bɑːriː/ A Nilotic (or, in some classifications, Nilo-Hamitic) language spoken by *c*.300,000 people, mainly in southern Sudan, with some in the Congo DR and Uganda. Many small and widely dispersed tribes use the language, which consequently has a wide range of dialects. It is written in the Roman alphabet. ➤Nilotic.

Bashkir /baʃ'kɪə/ A member of the Turkic branch of the Altaic family of languages, spoken by *c*.950,000 people in the Bashkir region of Russia (where it is an official language) and neighbouring regions. It is written in the Cyrillic alphabet. ➤Turkic.

Basic English A project to simplify the English language by reducing the size of its vocabulary, thus enabling it to be more easily put to international use. Devised in 1930 by Charles Kay Ogden (1889–1957), BASIC is an acronym of 'British American Scientific International Commercial'. It consists of a basic vocabulary of 850 words selected to cover general needs, supplemented by several international and scientific words (e.g. names of countries, chemical elements). The proposal achieved strong support in the 1940s, and still attracts enthusiasts, but is now largely of historical interest. ➤artificial language; English.

basilect ➤creole.

Basque /bask/ An isolated language spoken by *c*.590,000 people chiefly in northern Spain (*c*.580,000) and south-western France; it is an official regional language both in the País Vasco (Basque Provinces), Spain, and in the Pays Basque (Basque Country),

France. It is written in the Roman alphabet. Efforts have been made to show a relationship with Caucasian languages, North African languages, and Iberian, but none has been convincing. The written history of the language can be traced to Roman times through various inscriptions, with a continuous literary tradition from the 16th century. There is now intensive local concern to develop the language and introduce it into education, following a period under Franco (from the late 1930s to the mid-1950s) when its use was forbidden. The language (*Euskara* in Basque) is also closely associated with the demands of the political separatist movement, ETA (Euzkadi ta Azkatasuna, 'Basque Homeland and Liberty'). ➤➤isolate.

Batak /ˈbatak/ An Austronesian language spoken by *c.*2 million people in Sumatra, Indonesia; also called **Toba Batak** (from the name of the highland people who lived around Lake Toba). It is generally written in the Roman alphabet, but some use is still made of a local Batak script. ➤➤Austronesian.

Bazaar Malay ➤Malay.

BBC English ➤standard English.

Beach-la-Mar /ˈbiːtʃləˈmɑː/ ➤Bislama.

bel ➤decibel.

Belarus or **Byelarus** (population in 1995 estimated at 10,424,000) The official languages are Belorussian (spoken by *c.*98% of the population) and Russian (by *c.*10%). In the border areas, there are some speakers of languages used further west, especially Polish and German. ➤➤Belorussian; Russian.

Belau or **Palau** (population in 1995 estimated at 16,800) The official language is English. Most of the population speak an Austronesian language, Palauan (Belauan). ➤➤English.

Belgium (population in 1995 estimated at 10,099,000) The official languages are Dutch (Flemish, spoken in the north by *c.*57% of the population) and French (Walloon, spoken in the south by *c.*33%). The Brussels region is a bilingual zone. German is an official regional language in the eastern provinces of Eupen–Malmédy–St Vith, where it is spoken by *c.*150,000. Minority languages include Arabic, Turkish, Kabyle, Spanish, Portuguese and Lëtzebuergesch. ➤➤Dutch; French.

Belize (population in 1995 estimated at 212,000) The official language is English. Over 25% of the population have an English-based creole (Kriol) as a first language, and most people use it as a lingua franca. Spanish is spoken by over 20%, and over 15% use Amerindian languages, chiefly Carib and Quekchi. There are also *c.*5000 speakers of Mennonite German. ➤➤creole; English.

Belorussian or **Byelorussian** /belǝˈrʌʃn, bjelǝˈrʌʃn/ A member of the East Slavic group of languages, spoken by over 10 million people chiefly in the republic of Belarus (where it is the official language), and in parts of Poland; also formerly called

White Russian. It is written in the Cyrillic alphabet. Literary remains date from the 11th century, and the modern standard language is based on the dialect of the capital, Minsk. There has been considerable vocabulary borrowing from Polish. ➤➤Belarus; Slavic.

Bemba /ˈbembə/ A member of the Bantu group of the Benue-Congo family of languages, spoken by c.2.5 million people chiefly in Zambia (c.2 million) and the Democratic Republic of Congo (formerly Zaire). It is written in the Roman alphabet, and is an important lingua franca in the region. ➤➤lingua franca; Niger-Congo.

Bengali /benˈgɔːliː/ A member of the eastern group of Indo-Aryan languages, spoken by c.100 million people in Bangladesh (where it is the official language), by a further 68 million in India, chiefly in West Bengal, and by many more as an immigrant language in Great Britain and elsewhere – possibly 200 million, including second-language users. The language is diglossic in character, and is written in the Bengali alphabet. Its literature dates from the 12th century. In modern times, it was the first Indian language to show the influence of Western literary styles, and the poet and philosopher Rabindranath Tagore (1861–1941), who wrote in Bengali, was the first Asian to receive the Nobel Prize for Literature, in 1913. ➤➤Bangladesh; diglossia; Indo-Aryan.

Benin (population in 1995 estimated at 5,420,000) The official language is French. Over 50 local languages are in use, with Fon (1.5 million speakers) widely used as a lingua franca. Others include Yoruba (c.400,000), Burba, Fulfulde, Gun, and Tem. ➤➤French; lingua franca.

Benue-Congo /ˈbenuːɪ ˈkɒŋgəʊ/ The largest group of languages within the Niger-Congo family – c.800 languages spoken throughout central and southern Africa by c.150 million people. The vast majority are Bantu languages, such as Swahili, Rwanda, and Zulu. The most important non-Bantu languages are in Nigeria; they include Efik and Tiv. Several Nigerian and Benin languages formerly classified as part of the Kwa group are now placed under this heading (e.g. Edo, Idoma, Igbo, Nupe, Yoruba). ➤➤Bantu; Efik; Igbo; Niger-Congo; Rwanda 2; Shona; Sotho; Swahili; Tiv; Tswana; Yoruba; Zulu.

Berber /ˈbɜːbə/ A branch of the Afro-Asiatic family of languages, spoken by c.10 million people throughout North Africa, chiefly in Algeria and Morocco. The group of c.30 languages includes Riff, Kabyle, Shluh, and Tamashek, the widely scattered language of the Tuareg nomads. The Arabic alphabet is used for writing, in almost all cases (an exception is Tamashek, which uses a system derived from Old Libyan). There are some early inscriptions, but there is very little native literature. ➤➤Afro-Asiatic; Kabyle.

Bermuda (population in 1995 estimated at 62,000) The official language is English. The local dialect shows some creole influence. ➤➤creole; English.

BEV ➤African-American Vernacular English.

Bhojpuri /ˈbɒdʒpʊriː/ ➤Bihari.

Bhutan (population in 1995 estimated at 1,622,000) The official language is Dzongkha (Bhutani). About 10 other languages are in use, including Nepali (c.300,000). English is increasingly used for international trade and tourism. ➤➤Dzongkha.

Bhutani or **Bhutanese** /buˈtɑːniː/ ➤Dzongkha.

bidialectism The use by a person or community of two (or more) dialects of a language; also called **bidialectalism**. Following the increased mobility of populations, many people now have some degree of bidialectal ability, perhaps switching between regional dialects, or using the standard language at work and a local variety at home. In educational contexts, the term refers to the principle of attributing equal linguistic validity to different dialects – typically, between standard and nonstandard varieties, each of which is recommended for use in its appropriate settings. ➤➤bilingualism; dialect; English as a second dialect; standard.

Bihari /biˈhɑːriː/ Several varieties (considered by some to be separate languages) belonging to the Midland group of Indo-Aryan, spoken by c.60 million people in the state of Bihar, north-eastern India, with a further 3.5 million in Nepal, and some in nearby parts of adjoining countries. They comprise Bhojpuri (c.25 million) in the west, and Maithili (c.24 million) and Magahi (c.11 million) in the east. They are written in the Devanagari alphabet. Hindi/Urdu is spoken as an educated lingua franca by the majority of the population. ➤➤Devanagari; Indo-Aryan; lingua franca.

bilabial Descriptive of a consonant sound made with the two lips – most commonly, [p], [b], and [m]. ➤➤consonant; labial; rounding.

bilingualism A speech situation where an individual or community controls two (or more) languages; less usually called **polyglottism** (though the term **polyglot** for someone who speaks several languages is common enough; contrasting with **monoglot**). In **simultaneous** bilingualism, the languages are learned at the same time; in **sequential** bilingualism, the second is acquired after the first has been established. **Bilingual education** is the use of two languages of instruction at some point in a student's career. It also refers to the use of educational programmes designed to promote bilingual skills among students. The majority of the world's speakers are bilingual – a point which tends to surprise Britons and Americans, for whom knowledge of a single language (**monolingualism**) is traditionally the norm. ➤➤bidialectism; immersion; language learning; multilingualism; national language.

biliteracy ➤literacy.

binding ➤government and binding theory.

biolinguistics The study of the biological preconditions for language development and use, both in the human species and in individuals; also called **biological linguistics**. It includes such topics as the extent to which language can be said to be species-specific, the factors constraining the development of language in the child, and the neurophysiological processes involved in language disorders. ➤➤acquisition; language pathology; linguistics.

Bislama /bɪz'lɑːmə/ An English-based pidgin, with local language influences, widely used (over 150,000) in Vanuatu, Fiji, and surrounding areas as a lingua franca; also called **Beach-la-Mar**. The name derives from *bêche-de-mer*, a local variety of sea slug. There is now some use as a first language. ➤➤lingua franca; pidgin.

Black English Vernacular ➤African-American Vernacular English.

black letter writing A form of writing which developed out of the 9th-century minuscule associated with Emperor Charlemagne, in which the rounded strokes became straighter, bolder, and more pointed; often called **Gothic script**. Widely used in many variations between the 11th and 15th centuries, it became the earliest model for printer's type in Germany. ➤➤letter; minuscule; writing.

blade The part of the tongue between the tip and the centre; also known as the **lamina**. When the tongue is in a neutral position, the blade lies opposite the teeth and alveolar ridge. ➤➤tongue.

blasphemy ➤taboo language.

blend ➤cluster.

blending A process in grammar or vocabulary which takes place when two elements that do not normally co-occur are combined into a single linguistic unit (a **blend**). Examples in English vocabulary include *brunch* (from *breakfast* and *lunch*) and *Eurovision* (from *European* and *television*). When the process affects syntax, it is called a **syntactic blend**, as seen in *I think it's the money is one problem* (from *I think it's the money* and *The money is one problem*). ➤➤borrowing; word formation; *cartoon*, p. 39.

Blissymbolics /'blɪs sɪm'bɒlɪks/ A visual supplement to speech devised to help people with a communication handicap. Developed in Canada in the 1970s, it was created by a chemical engineer, Charles Bliss (1897–1985), whose aim was to devise a set of symbols which could be translated into any language (as could the symbols of chemistry). Blissymbols have since been used with a variety of clinical populations, such as the mentally handicapped and the autistic. ➤➤alternative communication system; language pathology.

blocking In stuttering, an obstruction experienced by the speaker that prevents the production of speech. The utterance is temporarily halted, and during the silence the speaker may make bodily movements (e.g. movement of the lips and jaw, swivelling of the head) indicative of the struggle going on inside. Blocks of several seconds may occur. ➤➤stuttering.

'Breakfast turned to brunch, then brunch became brinner and somehow brinner became brupper!' (**blending**)

block language The use of abbreviated structures in restricted communicative contexts, special use being made of the word or phrase rather than the clause or sentence. Examples include the language of posters, notice boards, book titles, and newspaper headlines. ➤ellipsis.

Bloomfieldian Adjective derived from Leonard Bloomfield (1887–1949), an American linguist whose thinking dominated the development of linguistics between the 1930s and the 1950s. He is known especially for his book *Language* (1933), the first major statement synthesizing the theory and practice of linguistic analysis. The Bloomfieldian approach later came to be called 'structuralist', because of the various kinds of technique it employed to identify and classify features of sentence structure. It also represented a behaviourist view of linguistics, especially in its approach to the study of meaning. ➤linguistics; structural.

body language Communication using body movement, position, and appearance, such as facial expressions, hand gestures, and the mutual body orientations of the speakers; called, more technically, **nonverbal communication**. The word 'language' is not being used here as strictly as in the case of speech, writing, and sign. The range of signals which can be sent using body 'language' is highly limited and unstructured compared with the virtually limitless and complex possibilities of language proper. ➤communication; kinesics; language 4; proxemics; semiotics.

Bokmål /'bʊkmɔːl/ ➤Norwegian.

bold A typeface in which the lines and dots which make up the symbols appear in thickened form, giving extra emphasis or prominence to the text; also called **bold-face**. Headings and sub-headings are typically printed in bold, which may also be used for technical terms and other special features within a text (as in its use for a synonymous term in the present entry). A typeface with strokes midway in thickness between ordinary roman and bold is called **semi-bold**. ➤typography.

Bolivia (population in 1995 estimated at 8,120,000) The official language is Spanish, spoken by c.43% of the population (3.5 million). Over 40 other languages are in use, including Quechua (c.34%), and Aymará (c.22%). There were c.18,000 speakers of Mennonite German in the mid-1980s. English is increasingly used, along with Spanish, for international trade and tourism. ➤Spanish.

borrowing The introduction of a word (or some other linguistic feature) from one language or dialect into another. Vocabulary borrowings are usually called **loan words**. Examples include *smoking* and *computer* (from English into French) and *restaurant* and *chic* (from French into English). In a **loan blend**, the meaning is borrowed but only part of the form, such as when English *restaurant* retains a French pronunciation of the final syllable. In **loan shifts**, the meaning is borrowed but the form is nativized, such as when *restaurant* is given a totally English pronunciation. These terms are all something of a misnomer, as the words are not given back, in any sense. ➤calque; vocabulary.

Bosnia and Herzegovina (population in 1995 estimated at 4,200,000) The official language is increasingly being referred to as **Bosnian** (before the civil war, Serbo-Croatian), but the unique ethnic mix in the country (c.2 million Bosnians, c.1.6 million Serbs, and c.500,000 Croats) means that several varieties of Serbo-Croatian currently co-exist. English is increasingly being used for international purposes. ➤Serbo-Croatian.

Bosnian ➤Bosnia and Herzegovina.

Botswana (population in 1995 estimated at 1,540,000) The official languages are Tswana (spoken by c.70% of the population) and English. Over 25 local languages are in use, including Shona and several Khoisan languages. ➤English; Khoisan; Tswana.

bound form A minimal grammatical unit which cannot occur on its own as a word, as in English *un-* and *-tion*; also called a **bound morpheme**. It contrasts with **free form**, where the unit can be used as a word without additional elements, as in *hope* and *on*. ➤free form; morpheme; word.

boustrophedon /buːˈstrɒfədn/ Writing in which the lines run in alternate directions; the name derives from Greek, and means 'ox-turning' (the reference is to the way an ox pulling a plough moves first in one direction then the other). It was especially used in an early period of Greek writing, but inscriptions using this method have been found in many other parts of the world. ➤➤graphology 1.

bow-wow theory The name of one of the speculative theories about the origins of language: it argues that speech arose through people imitating the sounds of the environment, especially animal calls. The main evidence is the use of onomatopoeic words (which are few, in most languages). ➤➤origins of language.

brace ➤brackets.

brachygraphy /brəˈkɪgrəfiː/ ➤shorthand.

bracketing A way of showing the internal structure of a string of elements. In a sentence, for example, the technique can be used to distinguish between subject and predicate, and within the predicate between verb and object: ((The cat) ((chased)

(a) This is an illustration of
writing of way possible one
in a boustrophedon style. The
but direction reverse lines
the words do not.
(b) This is another illustration
nI .gnitirw nodehportsuob fo
this case, both the lines and
.desrever era sdrow eht
(c) The third illustration shows
ƨɿɘttɘl nɘʜw ƨnɘqqɒʜ tɒʜw
are reversed as well as words
.ƨɘnil bnɒ

This drawing of an early Greek treaty (6th–5th century BC) is of the third kind, as can be seen most clearly from the reversed Es in the third and fifth lines.

There are three possible ways of writing **boustrophedon**. In (a) the lines reverse but the words do not. In (b) the words reverse as well as the lines. In (c) the letters reverse as well as words and lines.

(the leaf))). Working from the outside brackets inwards, the first pair encloses the whole construction (the sentence); within these there are two pairs which identify the subject and the predicate; and within the right-hand pair there are two further pairs identifying the verb and the object. ➤➤syntax.

brackets A pair of correlative punctuation marks which typically signals an included, parenthetic unit. In British English, the term is ambiguous, as it is used for both 'square brackets' [ ] and 'round brackets' ( ). American English tends to distinguish these, reserving 'brackets' for square brackets, and calling round brackets 'parentheses'. The latter usage has widespread British currency also. The **brace** { }, sometimes informally called 'curly brackets', tends to be restricted to technical writing. The less common **angle brackets** ⟨ ⟩ are likewise specialized in use. ➤➤parenthesis 1; punctuation.

Brahmi /'brɑːmiː/ An early script of southern Asia, found in various inscriptions from the 3rd century BC. The script, which was written from left to right, was the ancestor of many scripts used in southern Asia, such as Devanagari, Bengali, Tibetan, and Telugu. Its origins are controversial, most scholars deriving it from an earlier Semitic script, but with some linking it to the Indus Valley script of the 3rd millennium BC. ➤➤alphabet; Devanagari.

braille /breɪl/ A system devised to enable written language to be read by a blind person. It consists of a sequence of cells, each of which contains a matrix of embossed dots representing letters, numbers, punctuation marks, and a few other features. The blind person's fingers 'read' the brailled text, shapes being recognized through the sense of touch. The system was devised by French teacher Louis Braille (1809–52). ➤➤alternative communication system.

The **Braille** alphabet, with examples of word abbreviations.

Brazil (population in 1995 estimated at 159,233,000) The official language is Portuguese, spoken by over 96% of the population. There are about 190 Amerindian languages spoken, often by very small numbers, and all under threat from the encroaching Western economy – perhaps 150,000 speakers in all. The larger languages (whose numbers are likely to exceed 5000) include Baniwa, Guajajára, Guaraní, Kaingáng, Terêna, Ticuna, and Yanomámi. There are also c.6000 speakers of Mennonite German, and an uncertain (but probably large) number of speakers of

Romani. Several other immigrant languages are found, notably Japanese, standard German, and Italian. English is increasingly used for international purposes. ➤➤Amerindian; Portuguese.

breaking (of the voice) ➤voice mutation.

breathy voice A state of phonation in which the vocal folds are held somewhat apart, thus allowing the escape of audible breath during speech; also known as **murmur**. It is an important component of certain tones of voice, such as those associated with sexiness and secrecy. ➤➤paralanguage; phonation; voice quality.

Breton /'bretɒn/ A member of the Brythonic branch of the Celtic family of languages, spoken by *c*.500,000 people in France, chiefly in Brittany (where it is an official regional language), with a few thousand more speakers as a result of emigration to other parts of the world, especially the USA. There was a movement into Brittany from southern England during the 5th and 6th centuries, following the Anglo-Saxon invasions, and in its early period Breton was very close to Cornish. It is written in the Roman alphabet, and remains date from the 8th century. There was an increasing amount of literary writing in the 20th century, and a certain revival of interest in Breton language and culture, but there was a general decline in the number of speakers. ➤➤Celtic.

British National Corpus A computer corpus of 100 million words of contemporary spoken and written British English. It was compiled in a three-year project (1991–4) by a six-member consortium, based at Oxford, consisting of Oxford University Press, Longman Group UK, W. & R. Chambers, the British Library, and the universities of Oxford and Lancaster. Spoken material comprises 10% of the corpus. All words are tagged for their grammatical class. ➤➤corpus; tag 2.

British Sign Language ➤American Sign Language.

British Virgin Islands (population in 1995 estimated at 13,000) The official language is English. Most speakers use an English-based creole widespread throughout the Lesser Antilles. ➤➤creole; English.

broad transcription ➤transcription.

Broca's aphasia /'brəʊkə/ A type of aphasia which arises from damage to Broca's area, located towards the front of the left hemisphere of the brain; also called **expressive aphasia**. It is named after the French neurologist Paul Broca (1824–80), who first described the syndrome. It is characterized by effortful speech, with problems of word finding, and disruption to the grammatical system. Comprehension may be unimpaired. ➤➤aphasia; language areas.

Brown University Corpus of American English A corpus drawn from printed sources published in America in 1961. It comprises 500 samples of *c*.2000 words each, representing 15 main varieties of the language. Lexical concordances, word frequency lists, and other materials have been derived from the corpus. ➤➤corpus.

Brunei (population in 1995 estimated at 293,000) The official languages are Malay and English. Over half the population have Malay as a first language; less than 10,000 have English as a first language. Several varieties of Chinese are in use, spoken by *c.*12% of the population, with a number of local languages used by small numbers. Malay is a lingua franca, but English is increasingly the language of trade and tourism. ➤➤English; lingua franca; Malay.

Brythonic /brɪˈθɒnɪk/ ➤Celtic.

BSL An abbreviation of **British Sign Language**.

buccal sounds /ˈbʌkl/ Sounds made in or near the cavity of the cheek. One of the most famous buccal voices is that of Donald Duck. ➤➤articulatory phonetics; *cartoon below*.

Buginese /bəgəˈniːz/ A member of the Austronesian family of languages, spoken by *c.*3.5 million people in Sulawesi (Celebes); also called **Bugis**. It is written in both

'I'm terribly sorry – I can't understand a single word you're saying.'

the Buginese alphabet (as a result of influences from India) and the Roman alphabet. ➤➤Austronesian.

Bugis ➤Buginese.

Bulgaria (population in 1995 estimated at 8,670,000) The official language is Bulgarian, spoken by *c*.85% of the population. Minority languages include Turkish (*c*.9%), Albanian, Armenian, Gagauz, Greek, Macedonian, and Romanian. There are significant numbers of Romani speakers, perhaps 200,000. English, German, and Russian are all used for international purposes. ➤➤Bulgarian; Romani.

Bulgarian A member of the South Slavic group of languages, spoken by nearly 9 million people, chiefly in Bulgaria (where it is the official language) and also in parts of Greece, Romania, Moldova, and Ukraine. It is written in the Cyrillic alphabet. The closely related Macedonian is commonly included within these statistics. Old Bulgarian, the first Slavic literary language to develop, dates from the 10th century. ➤➤Bulgaria; Slavic.

Burkina Faso (population in 1995 estimated at 10,328,000) The official language is French. About 70 local languages are spoken, notably More (*c*.5 million), Bissa, Bobo, Dagari, Fulfulde, Gourma, and Lobi. French is the language used for international purposes. ➤➤French.

Burma ➤Myanmar.

Burmese A member of the Tibeto-Burman group of Sino-Tibetan languages, spoken by *c*.25 million people in Myanmar (Burma), where it is the official language. It is written in the Burmese alphabet, with records dating from the 11th century. ➤➤Myanmar; Sino-Tibetan.

burst A sudden, short peak of acoustic energy which occurs in the production of certain sounds. The clearest case is the release stage in the production of plosive consonants, such as [p] or [b]. ➤➤acoustic phonetics; plosive.

Burundi (population in 1995 estimated at 6,131,000) The official languages are Rundi (also called Kirundi or Urundi) and French. Swahili is quite widely used as a lingua franca, but French is normal for international purposes. ➤➤English; lingua franca; Rwanda 2.

Burushaski /bʊrʊˈʃaskiː/ An isolated language spoken in north-west Kashmir, India, and in a small part of nearby Pakistan, by *c*.50,000 people belonging to the Burusho tribe. It has no written form. ➤➤isolate.

Buryat /bʊrˈjat/ A member of the Mongolian group of the Altaic family of languages, spoken by *c*.320,000 people chiefly in the Buryat region of Russia (where it has official status). It is written in the Cyrillic alphabet. ➤➤Mongolian.

Byelarus ➤Belarus.

Byelorussian ➤Belorussian.

byname A supplementary name, added to someone's personal name in order to help identification, and sometimes replacing it completely. For example, several singers with identical surnames in North Wales are publicly known by their village of origin (e.g. *Williams Penygroes, Williams Brynsiencyn*). History is full of bynames – *Eric the Red, James the Bold, Ethelred the Unready*. A byname can in principle be distinguished from a surname, because it is not its purpose to be passed on between generations; however, many surnames undoubtedly started out life as bynames (e.g. *Michael Carpenter*). ➤➤nickname; onomastics.

C

C An abbreviation of **complement** or **consonant**.

CA An abbreviation of **conversation analysis** or **contrastive analysis**.

cacophony The use of unpleasant, harsh sounds, especially in speech. A similar term has been coined for unacceptable hand-writing or spelling – **cacography** – but is less used. A more general label for unacceptable uses of language also exists: **cacology**. None of these terms has developed a conventional use in linguistics; all have derived from popular reactions to language use. ➤euphony.

caesura /siˈzjʊərə/ A break in the rhythm of a line of poetry; the term derives from Latin, where it means 'cutting'. A caesura may occur anywhere in the line, and is usually (but by no means always) marked by punctuation. An example occurs in the second line of this extract from Pope's *An Essay on Man: Why has not man a microscopic eye? / For this plain reason, man is not a fly*. ➤metrics.

CAI ➤computer-assisted language learning.

CALL An abbreviation of **computer-assisted language learning**.

calligraphy /kəˈlɪgrəfiː/ ➤chirography.

calque /kalk/ A type of borrowing where the parts (morphemes) of the borrowed word are translated item by item into equivalent parts (morphemes) in the new language; sometimes called a **loan translation**. An example is English *power politics* from German *Machtpolitik*. ➤borrowing; morpheme.

Cambodia (formerly **Kampuchea**) (population in 1995 estimated at 9,692,000) The official language is Khmer, spoken by *c.*90% of the population. There are *c.*15 other languages in use, including Chinese (*c.*350,000) and Vietnamese (*c.*750,000). French is used for international purposes. ➤Khmer.

Cameroon (population in 1995 estimated at 13,986,000) The official languages are English and French. There are a remarkable number of languages found in this relatively small country (about twice the size of the UK) – about 280. The most widely used are Fang (*c.*1.7 million), Bamileke (*c.*1.2 million), and Duala (*c.*1.3 million). Fulfulde (*c.*700,000) and Arabic (*c.*60,000) are both used as lingua francas in the north of the country. The most important lingua franca, however, is Cameroonian Pidgin, used by about half the population. This is an English-based variety, now spoken by increasing numbers as a first language. ➤➤English; French; lingua franca; pidgin.

Canada (population in 1995 estimated at 28,972,000) The official languages are English and French, with French the official regional language of Québec. English is usually used for international purposes. There are many European immigrant languages, including three varieties of German associated with religious settlement (Hutterite, Mennonite, Pennsylvanian). Over 70 Amerindian languages are spoken by 100,000–150,000, notably Blackfoot, Chipewyan, Cree, Dakota, Eskimo, and Ojibwa. The chief families represented are the Algonkin, Athabaskan, Eskimo-Aleut, Iroquoian, Siouan, and Wakashan, with several isolated languages. ➤➤Amerindian; English; French; isolate.

Canary Islands (population in 1995 estimated at 1,468,000) The official language is Spanish. English is increasingly used in relation to tourism. ➤➤Spanish.

cant ➤argot.

Cantonese ➤Chinese.

Cape Dutch ➤Afrikaans.

Cape Verde (population in 1995 estimated at 394,000) The official language is Portuguese. About 70% of the people speak a Portuguese-based creole (Crioulo). Minority languages are Balanta and Mandyak. Some use is also made of English for international purposes. ➤➤creole; Portuguese.

capital letter ➤letter; majuscule.

cardinal number ➤numbers.

cardinal vowels A set of standard reference points for the articulation and recognition of vowels, devised by Daniel Jones. They provide a fairly precise way of identifying what the vowel sounds are in a language. The front, centre, and back of the tongue are distinguished, as are four levels of tongue height. A set of eight **primary** vowels is recognized, and a further set of **secondary** vowels is produced by reversing the lip position (rounded to unrounded, or vice versa). ➤➤Jones, Daniel; vowel.

caregiver/caretaker speech ➤motherese.

caret /'karət/ A diacritic (Λ) used to indicate that something needs to be inserted in a line of manuscript or typed text. It is used both informally and as a convention in proof correcting. ➤➤diacritic; proof.

caretaker speech ➤motherese.

Carib ➤Gê-Pano-Carib.

case (grammar) A way of showing the grammatical relationship between certain kinds of word and phrase by variations in word structure. Nouns, adjectives, and

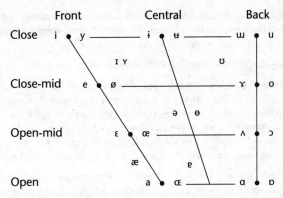

	Front	Central	Back
Close	i • y ——————— ɨ • ʉ ——————— ɯ • u		
	ɪ ʏ	ʊ	
Close-mid	e • ø ——————————————— ɤ • o		
		ə θ	
Open-mid	ɛ • œ ——————————————— ʌ • ɔ		
	æ	ɐ	
Open	a • ɶ ——————— ɑ • ɒ		

The **cardinal vowels**. (Where symbols appear in pairs, the one to the right represents a rounded vowel.)

pronouns are the main word classes affected. In European languages, case typically involves varying the word endings (the inflections), as in Latin (nominative *homo*, accusative *hominem*, genitive *hominis*, etc.). Each case is associated with a range of meanings – genitive, for example, typically conveys possession – and some approaches in linguistics use these meanings as a way of analysing all languages, whether they make use of a system of inflectional endings or not. ►►ablative/accusative/dative/genitive/instrumental/locative/nominative/vocative case; case grammar; inflection 1; typology of language.

case (typography) ►letter.

case grammar An approach to grammatical analysis which recognizes a set of syntactic functions ('cases') in the analysis of a sentence, giving these an interpretation in terms of the semantic roles that these functions express, such as agentive, dative, and locative. Devised by US linguist Charles Fillmore (1929–) in the late 1960s, in the context of generative grammar, it exercised considerable influence on subsequent developments in linguistic theory. ►►case; generative grammar; semantics.

catachresis /katəˈkriːsɪs/ ►malapropism.

Catalan /ˈkatəlan/ A member of the Romance family of languages, spoken by over 9 million people (by *c.*4 million as a first language) chiefly in north-eastern Spain, with some in southern France, Andorra, Sardinia, the Balearic Islands, and the USA. It is an official regional language in Catalonia (Spain) and Roussillon (France), and it has official status in Andorra and Valencia. It was the official language of the Kingdoms of Aragon and Valencia, and literary texts date from the 12th century. It is written in the Roman alphabet. The language (as the culture) is still recovering from long periods of repression, first under the Bourbon monarchy, and in the 20th century under Franco, and has been much influenced by Spanish (especially in vocabulary), but there has been a marked revival of interest and pride in its status and use in recent years. ➤Andorra; Romance; Spain.

cataphora /kəˈtafərə/ ➤anaphora; endophora.

catch phrase A phrase which is so appealing that people take pleasure from using it, and which for a time (often just a few months) is heard everywhere. Phrases derived from television advertisements or news stories are among the most transient. Some catch phrases become so popular that they emerge as long-term additions to the language: in English, these include Humphrey Bogart's *Here's looking at you, kid* (from the film *Casablanca*) and *Phone home* (from the film, *ET*). ➤set expression.

catenative /kəˈtiːnətɪv/ A lexical verb which governs the nonfinite form of another lexical verb, as with *try* in *She tried to leave*. Quite lengthy 'chains' of such verbs can be found (such as *She wanted to keep on trying to do the exam*) – hence the term (which derives from the Latin word *catena*, 'chain'). In linguistics, **catenation** or **concatenation** is often used to describe the serial linking of a series of forms. ➤finite; verb.

Caucasian A family of 38 languages spoken by nearly 8 million people in and around the Caucasus Mountains, between the Black Sea and the Caspian Sea. They are classified into three groups: Abkhazo-Adyghian, Nakho-Dagestanian, and Kartvelian. Several of the northern languages have a written form, using the Cyrillic alphabet, and have official status. There is much evidence of the influence of previous periods of contact with nearby languages, such as Arabic, Persian, and Slavic (Russian). ➤Abkhazo-Adyghian; Kartvelian; Nakho-Dagestanian.

causative A grammatical category which expresses a causal relationship, such as 'cause to eat'. Causatives are usually expressed by verbs (*kill*, for example, can be analysed as 'cause to die'), special conjunctions (such as *because*), or affixes (such as -*en*, as in *deafen*, 'to make deaf'). ➤affix; conjunction; verb.

cavity In phonetics, any of the anatomically defined chambers of the vocal tract which help to influence the character of a sound. The main cavities are the **esophageal** (from the esophagus to the stomach), the **pulmonic** (the lungs and trachea), the **pharyngeal** (the larynx to the base of the soft palate), the **oral** (the whole mouth area), and the **nasal** (the nose and that part of the pharynx above the soft palate). ➤vocal tract.

Cebuano /seɪˈbwaːnəʊ/ A member of the Austronesian family of languages, spoken by over 15 million people in the Philippines (nearly a quarter of the population). It is written in the Roman alphabet, but is little used as a literary language. ➤Austronesian; Philippines.

cedilla /səˈdɪlə/ A diacritic placed under a letter to indicate a change in the way the letter is normally pronounced. An example is French ç, as in *garçon* 'boy'. ➤diacritic.

Ceefax ►teletext.

Celtiberian /keltə'bɪərɪən/ ►Celtic.

Celtic An Indo-European family of languages, spoken originally by a group of peoples who emerged in south-west Europe around the 5th century BC. The Celts spread across Europe in a series of waves, reaching the Black Sea and Asia Minor, south-west Spain, central Italy, and Britain. The main migration was by the Galli, or Gauls, into northern Europe, and **Gaulish** is found in place names and inscriptions. **Galatian**, spoken by the Celts who went into Asia Minor, remained in use until around the 5th century AD. **Celtiberian** is the name given to the language of the Celts in Spain (the Celtiberi), known from a few inscriptions. The range of dialects spoken on the continent of Europe is called **Continental Celtic**, to be distinguished from the **Insular Celtic** spoken in the British Isles and Brittany, the ancestor of the modern Celtic languages. The first wave of invasion to the British Isles took place into Ireland in the 4th century, resulting in a variety now called **Goidelic** (or **Gaelic**); a later wave into southern England and Wales is called **Brythonic**. Goidelic spread from Ireland (Irish Gaelic) into the Isle of Man (Manx) and Scotland (Scottish Gaelic); Brythonic into Cornwall (Cornish), Wales (Welsh), Cumbria (Cumbric), and Brittany (Breton). There are currently *c.*1 million speakers of Celtic languages. ►►Breton; Cornish; Irish Gaelic; ogham; Scottish Gaelic; Welsh.

Central African Republic (population in 1995 estimated at 3,422,000) The official languages are French and Sango. Sango is a Ngbandi-based creole, now used in the media, commerce, and government; it is spoken by *c.*350,000 as a first language, and by most of the population as a second or third language. Over 60 other languages are spoken in the country, notably Banda, Gbaya, and Zande, but the status of several forms (as language or dialect) is unclear. French is the language used for international purposes. ►►creole; French.

central sound A sound made in the centre of the mouth or by the central part of the tongue. The notion is particularly used in describing vowels: the vowel of *bird* or the last vowel of *butter* would be described as 'central vowels'. If an articulation is made more towards the centre of the mouth than is normal, it is said to be **centralized**, and the process called **centralization**. ►►front sound; shwa; tongue; vowel.

centre (UK) or **center** (US) **1**. The top part of the tongue, between front and back, used especially in the production of vowels such as [ə]. ►►tongue; vowel. **2**. The most sonorous part of a syllable, typically consisting of a vowel; for example, [e] is the centre of the syllable [set]. ►►sonority; syllable.

centum language /'kentəm/ An Indo-European language in which the velar stop /k/ of Proto-Indo-European was retained in such words as Latin *centum* 'hundred'; contrasts with a **satem language** /'sɑːtəm/, where this sound changed to an alveolar fricative /s/, in such words as Avestan *satem* 'hundred'. Celtic, Romance, and Germanic languages are among the centum languages, according to this criterion. Balto-Slavonic and Indo-Iranian languages are among the satem languages. ➤➤Indo-European.

Chad (population in 1995 estimated at 6,424,000) The official languages are French and Arabic, the latter being an important lingua franca, spoken by about half the population. There are over 120 other languages, notably Kanuri, Marba, Mbai, Mosi, Sango, and Teda. Several have become lingua francas (e.g. Hausa, Ngambai, Sara). French is the language used for most international purposes. ➤➤Arabic; French; lingua franca.

Chadic /'ʧadɪk/ A branch of the Afro-Asiatic family of languages, *c.*160 languages spoken by *c.*30 million people in an area extending from northern Ghana to the Central African Republic. Hausa is the most important language of the group; other languages include Angas, Kotoko, and Mubi. ➤➤Afro-Asiatic; Hausa.

chain ➤speech chain.

character A graphic sign used in a writing system, especially one that is not part of an alphabet, but represents a word or morpheme directly. The best-known examples occur in Chinese and its derivative script, Japanese kanji, where the characters are often classified on the basis of the number of strokes used to write them. ➤➤alphabet; graphology 1; kanji; p. 53.

Chari-Nile /'ʃariː'naɪl/ ➤Nilo-Saharan.

Chechen /ʧe'ʧen/ A member of the Nakho-Dagestanian group of Caucasian languages, spoken by *c.*950,000 speakers in the Chechen-Ingush region of Russia (where it has official status, along with Ingush) and by several thousand more in Turkey, Jordan, and other nearby regions. It is written in the Cyrillic alphabet. ➤➤Nakho-Dagestanian.

Cheremis /'ʧerəmɪs/ ➤Mari.

cherology /kə'rɒlədʒiː/ The study of sign language. The term was coined on analogy with *phonology* to refer to the study of the smallest contrastive units (**cheremes**) which occur in a sign language. Signs are analysed into such features as the location in the signing space in which a sign is made, the hand configuration used, and the action of the active hand. ➤➤phonology; sign language.

chest pulse A contraction of the chest muscles which forces air into the vocal tract. It is a central notion in one theory of syllable production. ➤➤syllable.

Chewa /'ʧeɪwə/ ➤Nyanja.

chiasmus /kiː'azməs/ A balanced pattern of sentence construction in which the main elements are reversed. A Shakespearean example is *Love's fire heats water, water cools not love* (Sonnet 154). ➤➤figurative language.

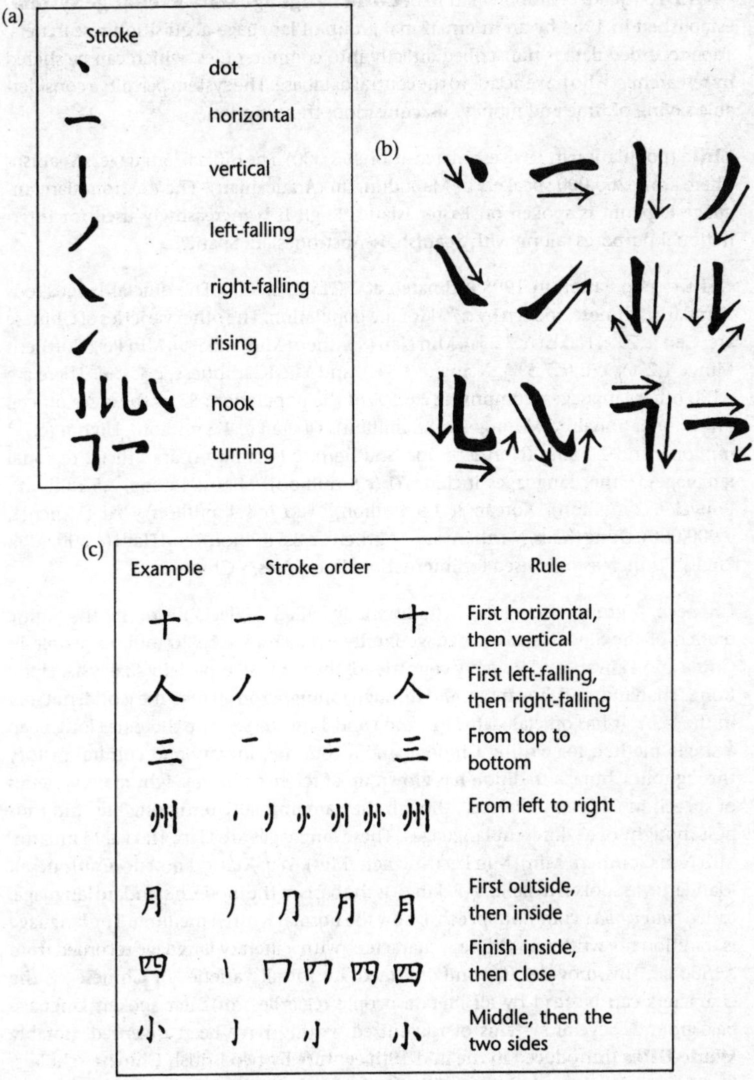

(a)

Stroke

` `	dot
`一`	horizontal
`丨`	vertical
`丿`	left-falling
`丶`	right-falling
`丿`	rising
`亅丨丨丶`	hook
`乛`	turning

(b)

(c)

Example	Stroke order	Rule
十	一 十	First horizontal, then vertical
人	丿 人	First left-falling, then right-falling
三	一 二 三	From top to bottom
州	丶 丿 丷 州 州 州	From left to right
月	丿 刀 月 月	First outside, then inside
四	丨 冂 冂 四 四	Finish inside, then close
小	亅 小 小	Middle, then the two sides

Chinese **characters**: (a) the eight basic strokes; (b) the directions in which the basic strokes are written; (c) the order of strokes of some simple characters.

CHILDES /ˈʧaɪldz/ An abbreviation of **Child Language Data Exchange System**, established in 1984 by an international group of language acquisition researchers. Tape-recorded data is transcribed directly into computer files, which can be shared by researchers who have access to the central database. The system permits a considerable saving of time and money. ➤acquisition; transcription.

Chile (population in 1995 estimated at 14,263,000) The official language is Spanish. There are *c*. 200,000 speakers of Mapudungun (Araucanian). The Austronesian language Rapanui is spoken on Easter Island. English is increasingly used for international purposes, along with Spanish. ➤Austronesian; Spanish.

China (population in 1995 estimated at 1,215,293,000) The official language is Mandarin Chinese, spoken by *c*.70% of the population. The other varieties of Chinese are: Gan (*c*.2%), Hakka (*c*.2.5%), Min Nan (Southern Min, *c*.2.5%), Min Pei (Northern Min, *c*.1.2%), Wu (*c*.7.5%), Xiang (*c*.3.5%), and Yue (Cantonese, *c*.4.5%). There are *c*.130 other languages, comprising *c*.6.5% of the population; 55 of these are official minority nationalities. Mongol (*c*.4.8 million), Tibetan (c.4.5 million), Uighur (c.7.2 million), and Zhuang (Northern and Southern, *c*.14 million) are official regional languages. Other languages include Yi (*c*.5 million), Miao (Hmong, *c*.5 million), Bouyei (*c*.2 million), Korean (*c*.1.9 million), Yao (*c*.1.4 million), Bai (Minchia, *c*.900,000), Dong (Kam, Northern and Southern, *c*.2.5 million), and Hani (*c*. 500,000). English is increasingly used for international purposes. ➤Chinese.

Chinese A group of languages (traditionally called 'dialects') forming the Sinitic branch of the Sino-Tibetan language family, spoken by *c*.1,220 million people in China and Taiwan, and in many countries of the Far East, especially Malaysia, Hong Kong, Thailand, and Singapore, and through immigration all over the world, notably in the USA. It has official status in China and Taiwan. Because there has long been a single method for writing Chinese, and a common literary and cultural history throughout China, a tradition has grown up of referring to the eight main varieties of speech in China as 'dialects', though they are mutually unintelligible, and thus best thought of as different languages. These languages are Gan, Hakka, Mandarin, Min Nan (Southern Min), Min Pei (Northern Min), Wu, Xiang, and Yue (Cantonese). Mandarin, as spoken in Beijing (Peking), is the basis of the modern standard language, called *putonghua* ('common speech'), now the normal written medium. The language is traditionally written in Chinese characters, with a literary language recorded from *c*.1500 BC; this provides the unifying medium for all varieties of Chinese, as the characters can be read by all literate people regardless of their spoken language background. Several systems of romanized writing have been invented, notably **Wade-Giles** (introduced in the mid-19th century by two British Chinese scholars, Sir Thomas Wade and Herbert Giles), which produced the traditional spellings familiar to Western eyes, such as *Peking* and *Mao Tse-tung*. This has been largely supplanted by **pinyin** ('phonetic spelling'), a system introduced in 1958, and now in widespread use; the above words (omitting symbols for tones) would be *Beijing* and *Mao-Zedong*. These developments are part of an ambitious modern programme of language reform, in which the classical characters have been reduced in number and complexity, and a single standard of spoken communication and spelling introduced. ➤character; China; kanji; logograph; Roman alphabet; Sino-Tibetan; Taiwan.

Chipewyan ➤Na-Dene.

chirography /kaɪˈrɒgrəfiː/ The study of handwriting forms and styles. The subject has attracted a wide range of aesthetic, psychological, and scientific approaches. There is no agreed system of classification, though several important notions have emerged from historical studies. Handwriting variation is analysed using several parameters, such as line direction, letter size, angle, and connection, and the thickness of strokes. The art of penmanship, or handwriting at its most formal, is called **calligraphy**. ➤black letter writing; cursive; graphology 2; italic; majuscule; minuscule; uncial; writing.

Chomskyan or **Chomskian** Adjective derived from (Avram) Noam Chomsky (1928–), an American linguist whose ideas have dominated the development of linguistic thought since the 1950s. As professor of linguistics at the Massachusetts Institute of Technology (MIT) he developed the conception of a generative grammar, which departed radically from the structuralism and behaviourism of the previous decades. His book *Syntactic Structures* (1957) proved to be a turning point in 20th-century linguistics. ➤competence; generative grammar; MIT; Standard Theory.

choral repetition The unison repetition of an example given by a teacher to a group of students. The technique is commonly used with those learning a foreign language. ➤method.

chrestomathy /kreˈstɒməθiː/ An anthology of passages compiled to help those engaged in learning a language. The term is derived from Greek words for 'useful' and 'learning'. ➤language learning.

chronogram /ˈkrɒnəgram/ A phrase or sentence in which letters that are also Roman numerals (e.g. C, I, X) combine to form a date. The significant letters are usually written in capitals, producing an odd graphic appearance to the line (e.g. *DoMVs* 'house' contains D, M, and V (for U)). Chronograms are often found on tombstones, foundation stones, and other items which mark the date of an event. ➤verbal play.

Chukchi /ˈtʃʊktʃiː/ A member of the Luorawetlan family of languages, spoken by *c.*12,000 people in the Chukchi region of Russia (where it has official status), in the northeasternmost corner of Siberia. It is written in the Cyrillic alphabet. ➤Luorawetlan.

chunking In the study of the psychology of language, the division of an utterance into parts, to make it easier to process. Some aphasic patients, for example, find it easier to say the sentence *The fat cat was chasing a big mouse* if it is 'chunked' into three parts: *the fat cat – was chasing – a big mouse*. Chunking is also used as a technique in foreign language teaching. ➤aphasia; psycholinguistics.

Chuvash /ˈtʃuːvaʃ/ A language spoken by *c*.1.7 million people in the Chuvash region of Russia (where it is an official language), in the middle Volga region. It is usually listed as a member of the Turkic branch of the Altaic family of languages, but often considered to be a separate branch within that family. It is written in the Cyrillic alphabet. ➤Turkic.

cipher or **cypher** A secret code in which letters are transposed or substituted. A message may be **enciphered** and **deciphered**. For example, using a simple **cipher alphabet** (in which each letter is replaced by the immediately preceding letter of the alphabet), the word *jewels* is enciphered as *idvdkr*. More complex cipher alphabets use several equivalents for a letter, such as when *j* might be replaced by either *gy, sf,* or *ni*. Modern cipher machines can produce highly complex systems using millions of (poly-alphabetic) transformations. ➤code 2; cryptology.

Circassian /sɜˈkasɪən/ ➤Adygey; Kabardian.

circumflex The accent ˆ, used to indicate the pronunciation of a particular letter, such as French *ê* in *même*. This accent may also be used to indicate other features of speech, such as a type of pitch movement in a tone language or phonetic transcription. ➤accent 3.

circumlocution The use of more words than is necessary to express a meaning. Circumlocution usually attracts criticism, when it is noticed, but it can have a positive value, such as when a speaker wishes to avoid an awkward or sensitive word. In some language pathologies (notably, in stuttering and certain kinds of aphasia), the term describes the roundabout expressions which a person may use in order to avoid a difficult word. ➤aphasia; language pathology; periphrasis; tautology.

citation form The form of a linguistic unit (typically, a spoken word) when this is produced in isolation for purposes of discussion. There are often substantial differences between a citation form and the way the word sounds in connected speech: *have*, for example, is pronounced [hav] in isolation, but may be reduced to [ə] in such phrases as *would have been*. In lexicography, the **citation slip** provides the written evidence, culled from books, magazines, and other sources, on which to base a dictionary entry. ➤lexicography.

class In language study, a set of entities sharing certain formal or semantic properties. The class of consonants, for example, has features which distinguish it from the class of vowels. The class of nouns is distinguishable from the class of verbs. ➤word class.

class dialect ➤sociolect.

Classical Greek ►Greek.

classical language A stage in the historical development of a language when it is thought to have reached its highest level of literary or cultural importance. The term is typically applied to Latin in ancient Rome and Greek in ancient Greece ('Classical Greek', as opposed to 'modern Greek'), but Hebrew, Sanskrit, and several other languages have recognized classical periods. ►►Greek; Hebrew; Latin; Sanskrit.

classifier A linguistic form which indicates the semantic class to which a group of words belongs; for example, the *-ess* suffix in English indicates membership of a noun class referring to females. In many languages, classifiers express a wide range of notions, such as size, animateness, and shape. ►►word class.

clause A type of grammatical construction intermediate between a sentence and a phrase, containing such major functional elements as subject and verb. It may be equivalent to a sentence (*I saw a cow*), but it need not be (*when I looked over the wall*). Clauses have been classified in many ways, but most distinguish between independent (**main**) and dependent (**subordinate**) kinds. The role of the clause in the sentence is also recognized, illustrated by the **subject clause** (performing the function of a subject as in ***What I said*** *was correct*), and the **adverbial clause** (performing the function of an adverb, as in the *when* example above). ►►finite; grammar 2; relative.

clear *l* A type of lateral sound which has a resonance similar to that of a front vowel of an [i] quality, as in English *leaf*. It contrasts with a **dark *l***, where the resonance is that of a back vowel with [u] quality, as in English *pool*. ►►lateral.

cleft palate speech Speech which results from a cleft palate – a congenital fissure in the middle of the palate, often found along with a single or double split in the upper lip and/or teeth ridge. The label 'hare lip' for the latter condition (once used because of the supposed similarity with the divided upper lip of members of the rabbit family) is now considered to be a demeaning form of description, and has been replaced in clinical usage by **cleft lip**. A nasal voice quality and an excessive use of glottal stops are among the most noticeable features of the early stages of cleft palate speech. ►►glottal; nasal; speech therapy.

cleft sentence A construction where a single clause has been divided ('cleft') into two separate sections, each with its own verb. For example, *Janet is looking at John* can be 'cleft' into *It is Janet who is looking at John*. ►►clause.

cliché or **cliche** An expression which has come to be so overused that it no longer conveys much meaning, and tends to attract criticism when people continue to use it. Examples from various contexts in present-day English include *at the end of the day*, *sick as a parrot*, and *someone who needs no introduction*. At times, clichés can be useful, in helping people to communicate in an awkward or stressful situation. ►►neologism.

click A type of consonant produced by the velaric airstream mechanism. The Khoisan languages have the most complex click systems. Click consonants are not used in European languages, but click sounds are common enough; they include the 'tut tut' effect, where the tongue articulates against the teeth (a dental click), and the noises of encouragement to horses and other animals (including people), made with the sides of the tongue (a lateral click). ➤Khoisan; velaric.

clinical linguistics The application of linguistics to the analysis of disorders of language, especially those involving the production or comprehension of speech. A development of the 1970s, the subject chiefly involves the transcription, description, and analysis of language samples obtained from patients (both children and adults), with the aim of relating the information to their diagnosis, assessment, and therapy. Other kinds of investigation (e.g. experimental, cross-linguistic) are also now practised as part of a concern to improve our understanding of the general nature of language disorder. ➤language pathology; linguistics; profile.

clipping A type of word formation in which a new word is derived by shortening another word. Examples include *exam* from *examination* and *ad* from *advertisement*. ➤abbreviation.

clitic A form which resembles a word, but which cannot be used on its own as a normal utterance because it is structurally dependent on a neighbouring word in a construction. Examples include the contracted forms of *be* in English (*I'm, he's*) and the pronoun *je* ('I') in French, which must always be followed by a verb. ➤contraction 1; enclitic.

closed class A word class whose membership is fixed or limited, such as the class of articles, pronouns, or conjunctions; also called a **closed system**. An **open class** or **open set**, by contrast, allows the unlimited addition of new items, the chief classes being nouns, verbs, adjectives, and adverbs. ➤word class.

closed syllable ➤open 2.

close vowel ➤high vowel.

closure An articulation where the contact between active and passive articulators obstructs the air flow through the mouth and/or nose. Closure is complete, in the case of plosives; partial, in the case of laterals; and intermittent, in the case of flaps. ➤articulation; flap; lateral; plosive.

cloze A technique used in the teaching and testing of reading comprehension, in which readers guess which words have been omitted at regular intervals from a text. The technique can be – from the present sentence, – every fifth word has – omitted. Some omissions are more predictable than others, of course, but working out the possibilities certainly demonstrates how well you know your language. ➤language teaching.

cluster A sequence of adjacent consonant sounds, occurring in restricted patterns at the beginning or end of a syllable. Initial clusters in English include [spr-] and [fl-]; final clusters include [-mps] and [-lt]. The notion is also used for consonant letters in the written language (where such clusters are sometimes referred to as **blends**). There is no one-to-one correspondence between clusters in speech and writing: the last letter of *fox* is a consonant cluster in speech, [ks]; and the last sound of [sik] is a consonant cluster in writing, *sick*. ►►consonant; syllable.

cluttering A disorder of fluency, in which utterances are produced in an excessively rapid way. Clutterers seem unable to control their speech rate, and as a result introduce distortions of rhythm and articulation into their speech. Sounds become displaced, mispronounced, or omitted, and syllables telescope into each other. The speed may increase as the utterance proceeds. ►►festination; fluency; stuttering.

coalescence The merging of linguistic units which occur in a sequence. In the history of English, for example, /z/ coalesced with the following sound /j/ to produce the /ʒ/ heard in such words as *measure*. In contemporary English, the same kind of effect can be heard in such phrases as *would you*, where the /d/ of *would* coalesces with the /j/ of *you*. ►►assimilation; convergence 2; sound change.

coarticulation The overlap of articulatory movements associated with different speech segments; for example, the /t/ of *too* is produced with rounded lips, because of the influence of the rounding which is part of the following vowel (compare the /t/ of *tea*, where there is no rounding). Simultaneous articulations of different consonants, such as [p] and [k], appear in several African languages. Coarticulation effects are extremely common, and the study of speech from this point of view has largely replaced the traditional study of articulation as a series of independently functioning segments. ►►articulation; assimilation; parametric phonetics; secondary articulation.

COBUILD /ˈkəʊbɪld/ An abbreviation of **Collins–Birmingham University International Language Database**, a research unit established in 1980 by Collins English Dictionaries and the University of Birmingham, under the direction of John Sinclair. It created a 20-million-word corpus during the 1980s, which led to the publication of a wide range of lexical reference works and teaching materials. ►►Bank of English; corpus.

Cockney The accent and dialect associated with people native to the East End of London. Several accents of south-east England, from the south coast to north of Cambridge and Oxford, now show the influence of Cockney speech. ►►Estuary English; rhyming slang.

cocktail party effect The process of selective listening. People listening to several utterances (or conversations) at once are able to attend consciously to one of them, and to ignore the others. The effect is studied as part of psycholinguistics. ►►psycholinguistics.

code 1. Any system of signals used for sending messages; the senders are said to **encode** the message, and the receivers to **decode** it. Specifically, the term is used for a system which converts one set of symbols into another, such as the alphabet (which converts sound units into letter units) or the Morse code (which converts letters into dot/dash sequences). **2.** A system of symbols used in the preparation (**encoding**) and interpretation (**decoding**) of secret messages. A code in this sense is a system of phrases, words, syllables, or letters, each of which has an associated 'code word' or 'code number', and which can be decoded using a 'code book'. The word *jewels*, for example, might be assigned the code word 'shape' or the code number '36598'. ➤cipher; cryptology. **3.** In the sociology of language, used loosely by some writers to mean a language, or a variety of a language. A code, in this sense, is chosen by a speaker for use in a particular speech situation (**code selection**). It may be used consistently, or changed midway (often several times) within a sentence or conversation (**code switching**). Different codes may also be used in an apparently haphazard way as part of a single system of communication (**code mixing**). ➤code mixing/switching; elaborated code; lect; variety.

code mixing In bilingual speech, the transfer of linguistic elements from one language into another. A single sentence might begin in one language, and then introduce words or grammatical features belonging to the other. The process can be illustrated from the kind of Spanish–English mixing used in the south-west USA ('Tex-Mex'). A shopper asks a supermarket clerk a question. *Shopper: Donde está el thin-sliced bread? Clerk: Está en aisle three, sobre el second shelf, en el wrapper rojo.* ('Where is the thin-sliced bread? It is in aisle three, on the second shelf, in the red wrapper.') ➤bilingualism.

code switching The use by a speaker of more than one language, dialect, or variety during a conversation. Which form is used will depend on such factors as the nature of the audience, the subject matter, and the situation in which the conversation takes place. An informal street conversation between friends will tolerate far more code switching than a job interview between strangers. ➤accommodation; bidialectism; bilingualism.

codification A systematic account of a language, especially of its grammar and vocabulary. This task is often undertaken when a language is being written down for the first time, but it can also happen when a language is developing a standard form, or after a period of considerable creativity and change (as in the case of the English grammars and dictionaries of the 18th century). The task is often delegated to an academy or special body, but in many instances it is carried out by individuals (as with Dr Johnson's dictionary). ➤academy; English; standard.

cognate A language or linguistic form which is historically derived from the same source as another. Spanish, French, and Portuguese are all cognate languages, deriving from Latin. Many of their words, accordingly, have a common origin, and are also said to be cognate, such as the various words for 'father' – *padre, père, pai.* ➤genetic classification; reconstruction.

cognitive meaning ➤reference.

coherence The underlying functional connectedness of a piece of language; opposed to **incoherence**. In some approaches, a distinction is drawn with **cohesion**, which refers to the specific features that link different parts of a discourse. A pronoun, for example, has a cohesive role to play, in the way it refers backwards or forwards to a noun phrase (as illustrated by the use of *it*, referring to *a pronoun*, in the present sentence.) ➤➤anaphora; discourse analysis; pronoun.

cohesion ➤coherence.

coinage ➤neologism.

collective noun A noun which denotes a group of entities, such as *government* and *committee*. In English, such nouns are formally different from others in that they have a distinctive three-way pattern of number contrast. *Committee*, for example, may be used as a singular with a singular verb (*The committee is interested*) and with a plural verb (*The committee are interested*), and again as a plural with a plural verb (*The committees are interested*). The difference between the first two patterns is one of point of view: in *committee is*, the committee is being seen as a single undifferentiated body; in *committee are*, the emphasis is on the individuals who comprise it. ➤➤noun; number.

collocation The habitual co-occurrence of individual lexical items, such as *auspicious* and *occasion*. The potential of items to collocate is called their **collocability**. ➤➤lexeme.

colloquialism A pronunciation, word, or grammatical construction which is heard in the most informal levels of speech, and which tends to be avoided in formal spoken and written language. The use of contracted forms (such as *I'm, can't*) is typical of colloquial speech, as is the use of slang (*Let's have a butcher's*) and nonstandard coinages (*Eurowimpishness* – said of one politician who was expressing his support for a common European currency in what was claimed to be an excessively weak manner). ➤➤formality.

Colombia (population in 1995 estimated at 35,021,000) The official language is Spanish. There are *c.*75 Amerindian languages, mostly spoken by very small numbers. An English-based creole is used on the San Andrés and Providencia Islands. ➤➤Amerindian; creole; Spanish.

colon A punctuation mark whose typical function is to express that what follows in the sentence is an expansion of what has preceded. *We have an important principle here: people must have freedom of choice*. There is a clear interdependence between the separated units, and in this respect the colon differs from the semicolon, where there is not usually such a close semantic relationship. In British English, it is not usual to have the clause following the colon begin with a capital letter; but this is more common in American English. ➤➤punctuation; semicolon.

comma A punctuation mark with a wide range of grammatical and prosodic functions, and displaying considerable flexibility in its use. Among its typical uses are the separation of a series of clauses within a sentence (*John sang, Mary played, and Mike drank*), the separation of a series of words of the same grammatical type within a phrase (*tall, dark, and handsome*), and the marking of an included unit (*the car, he was sorry to say, was a wreck*). Even in such straightforward grammatical contexts, however, there is much variation in usage, with many authors and publishers preferring not to use a comma before *and*. Certain rules do exist, especially stating where commas may *not* go; for example, phrases cannot be interrupted by a comma (we cannot write **a, car* or **they will, go*), and the comma is disallowed between subject and verb (**The car which I bought in France last year, has just been sold*). But apart from such contexts, authors vary greatly in the extent to which they use commas to reflect the rhythm, pace, and intonation of speech. ➤➤punctuation.

command A sentence whose typical function is to tell someone to do something. The form of such sentences typically involves the use of a verb in the imperative mood: *Leave!, Sit over there!*. ➤➤directive; imperative; sentence.

comment ➤given.

comment clause A type of clause whose function is to add a parenthetic comment to another clause; examples include *you know, you see, generally speaking*, and *to be honest*. Overuse of such clauses in conversation (especially on formal occasions) can lead to criticisms of 'empty speech'; but comment clauses have an important role to play in ensuring conversational naturalness and smoothness. ➤➤clause; parenthesis 2.

common core The range of linguistic features which would be used and understood by all speakers, regardless of their regional or social background. Common core features of a language would include its basic rules of word order and word formation, and its high frequency vocabulary. However, it is by no means clear just how many features can legitimately be called 'common core', because of the considerable divergence which actually exists between varieties, and it is very difficult to identify such features in some aspects of language structure (such as the vowel system). ➤➤Nuclear English; variety.

common noun A noun that refers to a class of objects or concepts, such as *chair, cat, information*. It is generally contrasted with a **proper noun** (or **proper name**), which refers to a unique person, place, animal, etc., such as *Fred, London, Mrs Jones*. The grammar of the two kinds of noun is different: for example, English common nouns typically express a contrast between singular and plural, whereas proper nouns do not – we can say *a chair* and *chairs*, but not *a Fred* and *Freds*. ➤➤noun.

communication The transmission and reception of information between a signaller and a receiver. Various steps in this process can be recognized. A message is formulated in the signaller's brain, and is then encoded in the nervous and muscular systems. It leaves the signaller (typically via the vocal tract or hands), and is trans-

mitted through air, paper, electrical system, or other medium to the brain of the receiver (typically, via the eye or ear), where it is decoded. The receiver may influence the nature of the message at any time by sending feedback to the signaller. In principle, any of the five senses can be involved, but humans tend to use only the auditory/vocal, visual, and tactile modes for active communication (the other two modes, smell and taste, being widely employed among certain animal species). ➤➤body language; communication board/disorder/science; feedback; miscommunication; zoösemiotics.

communication board A piece of apparatus which displays common words, the alphabet, numbers, and other important features of language, used by those who are unable to express themselves in any other way (such as the severely physically handicapped). People point to the item they wish to signal, either with their hands, or by using another part of the body (e.g. the shoulder or eyebrow) to move a pointer or other locater on the board. ➤➤alternative communication system; language pathology.

communication disorder A lack of development or breakdown in a person's ability to communicate. It may be mild, moderate, or severe, and affect any or all of the chief communication channels – auditory/vocal (speech), visual (writing, signing, facial expressions, bodily gesture), and tactile. The notion is much broader than that of a language disorder, and would include, for example, problems of maintaining or using eye contact efficiently (such as affect many autistic children). ➤➤alternative communication system; communication; language pathology.

communication science The scientific study of all aspects of communication; sometimes referred to as the **communication sciences**. The domain includes linguistics and phonetics, their various branches (e.g. psycholinguistics, sociolinguistics), and relevant applications of associated subjects (e.g. acoustics, anatomy, neurology). All modes of communication are involved – spoken, written, and signed. ➤➤communication; linguistics; phonetics.

communicative approach An approach to language teaching which focuses on language functions and communicative competence, and not on grammatical structure. Language functions include such notions as requesting, apologizing, narrating, commanding, and expressing dislike. The emphasis is on the processes involved in actual communication, and on the appropriate use of language in real situations. ➤➤communicative competence; language teaching; notional syllabus.

communicative competence A person's unconscious knowledge of the rules governing the appropriate use of language in social situations. It is usually contrasted with **linguistic competence**, the person's unconscious knowledge of the formal patterning of language. Communicative competence includes our formal knowledge of language, but in addition includes our awareness of the factors which govern acceptable speech, such as how to begin and end conversations, how to interrupt, how to address people, and how to behave in special speech situations (e.g. apologizing, thanking, and expressing formality or informality). ➤➤competence.

community language A language used by a particular community – typically, by an ethnic minority. In Britain, for example, there are over 100 community languages, including Bengali, Panjabi, Turkish, Italian, and Hindi. ➤➤speech community.

community language learning A method of foreign language teaching, devised by American educator Charles Curran, which uses techniques derived from group counselling for people with psychological problems. Learners are organized into small groups, great emphasis being placed on the students' personal thoughts and feelings while engaged in the task of language learning. They first express these feelings in their mother tongue. The utterances are then translated by the group leader into the foreign language, and the learner tries to repeat this translation, expressing the feelings again to the other members of the group. ➤➤humanistic; language learning.

Comoros (population for 1995 estimated at 600,000) The official language is French. A variety of Swahili is spoken as a first language by most people, and Malagasy is well represented among immigrants from Madagascar. ➤➤French; Swahili.

comparative A grammatical form used to make a comparison, such as the use of *-er* or *more* with adjectives in English (*taller, more necessary*). The construction which may follow the use of a comparative is a **comparative clause**: *That was easier than I expected.* ➤➤clause; degree.

comparative linguistics The branch of linguistics which interrelates the characteristics of different languages believed to have a common historical origin. The subject is sometimes still referred to by its older labels, **comparative philology** or **comparative grammar**. ➤➤linguistics; philology; reconstruction.

comparative method ➤reconstruction.

comparative philology ➤philology.

comparative reconstruction ➤reconstruction.

competence A person's unconscious knowledge of the system of rules underlying his or her language; contrasts with **performance**. The notion emerged in the 1960s as a tenet of Chomskyan linguistics. It has since led to the development of several related terms, notably **pragmatic** or **communicative competence**, referring to the ability to produce and understand sentences appropriate to the social context in which they occur. ➤➤Chomskyan; communicative competence; performance 1; pragmatics.

competence grammar ➤grammar 1.

complement An element of clause or sentence structure, traditionally associated with 'completing' the meaning specified by the verb. The domain of **complementation** may subsume all obligatory features of the predicate other than the verb (e.g. including objects) or it may be restricted to a single class of constructions (e.g. those following the verb *be* and semantically related verbs). In **subject complementation**, the complement element relates directly to the subject of the clause (*She is **a lawyer***); in **object complementation**, the complement element relates directly to the clause object (*She called him **a nuisance***). Categories other than the verb are sometimes said to take complements; for example, the item governed by a preposition can be called a **prepositional complement**. ➤➤clause; copula; object; preposition; subject; verb.

complementarity A type of oppositeness of meaning, in which the assertion of one term implies the denial of the other, as in *single* vs. *married*. The terms are sometimes called **contradictories**. They display no gradability – such phrases as **more single* and* *less married* are not normally possible. ➤➤antonymy; converseness.

complementary distribution The mutual exclusiveness of a pair of sounds in a certain phonetic environment. Sound A may appear only in environment B, and sound X only in environment Y; A may never appear in Y, and X never appear in B. In English, for example, voiceless and voiced varieties of /l/ are in complementary distribution: the voiceless sound heard in *play* can never replace the /l/ sounds in such words as *leap* or *pool*, and vice versa. ➤➤distribution; phoneme; voicing.

complex preposition A multi-word construction consisting of a noun or noun phrase both preceded and followed by a single preposition, as in *on account of* and *in accordance with*. The term is sometimes used to include any preposition consisting of more than one word, such as *next to*. ➤➤preposition.

complex sentence In its most general application, a sentence consisting of more than one clause. In a somewhat narrower sense, the term refers to a sentence consisting of a main clause and at least one subordinate clause; it thus contrasts with such notions as **compound sentence**. ➤clause; compound.

component 1. A major section of the organization of a generative grammar, used in such terms as the 'phrase structure component' or the 'syntactic component'. There may be further analysis of these sections into **sub-components**. ➤generative grammar. **2**. An irreducible feature in terms of which the sense of lexical items can be analysed. The item *girl*, for example, can in this approach be analysed into such semantic components as 'human', 'child', and 'female'. ➤componential analysis; lexicon.

componential analysis The analysis of a set of lexical items in terms of a semantic space structured by various semantic dimensions, such as sex, generation, colour, and shape. Each dimension is composed of contrasting semantic features (male vs. female, adult vs. child, etc.). The approach was developed in the 1960s by ethnosemanticists, and was particularly used for the analysis of kinship terms. ➤component 2; ethnosemantics; kinship terms; semantics.

composition In language teaching, a type of writing practice which makes the learner produce longer texts than a sentence, such as an essay, report, or story. In **free composition**, the student has total control over what is written about; in **controlled composition**, stimulus questions, pictures, or other techniques are used to guide the student's response. ➤language teaching; method.

compound Descriptive of a linguistic unit composed of two or more elements, each of which could function independently in other circumstances; usually contrasting with **simple**. A 'compound word', for example, consists of a combination of stems, such as *washing machine*. A 'compound sentence' consists of a combination of main clauses, such as *It rained and it snowed*. ➤clause; stem.

comprehension The ability to understand and interpret language, whether spoken, written, or signed; contrasts with **production**. The notion is used both theoretically (e.g. with reference to the psycholinguistic processes underlying language) and pedagogically (e.g. with reference to a pupil's ability to grasp the meaning of a particular text). ➤meaning; paraphrase; reading; speech perception/production; Wernicke's aphasia.

computational linguistics A branch of linguistics in which the techniques and concepts of computer science are applied to the investigation of linguistic and phonetic problems. Research areas include speech synthesis, the production of concordances, automatic translation, and the testing of grammars. ➤concordance; corpus; linguistics; machine translation; natural language; Standard Generalized Markup Language; system architecture.

computer language ➤language 2.

computer-assisted language learning (CALL) The use of a computer in the teaching of a language; also subsumed under the more general notion of **computer-**

assisted instruction (CAI). Typically, a computer screen presents a learner with a series of linguistic tasks, to which the student responds, and the program then indicates whether the responses are correct or in error. Other programs might perform such tasks as providing guidance about the syllabus to be followed, monitoring the student's progress, and testing. ➤➤language learning/teaching.

concessive Descriptive of a word or grammatical construction which expresses the meaning of 'concession'. The point expressed in the main clause continues to be valid despite the point which is being made in the subordinate clause (the **concessive clause**). In English, the most widely used markers of concession are *although* and *though*: *Although I went to bed early, I still felt tired*; *I felt tired though I went to bed early*. ➤➤clause.

concord The way in which a particular form of one word requires a corresponding form of another; also called **agreement**. In French, the gender of the noun requires a corresponding pronoun: masculine nouns take *il* ('he/it'), as in *Il est là, le sucre* ('It's there, the sugar'); feminine nouns take *elle* ('she/it'), as in *Elle est là, la table* ('It's there, the table'). In languages which have no fixed patterns of word order, such as Latin, concord is the main means of expressing grammatical relationships. ➤➤gender; government; word order.

concordance A list of words, usually organized alphabetically, which shows the frequency, citations, and locations for each item in a written text. If you wish to determine how often (and where) Shakespeare uses the word *fortune*, for example, a concordance of his works will tell you. Concordances are commonly used in projects in literary and linguistic computing. They may also be organized on the basis of principles other than the alphabet, such as subject matter or chronology. ➤➤computational linguistics.

concrete 1. Descriptive of nouns which refer to physical entities (*book, car, egg*); contrasts with **abstract**, which applies to nouns lacking physical reference (*information, idea, certainty*). The distinction is not clear-cut, as many nouns have properties which would allow either interpretation (*structure, music, version*). ➤➤noun. **2**. Descriptive of any analysis which emphasizes the phonetic reality of speech sounds; contrasts with **abstract**. ➤➤phonetics.

conditional A clause or sentence which expresses a hypothesis or circumstance under which a statement may be valid. In English, conditional constructions are typically introduced by *if* and *unless*, as in *If the bus comes soon, we'll be all right*. Some languages use distinctive verb forms to express conditional meaning, and these forms are then analysed as conditional tenses or moods (as in French *Je marcherais*, 'I would walk'). ➤➤clause; tense 1.

conductive deafness ➤deafness.

Congo 1. (country name) (population in 1995 estimated at 2,954,000) The official

67

language is French. There are over 50 local languages, including Kongo (spoken by nearly half the population) and the Teke group of languages (*c*.500,000). Lingala and Sango are important as lingua francas in certain areas. ➤➤French; lingua franca. **2.** (language name) ➤Kongo.

Congo, Democratic Republic of (formerly **Zaire**) (population in 1995 estimated at 41,837,000) The official language is French. Kongo (spoken by *c*.15% of the population), Bangala (Ngala, *c*.8%), Lingala (*c*.20%, mainly as a second language), Luba (*c*.19%), and Swahili (*c*.22% as a second language) also have special status, and are widely used as lingua francas. There are over 200 other languages, notably Ngala, Kituba (a Kongo-based creole, *c*.4 million), Songe (*c*.1 million), Lugbara, Mongo, Nandi, Rwanda, and Zande. French is used for international purposes. ➤➤creole; French; Kongo; lingua franca; Swahili.

conjoining ➤coordination.

conjugation In an inflecting language, a set of verbs which occur in the same range of forms. Latin verbs, for example, have four conjugations. In verbs of the first conjugation, traditionally illustrated using the forms of *amare* ('to love'), the endings of the active present tense are *amo, amas, amat, amamus, amatis, amant* ('I love, you love, he/she loves, we love, you love, they love'). Fourth conjugation verbs, typified by *audire* ('to hear') conjugate differently: *audio, audis, audit, audimus, auditis, audiunt* ('I hear, you hear, he/she hears, we hear, you hear, they hear'). These differences are systematic, applying to dozens of verb forms, and to hundreds of different verbs. ➤➤declension; inflection 1; Latin; principal parts; verb.

conjunct ➤conjunction.

conjunction A type of word whose chief function is to connect words or other constructions. Conjunctions are traditionally classified into **coordinating conjunctions** (the main items being *and, or*, and *but*) and **subordinating conjunctions** (e.g. *because, although, when*). Certain adverbs also have a primarily connective function (e.g. *however, moreover*), and these are sometimes called **conjunctive adverbs** or **conjuncts**. ➤➤coordination; subordination; word class.

connected speech Speaking as part of a natural discourse. It might be thought that all speech is, by definition, connected. The point of the term is to draw a contrast with certain speech styles which involve the use of isolated words and artificial pauses, such as can be found in some foreign language teaching or speech therapy exercises. A learner may be able to pronounce or recognize a word in isolation, but be unable to do so when it occurs within the rhythms of rapid connected speech. Several important features of language can be found only in connected speech, such as complex intonation patterns, and the modification or omission of sounds between and within words. ➤➤assimilation; discourse analysis; elision; intonation.

connective A word (or part of a word) whose chief function is to link linguistic units; also sometimes called a **connector**. Examples include the conjunctions (e.g. *and*, *because*), some adverbs (e.g. *nevertheless*, *otherwise*), and certain verbs (notably, *be*). ➤➤conjunction; correlative.

connector ➤connective.

connotation The personal or emotional associations which are suggested by words, and which thus form part of their meaning, for individual speakers; for example, the word *automation* may connote 'efficiency' to one person, and 'redundancy' to another. A contrast is drawn with **denotation**, which is the relationship between words and the entities in the world to which they refer – in the present example, reference to a particular automatic system or apparatus. The denotation is essentially the 'dictionary meaning' of the word, though information about the most widely shared connotations is usually given in dictionaries. ➤➤affective meaning; referential language; semantic differential.

consonance The harmonious use of sounds in speech; contrasts with **dissonance**. The term has a narrower use in the study of versification, referring to the correspondence of consonants, especially at the ends of words (e.g. *knife, leaf, brief*). ➤➤euphony.

consonant (C) In phonetics, a speech sound produced by a relatively constricted or totally closed configuration of the vocal tract; in phonology, a unit of the sound system which typically occupies the margins of a syllable. In both approaches, the term contrasts with **vowel** (as it does with the corresponding use in the writing system). The two views coincide in the classification of such sounds as /p/, /f/, and /tʃ/, but they do not always do so. It is possible for a sound to act like a consonant in the sound system, but to behave phonetically like a vowel. An example is /w/, which sounds like the vowel [u], but which only ever occurs before a vowel at the beginning of a syllable (as in *we*). Such cases are often called **semiconsonants** or **semivowels**. ➤➤cluster; semivowel; syllable; vowel.

consonant harmony ➤harmony.

constituent A linguistic unit which is an element of a larger construction. **Constituent analysis** is the process of analysing sentences into a series of constituents, which are organized in a hierarchical way. The major divisions made at a given level are called the **immediate constituents** (or **ICs**); the smallest units resulting from this process of analysis are the **ultimate constituents** (or **UCs**). A grammar which analyses sentences in this way is called a **constituency grammar**. ➤➤hierarchy; phrase-structure grammar; tree; p. 70.

constriction A narrowing within the vocal tract. Different kinds and degrees of constriction are the basis of the articulatory classification of sound qualities. A maximum constriction is a closure, as in the case of [p]. Less constriction is involved in fricative sounds, such as [f]. Open vowels are least constricted. ➤➤articulation; fricative; vocal tract; vowel.

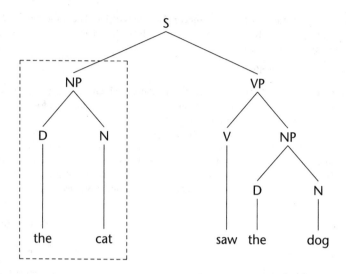

Constituent analysis. The immediate constituents of the sentence (S) are the NP (noun phrase) and VP (verb phrase). The immediate constituents of the first NP are D (determiner) and N (noun). The ultimate constituents of the sentence are the words in the bottom line – though *saw* could be further analysed into *see* + past tense.

constructional homonymity ➤ambiguous.

consultant ➤informant.

contact language ➤language contact; pidgin.

contentive ➤grammatical word.

content word ➤grammatical word.

context 1. The parts of an utterance next to or near a linguistic unit (such as a word) which is the focus of attention; also called **environment**. In that first sentence, for example, *focus* is being used in the context of *attention* (as opposed to, say, in the context of *camera*). Without knowing the context, the meaning of a word is likely to be ambiguous; providing this context is called **contextualization**. In generative grammar, forms can be classified in terms of whether they occur only in a specific structural context (they are **context-sensitive**) or are independent of context (they are **context-free**). In a context-sensitive grammar, the rules apply only in particular contexts; in a context-free grammar the rules apply regardless of context. ➤ambiguous; distribution; generative grammar. **2**. The features of the nonlinguistic world in relation to which linguistic units are systematically used; also called the **situational context** or **environment**. The historical context identifies the general time-period within which a language is being used (such as the 17th century). The geographical context identifies regional factors which correlate with the use of language (such as dialect). The social context identifies such features as the age, sex, or occupation of the speaker. ➤dialect; variety.

context-free/sensitive ➤context **1**.

continuant A sound made with an incomplete closure of the vocal tract, as can be heard with vowels and certain types of consonant (e.g. fricatives). Sounds which have a complete closure are called **noncontinuants** or **stops**. ➤closure; consonant; vocal tract; vowel.

continuous ➤progressive.

contour A distinctive configuration of tones in an utterance; also called an **intonation contour** or a **pitch contour**. Contours are usually classified into 'rising' and 'falling' basic types, with more complex variations recognized. A statement in English often has a falling contour; a question often has a rising one; and a hesitant or doubtful utterance often has a contour which falls then rises. ➤intonation; pitch; tone.

contraction 1. The shortening of a linguistic form so that it comes to be attached to an adjacent form, as in English *am* becoming '*m* in *I'm*; sometimes called **reduction**. The term also applies to cases of fusion, where both forms alter their shape, as in French *du* from **de le*, 'of the (masculine)'. ➤assimilation. **2**. ➤ellipsis.

contradictories ➤complementarity.

contrast A difference between linguistic units, especially one which serves to distinguish meanings in a language; also called an **opposition**, especially in phonology. Such differences, which will be found at all linguistic levels, may also be referred to as **distinctive**, **functional**, or **significant**. Contrasts in English include (in sounds) /p/ vs. /b/, (in grammar) *the* vs. *a* and *he is* vs. *is he?*, and (in vocabulary) *big* vs. *small*. ➤distinctive; level 1; markedness; redundant.

contrastive analysis (CA) In the study of foreign language learning, the identification of points of structural similarity and difference between two languages. The assumption is that points of difference will be areas of potential difficulty (called 'interference' or 'negative transfer') in the learning of one or other of the languages. A CA approach aims to predict what these difficulties will be, and to provide teaching materials which will help. ➤interference; language learning; transfer.

contrastive stress Extra emphasis given to a word, in order to draw special attention to its meaning. It often suggests a specific contrast with another word: *I need a RED pencil* (not a blue one). ➤stress.

conundrum ➤riddle.

convergence 1. In sociolinguistics, a process of linguistic change in which dialects become more like each other; contrasts with **divergence**, where dialects become less like each other. Convergence is widespread, being commonly found within adjacent speech communities, which tend to borrow words and sounds from each other. Also common are cases where a nonstandard variety becomes more like the standard language, as can be seen in several West Indian creoles. ➤accommodation; creole; dialect **2**. In historical linguistics, the merging of forms which were contrastive at an earlier stage of a language; also called **merger** or **coalescence**, and contrasted with **divergence**, where a form splits into two functional units. For example, in Middle English the vowels of *see* and *deep* were distinct, but these have now merged to /i:/. ➤coalescence; language change; syncretism.

conversational implicature ➤implicature.

conversational maxims ➤maxims of conversation.

conversation analysis (CA) The analysis of the methods people use to engage in conversation and other forms of social interaction involving speech. The central concern is to determine how individuals experience, make sense of, and report their interactions. Tape recordings are made of natural conversations, and the associated transcriptions are analysed to determine the properties which govern the way a conversation proceeds. ➤adjacency pair; cooperative principle; discourse analysis; implicature; interactional sociolinguistics; repair; sociolinguistics; turn.

converseness A type of oppositeness of meaning, in which one member of a pair of terms presupposes the other. Examples include *buy* vs. *sell* and *employer* vs. *employee*. ➤antonymy.

conversion A process of word formation in which an item comes to belong to a new word class without the addition of an affix; also called **functional shift**. Examples include the change of noun to verb in *carpet* (*I've bought a new carpet* vs. *I'm going to carpet the floor*), and (much less typical) the change of auxiliary verb to noun in *must* (*That's a must*). ➤affix, word formation.

cooing The earliest point in infant vocalization when speech-like sounds can be heard. The sounds are phonetically indeterminate, typically vowel-like in character (though some consonant-like noises can occur), and gradually develop into the more varied and definite sounds of babbling. The onset of cooing is usually around three months. ➤babbling; vocalization.

Cook Islands (population in 1995 estimated at 18,200) The official language is English. Cook Islands Maori (Rarotongan) is spoken by *c*.75% of the people as a first language. Four other Austronesian languages are also represented on the islands. ➤Austronesian; English.

cooperative principle A principle used in the analysis of conversations which states that speakers try to cooperate with each other when communicating; in particular, they try to be informative, truthful, relevant, and clear. Listeners normally assume that a speaker is following these conventions. ➤conversation analysis; implicature; maxims of conversation.

coordinating conjunction ➤conjunction.

coordination The linking of linguistic units which are usually of equivalent syntactic status, such as a series of clauses, or a series of nouns; also called **conjoining**; contrasts with **subordination**, where the units being linked are not equivalent. **Coordinate clauses** are illustrated by *Mary got a BA and Frank got a BSc*. Items which signal coordination are called **coordinators** or **coordinating conjunctions** – such as *and*, *or*, and *either/or*. ➤conjunction; subordination.

coordinator ➤coordination.

coprolalia /kɒprəˈleɪlɪə/ The uncontrolled use of obscene language – a symptom of certain rare neurological disorders, notably Giles de la Tourette syndrome. The term is used only in clinical contexts. ➤language pathology; taboo language.

Coptic ➤Egyptian.

copula /ˈkɒpjʊlə/ A verb with little or no independent meaning, whose primary function is to link elements of clause structure, typically the subject and the complement, to show that they are semantically equivalent; also called a **linking verb**. In English, the main copular verb is *be*, in its various forms, as used in such sentences as *She is a doctor*, *They are happy*. This somewhat unusual term derives from a Latin root meaning 'bond' or 'join' – as seen also in *couple* and *copulate*. ➤complement; subject; verb.

Cornish A member of the Brythonic branch of the Celtic family of languages, spoken chiefly in Cornwall from around the 5th century until the end of the 18th century. It is closely related to Breton. Written remains date from the early 15th century. Since the 1950s there has been an active revivalist movement. ➤Celtic.

corpus, plural **corpora** A collection of linguistic data, either compiled as written texts or as a transcription of recorded speech. The main purpose of a corpus is to verify a hypothesis about language – for example, to determine how the usage of a particular sound, word, or syntactic construction varies. **Corpus linguistics** deals with the principles and practice of using corpora in language study. A **computer corpus** is a large body of machine-readable texts. Very large computer corpora have been developed: the British National Corpus, for example, contains 100 million words. ➤Bank of English; British National Corpus; Brown University Corpus of American English; COBUILD; computational linguistics; International Computer Archive of Modern English; International Corpus of English; Lancaster–Oslo/Bergen Corpus of British English; London/Lund Corpus of Spoken English; Longman/Lancaster English Language Corpus; natural language; Survey of English Usage.

corpus planning ►language planning.

correctness An absolute standard of language use deriving from the rules of institutions (such as language academies) or respected publications (grammars, dictionaries, manuals of pronunciation and style). When applied to aspects of language where there is no usage variation among educated users, the notion is uncontroversial: the spelling form **langauge* is incorrect, as is the word order **Hardly he had left*. The notion becomes controversial only when it is used to condemn usages which are common within the whole or part of the speech community, such as the use of the split infinitive (*to really know*) or regional dialect forms (*It do no harm*). ➤➤appropriateness; normative; prescriptivism.

correlative Descriptive of constructions which use a pair of connecting words. A typical correlative construction is *Either we leave now or we'll have to stay until morning*. Other correlatives include *not only . . . but also, both . . . and*, and *if . . . then*. ➤➤connective; disjunction.

Corsican /'kɔ:sɪkn/ A variety of Romance spoken by *c.*340,000 people chiefly in the island of Corsica (by over half the population), where it is recognized as an official regional language (alongside French, the standard language) by the French government. There are also several thousand speakers in Italy and various countries of North and South America. Linguistically, the variety is closer to Tuscan (in Italy) than to French. ➤➤Italian; Romance.

Costa Rica (population in 1995 estimated at 3,383,000) The official language is Spanish, spoken by most of the population. About 2% speak an English-based creole widespread throughout the western Caribbean. There are also a small number of Amerindian languages spoken by a few thousand people, and an immigrant group of *c.*4500 Chinese (Yue). English is increasingly used for international purposes, along with Spanish. ➤➤creole; Spanish.

Côte d'Ivoire, formerly **Ivory Coast** (population in 1995 estimated at 14,651,000) The official language is French. There are *c.*70 local languages in use, notably Akar (Baule), widely used as a lingua franca, Bete, and Senufo. French is the language used for international purposes. ➤➤French; lingua franca.

countability A contrast in the grammatical classification of nouns, in which nouns denoting separable entities (**countable** or **count nouns**) are distinguished from those denoting continuous entities, having no natural bounds (**noncountable**, **uncountable**, **noncount** or **mass nouns**). English identifies count nouns by their co-occurrence with such forms as *a*, *many*, and the numbers; noncount nouns co-occur with such forms as *much* and *some*: compare *a table* vs. *some music*. Many nouns can be used in both contexts: *a cake* vs. *some cake*. ➤➤noun; number.

count noun ►countability.

covert prestige ►overt prestige.

creaky voice A vocal effect produced by a very slow vibration of only one end of the vocal folds; also called **creak** or **laryngealization**. Because the sound somewhat resembles that of frying, the effect has also been described as 'vocal fry'. Filmstar Vincent Price produced excellent creaky voice in his especially menacing moments. ➤➤larynx; paralanguage; phonation; vocal folds.

creativity, linguistic ➤productivity.

creole A pidgin language which has become the mother tongue of a speech community. The process of expanding the structural and stylistic range of the pidgin is called **creolization**. A process of **decreolization** takes place when the standard language begins to exert influence on the creole, and a whole range of varieties emerges to form a continuum between the standard and the creole (a **post-creole continuum**). Among the varieties which have been recognized are the **acrolect** (characterized by prestige or standardization), the **basilect** (most remote from the prestige variety), and the **mesolect** (intermediate between acrolect and basilect). ➤➤Black English Vernacular; Gullah; Jamaica; Krio; monogenesis; Papiamentu; pidgin; Sheldru.

critical linguistics An approach to language analysis which aims to reveal hidden power relations and ideological processes at work in linguistic texts. It is especially used in **critical discourse analysis**, the analysis of texts in relation to the social context which gave rise to them, and within which they need to be interpreted. ➤➤discourse analysis; linguistics.

critical period In child language acquisition, the hypothesis that there is a particular time-span during which a first language can be most easily acquired. The notion of a critical period is well supported in several areas of child development (e.g. with reference to the development of the mechanism of swallowing), and was felt to be also relevant to the emergence of language. It was argued that the critical period for language ends at puberty, because by this time the brain has become specialized in its functions, and no longer has the adaptability found at earlier stages of biological development. The hypothesis has proved to be extremely difficult to test, and remains controversial. ➤➤acquisition.

Croatia (population in 1995 estimated at 4,876,000) The official language is now called Croatian (before independence in 1991, Serbo-Croatian), spoken by most of the population. There are *c*.250,000 speakers of Italian, in the north of the country, and uncertain numbers of speakers of Slovak, Romani, and other people from nearby countries. English is increasingly being used for international purposes. ➤➤Serbo-Croatian.

Croatian The name increasingly being used since the early 1990s for the Slavic language spoken chiefly in Croatia by *c*.4.8 million people; before the civil war, considered a variety of Serbo-Croatian. It is also found in nearby territories, and through emigration is in Germany, Sweden, and several other countries. It is written in the Roman alphabet. ➤➤Croatia.

crossword A word game in which the aim is to fill out a symmetrically patterned grid of black and white squares by writing in the answers to a set of numbered clues. The location of the first letter of an answer is given by a number in a square, corresponding to the number of the clue, and answers interlock horizontally and vertically. The crossword is complete when all clues are answered correctly, so that all blank squares are filled. The origins of the puzzle are unclear, but it became widely known in 1913, when a US journalist, Arthur Wynne, devised a newspaper puzzle called a 'word cross'. Over the years, the game has developed several variant shapes and conventions, though a square grid is usual. ➤cryptic clue.

cryptic clue A type of clue in a crossword puzzle which is deliberately mysterious and ambiguous. Anagrams, hiding words in phrases, the use of puns, and other stratagems are all popular examples. Cryptic clues were introduced by Torquemada (Edward Powys Mathers), who composed puzzles for the *Observer* in the 1920s and 1930s. ➤crossword.

cryptology The study of how secret messages are constructed, using codes and ciphers (**cryptography** or 'code-making'), and then deciphered or decoded (**cryptanalysis** or 'code-breaking'). The messages themselves are called **cryptograms**. ➤cipher; code 2; steganography.

cryptophasia ➤idioglossia.

Cuba (population in 1995 estimated at 11,089,000) The official language is Spanish, spoken by almost everyone. There are a few speakers of Russian. English is increasingly used for international purposes, along with Spanish. ➤Spanish.

cued speech A method of speech reading in which manual cues help to distinguish sounds that have a visually similar articulation. The aim is to help a deaf person to 'see' the sounds of speech as they are spoken. Different positions and shapes of the hand are used near the speaker's mouth, chin, and throat to signal vowels and consonants. The system was devised in 1966 by the American educator R. Orin Cornett (1913–), and it has since been adapted for use in 56 languages (as of 1995). ➤sign language; speech reading.

cuneiform /ˈkjuːnɪfɔːm/ An ancient writing system using wedge-shaped characters. The name derives from Latin *cuneus* 'wedge', and refers to the technique used to make the symbols. A stylus was pressed into a tablet of soft clay to make a sequence of short straight strokes. The strokes are thicker at the top and to the left, reflecting the direction of writing. At first, symbols were written from top to bottom; later they were turned on their sides, and written from left to right. The system dates from the 4th millennium BC, and was used for over 3000 years throughout the Near East in a wide range of languages. Decipherment of these languages began only in the 19th century. ➤writing; p. 77.

curly brackets ➤brackets.

Original pictogram	Pictogram in position of later cuneiform	Early Babylonian	Assyrian	Original or derived meaning
				bird
				fish
				donkey
	Original pictogram			ox
				sun day
				grain
				orchard
				to plough to till
				boomerang to throw to throw down
				to stand to go

Examples of Sumerian pictograms and their meanings, seen in relation to later **cuneiform** developments. The signs were later rotated 90° anticlockwise, to facilitate writing, and thus lost their immediate pictorial recognizability. Two stages of cuneiform representation are shown.

cursive A form of handwriting in which the separate characters in a sequence have been joined together in a series of rounded, flowing strokes, promoting ease and speed; called informally (especially by children), 'joined-up writing'. It is found in general use from around the 4th century AD, and in time replaced uncial and half-uncial writing as a handwriting norm. ➤➤uncial.

Cushitic /kʊˈʃɪtɪk/ A branch of the Afro-Asiatic family of *c*.50 languages, spoken by *c*.24 million people in Ethiopia and nearby areas to the south and east. Galla, Somali, and Beja are the most widespread languages. A western group of languages is sometimes classified separately as Omotic. ➤➤Afro-Asiatic; Omotic; Oromo; Somali.

CV An abbreviation of **consonant–vowel** (when talking about sequences of sounds in syllables), often expanded to CVC, CVCC, etc.; also, an abbreviation of **cardinal vowel**.

cypher ➤cipher.

Cyprus (population in 1995 estimated at 600,000) The official languages are Greek (in the Greek part of the island) and Turkish (in the Turkish part) – *c*.77% and *c*.18% of the population, respectively. There are also several thousand speakers of Arabic, Armenian, and Syriac. English is the language used for international trade and tourism. ➤➤Greek; Turkish.

Cyrillic /sɪˈrɪlɪk/ An alphabet devised by Saints Cyril and Methodius in the 9th century AD for Eastern Orthodox Slavic speakers. Derived from the Greek uncial script, it came to be used (in various adaptations) for Russian, Bulgarian, Serbian, and several languages which fell under the influence of the Soviet Union during the 20th century (e.g. Ukrainian). ➤➤alphabet; Glagolitic; Russian; Slavic; uncial.

Czech A member of the West Slavic group of languages, spoken by *c*.12 million people chiefly in the Czech Republic, where it is the official language, and also in nearby parts of adjoining countries, the USA (*c*.1.5 million), and Canada. It is very closely related to Slovak (with which it is largely mutually intelligible). Written in the Roman alphabet, traces of the language can be found in 11th century texts in Old Church Slavonic. The standard language became established in the 16th century, based on the Prague dialect. ➤➤Czech Republic; Slavic; Slovak.

Czech Republic, formerly (to 1992) part of Czechoslovakia (population in 1995 estimated at 10,411,000) The official language is Czech, spoken by over 96% of the population. Other languages include German (both Bavarian and standard, *c*.200,000), Polish (*c*.50,000), and Romani (perhaps 150,000). English, German, and Russian are all used for international purposes. ➤➤Czech.

D

D An abbreviation of **determiner**.

DA An abbreviation of **discourse analysis**.

dactyl /'daktɪl/ ➤foot.

dactylology /daktɪ'lɒlədʒiː/ ➤finger spelling.

DAF An abbreviation of **delayed auditory feedback** (➤feedback 2).

Dagestanian ➤Nakho-Dagestanian.

dagger ➤obelisk.

Dalmatian ➤Romance.

dangling participle The use of a participle, or a phrase introduced by a participle, which has an unclear or ambiguous relationship to the rest of the sentence; also called a **misrelated participle**. If taken literally, the sentence often appears nonsensical or laughable: *Driving along the street, a runaway dog gave John a fright.* To avoid such inadvertent effects, manuals of style recommend that such sentences be rephrased, with the participial construction moved or replaced, as in *When John was driving along the street, a runaway dog gave him a fright.* ➤➤participle.

Danish A North Germanic language, a member of the East Scandinavian group, spoken by over 5 million people in Denmark, and also by the inhabitants of the Faeroe Islands and Greenland, where it is an official language (alongside Faeroese and Greenlandic Eskimo, respectively), in north Germany, and through emigration to the USA and Canada (a further *c*.300,000). The earliest traces of the language are runic inscriptions from the 3rd century. Danish began to emerge from common Old Norse in the 12th century, and literary texts date from a century later. It is written in the Roman alphabet. The political power of Denmark from the Middle Ages led to Danish being used as an official language in Norway for several hundred years, and its influence on all the Scandinavian languages is apparent. ➤➤Denmark; Norwegian; rune; Scandinavian.

Dardic /'dɑːdɪk/ A group of Indo-Iranian languages spoken in Pakistan, Kashmir, and Afghanistan. They are sometimes seen as a separate branch of Indo-Iranian, and sometimes placed within the Indo-Aryan branch (Northwestern group). The languages include Khowari, Kafiri, and Kashmiri. ➤➤Indo-Iranian; Kashmiri.

Dari /ˈdɑːriː/ ➤Afghanistan; Persian.

dark *l* ➤clear *l*.

dash A punctuation mark which typically signals an included unit – such as this one – especially in informal writing. A single dash may also precede an afterthought at the end of a sentence, and be used as a sign that a construction is incomplete. ➤➤punctuation.

dative case One of the ways in which inflected languages make a word change its form, in order to show a grammatical relationship with other words in the sentence. The dative mainly affects nouns, along with related words (such as adjectives and pronouns), and signals a range of meanings typically expressed in English by the prepositions *to* or *for* – for example, Latin *civi* is the dative of *civis* 'citizen', and would be translated as 'to/for the citizen'. ➤➤case; inflection 1; object; recipient.

daughter language ➤family of languages.

dB The symbol for decibel.

dead language A language which is no longer used as a natural daily means of spoken communication within a community; contrasts with **living language**. Latin is a dead language, in this sense, despite its continued use as an official language by the Roman Catholic Church. Attempts may be made to bring a dead language back to life, as in the case of Cornish and Manx, which both have enthusiastic groups of supporters. ➤➤Cornish; Hebrew; language death; Latin; Manx.

deafness Loss of the ability to hear, for whatever reason. In practice, total deafness (**anacusis**) is unusual, and more use is made of a scale of classification which recognizes levels of **hearing loss**. Six levels are often used: slight (a loss of up to 25 dB), mild (a loss of between 25 and 40 dB), moderate (a loss of between 40 and 55 dB), moderately severe (a loss of between 55 and 70 dB), severe (a loss of between 70 and 90 dB), and profound (a loss of over 90 dB). With a profound loss, a person may hear some loud sounds, but these are perceived more as vibrations than as speech patterns. If the hearing loss occurs before the normal development of speech in the child, it is referred to as **prelingual**; if it occurs after speech has begun to develop, it is **postlingual**. If sound fails to reach the cochlea, the hearing loss is described as **conductive**; if the loss arises from within the cochlea itself, it is described as **sensorineural**. ➤➤decibel; sign language; speech reading.

decibel (dB) A unit for measuring the relative intensity of sounds, especially used in the measurement of hearing loss. The term **bel** is named after Alexander Graham Bell (1847–1922). ➤➤deafness; p. 81.

decipher 1. To decode a writing system which is no longer in use and no longer comprehensible. ➤➤hieroglyphic. **2**. To work out the meaning of a message in code – especially one in cipher. ➤➤cipher.

(a)

0	threshold of audibility
10	rustle of leaves
20	ticking of watch (at ear); radio studio
30	quiet garden; whispered conversation
40	residential area, no traffic
50	quiet office; typewriter
60	conversation at 1 m; car at 10 m
70	very busy city traffic at 30 m
75	telephone bell at 3 m; shouting
80	noisy tube train; loud radio music
90	pneumatic drill at 1 m
100	car horn at 5 m; orchestra fortissimo
110	boilermakers' shop
120	pneumatic hammer, 1 m; amplified rock band
130	four-engined jet aircraft, 30 m

At around 120 dB, the sensation of hearing is replaced by that of pain.

(b)

ɔ:	29	e	23	l	20	ʒ	13	ð	10
ɒ	28	i:	22	ʃ	19	z	12	b	8
ɑ:	26	u:	22	ŋ	18	s	12	d	8
ʌ	26	ɪ	22	m	17	t	11	p	7
ɜ:	25	w	21	tʃ	16	g	11	f	7
a	24	r	20	n	15	k	11	θ	0
ʊ	24	j	20	dʒ	13	v	10		

Measurement in **decibels**. In (a) the relative intensity of different kinds of speech can be seen by relating them to the average intensities of some everyday sounds. In (b) the values of English sounds, expressed in decibels, are related to the sound with the lowest intensity, [θ], as in *thin*.

declarative /dɪˈklarətɪv/ Descriptive of a verb form or a type of sentence or clause which is typically used in the expression of a statement – that is, a 'declaration' that something is or is not the case. Most of the sentences in this book are declarative. A contrast is intended with other types of utterance, primarily question and command. ➤interrogative; statement.

declension In an inflecting language, a set of nouns, adjectives, or pronouns that share the same set of endings. In Latin, for example, the 'first declension' refers to nouns whose endings are -*a*, -*am* and -*ae*, in the various cases in the singular (e.g. *insula* 'island', *poeta* 'poet'). There are a further four declensions with different types of ending, as well as several nouns which decline in an irregular way. ➤case; conjugation; inflection 1; Latin; noun.

decode ➤code 1, 2.

deconstruction ➤logocentrism.

decreolization ➤creole.

deep structure In transformational grammar, the abstract or underlying syntactic representation of a sentence, specifying the factors which govern its interpretation; also called **deep grammar**; contrasts with **surface structure**. For example, the deep structure common to both active and passive sentences (*Mary kicked the ball* vs. *The ball was kicked by Mary*) would need to recognize an actor ('Mary'), action ('kick'), and goal ('ball'). The notion has been presented in several ways, and has proved to be a controversial issue in the recent history of grammatical thought. ➤➤surface structure; transformation; underlying.

defective Descriptive of words which do not follow all the rules of the class to which they belong. The English modal verbs, for example, are defective in that they do not permit the usual range of verb endings: *must, can, shall*, etc. do not vary (**musted, *cans, *shalling*). ➤➤mood; word class.

defective speech ➤speech defect.

deficit hypothesis The view that some children, especially those belonging to an ethnic minority or with a working-class background, lack a sufficiently wide range of grammar and vocabulary to be able to express complex ideas, such as will be needed for success in school. It is contrasted with the **difference hypothesis** – the view that the language used by such children is simply different from that found in middle-class children, though its social standing is lower. The difference hypothesis views all dialects as intrinsically equal and able to express ideas of any complexity, though children who speak nonstandard dialects may not have had the same kind of opportunity or motivation to use their language in demanding educational contexts. ➤➤educational linguistics; elaborated code; variety.

defining modification ➤restrictiveness.

defining vocabulary A set of words used as part of the definition of other words. The notion is found in such contexts as language teaching and dictionary preparation. Some dictionaries ensure that every word used in a definition is itself defined elsewhere in the book. ➤➤lexicography.

definiteness A feature of noun phrases, allowing a contrast between an entity (or class of entities) which is specific and identifiable (i.e. **definite**) and one which is not (**indefinite** or **nondefinite**). The contrast is generally conveyed through the use of a definite vs. indefinite determiner, especially the definite and indefinite article (English *the/a*). In some languages (e.g. Hungarian), verbs can express a contrast of definiteness, a verb agreeing with the definiteness of its direct object. ➤➤article; noun phrase.

degree A grammatical category which specifies the extent of a comparison between adjectives or adverbs. A three-way contrast is usually recognized, distinguishing **positive** from **comparative** from **superlative**, as in *big/bigger/biggest* or *interesting/*

more interesting/most interesting. Other types of comparative construction exist, such as the **equative**, illustrated by *as big as*. ➤➤adjective; adverb; comparative.

deixis /'daıksıs/ A grammatical category involving direct reference to the characteristics of the situation where an utterance takes place; also referred to as **indexicality**. The meaning of a deictic utterance is thus relative to the situation in which it is used. For example, the interpretation of the pronouns *I* and *you* varies, depending on who is doing the talking and who is being addressed. The location of the speaker in time and place governs the interpretation of certain temporal and spatial adverbs, such as *today*, *tomorrow*, *here*, and *there*. ➤➤adverb; pronoun.

delayed auditory feedback ➤feedback 2.

delayed language ➤language delay.

deletion The process of omitting a constituent from a construction. For example, in order to explain the structure of the sentence *The children sang and danced*, we can say that the subject of *danced* (which is also *the children*) has been deleted. Sounds, too, are often deleted, especially in rapid speech (as in *cup o' tea*). The notion has been particularly used as part of the approach to sentence analysis proposed by transformational grammar. ➤➤elision; ellipsis; transformation.

demonstrative A form whose chief function is to distinguish one item from other members of the same class. In English, the chief demonstratives are *this* and *that*, used alone (as pronouns) or with nouns (as determiners): *Look at this/that* and *Look at this/that book* illustrate the two possibilities. ➤➤determiner; pronoun.

demotic /dɪ'mɒtık/ Descriptive of a style of language used for or by ordinary people; usually contrasted with a **hieratic** style used for special (e.g. religious) purposes. Examples include the simplified hieroglyphic of Ancient Egyptian, and the vernacular variety of Modern Greek (➤**hieroglyphic** for an illustration). ➤➤diglossia; Egyptian; Greek; Rosetta Stone.

denasal /diː'neızl/ Descriptive of a sound or voice quality whose nasality has been reduced or removed. The notion is especially relevant as part of the description of voice disorders, where several clinical conditions give rise to voices with poor nasal resonance (such as adenoids). ➤➤nasal; voice quality.

Denmark (population in 1995 estimated at 5,188,000) The official language is Danish, spoken by almost everyone. Faeroese also has official status in the Faeroe Islands, as does Greenlandic Eskimo in Greenland. German is an official regional language in North Slesvig (Sydjylland), spoken by *c*.25,000. English is widely used for international purposes and tourism. ➤➤Danish; Eskimo; Faeroese.

denotation ➤connotation.

dental Descriptive of a consonant sound made by contact between the tongue tip or blade and the upper incisor teeth, as in the pronunciation of /t/ and /d/ in French or in certain dialects of English (e.g. Irish). Sounds made by the tongue tip between the teeth, like the 'th' sounds of such words as *this* and *thin*, are sometimes distinguished as **interdental**. ➤➤consonant; tongue.

dependent Descriptive of any element whose form or function is determined by another part of the sentence. In the phrase *the black book*, for example, the article and adjective both depend on the noun. In the sentence, *She said she was going*, the clause *she was going* depends on the verb *said*, and may thus be described as a **dependent clause**. ➤➤modification 1; qualification; subordination.

dependent clause ➤dependent; subordination.

deponent verb /dɪˈpəʊnənt/ A term from traditional Latin grammar, used for verbs which are passive in most of their forms, but active in meaning. Examples include *loquor* 'speak' and *hortor* 'I exhort'. They are called 'deponent' because they have 'put away' (*de* + *pono*) some of their parts – in other words, the inflections associated with the active voice. ➤➤verb; voice 1.

derivation 1. A major type of word formation, in which a certain kind of affix (a **derivational affix**) is used to form new words, as with *happiness* and *unhappy* from *happy*, or *determination* from *determine*. A contrast is intended with the process of inflection, which uses another kind of affix in order to form variants of the same word, as with *determine/determines/determining/determined*. ➤➤affix; inflection 1; morphology. **2**. In generative grammar, the structural history of a sentence – the formally identifiable stages which need to be recognized in order to generate a sentence from an initial symbol to a terminal string. ➤➤generative grammar. **3**. The origins or historical development of a language, or of a word or construction in a language. ➤➤etymology.

derivational morphology ➤morphology.

descender ➤ascender.

description A systematic, objective, and precise account of the patterns and use of a specific language or variety. The aim of **descriptive linguistics** is to account for the facts of linguistic usage as they are, in a particular language, and not as purist critics or prescriptive grammarians imagine they ought to be. A descriptive grammar (e.g. of English) may also be contrasted with a theoretical grammar, in which the aim is to make statements about language as a whole. ➤➤grammar 1; linguistics; prescriptivism; purism.

descriptive grammar ➤grammar 1.

det. An abbreviation of **determiner**.

determiner (D, det.) A grammatical element whose main role is to co-occur with nouns to express such semantic notions as quantity, number, possession, and definiteness; for example, *the, a, this, some, my, much*. These words 'determine' the way in which the noun is to be interpreted – *a car* vs. *the car* vs. *my car*, etc. The term is sometimes extended to include other types of word within the noun phrase (such as adjectives). ➤article; postdeterminer; predeterminer.

determinism, linguistic ➤Sapir–Whorf hypothesis.

Devanagari /devənə'gɑːriː/ An Indian alphabet used to write Sanskrit, Hindi, and several other languages of the Indian subcontinent; also called **Nagari**. As the script of Sanskrit literature (the name comes from the Sanskrit word *deva* 'holy'), it became the most widely used writing system in India. Its main visual feature is the use of a horizontal line on the top of a letter, which forms a continuous line when writing text. The alphabet, which can be traced from the 7th century AD, uses 48 letters, and is written from left to right. ➤alphabet; Brahmi; Sanskrit; p. 86.

developmental aphasia/dysphasia ➤aphasia.

developmental language disorder ➤acquired language disorder.

developmental linguistics A branch of linguistics concerned with the study of the acquisition of language in children – and, for some writers, with the continuing development of language through adulthood and into old age. Because psychological factors are so important in studying language acquisition, the subject is often called **developmental psycholinguistics**. ➤acquired language disorder; linguistics; psycholinguistics.

deviance Lack of conformity to the rules of a grammar. Deviant sentences are conventionally marked with a preceding asterisk, as in **Some the cars were damaged*. The notion is used both with reference to language in general (applying to any departure from linguistic norms by someone with normal language skills) and with reference to pathological conditions (applying to linguistic symptoms which could not be considered part of the usual developmental process). ➤grammar 1; language delay/disorder/pathology.

devoiced Descriptive of a sound in which the normal amount of vocal fold vibration ('voice') has been reduced. In English, for example, voiced consonants at the end of a word are generally devoiced, as in *bib* or *did*. ➤voicing.

Dhivehi ➤Maldivian.

diachronic linguistics /daɪə'krɒnɪk/ The study of languages from the viewpoint of their development through time; also called **historical linguistics**. Ferdinand de Saussure introduced the contrast between this approach and that of **synchronic linguistics**, where languages are studied at a theoretical single point in time, disregarding whatever changes might be taking place within them. ➤philology; Saussure.

diacritic /daɪə'krɪtɪk/ A mark added to a written symbol which alters the way it should be pronounced. The mark may be placed over it, under it, before it, after it,

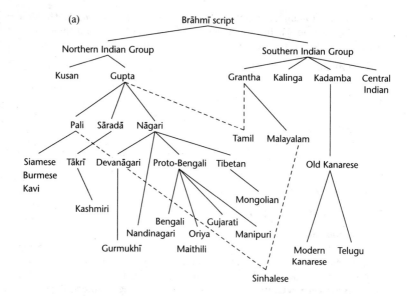

(a)

Brāhmī script

Northern Indian Group — Southern Indian Group

Kusan — Gupta — Grantha — Kalinga — Kadamba — Central Indian

Pali — Sāradā — Nāgari

Tamil — Malayalam

Siamese / Burmese / Kavi — Tākrī — Devanāgari — Proto-Bengali — Tibetan — Old Kanarese

Kashmiri

Mongolian

Bengali — Gujarati

Nandinagari — Oriya — Manipuri

Gurmukhī — Maithili

Modern Kanarese — Telugu

Sinhalese

(b)

Vowels		Consonants					
*श्र + अ	— a	क	k	gutturals	प	p	labials
आ	ा ā	ख	k-h		फ	p-h	
		ग	g		व	b	
		घ	g-h		भ	b-h	
		ङ	ṅ		म	m	
इ ि i		च	c	palatals	य	y	semivowels
ई ी ī		छ	c-h		र	r	
उ ु u		ज	j or झ j-h		ल	l	
ऊ ू ū		झ			व	v	
		ञ	ñ				
ऋ ृ ṛ (or ṛi)		ट	ṭ	cerebrals	श	ś (or ç)	spirants
ॠ ॄ r̄ (or ṛī)		ठ	ṭ-h		ष	ṣ	
ऌ ॢ ḷ (or ḷi)		ड	ḍ		स	s	
		ढ	ḍ-h		ह	h	
ए े e		ण	ṇ				
ऐ ै ai		त	t	dentals	:	ḥ (visarga)	
ओ ो o		थ	t-h		·	ṁ or ṁ (anusvāra)	
औ ौ au		द	d				
		ध	d-h				
		न	n				

* initial form of letters + medial form of letters

or through it. For example, in a phonetic transcription, the use of a small circle under a symbol indicates that the sound in question has been devoiced. In an alphabet, a diacritic used above a symbol is usually referred to as an **accent**. ➤accent 3; caret; cedilla; dieresis; macron; transcription.

diaeresis ➤dieresis.

diagramming ➤parsing.

dialect A language variety in which the use of grammar and vocabulary identifies the regional or social background of the user; the systematic study of dialects is known as **dialectology** or **dialect geography**. A **regional dialect** conveys information about the speaker's geographical origin; a **social dialect** conveys information about the speaker's class, social status, educational background, occupation, or other such notions. **Rural dialects** are heard in the country; **urban dialects** in the cities. The term is sometimes used in a pejorative way, as when someone refers to the speech of a primitive or rural community as 'just a dialect'. In fact, everyone speaks a dialect, even those who use a standard variety of a language (such as standard English – which is, technically, that dialect of English adopted as the norm for educated use). ➤accent 1; bidialectism; dialect atlas/continuum; dialectometry; idiolect; isogloss; language 1; patois; standard; variety.

dialect atlas A map (or series of maps) displaying dialect information within a geographical area; also known as a **linguistic atlas**. The first such atlas, of German, appeared in 1881, based on the analysis of over 50,000 questionnaires about local dialect use. The *Linguistic Atlas of England* appeared in 1978. Dialect surveys have now been carried out in many countries, and their results summarized in atlas form. ➤dialect; p. 88.

dialect continuum A chain of dialects spoken throughout an area; also called a **dialect chain**. At any point in the chain, speakers of a dialect can understand the speakers of other dialects who live adjacent to them; but people who live further away may be difficult or impossible to understand. For example, an extensive continuum links the modern dialects of German and Dutch, running from Belgium through the Netherlands, Germany, and Austria to Switzerland. ➤dialect; mutual intelligibility.

dialectology The study of dialects, especially regional dialects; also sometimes known as **dialect geography** or **linguistic geography**, though these terms usually suggest a much broader regional scope for the subject. In recent years, dialectologists have increasingly begun to study other factors than the purely regional, in order to explain linguistic variation (such as age, sex, and social class),

(*Opposite*) (a) The most important Brahmi-derived scripts of India. **Devanagari** is a member of the northern group. (b) The Devanagari alphabet for Sanskrit, showing the order devised by the ancient Indian grammarians. The colon (*visarga*) represents weak aspiration; the dot (*anusvara*) represents nazalization.

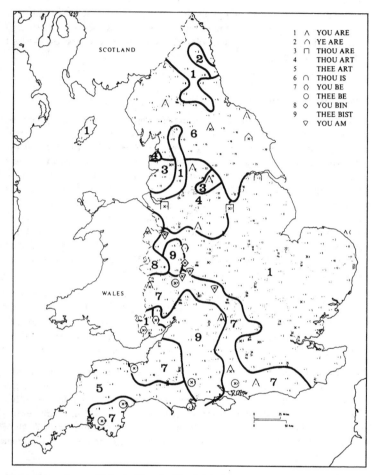

A map from a **dialect atlas**, the *Linguistic Atlas of England* (1978), showing variation in the forms equivalent to standard English *you are*.

and these emphases are reflected in such terms as **social** (as opposed to **regional**) dialectology, and **urban dialectology**. ➤dialect; dialect atlas; geolinguistics.

dialectometry A statistical method of analysing dialects. It measures the 'linguistic distance' between individual localities in a dialect region, based on the number of contrasts found in a large sample of linguistic features. Some dialects emerge as very closely related, while others diverge greatly. ➤dialect.

dialogue ➤monologue.

dichotic listening /daɪˈkɒtɪk/ A technique for determining which half of the brain is primarily involved in processing auditory effects. Subjects wear headphones, through which different sounds are presented to each ear. They are then asked to say what they hear. Some sounds are heard better through the right ear (a right-ear advantage), and some through the left (a left-ear advantage), suggesting that the two hemispheres of the brain play different roles in the perception of speech. Vowels and consonants, for example, seem to be mediated by the left hemisphere, in most people, whereas the right hemisphere is also involved in aspects of intonation. ➤➤auditory phonetics; intonation; psycholinguistics; speech perception.

diction The effective choice of words. The notion is usually employed in describing the vocabulary of a literary author, but any kind of writing can have its diction evaluated – as indeed can the spoken language, where clarity of pronunciation becomes an additional factor in achieving a particular effect. In traditional literary analysis, the notion is often used to refer to a specifically poetic kind of vocabulary, as illustrated by such words as *nymph* and *slumber*. ➤➤stylistics.

dictionary ➤lexicography.

dieresis or **diaeresis** /daɪˈerəsɪs/ A diacritic mark which indicates a change of vowel quality; often called an **umlaut**, from its use to mark the fronted pronunciations of certain vowels in German (e.g. *schön* 'beautiful'). It is sometimes used in English to mark the separate pronunciation of adjacent vowels, as in *naïve* and *coöperate*, especially in American texts, but this usage seems to be dying out. ➤➤diacritic.

difference hypothesis ➤deficit hypothesis.

diffusion The increased use of a language, or a feature of language (such as a sound or word), in a given area over a period of time. The notion emphasizes the view that change spreads gradually through a language, and not in an 'across-the-board' manner. Some speakers introduce a change into their speech before others; some use it more frequently and consistently than others; and some words are affected before others. ➤➤language/sound change; variable.

diglossia /daɪˈglɒsɪə/ A sociolinguistic situation where two very different varieties of a language – sometimes two languages – co-occur throughout a speech community, each performing an individual range of functions, and each having acquired some degree of status as a standard. The varieties are usually described as **high (H)** and **low (L)**, corresponding broadly to a difference in formality. H is used in such contexts as sermons, lectures, speeches, news broadcasts, and newspaper editorials, and is learned in school. L is used in everyday conversation, radio soaps, folk literature, and other informal contexts. Diglossic languages are widespread, and include Arabic, Modern Greek, (Swiss) German, and the Dravidian family. A situation where three varieties or languages are used with distinct functions within a community is called **triglossia**. An example is the use of French, Classical Arabic, and Colloquial Tunisian Arabic in Tunisia, the first two being rated H and the last L. ➤➤Arabic; Bengali; Dravidian; formality; German; Greek; standard; variety.

digraph /'daɪgraf/ **1**. A graphic unit in which two symbols are combined to function as a single element in a writing system. Digraphs such as æ and œ were formerly common in English, and are still used in the alphabets of some languages (e.g. Dutch, Swedish), as well as in special contexts, such as the phonetic alphabet. ➤➤graphology 1. **2**. In the study of reading and spelling, any sequence of two letters pronounced as a single sound (e.g. the first two letters of *ship* or the middle two letters of *wool*). ➤➤trigraph.

dimeter ➤metrics.

diminutive A form, usually expressed by an affix, with the general meaning of 'little', such as Italian *-ino*, Greek *-aki*, or English *-let* (*booklet, piglet*). It may be used either literally or metaphorically, often as a term of endearment. The term is usually contrasted with **augmentative**, where the general meaning is 'large', often implying awkwardness or ugliness, as in Italian *-one*. ➤➤affix.

ding-dong theory The name of one of the speculative theories about the origins of language; it argues that speech arose because people reacted to the stimuli in the world around them, and spontaneously produced sounds ('oral gestures') which in some way reflected the environment. The main evidence is the use of sound symbolism (which is, however, very limited in a language). The theory has also been called the **ta-ta** theory – a sceptical reference to the claim that the way the tongue moves while saying the words *ta-ta* reflects the physical act of waving good-bye. ➤➤origins of language; sound symbolism.

Dinka A Nilotic language spoken by *c*.2 million people in southern Sudan; also known as **Jieng**. It is written in the Roman alphabet. The Dinka are spread over a very wide area in the Nile basin, and consequently there are many dialects, some of which have been postulated as distinct languages. ➤➤Nilotic.

diphthong /'dɪfθɒŋ/ A vowel with a perceptible change of quality during a single syllable. It may be represented by a single letter (*my*) or a sequence of letters (*tie*); in the case of these words, the quality changes from a vowel of an [a] quality to one of an [i] quality. Phonetic symbols for diphthongs represent the beginning and the end of the vowel glide: [ai] in *my*, [ou] in *go*, etc. One element in the diphthong is always more sonorous than the other: if this is the first element, the diphthong is said to be 'falling' or 'descending'; if the second, it is 'rising' or 'ascending'. Other classifications of diphthong types have also been made. The process of forming a diphthong is **diphthongization**. ➤➤monophthong; triphthong; vowel.

diplomatics The study of legal and administrative documents. The name derives from Greek *diploma* 'folded'. One of its main aims is the identification of genuine documents as distinct from drafts, copies, and forgeries. ➤➤writing.

directive An utterance whose purpose is to get other people to do something for the speaker. The commonest method is to give a command, expressed either directly (*Sit down*) or indirectly (*I wonder if you'd kindly . . .*), but other formulations are possible, such as a noun said with appropriate intonation (e.g. *Window?* – meaning, 'Close it'). ➤➤command; imperative; speech act.

direct method A method of language teaching in which students speak only in the target language in the classroom. The teacher communicates with the students in as direct a way as possible, using mime, gestures, and other cues. The method avoids the conscious learning of grammar, and leaves work on reading and writing until after speaking and listening skills are well established. ➤➤language teaching; method; natural approach.

direct object ➤object.

direct speech The use of an actual utterance, without grammatical modification, as part of a narrative, such as *Hilary asked, 'Is the car ready?'* (a direct question). The term contrasts with **indirect speech**, also called **reported speech**, where the words of the speaker are subordinated to a verb (of 'saying') in the main clause, and several grammatical changes are introduced (such as in the use of tense forms): *Hilary asked if the car was ready* (an **indirect question**). ➤➤quotation marks.

disambiguate ➤ambiguous.

discontinuous construction A construction which is split by the insertion of another grammatical unit. Examples include the separation of the particle from the verb in such cases as *switch the light on*, and the use of the two-part negative construction in French *ne . . . pas*. ➤➤syntax.

discourse analysis (DA) The study of continuous stretches of language longer than a single sentence; also called **discourse linguistics**. It especially investigates the organization of such general notions as conversations, arguments, narratives, jokes, and speeches, looking out in particular for linguistic features which identify the structure of the discourse (**discourse markers**), such as *I mean to say* or *Well, anyway*. The term has been used to apply to both spoken and written language, but some authors restrict it to speech, and deal with the structural organization of writing under the heading of **text**. ➤➤connected speech; conversation analysis; monologue; narrative; paragraph; text.

discrete Descriptive of linguistic elements which have clearly definable boundaries, with no continuity between them. The units of a language's consonant system (e.g. [p] vs. [k]) are discrete. Features which do not have clear boundaries are said to be **nondiscrete**, such as the variations in pitch height which comprise a language's intonation system. ➤➤consonant; intonation.

disjunction The relating of two propositions so that they are in an alternative or contrastive relationship, as in *(Either) I'm late or you're early*. The either/or interpretation may be **inclusive** (either or both of the propositions is true) or **exclusive** (only one proposition is true). This distinction is often signalled by extra emphasis: compare *Would you like beans or peas*? ('You have the choice of both') and *Would you like beans OR peas*? ('Choose one only'). ➤correlative; proposition.

displacement A suggested defining property of human language, seen in contrast with other systems of communication: language can be used to refer to contexts removed from the immediate situation of the speaker (such as past and future time reference). The meaning of animal signals, by contrast, is restricted to the setting in which they are used; a hunger cry, for example, means that hunger is present 'now', not yesterday or tomorrow. ➤communication; language 1.

dissimilation The influence exercised by one sound segment upon another, so that the sounds become less alike; contrasts with **assimilation**. The effects are often seen in the history of a language, such as the change from /r/ to /l/ in the derivation of the word *pilgrim* from Latin *peregrinus*. ➤assimilation; sound change.

dissonance ➤consonance.

distinctive Descriptive of any feature which enables a contrast to be made between linguistic units; distinctive contrasts are also called **functional** or **significant**. The main use of the term has been in phonology, where **distinctive features** (such as voicing, tongue height, lip rounding) are the smallest contrastive units proposed to explain how the sound system of a language is organized. ➤contrast; phonological feature theory.

distribution The total set of linguistic contexts in which a unit can occur. A **distributional analysis** plots the places in larger linguistic units in which smaller units appear, such as the distribution of sounds within a word, or the distribution of words within a phrase. In English, for example, the sound *ng* [ŋ] is used at the end and in the middle of words (*sing, banger*), but not at the beginning. ➤complementary distribution; context 1; phonotactics.

disyllable /dɪˈsɪləbl/ A linguistic unit (typically a word) consisting of two syllables. *Unit, bottle*, and *seven* are disyllabic words. ➤syllable.

ditransitive Descriptive of a verb which can take both a direct and an indirect object (e.g. *give*). A contrast is drawn with **monotransitive** verbs, which take only one object. ➤object; transitivity.

Divehi ➤Maldivian.

divergence ➤convergence.

Djibouti (population in 1995 estimated at 607,000) The official languages are French (spoken by *c*.3% of the population) and Arabic (*c*.11%). Two of the local languages – Afar (Danakil, c.55%) and Somali (c.33%) – are used on the radio. French is the language mainly used for international purposes. ➤Arabic; French.

DO An abbreviation of **direct object**.

Dolomitic /dɒlə'mɪtɪk/ ➤Rhaetian.

Dominica (population in 1995 estimated at 83,900) The official language is English. Over 96% of the population speak a French-based creole (Patwa), widely used throughout the Lesser Antilles. ➤creole; English; Patwa.

Dominican Republic (population in 1995 estimated at 7,994,000) The official language is Spanish, spoken by c.87% of the population. About 2% speak Haitian Creole French, and there are a few thousand speakers of an English-based creole (Samaná). English is increasingly used for international purposes, along with Spanish. ➤creole; Spanish.

dorsal Descriptive of any sound made with the back ('dorsum') of the tongue in contact with the roof of the mouth. Examples include [k] and [g]. ➤tongue.

double articulation ➤duality of structure.

double negative A construction in which more than one negative word is used within the same clause. The two negative words do not cancel each other out (as negative signs do in mathematics), but simply add emphasis. This kind of construction is common in many languages. French uses a double negative construction (*ne . . . pas*), as do many dialects of English. However, standard English condemns the construction as uneducated, and eliminating the use of the double negative (such as *I didn't give him nothing*) is one of the chief targets of prescriptive approaches to English grammar. ➤negation; prescriptivism.

Doublespeak Awards ➤Plain English Campaign.

doublet 1. A pair of different words in a language which have a common origin and display similarities of form and meaning (e.g. *wine/vine, poison/potion*). ➤etymology. **2**. A type of word game in which a series of single-letter substitutions links pairs of words. The challenge is to carry out this task in as few steps as possible. The game was invented by Lewis Carroll, who gave as one of his first examples, *Drive PIG into STY*. His solution involved five steps: PIG-WIG-WAG-WAY-SAY-STY. ➤word game.

Dravidian A family of over 25 languages, most of which are found close together in the southern and eastern areas of India, and now widely represented in south-east Asia, Africa, and the Pacific through emigration. There is little agreement about the origins of the family, with some scholars arguing for a movement to the area from Asia, others for a movement from lands to the south, now submerged. There is evidence that Dravidian languages were formerly spoken in the north of India, being displaced by the arrival of the Indo-European invaders. The main languages are

Telugu, Tamil, Kannada, and Malayalam, each of which is identified with a state in southern India. Other languages include Gondhi, Kurukhi, Tulu, Kui, Malto (an isolated language in the north-east), and Brahui (curiously isolated 1000 miles away from the rest of the family, in the north of Pakistan). Distinctive Dravidian features include the widespread use of retroflex consonants, and a sociolinguistic situation of diglossia. Speakers of Dravidian languages total over 160 million. Several other languages have been proposed as belonging to the family. ➤➤diglossia; Kannada; Malayalam; retroflex; Tamil; Telugu.

drill In language teaching, the use of guided repetition to instil a particular aspect of language in a learner; when practising a grammatical construction, often called a **pattern drill**. Three main types of drill are common: an imitation technique, in which the student repeats the stimulus sentence without changing anything; a substitution technique, in which the student has to replace a target word in the stimulus sentence; and a transformational technique, where the student has to change the construction into a related form (e.g. statement into question). ➤➤language teaching; method.

drum language The use of a drum to simulate selected features of speech (primarily, tones and rhythms). The signals consist mainly of short, formulaic utterances, but are used to build up quite elaborate systems of communication, especially in Africa. Drum signalling is used both within villages (e.g. in summoning people, controlling meetings) and between communities. ➤➤speech surrogate.

dual A grammatical contrast of number in some languages (e.g. Eskimo, Old English), referring to 'two of', and contrasting with singular ('one of') and plural ('more than two'). Some languages (e.g. some Australian languages) have a **trial** category ('three of'). ➤➤number.

dual alphabet ➤majuscule.

duality of structure A suggested defining property of human language, which sees language as structurally organized into two abstract levels; also called **double articulation**. At one level, language is analysed into combinations of meaningful units (such as words and sentences); at the other level, it is analysed as a sequence of phonological segments which lack meaning. Facial expression, body gesture, and animal systems of communication are said to lack duality of structure. ➤➤language 1; zoösemiotics.

duration The length of time involved in the articulation of a sound or syllable. Vowels, for example, may be long (as in *car*) or short (as in *cat*). Consonants in some languages (e.g. Hungarian) may also contrast in duration. Some sounds are intrinsically short (e.g. a flapped *r*, as in *very*), whereas others can be held for varying periods of time (e.g. fricatives and trills). ➤➤consonant; length; syllable; vowel.

durative In the grammatical analysis of aspect, descriptive of a category expressing an event which involves a period of time; contrasts with **nondurative** or **punctual**, where there is no duration implied. Some verbs are essentially durative in character (e.g. *grow*); others are essentially punctual (e.g. *kick*). ►►aspect; verb.

Dutch A West Germanic language spoken by *c.*20 million people, chiefly in The Netherlands (14 million) and Belgium (5 million), with others in a small adjacent area of north-east France, in Suriname and the Netherlands Antilles (where it has official status), and by immigrants in several other countries. In Belgium, the language is called **Flemish** and is the official language in the northern part of the country. The Flemish/French language issue continues to divide the Belgian population. There is very little structural difference with the language spoken in The Netherlands, and the name **Netherlandic** has been proposed as a single term for all varieties of the language. Dutch is written in the Roman alphabet, and texts date from the end of the 12th century. ►►Afrikaans; Belgium; Germanic; Netherlands, The.

dynamic linguistics The study of language variation in terms of the processes of change which give rise to it. The term 'dynamic' refers to the way a particular linguistic feature moves throughout a speech community in different directions at different rates, being affected by such factors as the age, sex, class, and occupation of the speakers. ►►linguistics; variable.

dynamic verb A type of verb which typically occurs in the progressive form and in the imperative, and which expresses such meanings as activity, process, and bodily sensation (e.g. *run, kick, change*). A contrast is drawn with **stative verbs** (also called **static** or **state verbs**), which do not usually occur in the progressive nor in the imperative, and which express a state of affairs rather than an action (e.g. *know, seem, suppose*). Thus, we may say *They are running* and *Run!*, but not **They are seeming* and **Seem!*. ►►imperative; progressive; verb.

dysarthria /dɪsˈɑ:θrɪə/ A motor speech disorder which leaves someone unable to articulate speech sounds, caused by an impairment in the nervous system; in severe form, sometimes called **anarthria**. The disorder may affect any part of the vocal tract, and any aspects of speech sound production can be impaired. ►►language pathology.

dysfluency The loss of ability to control the smooth flow of speech production, resulting in hesitancy, poor rhythm, and stuttering; also called **nonfluency**. ►►fluency; stuttering.

dysgraphia /dɪsˈgrafɪə/ ►dyslexia.

dyslexia A serious disturbance in the ability to read. The term is used both for literate adults who lose their reading ability after brain injury (**aquired dyslexia**), and for children who encounter special difficulties as they try to learn to read, in the absence of evident brain injury (**developmental dyslexia**). The term **alexia** replaces dyslexia in many (especially American) studies, and from time to time several other terms have been used for the condition, such as 'word blindness'. Several types of dyslexia are now recognized. A commonly associated disorder is **dysgraphia** (or **agraphia**), a disturbance in the normal ability to write. ➤➤language pathology; literacy.

dysnomia /dɪsˈnəʊmɪə/ ➤anomia.

dysphasia /dɪsˈfeɪʒə/ ➤aphasia.

dysphasic children ➤language delay.

dysphemism /ˈdɪsfəmɪzm/ The use of an offensive or disparaging expression instead of a neutral or pleasant one. Examples include *mug* for *face*, and *boneshaker* for *car*. ➤➤euphemism.

dysphonia /dɪsˈfəʊnɪə/ The loss of ability to use the vocal folds to produce normal voice; also, especially in severe form, called **aphonia**. The term is chiefly used in speech therapy. ➤➤language pathology; voice disorder.

dyspraxia /dɪsˈpraksɪə/ ➤apraxia.

dysprosody /dɪsˈprɒsədiː/ The loss of ability to produce speech with a normal intonation, loudness, and rhythm. Rhythmical difficulty is often labelled separately as **dysrhythmia**. Both terms are used mainly in clinical linguistic contexts. ➤➤language pathology; prosody; rhythm.

dysrhythmia ➤dysprosody.

Dyula or **Jula** /ˈdjuːlə/ A Mande language spoken by *c*.1 million people in the Côte d'Ivoire, Burkina Faso, and parts of Mali and Ghana, with over 3 million second-language users. It is written in the Roman alphabet. ➤➤Mande.

Dzongkha or **Dzongka** /ˈdzɒŋkə/ A member of the Tibeto-Burman group of Sino-Tibetan languages, spoken by *c*.400,000 people chiefly in Bhutan (where it is the official language); also called **Bhutani** or **Bhutanese**. It is written in the Dzongkha alphabet. ➤➤Bhutan.

E

EAP ➤English for Special Purposes.

ear training A technique in phonetics which trains aspiring phoneticians to discriminate and identify the whole range of human speech sounds. It is usually complemented by training in **performance** – the controlled movement of the vocal organs to produce any of these sounds. ➤➤auditory phonetics; *cartoon below*.

Easter Island ➤Chile.

Ebonics /iːˈbɒnɪks/ The name given to African-American Vernacular English when given the status of a language distinct from standard English; derived from *ebony* and *phonics*. Although the name was coined as long ago as 1973, it did not become

'I can try to pronounce your illness, Mrs Creedmore, but I would highly recommend your getting a second opinion.'

widely known until December 1996, when the local school board in Oakland, California, concerned about the low level of achievement among the African-American children in its care, and anxious to increase the respect for the language the children used at home, decided to give the variety official status – the first school district in the USA to do so. The decision proved to be enormously controversial – among both black and white populations – and was dropped a month later. ⟫African-American Vernacular English.

echo A type of sentence which repeats, in whole or in part, what has just been said by another speaker; also called an **echo utterance**. An example is the following sequence: *A: I told him he was fired. B: You told him he was what?'* (an instance of an **echo question**). ⟫question.

echolalia /ekəʊˈleɪlɪə/ The automatic repetition of all or part of what someone has said. It is often heard at an early stage of normal language development, and is also a symptom of certain language disorders, especially those in which comprehension is poor. The meaning of the speech is usually not apparent to the speaker – a situation which distinguishes echolalia from the controlled, contrastive focus of other kinds of echo utterance. ⟫echo; language pathology.

ecolinguistics An emphasis within language study – reflecting the notion of *ecology* in biological studies – in which the interaction between language and the cultural environment is seen as central; also called the **ecology of language**, **ecological linguistics**, and sometimes **green linguistics**. An ecolinguistic approach highlights the value of linguistic diversity in the world, the importance of individual and community linguistic rights, and the role of language attitudes, awareness, variation, and change in fostering a culture of communicative peace. ⟫endangered languages; peace linguistics; Universal Declaration of Linguistic Rights.

Ecuador (population in 1995 estimated at 11,423,000) The official language is Spanish, spoken by *c*.80% of the population. Quechua is spoken in several varieties by *c*.15%. About 10 other Amerindian languages are spoken by small numbers. There is some use of English for international purposes. ⟫Spanish.

-ed form An abbreviated way of referring to the simple past tense form of verbs in English. The addition of an *-ed* ending to the present tense is the commonest way of making this form (*walked, jumped*), but the term is used for all past tense forms, whether they are regular or not (e.g. *took, went*). ⟫past tense; verb.

educational linguistics The application of linguistics to the teaching and learning of a native language, in both spoken and written form, in schools and other educational settings; also called **pedagogical linguistics**. It thus includes the study of the various problems associated with literacy, as well as more advanced topics in grammar, vocabulary, stylistic appreciation, and language use. In a broader sense, the subject deals with the application of linguistics to all contexts of teaching, such as the way language is used in scientific texts and materials, or the nature of the dialogue between teachers and students. ➤➤deficit hypothesis; knowledge about language; language in use; linguistics; literacy; oracy; parsing.

Efik /'efɪk/ A language spoken in the Cross River area of southern Nigeria by *c.*400,000 people. A non-Bantu member of the Benue-Congo family, it became a literary language in the 19th century, written in the Roman alphabet, and a local lingua franca (*c.*2 million speakers). The Efik belong to the Ibibio group of peoples, and the language is closely related to **Ibibio** (*c.*3 million speakers). ➤➤Benue-Congo; lingua franca.

EFL ➤Teaching English to Speakers of Other Languages.

egocentric speech Speech which does not take into account the needs of the listener, but is used for such purposes as self-expression and language play. The notion was introduced by Swiss psychologist Jean Piaget (1896–1980) as part of a basic classification of types of speech observed in young children; it contrasts with the socialized speech which is used for communication with others. ➤➤acquisition.

EGP ➤English for Special Purposes.

egressive /iːˈgresɪv/ Descriptive of a speech sound produced using an outward-moving airstream, which is the norm for speech production; it contrasts with **ingressive**, where the air moves towards the lungs (heard, for example, when people try to speak while out of breath). A few speech sounds in some languages make use of ingressive air. ➤➤glottalic; pulmonic; velaric.

Egypt (population in 1995 estimated at 60,284,000) The official language is Arabic, spoken by most of the population. Several varieties of colloquial Arabic are in use. Other languages include Domari (a Gypsy language, spoken by perhaps half of the *c.*1 million Muslim Gypsies in the country), Armenian, Greek, and Nile Nubian. Coptic has a restricted, liturgical use. English is increasingly used for international trade and tourism. ➤➤Arabic; Coptic.

Egyptian A branch of the Afro-Asiatic family of languages, formerly spoken throughout the Nile Valley. Its history dates from before the 3rd millennium BC, preserved in many hieroglyphic inscriptions and papyrus manuscripts. Five periods in the history of the language are distinguished: Old Egyptian (*c.*3000–*c.*2200 BC), Middle Egyptian (*c.*2200–*c.*1600 BC, regarded as the classical period of the language), Late Egyptian (*c.*1500–*c.*700 BC), Demotic (*c.*700 BC–*c.*AD 400), and **Coptic** (from the 2nd century AD). Egyptian was originally written in hieroglyphic, and developed both a hieratic form, used mainly for religious texts, and a demotic form, used for everyday purposes. Coptic, the final stage of development in the language, was employed mainly for Christian religious writing. It used a modified Greek alphabet, and introduced a great deal of Greek vocabulary. Its latest texts date from the 14th century, but the language is still in ritual use by Coptic Christians in their liturgy. ➤➤Afro-Asiatic; demotic; hieroglyphic.

Eire ➤Ireland.

ejective /ɪ'dʒektɪv/ A type of consonant produced with the glottalic airstream mechanism. A closure is made in the vocal tract while the vocal folds are brought together, impounding the air. The closed glottis is then elevated, increasing the air pressure. When the closure is released, an egressive airstream is produced, which can be used to make a wide range of sounds, such as ejective (also called 'glottalized') stops. Ejective sounds are transcribed with a following apostrophe: [p'], [f'], etc. ➤➤consonant; egressive; glottalic.

elaborated code A relatively formal, educated use of language, involving a comparatively wide range of linguistic structures; contrasts with the notion of **restricted code**, which displays a limited range of structures. The concepts, associated chiefly with the work of British sociologist Basil Bernstein (1924–   ), are part of an explanation of how a society's distribution of power can shape modes of communication which carry the cultures of different social classes and that of the school, and so reproduce unequal educational advantages. Restricted codes arise where meanings are particular to a local context, and the need to make meanings explicit is reduced because of shared understandings, values, and identifications. By contrast, the forms of elaborated codes arise out of social relations where less is taken for granted, and so where explicitness is more likely to be demanded. The theory asserts that middle-class children have access to both of these codes, whereas lower-working-class children are more likely to be initially limited to a restricted code, and to experience difficulty in acquiring the form of the elaborated code required by the school. ➤➤code 3; variety.

Elamite /'iːləmaɪt/ A language spoken in the ancient country of Elam (Khuzistan, south-west Iran). The oldest writings are pictographic inscriptions from the 3rd millennium BC. Later writing is in cuneiform script. The language was still in use at the end of the 1st millennium BC. No clear relationship exists with other languages. ➤➤cuneiform; isolate; pictograph.

electroaerometer ➤aerometry.

electrokymograph /ɪlektrəʊ'kaɪməgraf/ An instrument which records changes in the air flow from mouth and nose during speech, in the form of traces on paper (**kymograms**); also called a **kymograph**. It was an important tool in the early days of instrumental phonetics. ➤➤experimental phonetics.

electrolaryngograph /ɪlektrəʊlə'rɪŋgəʊgraf/ ➤larynx.

electromyograph /ɪlektrəʊ'maɪəgraf/ An instrument which records muscular contractions during speech. The technique uses electrodes which are applied to the muscles in the vocal tract, and the results are recorded as visual traces (**electromyograms**). ➤➤experimental phonetics; speech production.

electropalatograph /ɪlektrəʊ'palətəʊgraf/ An instrument which records the con-

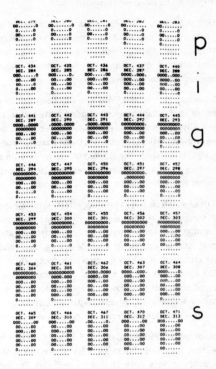

Computer printout of **electropalatographic** data showing patterns of tongue contact (represented as zeros) from the release of the [p] to the first part of the [s] in the word *pigsty*. A phonemic transcription is included on the right of the printout to aid segmentation.

tacts made between the tongue and the palate during speech. The technique uses an artificial palate containing electrodes which register an articulatory contact as it is made. The results are presented visually (e.g. on a computer screen) as **electropalatograms**. ➤ palate; phonetics; speech production.

elicitation A method of obtaining reliable linguistic data from native speakers – either utterances, or judgements about utterances (e.g. whether they are acceptable); also called **direct elicitation**. A great deal of effort is devoted to obtaining this information in an indirect and unselfconscious manner, so that informants do not provide artificial or misleading data. ➤informant.

elision The omission of sounds, syllables, or words in connected speech, as shown in such forms as *Febr'y, y'know*, and *cup o' tea*; contrasts with **intrusion**. Elision is a normal and unavoidable feature of informal discourse, though it is condemned as 'lazy' speech by purist critics. Some elisions may be standard usage, e.g. French *j'ai* ('I have'). ➤apocope; assimilation; purism; syncope.

ellipsis A sentence where part of the structure has been omitted, for reasons of economy, emphasis, or style; also sometimes called **reduction**, **contraction**, or **abbreviation**. Typically, the omitted element can be recovered from a scrutiny of the context (and some grammatical approaches insist that this must be possible): *A Where are you going? B: Town* (where the ellipted utterance is 'I am going to'). Using this criterion, a sentence such as *Thanks* would not be a clear example of ellipsis, as it is unclear what other words have been omitted. ➤syntax.

elocution The art of speech training to produce effective public speaking, practised since ancient times (originally as part of rhetoric). It was a fashionable activity in Britain in the 18th and 19th centuries, when it became strongly associated with the achievement of excellence in the use of a single accent, Received Pronunciation, other accents being criticized as inferior or ugly by comparison. In recent years, elocution has fallen somewhat out of fashion, as a result of people adopting a more tolerant and egalitarian attitude towards regional accents. However, there are contemporary signs of a revival of interest, with a fresh focus on the need for effectiveness and clarity, whichever accent is employed. ➤rhetoric.

El Salvador (population in 1995 estimated at 5,811,000) The official language is Spanish, used by almost everyone. There are a few thousand speakers of Quekchí, but other Amerindian languages have almost all died out. English is increasingly used for international purposes, along with Spanish. ➤Spanish.

ELT An abbreviation of **English Language Teaching**.

embedding In generative grammar, the process or result of including one sentence within another. The sentence *I went to the shop* can be embedded within the sentence *The shop was open* by turning it into a relative clause within the noun phrase: *The shop which I went to was open*. ➤generative grammar.

EmergencySpeak ➤Seaspeak.

emic vs. **etic** /'i:mɪk, 'etɪk/ Terms which characterize contrasting approaches to the study of linguistic data. An **etic** approach is one where the physical patterns of language are described with a minimum of reference to their function within the language system. An **emic** approach takes full account of functional relationships, setting up systems of contrastive units. In studying intonation, for example, an etic approach would describe a very large number of rises and falls in pitch, whereas an emic approach would propose a small number of basic contrasts, such as 'low rising', 'high falling', and 'level'. ➤➤intonation; phonetics; phonology.

emotive language Language whose primary function is the expression of emotion; also called **expressive language**. The clearest case is the use of swearing or obscenity as a means of getting rid of nervous energy when people are under stress. Other emotive utterances include involuntary responses to beautiful art or scenery, expressions of fear or affection, and the outpourings found in a great deal of poetry. ➤➤figurative/taboo language.

empty word ➤grammatical word.

encipher ➤cipher.

enclitic /enˈklɪtɪk/ An unstressed form attached to a preceding word (e.g. can**not**). Enclitics are common in informal speech, and this is occasionally reflected in writing, as in *cuppa* ('cup of ') and *pinta* ('pint of '). There is a contrast with **proclitic**, where the unstressed form depends on and is pronounced with the following word: an example is English indefinite article *an*, used before words begining with a vowel. ➤➤clitic; stress.

encode ➤code 1, 2.

endangered languages Languages which are at risk of becoming extinct within the foreseeable future. As a result of increased survey information during the 1980s, it is now thought that over half the world's languages are moribund – not being effectively passed on to the next generation. The 1990s, accordingly, saw a significant growth in international professional linguistic concern, including the formation of national and international organizations devoted to gathering data, developing international policies, raising public awareness, and promoting means of improving the documentation of endangered languages. In particular, efforts were being made to draw public attention to the irreparable loss of knowledge for the human race which takes place when an unrecorded language dies. A UNESCO-sponsored clearing-house was established at the University of Tokyo in 1995, and other important bodies established at around that time include the Foundation for Endangered Languages in the UK and the Endangered Languages Fund in the USA. Although these organizations recognize that it is impossible to stem the global forces which are at the root of language decline and loss, and that it is too late to do a great deal in many cases, their aim is to work as much as is practicable with endangered communities to provide support for their languages (e.g. through the provision of literacy programmes), and to try to lessen the damage by recording as much as possible of those languages which are in terminal decline. It is an expensive task, however, and the amount that can be done will very largely depend on the money which will become available through private and public fund-raising. ➤➤ecolinguistics; language death/maintenance/planning/shift; Universal Declaration of Linguistic Rights.

endearment, terms of Forms of address used between people who mutually perceive their relationship to be one of intimacy (e.g. *love, dear, honey, darling, mate*). These forms can also be used in an asymmetrical way, when one participant uses them and the other does not. This happens, for example, in service encounters, such as when a customer treats a clerk in a familiar manner by using one of these labels (or, of course, the other way round). Whether the result is viewed by each participant as friendliness, condescension, or some other attitude is not always predictable. ➤address, forms of.

end matter The material which is placed at the end of a book, following the text proper; it includes appendices, bibliographies, and indexes. A contrast is drawn with the **front matter** or **prelims** – containing the title page, contents list, preface, and other preliminary information. The prelims are often numbered separately (in Roman numerals). ➤typography.

endocentric construction A group of syntactically related words where one word can be shown to be the most important (the **head**), governing the way the group works in the sentence. In the sentence *The three red cars are expensive, cars* is the head of the noun phrase, its plural form forcing the selection of a plural verb (*are*). Other words in the noun phrase are subordinate to the head in various ways. A contrast is drawn with an **exocentric construction**, where no single word can be identified as the head: in a subject–predicate construction, for example (such as *She asked*), neither element can be seen as the head of the sentence as a whole. ➤modification 1; phrase; syntax.

endoglossic /endəʊˈglɒsɪk/ Descriptive of a language which is the native language of most (or all) of the population in a geographical area; contrasts with **exoglossic**. English, for example, is endoglossic for Australia and England, but not for Québec or Singapore. ➤geolinguistics.

endophora /enˈdɒfərə/ The relationships of cohesion which help to define the structure of a text, usually classified into **anaphora** (items which refer in a backward direction) and **cataphora** (items which refer in a forward direction). A contrast is drawn with **exophora**, where the interpretation requires reference to the extralinguistic situation: the meaning of *that* in *Look at that* requires a knowledge of what is going on in the real world, and not of other words in the previous or subsequent discourse. ➤anaphora; cohesion.

-en form An abbreviated way of referring to the past participle form of the English verb, which often ends in the suffix *-en* (e.g. *taken, stolen*). The term is used for all past participle forms, whether regular or not; thus, *gone, dealt*, and *walked* (as in *I have walked*) can all be described in this way. ➤participle; verb.

England ➤United Kingdom.

English A Germanic language which has come to be spoken worldwide by a large and ever-increasing number of people – 1,000,000,000 by a conservative estimate, 1,500,000,000 by a liberal estimate. Some 400,000,000 use the language as a mother tongue, chiefly in the USA (*c*.227 million), the UK (*c*.57 million), Canada (*c*.20 million), Australia (*c*.15 million), New Zealand (*c*.3.4 million), Ireland (*c*.3.5 million), and South Africa (*c*.3.6 million). A further 400 million use it as a second language, in such countries as Ghana, Nigeria, Tanzania, Pakistan, and the Philippines. It has official status in over 60 countries. At least 150 million people use English fluently as a foreign language, and four or five times this number with some degree of competence. A British Council estimate is of a thousand million people learning English worldwide in the year 2000. In India, China, and most of the countries of western Europe, the presence of English is noticeable or rapidly growing. English is also the language of international air traffic control, and the chief language of world publishing, science and technology, conferencing, and computer storage.

English developed in England as a consequence of the Anglo-Saxon invasions of the 5th century, and is often accordingly referred to as **Anglo-Saxon**; however, its oldest extant form, found in texts from the 7th century, is generally called **Old English**, an inflecting language which preserves many features of Germanic. The epic poem, *Beowulf*, preserved in manuscript from *c*.AD1000, is the chief example of this period. The **Middle English** period, from the 11th to the 14th centuries, saw the emergence of a language in which word order came to replace inflections as the chief grammatical characteristic, and in which vocabulary was vastly increased through recurring waves of borrowing, especially from Latin and French. Literary excellence in this period is chiefly preserved in the work of Chaucer (*c*.1345–1400). After this time the language rapidly evolved into a recognizable modern form, with the process of standardization hastened in the later 15th century through the invention of printing. Shakespeare and the Authorized Version of the Bible represent the peak of literary achievement of a post-Renaissance era that produced a highly diversified and wide-ranging language, which in due course motivated the concern to codify grammar and vocabulary. The resulting dictionaries, grammars, and manuals of the 18th century, notably Johnson's dictionary, heralded an age of analysis whose attitudes and recommendations are still to be found in the prescriptive concerns of modern grammars and usage books. However, fresh perspectives have been generated by the post-colonial expansion of English around the world, which has led to the rise of new regional varieties, both first language (e.g. American, Australian, South African) and second language (e.g. Indian, Nigerian, Singaporean), the nature of which has begun to be investigated only in recent times. ⟫Basic English; Black English Vernacular; codification; corpus; English as an International Language; English as a Second Dialect; English for Special Purposes; Germanic; New Englishes; Nuclear English; second language; standard English; Teaching English to Speakers of Other Languages; typology of language; vowel shift.

English as an International Language The use of English for purposes of international communication, as encountered especially among people who do not have the language as a mother tongue. The language is widely used among the international political, business, academic, and scientific communities, for example. It is often one of the standard varieties (such as British or American English), but need not be so, as there may be many local forms which reflect features of the speakers' mother tongues. The kind of English used in a meeting between a Nigerian and a Japanese businessman, for example, will contain several different features from that used between an Arab and a Ugandan – though very little study has been made of the nature and extent of this kind of variation. ➤➤non-native varieties.

English as a Second Dialect A name sometimes given to standard English when it is being taught to someone who already speaks a regional dialect of the language. This situation obtains both internationally (when a speaker of a creole, for example, might wish to learn standard English) and intranationally (when children from a regional background are taught standard English in school). ➤➤bidialectism.

English for Special Purposes (ESP) The name given to courses for foreigners where the kind of English taught is determined by the professional needs of the students; contrasts with **English for General Purposes (EGP)**, where the courses aim to establish a general level of proficiency. Several areas have been recognized, including English for Academic Purposes (EAP) and English for Science and Technology (EST), but any specific domain might be the focus of attention, such as medicine, law, or commerce. ➤➤Language(s) for Special Purposes; Teaching English to Speakers of Other Languages.

English Vowel Shift ➤vowel shift.

enigma Intentionally obscure language; also, a word game which takes the form of a riddle in verse. Popular in the 18th and 19th centuries, enigmas are now heard only in traditional children's verse (e.g. *My first is in apple and Albert and Ann . . .*). ➤➤riddle.

enjambement /ɪnˈʤambmənt/, French /ɑ̄ʒɑ̄b'mɑ̄/ The running on of a sentence between two lines of verse without pause; the term derives from French 'striding over'. A famous example is Wordsworth's *I wandered lonely as a cloud / That floats on high o'er vales and hills.* ➤➤metrics.

entailment A semantic relationship between a pair of sentences, such that the truth of the second necessarily follows from the truth of the first. If you say *I have seen a cat*, it follows that *I have seen an animal* is true. The first sentence entails the second. ➤➤presupposition; semantics.

environment ➤context; distribution.

epenthesis /epənˈθiːsɪs/ A type of intrusion, in which an extra sound is inserted in a word. In traditional description, a distinction is often made between cases where the sound is added initially (**prothesis**) and those where it is added between two consonants (**anaptyxis**). An example of the former is the sergeant major who adds a brief vowel before shouting *Left turn!* ('uh-left turn'); an example of the latter is the pronunciation of *film* as 'fillum'. These processes are common in historical sound change; for example, Latin *schola* 'school' became Spanish *escuela* – an instance of prothesis. ➤intrusion; sound change.

epicene /ˈepɪsiːn/ A noun which can refer to either sex without changing its form. The term is from Greek *epikoinos* 'common to many', and was used in Latin and Greek grammar for nouns which stayed in the same gender regardless of the sex of the being referred to (e.g. Latin *vulpes* 'fox/vixen'). English examples include *teacher* and *doctor*. ➤gender; noun.

epiglottis /epɪˈglɒtɪs/ An anatomical structure which closes over the larynx during swallowing. It is not used as an active articulator in speech, though it can produce an audible trill. ➤trill.

epigram A short, witty statement in verse or prose. An example of an epigrammatic utterance is Dr Johnson's *Love is the wisdom of the fool and the folly of the wise.* A poetic example is Pope's *True wit is nature to advantage dressed, / What oft was thought but ne'er so well expressed (An Essay on Criticism).* ➤aphorism.

epigraph 1. An inscription on stone, buildings, pottery, and other hard, durable artefacts. The techniques include engraving, carving, embossing, and painting. The study of inscriptions, and especially of their interpretation in ancient times, is **epigraphy**. When the inscriptions appear on coins, medals, and similar artefacts, the subject is known as **numismatics**. ➤petroglyph; writing. 2. A phrase or quotation above a section in a book or immediately before the book begins. Epigraphs are especially common at the beginning of chapters.

epitaph A commemorative inscription on a tombstone or monument. The term is also used for a brief statement, either in verse or prose, remembering a dead person or past event. ➤epigraph 1.

epithet A word or phrase which characterizes a noun and is regularly associated with it. Examples include *the **haunted** house, the **iron** lady* (when Mrs Thatcher was British prime minister), and *William **the Conqueror.*** The term can also be found in pejorative contexts (as in *They hurled foul epithets at each other for several seconds*). ➤adjective.

eponym /ˈepənɪm/ The name of a person after whom something (such as an invention, or the title of a book or film) is named; also called an **appellative.** Examples include *Hamlet, biro,* and *sandwich.* Place names are often eponymous, as with *Washington, San Antonio,* and *Sydney.* ➤onomastics.

Equatorial Guinea (population in 1995 estimated at 472,000) The official language is Spanish. About 75% of the population speak Fang, and there are a few thousand speakers of other Benue-Congo languages, and a number of creole languages. Some use is made of English for international purposes. ➤creole; Spanish.

Eritrea (population in 1995 estimated at 3,950,000, though figures are uncertain because of famines) About half the people speak Tigrinya; other languages of over 100,000 speakers are Afar, Kunama, Saho, Bedawi, and Tigré. Several varieties of spoken Arabic are used in the country, and English is increasingly found as a lingua franca. ➤Tigrinya.

error analysis In language teaching and learning, the study of the unacceptable forms produced by someone learning a language, especially a foreign language. Errors are considered to be systematic, governed by rules, and appear because a learner's knowledge of the rules of the target language is incomplete. They are of particular interest in linguistic research because they provide evidence about the nature of the language learning process. A contrast is drawn with **mistakes**, which are unsystematic features of production that speakers would correct if their attention were drawn to them (e.g. those arising out of tiredness or a lapse of memory). ➤interference.

Erse ➤Irish Gaelic; Scottish Gaelic.

Eskimo A member of the Eskimo-Aleut family of languages, spoken in many dialects by *c.*100,000 people in the Arctic, chiefly in Greenland (*c.*40,000), with some in Alaska, Canada, and Russia. Its two main branches – **Yupik** in Alaska and Siberia, **Inupiaq** or **Inupik** (also called **Inuit** or **Inuktitut**) elsewhere – are sometimes classified as separate languages. Greenlandic Eskimo has official status in Greenland (along with Danish). The language has used several orthographies since the mid-18th century, when missionaries first wrote it down; modern Greenlandic uses the Roman alphabet, and Cyrillic is now used in Asia. ➤Eskimo-Aleut; Greenland.

Eskimo-Aleut /ˈeskɪməʊ əˈljuːt/ A small group of Amerindian languages spoken in Alaska, Canada, and Greenland; and stretching along the Aleutian Islands into Siberia. Eskimo is the main language, but there are also a few hundred speakers still using Aleut, in the Aleutian, Pribilof, and Commander Islands. ➤Amerindian; Eskimo.

ESL and **ESOL** ➤Teaching English to Speakers of Other Languages.

esophageal or **oesophageal** /iːsɒfəˈdʒiːəl/ Descriptive of voice or sounds which originate at or below the esophagus. The notion is chiefly used with reference to the 'throaty' voice quality produced by some people who have had their larynx removed. ➤laryngectomy.

ESP An abbreviation of **English for Special Purposes**.

Esperanto A language invented in 1887 by a Polish oculist, Ludwig Lazarus Zamenhof (1859–1917). The scheme was first published using the pseudonym Doktoro Esperanto ('Doctor Hopeful'). The language was first called 'Lingvo Internacia', but the name 'Esperanto' quickly caught on, and in due course became the official title. There is now a large translated literature in Esperanto, and several countries transmit radio broadcasts in it. Estimates vary about the number of fluent speakers, from less than 1 million to over 15 million. Most seem to be in the countries of Eastern Europe, but there are significant numbers in Japan, China, and elsewhere. ➤artificial language.

EST An abbreviation of **English for Science and Technology** and also of **Extended Standard Theory**.

Estonia (population in 1995 estimated at 1,568,000) The official languages are Estonian (spoken by *c*.62% of the population) and Russian (*c*.30%). Finnish, Ukrainian, Belorussian, and Romani are among the other languages used. ➤Estonian; Russian.

Estonian A member of the Finnic group of the Finno-Ugric family of languages, spoken by over 1 million people in Estonia, where it is an official language, in nearby parts of Latvia and Russia, and through immigration in several other countries (e.g. the UK, the USA, Finland, Sweden). The northern dialect, centred on Tallinn, is the basis of the literary language, using the Roman alphabet. Estonian literature dates from the 16th century, though the dominance of Russian and Swedish resulted in little work being produced in the vernacular before the 19th century. Linguistically, the Estonian sound system is noted for its three degrees of contrastive consonant and vowel length. ➤Finno-Ugric; length.

Estuary English A variety of British English originating in the counties adjacent to the estuary of the River Thames, and thus displaying the influence of London regional speech (Cockney), especially in pronunciation; also called simply **Estuary**. The variety has now a considerable presence in the London hinterland, reaching towns over 100 miles away along the commuter roads and railways, and interacting with other regional dialects. It achieved considerable public attention during the 1990s, when it was reported that several commercial organizations were finding it a more attractive ('customer friendly') accent than RP. ➤Cockney; language attitudes; Received Pronunciation.

eth /eð/ The name of the symbol ð used in Old English and Icelandic manuscripts to represent the sounds spelled *th* in Modern English. It is also used in phonetic transcription, as at the beginning of this entry, for the voiced interdental fricative in such words as *the* – and *eth*. ➤English.

Ethiopia (population in 1995 estimated at 57,919,000) The language of administration is Amharic. English has auxiliary official status, being used in education, trade, and for other international purposes. Over 80 languages are spoken in the country, notably Oromo (*c*.14 million), Tigrinya (*c*.4 million), Gurage (*c*.1 million), Welamo (Wolaytta, *c*.2 million), Afar, Somali, and Arabic. Figures for minority languages are very uncertain. Amharic is spoken as a first language by *c*.25% of the population, but is widely used as a lingua franca, as is Tigrinya (in the north), Oromo (in the south), Arabic (especially among the Muslim population), and Italian. Ge'ez

(Ethiopic) is used as a liturgical language in the Ethiopian Christian Church. ➻Amharic; English; lingua franca.

Ethiopic ➤Ethiopia.

ethnography of speaking An approach within linguistic anthropology which views speech as a social institution, to be investigated using ethnographic techniques; also called **ethnography of communication**. It typically involves the participant observation of naturally occurring discourse within particular social groups and communities. ➤anthropological linguistics; ethnolinguistics.

ethnolinguistics The study of language with reference to its cultural context. The term is often used in a very general way, to include the subject-matter of anthropological and ethnographic approaches to language. ➻anthropological linguistics; ethnography of speaking; ethnosemantics.

ethnopoetics The study of the way verbal art is learned, practised, represented, and interpreted. Close attention is paid to linguistic detail and verbal form, and to ways of reflecting on the page the characteristics of an oral original. ➻ethnolinguistics; poetics.

ethnosemantics The study of the meanings of linguistic expressions with particular reference to the cultures in which they are found. The approach was introduced in the 1960s by anthropologists working within ethnoscience. A particular application is **historical ethnosemantics**, the study of the development of the vocabulary reconstructed in a proto-language, and of the cultural and historical contexts in which the words came to be used in individual languages. ➻ethnolinguistics; proto-language; semantics.

etic ➤emic vs. etic.

Etruscan /əˈtrʌskn/ A non-Indo-European language spoken in the ancient country of Etruria (Tuscany, Italy) where a civilization was at its height in the 6th century BC. It is known mainly from *c.*10,000 inscriptions, written in an alphabet probably derived from Greek, from which the Roman alphabet was later derived. The Etruscan alphabet had 20 letters in its classical form (*c.*400 BC), and was usually written from right to left. The language may still have been spoken as late as the 4th century AD. Only a few words have been deciphered, and its relationship to other languages is unclear. ➻alphabet; isolate.

etymology The study of the origins and history of the form and meaning of words. The linguistic form from which a later form derives is called its **etymon**. A **popular** or **folk etymology** arises when a word is assumed to come from a particular etymon, because of some association of form or meaning, whereas in fact the word has a different derivation. Examples include *sparrow-grass* as a gloss for *asparagus*, and *spitting image* for *spit and image*. The **etymological fallacy** is the view that an earlier (or the earliest) meaning of a word is the correct one – as when someone argues that the 'true' meaning of *history* is 'investigation' or 'enquiry', because that is what the word meant in Classical Greek. The view is fallacious because there are always several earlier meanings which could claim to be the 'true' sense, though they may no longer be in use at all, and the earliest senses of a word are always unknown. ►►metanalysis; paronymy; semantics.

euphemism The use of a vague or indirect expression in place of one which is thought to be unpleasant, embarrassing, or offensive. Euphemisms are typically used to replace expressions to do with death, sexual activity, and other bodily functions; examples include *pass on* for *die*, or *powder my nose* for *go to the toilet*. ►►dysphemism.

euphony A pleasing or harmonious sequence of sounds. The notion is an inherently subjective one, commonly used in the impressionistic description of poetry, but not readily yielding to analysis in phonetic terms. ►►cacophony; consonance.

Eurodicautom /jʊərəʊdɪˈkɔːtm/ ►term bank.

eurythmy, formerly **eurhythmy** /juːˈrɪðmiː/ A system which aims to promote a close harmony between the sounds of speech and the patterns of body movement. The approach was developed by Rudolf Steiner (1861–1925) as a kind of 'visible speech', in which the body reflects in its physical shape the forms of sounds as they are articulated. For example, the open articulation of /a/ is reflected in the stretching of the arms upwards and outwards, and is interpreted as expressing the meaning of astonishment and wonder. ►►sound symbolism.

Evenki /əˈveŋki:/ A member of the Manchu-Tungus group of the Altaic family of languages, spoken by *c*.12,000 people in the Evenki region of north central Russia (where it is an official language); formerly called **Tungus**. It is written in the Cyrillic alphabet. ►►Manchu-Tungus.

Ewe /ˈeveɪ, ˈeɪweɪ/ A Kwa language spoken by *c*.2.5 million people in south-east Ghana, south Togo, and south Benin, and also used as a lingua franca in several areas. It is written in the Roman alphabet. ►►Kwa; lingua franca.

exclamation In traditional grammar, an emotional utterance which lacks the grammatical structure of a full sentence, and is marked by strong intonation (e.g. *Gosh!*); usually contrasted with statements, questions, and commands. In writing, exclamations are signalled by special punctuation (an **exclamation mark** or **exclamation point**). In modern grammars of English, **exclamatory sentences** are sometimes given a more restricted sense, referring to constructions which begin with *how* or *what* without a following subject–verb inversion (*What a lovely day it is!*). ►►intonation; inversion; sentence.

exclusive ►disjunction; inclusive.

exegesis /eksəˈdʒiːsɪs/ A critical and systematic interpretation of a text. In classical Rome, exegetes were professional interpreters of omens, dreams, oracles, and other such phenomena. The term came later to apply to the explanation of a sacred text, especially the Bible, the branch of study being known as **exegetics**. It broadened still further to include the critical exposition of any difficult work of literature. ➤➤hermeneutics.

existential Descriptive of a sentence which emphasizes the idea of existence. In English, the commonest type of existential sentence begins with unstressed *There: There are three books on the table.* ➤➤sentence.

existential quantifier ➤quantifier.

exocentric construction ➤endocentric construction.

exoglossic /eksəʊˈglɒsɪk/ ➤endoglossic.

exophora /ekˈsɒfərə/ ➤endophora.

expansion 1. In grammar, the process of adding extra elements to a construction, without its basic structure or function being affected; for example, the noun phrase *the car* can be expanded by the addition of adjectives and other modifiers (*the new car in the street*). ➤➤syntax. **2**. In the study of child language acquisition and foreign language learning, a response which adds extra elements that the speaker has omitted. A child might say *Man gone*, to which the adult listener might reply, *Yes, the man's gone*. This type of response is thought to play an important role in guiding the learner towards the rules of the target language, without the need to make explicit corrections. ➤➤acquisition; language learning.

experimental phonetics The use of instruments and experimental techniques to investigate the acoustic, articulatory, or auditory properties of speech sounds; also called **instrumental phonetics**. A wide range of devices is now available, particular use being made of advances in electronic and computational technology. ➤➤acoustic phonetics; aerometry; electromyograph; electropalatograph; larynx; phonetics; pneumotachograph; segmentator; spectrograph; speech recognition/science/stretcher/synthesis.

expletive ➤taboo language.

Expolangues /ekspoːˈlãg/ An annual languages exhibition, held in Paris since 1983. It reflects ongoing language-related activities in commerce, technology, culture, education, publishing, and several other fields. About 500 languages have been represented.

expressive 1. Descriptive of any use of language which displays or affects a person's emotions. Poetic language is usually highly expressive, as is the language of prayer, political speaking, and advertising. ➤➤affective meaning; emotive language. **2**. Descriptive of a disorder of language production, as opposed to reception. Aphasia, for example, is commonly classified into expressive and receptive types. ➤➤aphasia; language pathology.

expressive aphasia ➤Broca's aphasia.

extension 1. The class of entities to which a word or expression is correctly applied. The extension of the word *flower* is rose, daffodil, crocus, and all the other entities in the world which we recognize as flowers. ➤➤reference 1. **2**. In historical linguistics, the widening of a word's meaning over time. In Latin, for example, *virtue* was a male quality (*vir* 'man'); today it applies to both sexes. ➤➤narrowing.

extensive Descriptive of a construction where there is no close semantic relationship between the elements; contrasts with an **intensive** construction, where such a relationship exists. An example of an extensive construction is the verb + object construction, as in *Mary saw a cow*, where there is no especial semantic link between the seeing and the cow. In an intensive construction, such as *Mary is my sister*, there is a very close link (in this case, one of identity) between the elements of subject and complement. **Extensive verbs** are typically transitive; **intensive verbs** are typically forms of the verb *be*, and are also called **linking verbs**. ➤➤clause; complement; copula; transitivity; verb.

external speech ➤inner speech.

extralinguistic Descriptive of anything (other than language itself) to which language can relate. The objects in the world to which language refers are extralinguistic, therefore, as are the facial expressions and bodily gestures which accompany speech. ➤➤language 4.

eye dialect A way of spelling words which suggests a regional way of talking, such as *wuz* for *was* or *wimmin* for *women*. The point of the term is that there is no regional pronunciation involved: *wimmin* is pronounced /'wɪmɪn/ in Received Pronunciation, too; but by using a nonstandard spelling, a nonstandard pronunciation is suggested. ➤➤dialect.

eye rhyme A pair of words which seem to rhyme from the spelling, but which have different pronunciations. Examples include *come* and *home*, or *love* and *prove*. ➤➤rhyme.

F

Faeroese or **Faroese** /fɛərəʊˈiːz/ A North Germanic language, a member of the West Scandinavian group, spoken by the people in the Faeroe Islands (population in 1995 estimated at 47,000), located between Iceland and Shetland. The islands are part of Denmark, but form a self-governing community in which Faeroese now has official status, being taught alongside Danish in schools. Faeroese is closely related to Icelandic. It has had a written form (using the Roman alphabet) only since 1846, but a growing local literature exists. ➤➤Denmark; Icelandic; Scandinavian.

Falkland Islands (population in 1995 estimated at 2100) English is the official and only language in the Islands. ➤➤English.

falling tone Descriptive of a pitch movement from relatively high to relatively low within a syllable, encountered in the study of tone languages and of intonation. In many varieties of English, a low falling tone is associated with an unemotional tone of voice, often used on statements. It contrasts with such pitch movements as **rising tone**, where the pitch movement goes from relatively low to relatively high (often associated with a questioning tone of voice), **level tone**, where the pitch movement stays constant throughout the syllable, and **falling-rising tone** (often associated with a hesitant or doubtful tone of voice), where the pitch first falls and then rises. ➤➤intonation; tone.

false friends Words in different languages which resemble each other in form, but which express different meanings; also called **false cognates**, and often known by the French equivalent expression **faux amis** /foːzamiː/. Examples include French *demander*, which translates into English as 'to request' not 'to demand', and Italian *caldo*, which translates as 'warm' not 'cold'. ➤➤translation.

falsetto An unnaturally high-pitched voice produced by the vibration of the front part of the vocal folds, either in speaking or singing. It is viewed as a voice disorder (most noticeably in males), especially if it persists into adulthood. ➤➤voice disorder/ mutation.

family of languages A set of languages deriving from a common ancestor, or 'parent'; the derived languages are called 'daughter-languages', and are 'sisters' of each other. A diagrammatic representation of these languages is a **family tree**. ➤➤genetic classification; Indo-European; isolate; phylum; p. 115.

Faroes ➤Denmark.

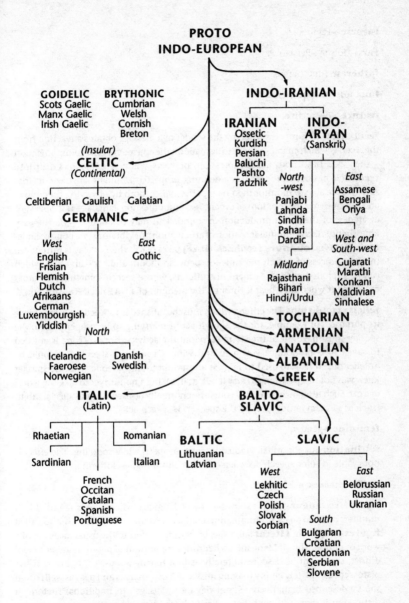

A **family of languages**: the Indo-European family tree, reflecting geographical distribution.

Faroese ➤Faeroese.

Farsi /'fɑːsiː/ ➤Persian.

fatherese ➤motherese.

faux amis ➤false friends.

feature ➤distinctive.

feedback 1. The process whereby the sender of a message obtains a reaction from the receiver which enables a check to be made on the efficiency of the communication – such as a head nod, facial expression, or vocalization (e.g. *mhm*). **Complete feedback** has been proposed as a defining property of human language, in that speakers are able to monitor their own performance, both by observing themselves and by observing the reactions of others. ➤➤communication; language 1. **2**. Speakers' awareness of their own production of sound. This may be auditory (via the ear), kinesthetic (via the internal sensation of articulation), or vibratory (via bone conduction). **Delayed auditory feedback (DAF)** takes place when a delay is introduced into the process of speech transmission between mouth and ear – an effect which can be exploited in the treatment of stutterers, whose speech sometimes becomes more fluent when they hear it through the medium of a DAF device. ➤➤stuttering.

felicity conditions The criteria which must be satisfied if a speech act is to achieve its purpose. For example, for the speech act of marrying to be properly used, the speaker must have the authority to carry out the activity: not everyone is entitled to say 'I now pronounce you man and wife'. Or again, a speech act would be 'infelicitous' if it were used to request a response from someone who the speaker knew was not in a position to carry it out, as in asking a non-driver to take the wheel of a car. Such utterances would of course not normally be used without special intent (such as sarcasm or humour) by the speaker. ➤➤speech act.

feminine ➤gender.

festination An abnormal, gradual increase in speed while speaking. The effect is noticeable in some speech disorders, notably cluttering. ➤➤cluttering.

field ➤semantic field theory.

figurative language An expressive use of language where words are used in a nonliteral way to suggest illuminating comparisons and resemblances; also called **figures of speech**. **Literal** language, by contrast, refers to the usual meaning of a word or phrase. Thus if Marie misses her turn for a portion of pig-meat at her school dinner, she might be described literally as 'not having a sausage'; but only if her plate were completely empty (having missed out on potatoes and peas as well) could she be described figuratively as 'not having a sausage'. In traditional rhetoric, a distinction is drawn (though not entirely clearly) between two types of figurative language: an effect (such as rhyme) which changes the structure of language without affecting its meaning is a **scheme**; one which does affect the meaning (such as metaphor) is a **trope**. ➤➤apostrophe 2; chiasmus; hyperbole; imagery; irony; litotes; metaphor; metonymy; oxymoron; paradox; personification; rhetoric; simile; synechdoche; zeugma.

figure of speech ➤figurative language.

Fiji (population in 1995 estimated at 775,000) The official language is English. Fijian is spoken by *c.*45% of the population. Nearly half the population (those of Indian origin) speak Hindi, and *c.*10 other languages are represented, mainly other Austronesian languages. ➤➤English; Fijian.

Fijian /fɪˈdʒiːən/ A member of the Austronesian family of languages, spoken by *c.*380,000 people in the Fiji Islands. The standard form, based on the Bauan dialect, is used in broadcasting and the press. It is written in the Roman alphabet. ➤➤Austronesian; Fiji.

Filipino /fɪləˈpiːnəʊ/ ➤Pilipino.

filled pause ➤pause.

filtered speech Speech which has been passed through filters to alter its acoustic characteristics. The distorted speech produced is often used in research into auditory perception – for example, determining the extent to which words can still be recognized after certain frequencies have been removed. ➤➤acoustic phonetics.

finger spelling A communication system which uses movements of the fingers to represent letters of the alphabet (a **manual alphabet**); also called **dactylology**. It is widely used by the deaf, especially for communicating words that do not have conventional signs, and which thus have to be 'spelled out' (such as names of people and places). ➤➤sign language; p. 118.

finite Descriptive of a verb or construction which can occur on its own in an independent clause, permitting formal contrasts of tense, number, and mood; contrasts with a **nonfinite** verb or construction, which occurs on its own only in a dependent clause, and which lacks these contrasts. The notion of finiteness basically refers to the extent to which a verb is limited by tense, number, and mood. Thus, *I walk* is a finite use of a verb, because it expresses only one tense, number, and mood (1st person present indicative), as can be shown by such contrasts as *I walked* and *He walks*. The verb in *Walking in the street* . . . , however, is nonfinite, as it is not limited in this way: all options are available to continue this sentence – such as *Walking down the street, I/he/they felt happy* or *Walking down the street, they were/are/will be/must be satisfied*. ➤➤infinitive; mood; number; participle; tense 1; verb.

finite state grammar A simple kind of generative grammar, which generates sentences by working through them from left to right. An initial element is selected, and thereafter the possibilities of occurrence of all other elements are determined

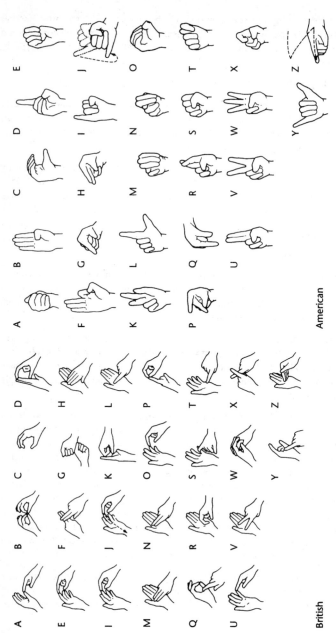

British

American

Two-handed and one-handed examples of **finger spelling** for English.

by the nature of the elements preceding them. The selection of *a*, for example, would require a singular noun to follow, which would in turn require a singular form of the verb, and so on. The perceived limitations of this way of proceeding is part of the argument in favour of more ambitious kinds of grammar. ➤➤generative grammar.

Finland (population in 1995 estimated at 5,110,000) The official languages are Finnish and Swedish. Swedish is spoken as a first language by *c*.6% of the population, and is an official regional language in the Ahvenanmaa/Åland islands. Same (Lappish) is used by *c*.3000 in the northernmost part of the country. A few other Finnic languages are represented (e.g. Estonian, Karelian). English is used for international purposes. ➤➤Finnish; Swedish.

Finnic ➤Finno-Ugric.

Finnish The chief member of the Finnic group of the Finno-Ugric family of languages, spoken by *c*.6 million people, chiefly in Finland (*c*.4.7 million), with some in nearby parts of Sweden (where it is an immigrant language), Estonia, Norway, and Russia (Karelia), and also through immigration especially in the USA and Canada. It is written in the Roman alphabet. The language's official status in Finland dates only from 1863 (Swedish being used there previously). Its written literature dates from a 16th-century Bible translation. An important factor in raising national consciousness about Finnish was the publication in the mid-19th century of the *Kalevala*, an epic poem constructed by Elias Lönnrot out of a collection of oral folk tales. ➤➤Finland; Finno-Ugric.

Finno-Ugric A branch of the Uralic family of languages, found in one part of central Europe, and in those northern territories where Europe and Asia meet. In the north, the **Finnic** branch is located in the region between northern Norway and the White Sea, the whole of Finland, and parts of nearby Russia. The languages of this group include Finnish, Estonian, and Same (Lappish). Curiously isolated from the rest of the group is the main language of the **Ugric** branch, Hungarian; other Ugric languages include Khanty and Mansi, spoken in the region of the River Ob (and sometimes described separately as **Ob-Ugric**). Other Finno-Ugric languages are spoken in various parts of northern and central Russia, several with official regional status, notably Mordvin, Mari, Udmurt, and Komi. The total number of Finno-Ugric speakers is *c*.24 million. ➤➤Estonian; Finnish; Hungarian; Khanty; Komi; Mari; Mordvin; Same; Udmurt; Uralic.

first language The language first acquired by a child (also called the **mother tongue** or **native language**) or preferred in a multilingual situation. The second context may not be identical to the first; for example, the children of many European emigrants to the USA have come to use English as a first language. A **native speaker** is someone for whom a particular language is a first language. ➤➤second language.

first person ➤person.

Firthian linguistics An approach to linguistics based on the thought of J(ames) R(upert) Firth (1890–1969), professor of general linguistics at the University of London (1944–56), and the formative influence on the development of linguistics in Great Britain. A central notion is his view that language cannot be accounted for in terms of a single system of analytic principles and categories, but that different systems must be established at different places within a given level of description (**polysystemicism**). Many of his ideas were developed by a **neo-Firthian** group of scholars in Britain, whose main theoretician, M(ichael) A(lexander) K(irkwood) Halliday (1925–), was professor of general linguistics at London (1965–70) before moving to Australia. ➤➤level 1; linguistics; scale and category grammar; systemic grammar.

fixed expression ➤set expression.

flap A type of consonant in which an articulator (usually the tongue tip) strikes another a glancing blow with a very short contact duration; also called a **tap**. Examples include the standard pronunciation of *r* in *very*, or of the *d* in the American pronunciation of *ladder*. ➤➤articulation.

flash card ➤sight vocabulary.

Flemish ➤Dutch.

flexion ➤inflection.

fliting ➤flyting.

fluency Smooth, rapid, effortless, accurate use of language. The notion is chiefly applied to oral fluency (speech), but is also used with reference to ability in writing, reading, and signing. Curiously, the skill of listening is not usually considered in terms of fluency. In foreign language teaching, the notion of fluency is sometimes contrasted with that of accuracy: the laboured production of grammatically correct sentences may be accurate but is not fluent. In this domain, also, somewhat different criteria for the evaluation of fluency may be found – for example, speed of speech is not so critical, and an imperfect command of sounds, grammar, and vocabulary is common in foreign speakers who would none the less be considered fluent. ➤➤dysfluency.

flyting or **fliting** /ˈflaɪtɪŋ/ An exchange of curses or personal abuse in verse form; a war of words. It is found in Anglo-Saxon, Gaelic, and other early or medieval epic literature. There is a famous exchange between Anglo-Saxon and Viking leaders in the Old English poem *The Battle of Maldon* (991). ➤➤verbal duelling.

focus An element in a sentence to which the speaker wishes to draw special attention. For example, in *It was the EXPLOSION which first told us that there was trouble*, the word order and intonational emphasis combine to draw our attention to *explosion*. ➤➤information structure; intonation; word order.

folk etymology ➤etymology.

font A complete set of type of a particular design and size (e.g. Times, Helvetica); in Britain also spelled **fount**. It includes all the letters of the alphabet, along with numerals, accents, punctuation marks, and several other symbols. ➤➤sort; typography.

foot Traditionally, a unit of rhythm in the metrical system of a language, described in terms of a sequence of stressed and unstressed syllables; for example, the line *The curfew tolls the knell of parting day* is said to consist of five unstressed + stressed units (each called an **iamb**, or **iambic foot**). Other basic types include: the **trochee**, or **trochaic foot**, a stressed + unstressed unit, as heard in the word *David*; a **spondee**, or **spondaic foot**, for a unit consisting of two stresses, as in *James Bond*; a **dactyl**, or **dactylic foot**, for a combination of one stressed syllable followed by two unstressed syllables, as in *Hilary*; and an **anapest**, or **anapestic foot**, for a combination of two unstressed syllables followed by a stressed syllable, as in *(middle) of the night*. The notion is no longer restricted to the analysis of poetic metre, but can also be found as part of a general linguistic description of the rhythmical patterns of words and phrases in speech. ➤➤alexandrine; metrics; rhythm.

foregrounding Relative prominence in a discourse; being in the foreground of the communication, as opposed to being in the background (**backgrounding**). It often involves deviation from a linguistic norm, as when a line of poetry is given a distinctive rhythm, or an author radically alters the word order of a sentence. In advertising, a brand name might be foregrounded by being given a special spelling (*Krunchy Krakkers*). In a narrative, events belonging to the story line are foregrounded, whereas supporting or clarifying events are backgrounded. ➤➤narrative; style.

foreigner talk A variety of speech used by native speakers when they talk to foreigners who are not proficient in the use of their language. It adapts to the speech of the outsider in various ways, such as by being slower, louder, more simplified, more repetitive, and more formal. ➤➤variety.

foreign language A language which is not the mother tongue of a speaker. The term is often used to exclude cases where a language has a special status within a country (such as English used as a second language in Nigeria). Although the second language is not a mother tongue, there is reluctance to see it in the same terms as other foreign languages which have no such status (e.g. German and Russian in the UK). However, the distinction between 'foreign' and 'second' language came to be less used in the early 1990s. ➤➤first/second language; *cartoon*, p. 122.

forensic linguistics The use of linguistic techniques to investigate crimes in which language data forms part of the evidence. The field of **forensic phonetics** is often distinguished as a separate domain, dealing with such matters as accent and voice identification. ➤➤linguistics.

'No worries. If it can't be said in English, it ain't worth saying at all.' (**foreign language**)

foreword Introductory remarks about a book or its author, often written by someone else. The notion contrasts with the **preface**, which is a personal note by the author explaining how the book came to be written, and often including acknowledgements and other incidental details.

form 1. The abstract structural character of language, as defined in terms of the sound or writing system, grammar, and vocabulary. The term enters into two kinds of contrast: on the one hand, it contrasts with the **meaning** or **function** of language; on the other hand, it contrasts with the **substance** of linguistic expression – the physical sounds or marks which language uses in order to build up a system of communication. ➤formalization; graphetics; phonetics; semantics. **2.** A linguistic unit established at a particular level of analysis, or the variations in that unit which occur; for example, we might talk of the 'forms' of the verb *go*, by which we would mean *go, goes, going, gone, went*. A set of forms which display similar or identical grammatical features is a **form class** – a notion which includes not only word classes (parts of speech) but also morpheme classes (such as types of affix). ➤affix; morpheme; word class.

formal grammar An approach to grammatical study which focuses on the forms which make up the patterns of word and sentence structure; the implication is that the analysis is carried out without relying on the meanings of these forms (a 'notional' approach). Notional grammar would analyse nouns, for example, as 'names of persons, places, and things', whereas formal grammar would describe nouns in terms of their location in sentences and the types of words which co-occur with them (articles, determiners, etc.). ➤form 1; grammar 1; string; syntax.

formalist Descriptive of an approach to stylistic analysis which looks at texts as formal objects of study, comprising an internal structure which can be objectively identified. The approach has been particularly associated with structural linguistics, especially as practised in eastern Europe. ➤➤form 1; structural; stylistics.

formality A dimension of social behaviour, ranging from the most strictly regulated to the least regulated, and reflected in language by varied linguistic features. Highly formal language involves carefully organized discourse, often with complex syntax and vocabulary, which closely follows the standard language, and which is often sensitive to prescriptive judgements. Highly informal language is very loosely structured, involving a high level of colloquial expression, and often departing from standard norms (such as by using slang, regionalisms, neologisms, and code mixing). ➤➤code 3; diglossia; style; variety.

formalization A characteristic of formulations in linguistics, whereby rules, statements, and other features of language are capable of being specified in a precise and rigorous way, especially in logical or mathematical terms. A 'formalized' account contrasts with an 'informal' one. Formalized accounts make use of **formalisms** – artificial languages devised to make precise statements about the grammatical properties of a language (whether natural or artificial). ➤➤form 1; formalist; semantics.

formal semantics ➤semantics.

formal universal ➤universal.

formant A concentration of acoustic energy. The notion is important in acoustic phonetics as part of the classification of vowels, vowel-like sounds, and the transitional features between vowels and adjacent sounds. ➤➤acoustic phonetics; transition 2; vowel.

formative A formally identifiable, irreducible grammatical element which enters into the construction of larger linguistic units, such as the affixes *-ing* and *-ed* in English. The notion is especially used in generative grammar for the terminal elements in a surface structure representation of a sentence. ➤➤generative grammar; morpheme; surface structure.

form class ➤form 2.

formula A fixed form of words serving a conventional purpose; examples include greetings (*Pleased to meet you*), formal declarations (*Not guilty*), and letter-openings (*Dear Madam*). Language which is characterized by many such fixed forms (or **routines**) is called **formulaic** or **prefabricated**. A contrast is sometimes drawn with **free discourse**, where there is a relatively wide choice over what to say and how to say it. The term **formula** can also refer to any idiomatic word sequence or set expression, such as *spick and span*. ➤➤idiom; set expression.

form word ➤grammatical word.

fortis Descriptive of sounds made with a relatively strong degree of muscular effort and breath force, compared with other sounds (**lenis** sounds). Typically, voiceless sounds are fortis; voiced sounds are lenis. The strengthening of the overall force of a sound (e.g. a fricative becoming a stop) is called **fortition**, a process which occurs in sound changes both historically and synchronically. This process contrasts with **lenition**, which is a weakening in overall force (e.g. voiceless sounds becoming voiced). ➤tension.

fossilized Descriptive of a construction which is no longer productive in a language, but is still in use. Many constructions involving the subjunctive are fossilized, such as *Come what may* and *So be it*. In foreign language learning, the term describes those incorrect linguistic features which have become a permanent part of a learner's production – such as the features which identify a foreign accent. ➤productivity; subjunctive.

found poem A text which is identified as a poem though not intended to be one by the author. Usually, the discovery takes the form of a rhyme scheme or metrical pattern which is part of a piece of prose. Accidental poetry can easily be found in the prose passages of great descriptive writers, such as Dickens (and the term **prose poem** has been suggested to cope with the result). Some authors consciously build a poetic structure into their prose. A tongue-in-cheek example is Lewis Carroll's preface to his poem 'Hiawatha's photographing' (1857), which incorporates Longfellow's famous rhythm: *In an age of imitation, I can claim no special merit for this slight attempt at doing what is known to be so easy. . .* In everyday speech, inadvertent rhyme can bring forth such a comment as *I'm a poet and I don't know it*. ➤verbal play.

fount ➤font.

fourth person ➤person.

frame The structural environment within which a class of items can be used; also called a **syntactic frame** or a **substitution frame**. For example, *I – cross* provides a frame for a particular class of verbs (e.g. *am, become, feel*) ➤word class.

France (population in 1995 estimated at 58,333,000) The official language is French (spoken by *c*.53 million). Official regional language status has been given to Basque (*c*.75,000), Breton (*c*.500,000), Catalan (*c*.250,000), and Corsican (*c*.280,000). There are *c*.250,000 speakers of Occitan (Provençal). German (Alsatian, *c*.1.5 million) and Dutch (*c*.90,000) are used in the border areas of Alsace-Lorraine and Westhoek, respectively. Immigrant languages include varieties of Arabic (*c*.1 million), Armenian (*c*.70,000), Italian (*c*.1 million), Kabyle (*c*.500,000), Portuguese (*c*.750,000), Turkish (*c*.135,000), and Wolof (*c*.35,000), and there are many (50,000–100,000) speakers of Romani. ➤Basque; Breton; Catalan; Corsican; French; Kabyle; Occitan.

Franglais A language variety which is a nonstandard mixture of French and English, and recognized by both the French and the English. To the French, it generally refers to any instance of the language using too many English words. To the English, especially since Miles Kington began writing on the subject, it refers to a form of French which has been distorted by the use of English grammar, vocabulary, and idiom – a pastiche on the poor quality of French often heard by English learners. ➤Spanish.

free discourse ➤formula.

free form A minimal grammatical unit which can be used as a word without additional elements; also called a **free morpheme**. Free forms used in the first sentence of this entry include *as, unit, which* and *word*, but not, for example, *additional*, which is not a minimal unit (as it is analysable into *addition* and *-al*). ➤bound form; morpheme; word.

free translation ➤translation.

free variation The ability of one sound to be substituted for another within a word, without this affecting the word's meaning. For example, the vowels /e/ and /ɒ/ are in free variation in the first syllable of *envelope*. ➤allo-; phoneme.

French A member of the Romance family of languages, spoken by *c*.72 million people as a first language, by at least a further 50 million as a country's second language, and by many more as an international foreign language. First language use is chiefly in France (*c*.53 million), Canada (*c*.6 million, primarily in Québec), Belgium (4 million), Switzerland (1.3 million), and the USA (*c*.2.5 million), with substantial numbers also in Réunion, Mauritius, Guadeloupe, Martinique, and other former French colonies. French has official status in over 30 countries, and is spoken by many as a second language, notably in Cameroon, Madagascar, Côte d'Ivoire, Mali, Niger, Senegal, Burkina Faso, and Haiti. Its written form (in the Roman alphabet) can be traced back to the 9th century AD, with a literature emerging in the 12th century, in the form of the *chansons de geste* ('songs of deeds') and courtly romances. The 17th century was the golden age of French literature, including the work of the dramatists Corneille, Racine, and Molière, and this century also saw the creation of the *Académie française* (1635), which has continued to exercise a far-reaching, conservative influence on the language down to the present day. French developed as the international language of culture, politics, and education during the 18th century, and continued to play this role until largely supplanted by the growing dominance of English since the 1950s. It none the less plays an important role, being an official language of most international political bodies. In France, regional dialects tend to be grouped into two broad types: in the north, there is the *langue d'oï* (the name deriving from an old form of the word *oui* 'yes'); in the south the *langue d'oc* (from the Provençal word *oc* 'yes'). There are several French-based creoles in the former colonies. Standard French is based on the dialect of the Paris region, recognized as such since the 16th century. ➤Académie française; creole; France; Occitan; Romance.

French Guiana (population in 1995 estimated at 120,000) The official language is French. A French-based creole (Patois) is used by *c*.75% of the population, by at least 50,000 as a first language. There are a few Amerindian languages in use, as well as some speakers of Chinese, Hindi, and an English-based creole (Aucaans). ➤French; Patwa.

French Polynesia (population in 1995 estimated at 215,000) The official language is French. Tahitian is an official regional language in Tahiti, and an important lingua franca. A few other Austronesian languages are spoken on various islands (e.g. Paumotu, Marquesan). Chinese (Hakka) is used by *c*.2% of the population. ➤French; Tahitian.

frequency In acoustics, the number of sound waves per second produced by a source of vibration. Formerly expressed in 'cycles per second' (cps), it is now measured in hertz (Hz). ➤fundamental frequency; hertz.

fricative /'frɪkətɪv/ Descriptive of a type of consonant where there is sufficient articulatory constriction to produce friction as its main auditory feature; also sometimes called **spirant**. Fricatives may be voiceless (e.g. [f], [s]) or voiced (e.g. [v], [z]). ➤affricate; consonant; friction.

friction The auditory effect of air passing a constriction in the vocal tract. Friction is part of the phonetic definition of consonants; the phonetic definition of vowels requires that they be **frictionless**. However, from a phonological point of view **frictionless continuants** do occur as consonants: these are sounds (such as nasals or laterals) which function as a consonant in speech but which lack the closure or friction that identifies most consonantal articulations. ➤consonant; lateral; nasal; phonology; vowel.

Frisian A West Germanic language spoken by *c*.700,000 people, 400,000 in The Netherlands, mainly in the province of Friesland (population in 1995 estimated at 615,000), with some in north-west Germany. It is written in the Roman alphabet, and is the language most closely related to English. Written remains in Old Frisian date from the end of the 13th century. A 20th-century revival of interest in the language has resulted in its being given official regional status in Friesland, and there is now a Frisian Academy. ➤academy; Germanic.

Friulian /friˈuːlɪən/ ➤Rhaetian.

fronting 1. The articulation of a sound further forward in the mouth than is expected, such as when a child pronounces *car* as [tɑ:]. ➤front sound. **2**. The moving of a sentence element from the middle or end of a sentence to initial position; for example, we can front the final element of *We turned left at The Rose* to get *At The Rose we turned left*. ➤transformation; word order.

front matter ➤end matter.

front sound A sound made in the front part of the mouth (e.g. [m]) or by the front part of the tongue (e.g. [a]); contrasts with **back sounds**, made in the back part of the mouth (e.g. [h]) or by the back part of the tongue (e.g. [k]). The term is most commonly used with reference to vowel classification, where **front vowels** (e.g. [i], [e]) are those produced with the highest point of the tongue as far forward as possible. The contrast is with **back vowels** (e.g. [u], [o]), where the highest part of the tongue is as far to the rear as possible. ➤central sound; fronting.

frozen expression ➤set expression.

FSP ➤functional.

Fula /'fu:lə/ A West Atlantic language spoken by *c*.15 million people, in Nigeria (*c*.8 million), Guinea, Senegal, and other countries in the western part of the African bulge; also called **Ful**, **Fulfulde**, or (after the name of the people) **Fulani**. It is a lingua franca throughout the region, and also in the Central African Republic. It is written in the Roman alphabet. ➤lingua franca; West Atlantic.

Fulani /'fu:ləni:/ ➤Fula.

Fulfulde /fʊl'fʊldi:/ ➤Fula.

full stop ➤period.

full verb ➤lexical verb.

full word ➤grammatical word.

function 1. The relationship between a linguistic form and other parts of the sentence (or other unit) in which it is used; for example, the functions of a noun phrase include its use as the subject or object of a sentence. Any element which is part of a system can be said to 'function' or 'contrast' within that system; for example, vowels and consonants function within the sound system. The use made of a linguistic contrast in a system is called its **functional load** or **functional yield**: for example, a great deal of use is made in English of the contrast between /p/ and /b/ (this has a heavy functional load), whereas the contrast between /ʃ/ and /ʒ/ (sh and zh) is very little used. ➤form 1; phonology. **2**. The relationship between a linguistic form and the social or interpersonal setting in which it is used, as when we refer to the various functions of language to communicate ideas, express attitudes, generate rapport, and so on. Different kinds of utterance (e.g. questions, statements) can also be described in this way, in terms of the interactive functions they perform. ➤functional; pragmatics; speech act.

functional Descriptive of any approach in which the notion of 'function' is central. **Functional grammar**, for example, was devised as an alternative to the abstract view of language presented by transformational grammar; based on a pragmatic view of language as social interaction, it focuses on the rules governing the linguistic expressions that are used as instruments of this activity. In foreign language teaching, a **functional syllabus** is one where the syllabus content is organized in terms of language functions, such as requesting, persuading, and inviting. **Functional sentence perspective (FSP)** is a linguistic theory devised by Czech linguists which analyses utterances in terms of the information they contain; the role of each utterance part is evaluated for its semantic function in relation to the whole. ➤➤contrast; distinctive; function 1, 2; Prague School.

functional change 1. The use of a word in different grammatical roles, such as *round* being used as adjective (*a round table*), verb (*we rounded the corner*), and noun (*It's your round*). ➤➤conversion. **2**. In historical linguistics, the alteration of the role of a linguistic feature over time – especially, when a sound takes on or loses the status of a phoneme. For example, in Old English, /s/ was heard as [z] only between voiced sounds, but in modern English /z/ has become a phoneme in its own right, as shown by such contrasts as *Sue* vs. *zoo*. ➤➤phoneme; sound change.

functional literacy ➤literacy.

functional load ➤function 1.

functional phonetics ➤function 1; phonology.

functional shift ➤conversion.

functional yield ➤function 1.

function word ➤grammatical word.

functor ➤grammatical word.

fundamental frequency The lowest frequency component in a complex sound wave, of particular importance in determining a sound's pitch; also called **the fundamental** or **F nought**, and symbolized as F_0. Multiples of this frequency are called the **harmonics**; for example, if the fundamental is 200 Hz, the harmonics are 400, 600, etc. A frequency which is twice the fundamental is the 'second harmonic'; one three times the fundamental is the 'third harmonic'; and so on. ➤➤frequency; intonation.

Fur /fʊə/ A Nilo-Saharan language spoken by *c*.500,000 people in western Sudan, largely in the province of Darfur. The language has no clear relationships with other members of the family. It is written in the Roman alphabet. Arabic influence is evident, as the people are now entirely Muslim. ➤➤Nilo-Saharan.

fusion A type of assimilation in which two adjacent sounds influence each other, losing their identities to emerge as a single different sound; for example, the final /t/ of *don't* and the initial /j/ of *you* readily fuse to produce the affricate /tʃ/. ➤➤assimilation.

fusional language ➤typology of language.

futhork or **futhark** /ˈfʌðɔːk/ ➤rune.

future tense A form of the verb which refers to future time, as in French *J'irai* 'I'll go'. English has no formal future tense, but has many ways of referring to future time, such as through the use of the modal verbs *will/shall*, future-time adverbials (e.g. *tomorrow*), and such verbs as *be about to*. The *will/shall* forms are usually called 'future tenses' in traditional grammar, but many linguists consider this to be misleading, as these forms express several other meanings than future time (such as timelessness, as in *Stones will sink in water*). The use of *will/shall* followed by *have* is traditionally called **future perfect tense** (or 'future in the past') in traditional grammar. ➤tense 1.

G

Gabon (population in 1995 estimated at 1,379,000) The official language is French. There are *c*.35 local languages, including Fang (spoken by *c*.30% of the population), Myene, and Punu. Several of these languages are spoken by very small numbers. ➤French.

Gaelic /ˈɡeɪlɪk, ˈɡalɪk/ ➤Celtic; Irish Gaelic; Scottish Gaelic.

Galatian /ɡəˈleɪʃn/ ➤Celtic.

Galician /ɡəˈliːʃn/ ➤Portuguese.

galley ➤proof.

Gallinya /ɡəˈlɪnjə/ ➤Oromo.

Gambia, The (population in 1995 estimated at 1,053,000) The official language is English. There is an English-based creole (Krio) quite widely used as a lingua franca, and a Portuguese-based creole (Crioulo). The chief language in the middle of the country is Mandinka (Malinke), spoken by *c*.40% of the population. There are *c*.15 other local languages, including Ful and Wolof. ➤creole; English; lingua franca.

gap The absence of a linguistic unit at a place in a pattern of relationships where one might have been expected. For example, because of the widespread use of the male/female contrast in English kinship terms (*mummy/daddy*, *brother/sister*, *uncle/aunt*, etc.), we might expect there to be words for male and female cousin, too – but there is a lexical gap here. The same kind of notion, often referred to as **gapping**, is also used in some approaches to grammatical analysis for the omission of an element from certain types of sentence, such as *Mary likes drawing and John driving*, where there is a gap between subject and object in the second clause. ➤ellipsis; kinship terms.

Gaulish /ˈɡɔːlɪʃ/ ➤Celtic.

GB An abbreviation of **government and binding theory**.

Ge'ez ➤Ethiopia.

gender A grammatical category which displays such contrasts as masculine/femine/neuter or animate/inanimate. A distinction is drawn between **natural gender**, which involves reference to the sex of real-world entities, and **grammatical gender**, which is associated with arbitrary word classes, and signals grammatical relationships between words in a sentence. English has natural gender – words such as *he* and *she* are used only with reference to male and female entities (or entities which can be personified in this way). French, by contrast, also has grammatical gender: a word which is 'feminine' (signalled by the use of *la* and certain other words before a noun) does not necessarily refer to a female, as in *la gare* 'the station', *la discussion* 'discussion', and thousands of other cases. ➤➤animate; noun.

genealogical classification ➤genetic classification.

generalization In psycholinguistics, the process whereby children extend their initial use of a linguistic feature to a class of items, such as gradually coming to use the *-s* ending to express noun plurals. **Overgeneralization** takes place when the feature is extended beyond its limits in the adult grammar, such as when the *-s* ending is used in *mouses* and *mans*. Overgeneralization is also found in foreign language learning, when the rules of the foreign language are applied too liberally. Forms such as *mouses* can be heard in the speech of adult foreigners too. ➤➤acquisition; language learning; psycholinguistics.

generalized phrase-structure grammar (GPSG) A framework for writing fully explicit formal grammars for natural languages, developed in the 1980s as an alternative to transformational accounts of language. It was originally formulated as a notationally elaborated variant of context-free phrase-structure grammar. ➤➤context 1; phrase-structure grammar.

general linguistics ➤linguistics.

general phonetics ➤phonetics.

general semantics, now officially **general-semantics** A philosophical movement developed in the 1930s by a Polish-American scientist and philosopher Alfred Korzybski (1879–1950), which aimed to make people aware of the conventional relationships between words and things, as a means of improving systems of communication and clear thinking. It attracted considerable popular interest in the 1930s and 1940s, and there is an Institute of General Semantics in Maryland, USA. ➤➤semantics.

generative grammar A grammar which defines the set of grammatical sentences in a language: formal rules project a finite set of sentences upon the potentially infinite set which constitutes the language as a whole. The term is also used as a label for the theoretical approach, associated primarily with the thought of Noam Chomsky, which developed the scope and aims of such a grammar. The two main branches of generative grammar are **generative phonology** and **generative syntax**. The word 'grammar' in this label thus has a much broader range than that encountered in traditional language study, including phonology and semantics alongside syntax. ➤➤Chomskyan grammar 1; innateness hypothesis; syntax; transformation; tree; universal.

generic /dʒəˈnerɪk/ Descriptive of a class of word which refers to a class of entities.

Examples include certain uses of nouns (e.g. *A lion is a fierce animal*, where *A lion* means 'the class of all lions'), adjectival nouns (e.g. *the Chinese, the rich*), and general semantic labels such as *fruit* (which subsumes apples, oranges, etc.). ➤hyponymy; noun; sexist language.

genetic classification The classification of languages according to a hypothesis of common origin; also called a **genealogical classification**. It typically produces a family tree for a group of languages which displays their relative chronology. The members of the family are brought together by a meticulous process of comparison of individual linguistic forms. ➤family of languages; phylum; typology of language.

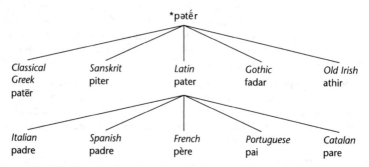

Genetic classification. Reconstruction of the Indo-European form **pətḗr* by a comparison of cognate forms in attested languages. The families of languages begin to emerge in the process.

Geneva School ➤Saussure, Ferdinand de.

genitive case One of the common ways in which an inflected language makes a word change its form, in order to show a grammatical relationship with other parts of the sentence. The genitive is used with nouns (or noun phrases) typically to express a possessive relationship (e.g. *the lady's hand*) or some other close semantic connection (e.g. *a summer's day*). The term is also used for constructions which are formally related to the genitive case form, such as the **postmodifying genitive**, using *of*, in English: *the bottom of the page*. The English **group genitive** is a construction where the genitive ending is added to the last element in a noun phrase containing postmodification or coordination, as in *the University of Bangor's team* or *the prince and princess's opinion*. ➤case; inflection 1; subject.

genre /ˈʒɔːnrə/ An identifiable category of artistic composition – in the literary domain, subsuming such general notions as poetry, drama, and novel as well as such lower-order notions as science fiction, crime, and romance. The term is also used in a more abstract way, to refer to any formally distinguishable variety, whether of speech or writing, such as a song, sermon, or conversation. ➤variety.

geographical linguistics ►dialectology; geolinguistics.

geolinguistics A branch of linguistics which studies the geographical distribution of languages in the world, with reference to their political, economic, and cultural status; also called **geographical linguistics**. More narrowly, the term is used for an approach which relates dialect geography, urban dialect study, and human geography within a sociolinguistic perspective. ►dialect; sociolinguistics.

Geordie /'dʒɔːdiː/ The accent and dialect associated with the Tyneside area in the north-east of England. The name is a diminutive form of *George*. ►accent 1.

Georgia (population in 1995 estimated at 5,481,000) The official languages are Georgian, spoken by c.70% of the population, and Russian (c.7%). There are c.10 other languages, notably Abkhaz, Armenian (c.8%), Azerbaijani, Chechen, and Ossetic. ►Georgian; Russian.

Georgian The chief member of the Kartvelian group of Caucasian languages, spoken by over 4 million people, chiefly in Georgia (where it is an official language), and in nearby countries. There is a literary tradition dating from the 5th century AD, when an alphabet was first devised to permit the translation of the Bible into Georgian. This was followed by a period of Old Georgian which lasted as a literary medium until the 11th century (continuing in religious use until the 19th century). New Georgian developed as a secular literary medium in the 12th century. The language is written in the Georgian alphabet (Mkhedruli), from left to right. ►Georgia; Kartvelian.

Gê-Pano-Carib /'geɪ 'panəʊ 'karɪb/ A group of c.200 Amerindian languages, spoken east of the Andes along most of the length of South America, and along the Brazilian Amazon basin. It has a very small number of speakers (perhaps a million) for such a vast area. The group contains the **Carib** family, one of the largest in South America, with over 80 languages spoken by tiny numbers throughout the whole northern region. Only Carib itself has as many as 5000 speakers. **Macro-Panoan**, also within this group, is a family of c.70 languages spoken from Peru and Bolivia eastward to Brazil, and southward to Paraguay and Argentina. Mataco is the only language with more than 10,000 speakers. The **Macro-Gê** family has c.30 languages, spoken mainly in eastern Brazil. All these languages use the Roman alphabet when written down. ►Amerindian.

German A West Germanic language spoken by c.100 million people, chiefly in Germany, Austria, Switzerland, and Liechtenstein, and spilling over into nearby countries, notably France, Denmark, Belgium, Hungary, Italy, Poland, the Czech and Slovak republics, Romania, and Kazakhstan. It is the official language of Germany and Austria, and one of the official languages of Switzerland, and is used as a lingua franca in much of eastern Europe by c.20 million people. Large numbers of German-speaking immigrants are to be found in the USA, Brazil, and several other countries. German is written in the Roman alphabet, sometimes in the form of the traditional 'Gothic' script. Two main varieties are recognized. High German (**Hochdeutsch**) is the language of the southern highlands, and the basis of the modern written language. Low German (**Plattdeutsch** or **Niederdeutsch**) is the spoken language of the northern lowlands. The period around 1100 is recognized as the boundary between Old High German (in evidence from the 9th century) and Middle High German, the latter preserved in many texts, such as the epic *Nibelungenlied* and the many courtly poems of the troubadours (minnesingers). Several important regional varieties of Modern High German exist, notably those of Austria and Switzerland. Three varieties associated with emigrant religious settlements are spoken in other countries (especially the Americas): **Mennonite** (introduced by a 16th-century Anabaptist group, named after the reformer Menno Simons), **Hutterite** (introduced by another Anabaptist group, named after Jakob Hutter), and **Pennsylvanian** (introduced by later settlers in Pennsylvania), also known as *Pennsylvanian Dutch* (a popular etymology from *Deutsch* 'German'). ➤black letter writing; diglossia; etymology; Germanic; Yiddish.

Germanic An Indo-European family of languages, spoken by over 550 million people as a first language (largely because of the worldwide distribution of English), descended from the Germanic tribes who lived in northern Europe during the first millennium BC. Some Germanic words are recorded in Latin authors, and Scandinavian inscriptions in the runic alphabet are recorded from the 3rd century AD. The languages are usually classified into three groups. **East Germanic** is now extinct, with only Gothic recorded in manuscript to any extent. **North Germanic** includes the Scandinavian languages of Swedish and Danish (East Scandinavian), and Norwegian, Icelandic, and Faeroese (West Scandinavian), along with the older states of these languages (Old Norse), notably the literary variety of Old Icelandic. Within **West Germanic**, English and Frisian are often grouped together as **Anglo-Frisian**; German, Yiddish, Netherlandic (i.e. Dutch, including local Flemish dialects in Belgium), and Afrikaans are often grouped together as **Netherlandic-German**. ➤Afrikaans; Dutch; English; Faeroese; Frisian; German; Gothic; rune; Scandinavian; Yiddish.

Germany (population in 1995 estimated at 82,235,000) The official language is German. There are *c.*20 languages spoken by various immigrant groups, notably Arabic (*c.*70,000), Greek (*c.*318,000), Italian (*c.*550,000), Kurdish (*c.*500,000), and Turkish (*c.*1.5 million). Sorbian in Lusatia (*c.*70,000) and Danish in South Slesvig (*c.*50,000) have official regional status. Frisian is spoken in the coastal islands region. There are *c.*240,000 Polish speakers near the eastern border, *c.*100,000 Dutch speakers in the north-west, and an uncertain number of speakers of Romani. ➤German.

gerund /'ʤerʌnd/ ➤participle.

gerundive /ʤə'rʌndɪv/ ➤participle.

Ghana (population in 1995 estimated at 17,086,000) The official language is English, spoken by *c*.1 million as a second language. There are *c*.70 local languages, notably Akan (spoken by *c*.45% of the population), More, Ewe, and Ga-Adangme (Ga is the chief language used in the capital, Accra). Hausa is used as a lingua franca in the north. Several of the languages have official literary status. ➤➤English; lingua franca.

Gheg /geg/ ➤Albanian.

ghost form A word originating in error during the copying, analysing, or learning of a language, which does not exist in the original language. An example is *Dord*, printed in one dictionary as a headword, though it was a misinterpretation of a card heading 'D or d'.

Gibraltar (population in 1995 estimated at 30,700) The official language is English, used by about a third of the population (by *c*.3000 as a first language). Spanish is used by another third, and several other languages are spoken by small numbers, notably Arabic (*c*.3000). ➤➤English.

Gilyak /ˈgɪljak/ A language generally placed within the Paleosiberian grouping, spoken by *c*.400 people around the Amur River estuary and in the north of Sakhalin Island; also called **Nivkhi**. It is written in the Cyrillic alphabet. The language has no known relatives. ➤➤isolate; Paleosiberian.

given Descriptive of one of the two main constituents comprising the information structure of an utterance. Given information is that already supplied by the previous linguistic context; also called the **topic**. It contrasts with **new** information, which has not been previously supplied; also called the **comment**. For example, following the sentence *Jane arrived in a taxi*, the sentence *The taxi had a bent bumper* can be analysed as containing a given constituent (the topic is *the taxi*) and a new constituent (the comment is the rest of the sentence). **Topicalization** is the movement of a constituent to the front of a sentence to act as topic, as in *On the bumper was a big scratch*. ➤➤information structure.

Glagolitic script /glagəˈlɪtɪk/ An early Slavic script, possibly invented by St Cyril in the 9th century, but according to some views deriving from Greek cursive writing current in the 7th or 8th centuries. Glagolitic became widely used alongside Cyrillic in Bulgaria, Macedonia, and nearby regions, but was gradually replaced by Cyrillic, though surviving in Croatia, especially in religious settings, until the beginning of the 19th century. There was renewed interest in the script in the early 1990s. ➤➤Cyrillic; Slavic.

glide 1. A transitional sound produced as the vocal organs move towards or away from an articulation (or a position of rest). A movement towards a target position is called an **on-glide**; a movement away is called an **off-glide**. ➤➤articulation. **2**. A vowel where there is an audible change of quality; diphthongs and triphthongs are both types of glide. ➤➤vowel. **3**. A tone involving a change of pitch level; falling tones and rising tones are both glides, in this sense. ➤➤tone.

global aphasia ➤aphasia.

Glosa /ˈɡlɒsə/ ➤Interglossa.

glossary An alphabetical list of the terms used in a special field, along with brief explanations (**glosses**). A word which provides a translation or explanation of another word (such as one in a foreign language) is also known as a gloss. ➤➤lexicography.

glossogenetics /ɡlɒsəʊʤəˈnetɪks/ The study of the origins and development of language, both in the child and in the race. It involves a wide range of contributing sciences, including biology, anthropology, psychology, semiotics, neurology, and primatology, as well as linguistics. ➤➤origins of language.

glossographia ➤glossolalia.

glossolalia /ɡlɒsəˈleɪlɪə/ The religious practice of speaking in tongues – a widespread phenomenon within the Pentecostal tradition of Protestantism and charismatic Roman Catholicism. Many glossolalists believe they are speaking a real but unknown language, but linguistic analysis has shown the utterance patterns to be quite unlike ordinary language, being simpler and more repetitive. Glossolalic speech is interpreted in a general way, usually as a sign of a person's belief or as evidence of conversion. Its written equivalent is called **glossographia**. ➤➤xenoglossia.

glottal Descriptive of sounds made in the larynx, due to closure or narrowing of the **glottis** (the aperture between the vocal folds). The audible release of a complete closure at the glottis is a **glottal stop**, symbolized as [ʔ] – heard, for example, in a Cockney or Cockney-influenced accent, where it replaces the [t] in such words as *bottle*. **Glottalization** is a general term for any articulation involving a simultaneous glottal constriction. ➤➤glottalic.

glottalic /ɡləˈtalɪk/ Descriptive of the use of the glottis to initiate an airstream capable of making consonant sounds. Ejective sounds result from an outward flow of air; implosive consonants result from an inward flow. ➤➤airstream; ejective; glottis; implosive.

glottis ➤glottal.

glottochronology A controversial approach to language history in which a statistical technique (**lexicostatistics**) is used to quantify, in units of time, the extent to which languages have diverged from a common source. A sample of vocabulary is taken from two languages, using a basic word list, and the number of similar words between the languages is counted. Glottochronologists assume that the lower the number of vocabulary agreements between the two samples, the longer the languages have been separated. ➤➤diachronic linguistics.

goal In grammatical analysis, the entity that is affected by the action of the verb. It is usually equivalent to the grammatical object (e.g. *the balloon* in *The pin burst the* *balloon*), but it may appear in other grammatical locations (e.g. as subject in the passive construction, *The balloon was burst by the pin*). ➤➤actor–action–goal; object.

gobbledegook ➤Plain English Campaign.

Goidelic /gɔɪ'delɪk/ ➤Celtic.

Golden Bull Awards ➤Plain English Campaign.

Gothic An East Germanic language, now extinct, spoken by the Goths, a people who migrated from southern Scandinavia throughout eastern and south-eastern Europe during the later 2nd century AD. There is evidence of two dialects, relating to the two chief tribes: Ostrogothic, spoken chiefly in the east, and Visigothic, spoken chiefly in the west. Gothic provides the earliest evidence of the Germanic language family, and is largely attested in the remains of a translation of the Bible made by Bishop Ulfilas (or Wulfilas) in the 4th century AD – the Codex Argenteus, so-called from its gold and silver writing on purple-red parchment. In Spain and Italy, the language died out in the 6th–7th centuries, following the various defeats of the Gothic tribes. In the Crimea, however, a variety of Gothic was still being recorded in the 16th century (Crimean Gothic). The Gothic alphabet had 27 letters, chiefly derived from Greek, with some Latin and runic symbols. This alphabet should be carefully distinguished from **Gothic script**, which is a black-letter form of the Roman alphabet. ➤➤black letter writing; Germanic; Gothic script; rune.

Gothic script ➤black letter writing.

government A type of syntactic linkage whereby one word (or word class) requires that another word (or class) be in a particular form. In Latin, for example, a preposition governs a noun in a specific case: *cum* 'with' takes the ablative case; *ad* 'to' takes the accusative. ➤➤case; concord; preposition; word class.

government and binding theory (GB) A model of generative grammar which involves three main levels of structure (known as D-structure, S-structure, and Logical Form) and a set of interacting sub-theories. The model takes its name from two of these sub-theories: 'binding' deals with the conditions which formally relate (or 'bind') certain elements of a sentence; 'government' deals with the structural contexts within which these binding relationships obtain. The approach is also described by the phrase **principles and parameters**, for its view that the same principles of syntax are operative in all languages, though they can take a slightly different form in different languages. The approach is also described as **modular**, because of the way its explanations may derive from different principles (or **modules**) of the grammar. ➤➤generative grammar; parameter.

GPSG An abbreviation of **generalized phrase-structure grammar**.

Grabar /gra'bɑː/ ➤Armenian.

gradability Variability in degree, viewed grammatically or semantically. A word is **gradable** if it allows the possibility of comparison or intensification, using such means as comparative/superlative form (e.g. *slower, most interestingly*) and adverbs of degree (*very big, especially small*). If these possibilities are not available, the word is **ungradable** (e.g. **most upstairs*). ➤➤antonymy.

gradation ➤ablaut.

grammar 1. A systematic analysis of the structure of a language. A contrast is often drawn between a **descriptive grammar**, which provides a precise account of actual usage, and a **prescriptive grammar**, which attempts to establish rules for the correct use of language in society. A comprehensive practical description of the structure of a language is a **reference grammar**. A **theoretical grammar** goes beyond the study of individual languages, and uses linguistic data as a means of developing insights into the nature of language as such, and into the categories and processes needed for linguistic analysis. A **performance grammar** analyses the structures found in a corpus of speech or writing; this contrasts with a **competence grammar**, which is predictive of a speaker's knowledge. A grammar of the latter kind is usually thought of as a **generative grammar**, a device which gives a finite specification of the sentences of a language. A grammar which tries to establish the defining (universal) characteristics of human language is a **universal grammar**. In so far as grammar concentrates on the study of linguistic forms, or analyses language using the formalized techniques of logic or mathematics, it may be referred to as **formal grammar**; this is often contrasted with **notional grammar**, which assumes the existence of extralinguistic categories in order to define grammatical units. **Traditional grammar** refers to the range of attitudes and methods found in the prelinguistic era of grammatical study, and especially in the European school grammars of the 18th and 19th centuries. ➤➤case/finite state/formal/generalized phrase-structure/generative/lexical-functional/phrase-structure/relational/scale and category/systemic grammar; clause; competence; corpus; prescriptivism. **2**. A level of structural organization which can be studied independently of phonology and semantics, generally divided into the branches of **syntax** and **morphology**. It is the study of the way in which words, and their component parts, combine to form phrases, clauses, sentences, and other units. ➤➤clause; morphology; parsing; phrase; rule 1; syntax.

grammar–translation method A method of foreign language teaching in which grammatical analysis and translation exercises have a dominant role. This was the main way in which Latin and Greek were traditionally taught in European schools, and the method was automatically introduced into the teaching of modern languages. The present-day emphasis on the need to teach the spoken language has reduced the use of the grammar–translation method (which was based almost exclusively on the study of reading and writing), but it is still widely practised. ➤➤direct method; language teaching; method.

grammatical Descriptive of a sentence (or part of a sentence) which conforms to the rules defined by a specific grammar of a language; also called **well-formed**. A preceding asterisk is commonly used to indicate that a sentence is incapable of being accounted for in this way – in other words, it is **ungrammatical** or **ill-formed** (e.g. *Sentence this is ill-formed*). ➤➤acceptable; semi-sentence.

grammatical gender ➤gender.

grammatical word A word with no lexical meaning, whose function is solely to express a grammatical relationship; also called a **form word**, **function word**, **structural word**, **functor**, or **empty word**. English examples include *the, of*, and *to* (as in *I want to see*). Far more frequent in a language are words which have a statable lexical meaning (e.g. *book, red, run*); these are called **lexical words**, **content words**, **contentives**, or **full words**.

graph The smallest separable segment in a stretch of writing or print. The notion includes letters, punctuation marks, and special symbols such as & and *. ➤➤graphology 1.

grapheme The smallest contrastive unit in the writing system of a language – a notion devised on analogy with that of the phoneme, used in the study of a language's sound system. In alphabetic languages, the chief graphemes are the letters. Graphemes are usually transcribed within angle brackets: ⟨e⟩, ⟨E⟩, ⟨,⟩, ⟨$⟩, etc. ➤➤graphology 1; letter; phoneme.

graphetics The study of the graphic substance of written or printed language – a term coined on analogy with phonetics. Graphic substance is the written or printed form of language, seen as a set of physically definable marks on a surface. ➤➤graph; graphology 1; phonetics; phonic substance.

graphic substance ➤graphetics.

graphic translatability The conversion of graphic expression from a medium with one range of resources into another in which the range is different. The problem arises between any two mediums (e.g. handwriting and typescript), but has become especially prominent in relation to the properties available in electronic displays, where often a very limited range of characters is available. For example, consideration needs to be given to the range of options available for the expression of emphasis on the screen (e.g. underlining, capitalization, typeface change, spacing, flashing lights, colour, movement), and to the implications of choosing one option rather than another. ➤➤typography.

graphology 1. The writing system of a language, or the linguistic study of that system, using analogous techniques to those devised for phonology. The data includes handwriting, print, and the forms displayed on computer screens. An interesting question is the extent to which there is 'graphic translatability' between these mediums: the range of options routinely available in print is rather different from the range of options routinely available on a screen (e.g. typefaces, special

Top stroke roofing over the whole word
Spirit of protection, patronizing

Arcs extending to the left
Fussiness, bad taste, vulgarity

Knotted
Toughness, thoroughness

With large loop
Pride in own achievements

Cross going down
*Disappointed, sulky, resentful,
low opinion of others*

Low crossing
Subordination

Cross broadening
Vigour, brutality

Cross sharpening
Malicious criticism

Hooks
Sulkiness, persistence, pigheadedness

Inverted, ending in an arc
Quick, ready liar

Loop at the top
Vanity, prejudice

Mounting stroke
Aggressive, ambitious

Cross at the top
Longing to get to the top, bossiness

Cross right over the top
*Idealism, high-flying dreams,
neglect of realities*

Cross to the right
*Quick thinking, thoughts running
before actions*

Cross to the left
Caution, procrastination

Missing cross
*Weakness, carelessness, lack of
consideration*

Cross in wavy line form
Sense of fun

Curved cross
Weak health

Cross going down and left
Material greed, rascal

Cross going up and left
Egoism

Down-stroke going up and left
Egoism

Twenty-two ways of writing *t*, and their interpretations – according to one
graphology manual.

symbols, spacing and layout conventions). ➤alphabet; graphetics; graphic translatability; orthography; script; writing. **2**. The study of handwriting to obtain information about a person's character and personality. The analyst is called a **graphologist**. Handwriting characteristics have been studied with reference to all kinds of normal and pathological states – as encountered in samples obtained from the famous (e.g. monarchs, criminals, authors, and politicians) or the ordinary (e.g. determining someone's employment suitability or marriage compatibility). The subject is controversial, given the limited evidence concerning the accuracy or reliability of its procedures and conclusions. ➤chirography.

grave accent /grɑːv/ The accent `, used to distinguish the sound values of letters in several languages, such as in French *mère* 'mother'. It is sometimes used in English, as in the word *learnèd* 'scholarly'. The symbol can also be used to mark certain kinds of pitch movement in a tone language or phonetic transcription. ➤accent 3.

Greece (population in 1995 estimated at 10,513,000) The official language is Greek (spoken by over 98% of the population). Other languages include Albanian, Arabic, Armenian, Bulgarian, Macedonian, Romanian, Romani, and Turkish. English is increasingly used for international trade and tourism. ➤Greek.

Greek An Indo-European language, spoken by *c*.12 million people in Greece, in the Greek part of Cyprus, in nearby areas of adjacent countries, and as an immigrant language in several countries of Europe and America. The modern language is found in two main varieties: **Dimotiki** ('popular language') is based on the spoken language, and is widely used in everyday communication; **Katharévusa** ('pure language') reflects the classical language more closely, and is found in official documents, newspapers, and other formal contexts. It is written in the Greek alphabet. The language is attested from around the 14th century BC, the earliest evidence coming from the inscriptions discovered on Crete, known as Linear B. The language of this period is known as **Mycenaean Greek**, which needs to be distinguished from the later **Classical** or **Ancient Greek**, dating from the 8th century BC, when texts came to be written in the Greek alphabet, notably the epic poems *Iliad* and *Odyssey*. Several major dialect groups are in evidence at that time (e.g. Doric, Ionic, Aeolic). The great period of classical drama, history, philosophy, and poetry lasted until the 4th century BC. A later variety, known as **Koiné** ('common') or **Hellenistic Greek**, was spoken throughout the eastern Mediterranean from the 4th century BC for *c*.800 years. In its written form, this was the language of the New Testament. A period of **Byzantine Greek** followed, until the 15th century, after which the language developed into **Modern Greek**, the foundation of the varieties in use today. ➤demotic; diglossia; formality; Greece; Indo-European.

Greenland ➤Denmark.

Greenlandic ➤Eskimo.

Grenada (population in 1995 estimated at 91,900) The official language is English.

Nearly half the population speak an English-based creole (Patwa) widely used throughout the Lesser Antilles. ➤➤creole; English.

grid game A visual word game which operates on the principle of building up words on a predetermined grid. Familiar examples include crossword puzzles, Scrabble, and a number of card or tile games in which letters have to be laid out according to certain rules (e.g. the game of Lexicon). ➤➤crossword.

Grimm's law A sound law first worked out in 1822 by Jakob Grimm (1785–1863) which shows the regular way in which the Germanic sound system diverged from that of Indo-European. Nine sets of correspondences were shown, which fell into a clear phonetic pattern. Voiced aspirates (a term which includes both aspirated plosives and fricatives) in Indo-European became voiced plosives in Germanic; voiced plosives became voiceless plosives; and voiceless plosives became voiceless aspirates. These relationships explain, for example, why words which begin with /p/ in Latin, Greek, or Sanskrit generally have /f/ in English (e.g. *pater – father*). Certain exceptions to this law were explained by later philologists. ➤➤sound change; Verner's law.

Grishun /'grɪʃn/ ➤Rhaetian.

groove A slight hollowing along the central line of the tongue, used in producing the type of fricative called a sibilant, in which the passage of air creates a sound with a higher frequency than other fricatives (e.g. [s]). The notion contrasts with **slit** fricatives (e.g. [f]), where there is no such groove. ➤➤fricative; sibilant.

grounding ➤foregrounding.

group ➤phrase.

group genitive ➤genitive case.

Guadeloupe (population in 1995 estimated at 431,000) The official language is French. Almost everyone speaks a French-based creole (Patois) widely used throughout the Lesser Antilles. ➤➤creole; French; Patwa.

Guam (population in 1995 estimated at 155,000) The official language is English, spoken by *c.*28,000 people as a first language (mostly US military personnel and their families). About half the population speak Chamorro, which is an important lingua franca; about 20% speak Tagalog. ➤➤English; lingua franca.

Guaraní /gwarə'niː/ A member of the Tupian family of Andean-Equatorial languages, spoken by *c.*4.6 million people in Paraguay (where it is an official language, along with Spanish), with some in nearby parts of Brazil. It is written in the Roman alphabet, and there is a growing popular literature. Guaraní is now the majority language of Paraguay, spoken by *c.*95% of the population, the only Indian language ever to achieve such a status. ➤➤Amerindian; Andean-Equatorial.

Guatemala (population in 1995 estimated at 10,557,000) The official language is

Spanish. There are c.20 Amerindian languages (several split into major dialects of uncertain mutual intelligibility) spoken by about half the population, notably Quiché (c.700,000), Cakchiquel, Quekchi (Kekchí), and Mam. English is increasingly used along with Spanish for international purposes. ➤Spanish.

Guinea (population in 1995 estimated at 6,543,000) The official language is French. There are c.30 local languages, notably Fula (Fuuta Jalon, spoken by c.40% of the population), Maninka (c.25%), and Susu (c.10%). ➤French.

Guinea-Bissau (population in 1995 estimated at 1,070,000) The official language is Portuguese. There are c.20 local languages, notably Balanta (spoken by c.30% of the population), Fulfulde (Fulacunda, c.20%), Mandinka, and Mandyak. A Portuguese-based creole (Crioulo) is spoken by c.150,000 as a first language, and a further 600,000 as a second language. English is increasingly used along with Portuguese for international purposes. ➤creole; Portuguese.

Gujarati /gʊʤə'rɑːtiː/ A language belonging to the western group of Indo-Aryan languages, spoken by c.43 million people chiefly in the state of Gujarat, western India (where it is an official regional language), with some 400,000 in Pakistan. It is written in the Gujarati alphabet, a variant of Devanagari. Literary texts date from the 12th century. Gujarati was the mother-tongue of M.K. Gandhi, who was born in Porbandar, Gujarat. A variety of the language is used in the Parsi religion. ➤Devanagari; Indo-Aryan.

Gullah /'gʌlə/ ➤Sea Islands Creole English.

Gur /gʊə/ ➤Voltaic.

Gurkhali /gɜː'kaliː/ ➤Nepali.

guttural A popular impressionistic label for a consonant sound made towards the back of the mouth, or for a low-pitched, throaty voice quality. It is not used in phonetic description, which instead uses such terms as velar, uvular, and pharyngeal – notions capable of more precise articulatory location. ➤articulation; pharyngeal; uvular; velar.

Guyana (population in 1995 estimated at 750,000) The official language is English. An English-based creole (Guyanese) is spoken by over 85% of the population. Several Indian languages are represented, notably Hindi. There are some speakers of creole Dutch, and c.10 Amerindian languages spoken by a few thousand. ➤creole; English.

Gypsy ➤Romani.

H

H ➤diglossia.

habitual Descriptive of a form (typically, a verb or adverb) which expresses the repetition of an action. English makes use of a wide range of adverbials which convey habitual meaning (e.g. *often, regularly, three times a week*). ➤➤adverb; verb.

Haida /'haɪdə/ ➤Na-Dene.

Haiti (population in 1995 estimated at 6,472,000) The official languages are French and Haitian. Haitian, a French-based creole, is the first language of almost the whole population. ➤➤creole; French.

half-close/half-open vowel ➤high vowel.

half-rhyme ➤pararhyme.

half-uncial ➤uncial.

Halliday, Michael ➤Firthian linguistics.

Hamito-Semitic /'hamɪtəʊ sə'mɪtɪk/ ➤Afro-Asiatic.

hanging indention ➤indention.

hapax legomenon /'hapaks lɪ'gɒmənən/ A word which occurs only once in a text, author, or extant corpus of a language; often shortened to **hapax**. The expression is from Greek, 'something said only once'. The word following *hapax* in the headword of this entry is itself a hapax in the present book. ➤➤corpus.

haplography /hap'lɒgrəfi:/ An omission made in a sequence of identical letters, as when *occurrence* is spelled *ocurrence* or *occurence*. It is one of the commonest kinds of spelling mistake. ➤➤spelling.

haplology /hap'lɒlədʒi:/ The omission of one or more sounds occurring in a sequence of similar articulations, as takes place in the common colloquial pronunciation of such words as *library* /'laɪbri:/ and *probably* /'prɒbli:/. The process is common in the study of historical sound change; for example, Old English *Englalond* became Modern English *England*. ➤➤elision; sound change.

hard palate ➤palate.

hard sign A symbol (ъ) used in the Cyrillic alphabet to show that the preceding sound is 'hard' – that is, not palatalized. In modern transcriptions of Russian, it is often replaced by an apostrophe. It contrasts with the **soft sign** (ь), which shows that the preceding sound is 'soft' – palatalized. ➤Cyrillic; palate.

hare lip ➤cleft palate speech.

harmonic ➤fundamental frequency.

harmony A type of assimilation which takes place when sounds of a particular class (consonants or vowels) come to share certain features with other sounds of the same class, elsewhere in a word or phrase; usually classified into **consonant harmony** and **vowel harmony**. The sounds are not adjacent to each other, but are often within the same word – for example, a front vowel in the first syllable might require the presence of a front vowel in the second syllable, or the occurrence of one consonant with lip rounding might require that other consonants in the word are also lip rounded. Languages which display harmony as a systematic feature of their sound system include Turkish and Hungarian. When young children are learning to talk, their early efforts often display harmony – as can be seen from one English child's version of *window*, /wawa/, which displays both vowel and consonant harmony. ➤assimilation; consonant; front sound; rounding; vowel.

Hausa /ˈhaʊsə, ˈhaʊzə/ A member of the Chadic family of languages, spoken by *c*.22 million people as a first language, and a further 15 million as a second language, chiefly in Nigeria (*c*.19 million), Niger, and nearby parts of Cameroon, Chad, and Ghana. It is an official regional language in northern Nigeria, and widely used as a lingua franca throughout West Africa. It has the largest number of speakers of any language in Africa below the Sahara. Literary Hausa, based on the Kano dialect, was written in the Arabic alphabet from the 16th century, but this has been largely replaced by the Roman alphabet in the present century. It is the only Chadic language to have a written form. ➤Chadic.

Hawaiian Islands (population in 1990 estimated at 1,243,000) The official language is English. About half the population speak an English-based creole, which is receiving increased official and literary recognition. Hawaiian (an Austronesian language) is spoken as a first language by *c*.1000 people in the state of Hawaii, where it has some official status, and by a further *c*.8000 as a second language. ➤creole; English.

head ➤endocentric construction; headline.

header ➤headline.

headline A heading which indicates in summary form the subject-matter of a piece of text, often set in larger type than the rest of the text; in typography, also called the **head** or **header**. The notion is well-known in the context of newspapers. In book publishing, it refers to the heading set at the top of most pages (but not over chapter openings); when this heading is the same throughout a chapter or section, it is usually called a **running head**. ➤typography.

headword The item which occurs at the beginning of a dictionary entry. It is essentially an abstract representation, or **lemma**, subsuming all the formal variations which may occur: *walk*, for example, subsumes *walks*, *walking*, and *walked*. In the present entry, the headword is *headword* (and, by implication, *headwords*). ➤lexicography.

hearing loss ➤deafness.

Hebrew A Semitic language spoken by *c*.4.5 million people in Israel (where it is the official language), and used with varying levels of fluency, often only in religious contexts, by Jewish people all over the world (*c*.14 million in 1997). It is written from right to left in a 22-letter alphabet. Hebrew was spoken throughout ancient Palestine until about the 3rd century BC (when it gave way to Aramaic), but continued in use as the liturgical and literary language of Judaism. The classical written form was revived as a spoken language in the 19th century, associated with the Zionist movement – **Modern Hebrew**, a unique linguistic development. Written records date from the 2nd century BC, and the period of **Classical** (or **Biblical**) **Hebrew** continues until around the 3rd century BC. **Mishnaic Hebrew** is a later form of the language used in the collection of rabbinical writings (the Mishna) compiled *c*. AD 200, and later expanded (as the Gemara), the whole set of commentaries comprising the Talmud. Medieval Hebrew is the form of the written language as it developed in religion and scholarship between the 6th and 13th centuries, when it was much in contact with other languages in Europe and the Middle East. Several varieties and mixed forms of the language have since developed (e.g. Yiddish), along with the spread of Judaism around the world. ➤Israel; Semitic; Yiddish.

hermeneutics /hɜːmən'juːtɪks/ The study of the principles and methodology involved in textual interpretation. The subject developed as a branch of theology, studying the principles of biblical exegesis, but it later broadened to include literary and other texts. The term is also used in sociolinguistics, where it refers to the task of interpreting specific instances of discourse. ➤exegesis; *cartoon*, p. 147.

hertz The unit for measuring sound vibration; abbreviated as **Hz**. It has replaced an earlier measure, which used the notion of 'cycles per second'. The name derives from German physicist Heinrich Hertz (1857–94), the discoverer of radio waves. ➤frequency; intonation.

hesitation A pause or meaningless noise (typically, *er* or *erm* in English) which breaks up the flow of speech. Hesitations have a variety of functions: some indicate that the speaker is thinking what to say next; some express an attitude, such as doubt or uncertainty. ➤pause.

heterography /hetə'rɒgrəfiː/ ➤homography 1.

heteronyms /'hetərənɪmz/ Words which display partial homonymy, differing in meaning, but identical in form in one medium only (speech or writing). *Threw* and

'You mean that's it – this one went to market and this one didn't?' (**hermeneutics**)

through are heteronyms, identical in sound but not in spelling, as are *tear* (in clothing) and *tear* (from the eye), identical in spelling but not in sound. ➤homonyms.

heterophemy /hetəˈrɒfəmiː/ An unintentional error in spoken or written language; the term derives from Greek words meaning 'other' and 'speech'. Such errors may occur in everyday speech (as when we have a slip of the tongue) or in clinical conditions (such as aphasia). ➤malapropism.

heterotopy /hetəˈrɒtəpiː/ A misplaced sound during speech, especially when someone is speaking very quickly; the term derives from Greek words meaning 'other' and 'place'. It may occur both in everyday speech and in certain clinical conditions (notably, cluttering). ➤cluttering.

hexameter ➤metrics.

hierarchy A classification of linguistic units which recognizes a series of successively subordinate levels. An example is the analysis of a sentence into constituents, or the relationship between different linguistic levels, such as sentence, clause, phrase, word, and morpheme. ➤level 3; morpheme.

hieratic /haɪəˈratɪk/ ➤demotic.

hieroglyphic /haɪərəˈglɪfɪk/ A writing system which uses mainly pictorial symbols; also called **hieroglyphics**. The name comes from the Greek, meaning 'sacred carving', so called because of its prominent use in temples, tombs, and other special

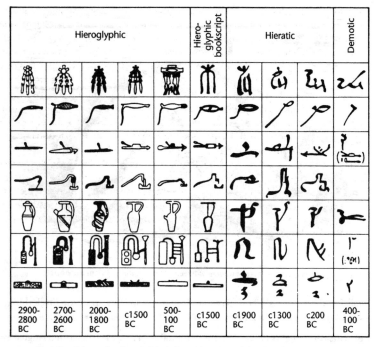

Hieroglyphic					Hiero-glyphic bookscript	Hieratic			Demotic
2900-2800 BC	2700-2600 BC	2000-1800 BC	c1500 BC	500-100 BC	c1500 BC	c1900 BC	c1300 BC	c200 BC	400-100 BC

Egyptian **hieroglyphs**, and their later hieratic and demotic forms.

places. It is especially applied to the form of pictography developed in Egypt *c.*3000 BC, though other systems can be found in China, the Indus Valley, Central America, and elsewhere. The units of the writing system are called **hieroglyphs**. ➤Egyptian; Mayan; pictogram; Rosetta Stone.

high tone ➤tone.

high variety ➤diglossia.

high vowel A vowel produced in the upper region of the mouth, with the tongue close to the palate or velum, such as [i] or [u]; also called a **close vowel**. It contrasts with a **low vowel**, which is produced with the body of the tongue relatively low in the mouth, such as [a]; also called an **open vowel**. A further distinction is sometimes made with a **mid** or **medial** vowel, such as [e], which is articulated between these two extremes. Another classification recognizes two intermediate qualities, called **mid-close** or **half-close**, such as [e], and **mid-open** or **half-open**, such as [ɛ]. This dimension of vowel classification is strongly related to the close/open position of the lower jaw. ➤central sound; tongue; vowel.

Hindi /'hɪndiː/ A member of the Midland group of Indo-Aryan languages, spoken as a first language by *c.*180 million people throughout India, and by a similar number as a second language in India. It is also used by significant numbers in South Africa (*c.*890,000), Mauritius (*c.*685,000), Bangladesh (*c.*346,000), and many other countries, so that the total for all first and second language users worldwide is now *c.*420 million. It is a union language, along with English, in the Republic of India (1995 population, 944 million), the official language of a number of Indian states, and a lingua franca in India for about half the population. There is little structural difference between Hindi and Urdu, and the two varieties are often grouped together under the single label **Hindi/Urdu**, sometimes abbreviated to **Hirdu**, and formerly often called **Hindustani**. However, there is a considerable cultural distance, Hindi being the variety in use by Hindus (Urdu by Muslims), and displaying the marked influence of Sanskrit in its vocabulary. A literary language dates from the 7th century AD. The variety known as Braj Bhasa was the chief literary medium between the 15th and 18th centuries, but the modern literary language is based on a different variety, known as Khari Boli. It is written in the Devanagari alphabet. ➤➤Devanagari; India; Indo-Aryan; lingua franca; Urdu.

Hindustani /hɪndʊ'stɑːniː/ ➤Hindi; Urdu.

hiragana /hɪrə'gɑːnə/ ➤kana.

Hirdu /'hɪəduː/ ➤Hindi; Urdu.

Hiri Motu /'hɪriː 'məʊtuː/ ➤Motu.

historical linguistics ➤diachronic linguistics; philology.

historic(al) present The use of a present tense form while narrating events which happened in the past; for example, *Three weeks ago I'm walking down this road, when I see Smithers coming towards me*. . . This usage is common in contexts where the speaker wishes to convey a sense of drama, immediacy, or urgency. ➤➤tense 1.

Hittite /'hɪtaɪt/ ➤Anatolian; ideogram; p. 156.

Hokan /'həʊkn/ A group of *c.*20 Amerindian languages spoken by small numbers in parts of western and south-western USA, and eastern Mexico. It includes some North American and some Meso-American families of languages, and thus forms part of a linguistic continuity between the Americas. Tlapanec is the only language with over 20,000 speakers. Several Hokan languages have become extinct in recent times. When written down, they use the Roman alphabet. ➤➤Amerindian.

Holland ➤Netherlands, The.

holograph /'hɒləgraf/ A document which is entirely written in the handwriting of its author. Informal letters are the commonest examples of holographic writing, but certain formal documents may also be produced in this way, notably wills (in some legal systems). ➤➤paleography.

holophrase /'hɒləfreɪz/ A word which expresses the meaning of a whole sentence. It is a grammatically unstructured utterance, characteristic of the earliest stage of language learning in children, typically appearing between 12 and 18 months. For example, a child saying *more* might mean 'I want some more'. Holophrastic utterances sometimes contain several elements which would be separate words in the adult language, such as *allgone*. ➤➤acquisition; sentence.

homographs /'hɒməgrafs/ Words which have the same spelling but different meanings, as in *wind* ('which blows' vs. 'a clock'). Homography is one of the main types of homonymy. ➤➤homonyms.

homography /hə'mɒgrəfi:/ **1.** An orthographic system where there is a one-to-one correspondence between symbols and sounds, as in some alphabets. It contrasts with **heterography**, where the system lacks this correspondence. The clearest example of a homographic system is the International Phonetic Alphabet. ➤➤International Phonetic Association; orthography. **2.** ➤homographs.

homonyms /'hɒmənɪmz/ Words which have the same form but different meanings, as in *ear* ('of a body' or 'of corn'). Partial homonymy (**heteronymy**) takes place when the identity is within a single medium, as in **homophony** (for sounds) and **homography** (for spellings). When there is ambiguity between homonyms, a **homonymic clash** is said to have occurred. ➤➤heteronyms; homographs; homophenes; homophones; polysemy.

homophenes /'hɒməfi:nz/ Words which are visually identical, when seen on the lips; examples are *fan* and *van*. The notion has developed chiefly in relation to the study of deaf communication. ➤➤homonyms; speech reading.

homophones /'hɒməfəʊnz/ Words which have the same pronunciation but different meanings, as in *rode* and *rowed*. Homophony is one of the main types of homonymy. ➤➤homonyms.

Honduras (population in 1995 estimated at 5,628,000) The official language is Spanish, used by most of the population. There are a few Amerindian languages spoken by perhaps 90,000 people, and a few thousand speak an English-based creole. English is used along with Spanish for international purposes. ➤➤Spanish.

Hong Kong (population at the time of the change of rule in 1997 estimated at 6,083,000) The official languages are English and Chinese. Yue Chinese (Cantonese) is spoken by *c.*98% of the population. A few thousand speak a Portuguese-based creole (Macanese), derived from Macao, and there are several immigrant languages, notably Vietnamese and Philippines languages. ➤➤Chinese; creole; English.

honorific /ɒnə'rɪfɪk/ A grammatical form used to express a level of politeness or respect, related to the social status of the participants in a conversation. Many languages of the Far East, such as Japanese, have a well-developed honorific system, containing several levels of politeness, and often distinguishing between male and female participants. ➤➤Japanese; politeness phenomena.

hortative /ˈhɔːtətɪv/ ➤mood.

Hottentot ➤Khoisan.

humanistic Descriptive of approaches to foreign language teaching which emphasize the need for the student to develop self-awareness, sensitivity to the feelings of others, and a sense of human values. Such approaches require students to be actively involved in understanding the processes of learning, as they work with a foreign language. ➤➤community language learning; silent way; suggestopedia.

Hungarian The chief language of the Ugric branch of the Finno-Ugric family, spoken by *c*.14.5 million people, chiefly in Hungary (*c*.10 million), Romania (*c*.2 million), the Czech and Slovak republics, Yugoslavia (in Voivodina, where it has official status), and Ukraine; also called **Magyar**. It is written in the Roman alphabet, modified with certain diacritics (notably, the use of the acute accent to mark long vowels, as in ó, and the double acute accent to mark front long rounded vowels, as in ő). A characteristic feature of the sound system is vowel harmony. A literary tradition dates from the early 13th century, but a standard orthography did not emerge until the 16th century. ➤➤Finno-Ugric; Hungary; vowel.

Hungary (population in 1995 estimated at 10,220,000) The official language is Hungarian, spoken by *c*.98% of the population. Other languages include German, Romani, varieties of Serbo-Croatian, and Slovene. English and German are used for international purposes. ➤➤Hungarian.

Hutterite German ➤German.

hybrid A word composed of elements from different languages; for example, *television* comprises elements from both Latin and Greek. ➤➤neologism.

hydronymy /haɪˈdrɒnəmiː/ The study of the names of rivers, lakes, and other bodies of water. It is a domain within onomastics. ➤➤onomastics.

hyperbole /haɪˈpɜːbəliː/ A figure of speech which involves emphatic exaggeration. Often recognized in literature (as in Hamlet's *forty thousand brothers could not, with all their quantity of love, make up my sum*), it is far more often encountered in everyday conversation (*where there are millions of examples*). ➤➤figurative language.

hypercorrection The use of a linguistic form which goes beyond the norm of a target variety, because of the speaker's desire to be correct, and thus results in a form which is not part of the target variety; also called **hyperurbanism** or **overcorrection**. This usually happens when a nonstandard speaker tries to use the standard language or a prestige accent. An example is the first vowel of *butcher*, which is sometimes pronounced with an open unrounded articulation (using the vowel of *cup*, /ʌ/) instead of with a close rounded articulation (using the vowel of *put*, /ʊ/) by speakers who have noticed the distinctive quality of the /ʌ/ vowel in Received Pronunciation and are trying to reproduce it. RP speakers, however, use /ʊ/ in *butcher*. ➤➤Received Pronunciation; standard.

hypernasality Excessive nasal resonance in speech, usually the result of a clinical condition. It contrasts with **hyponasality**, which is the lack of normal nasal resonance in speech. Cleft palate speech, for example, is typically hypernasal. The speech of someone suffering from a bad cold is typically hyponasal. ➤➤nasal.

hypernym /'haɪpənɪm/ ➤hyponymy.

hyperurbanism ➤hypercorrection.

hyphen A punctuation mark which indicates a division within a word. Such divisions take place at the end of a line of print, where a word will not fit without a break (*exclam- ation*), and to mark the parts of a complex word, such as a compound (*mother-in-law*) or certain prefixed forms (*ex-husband*). The conventions governing use are not clear-cut, however, in either function. Some dictionaries print guidelines for word division, but there is often disagreement about what counts as a 'natural' dividing point for a word (to continue the above example, should it be *excla- mation* or *exclama- tion*?), and different practices will be encountered between the UK and USA, and between publishers. Similarly, there is widespread divergence over the use of the hyphen within compound words: one will find all three possibilities – *flowerpot* (written **solid**), *flower-pot*, and *flower pot* (written **open**). Consistency is important in formal work, and publishing houses make recommendations about how to handle such forms in their style guides. ➤➤punctuation.

hypocoristic /haɪpəkə'rɪstɪk/ A pet name, such as *Willie* or *honey*. Ingenious and bizarre coinages may be encountered, as seen in the love messages published in some British national newspapers on St Valentine's Day. ➤➤Valentine.

hyponasality ➤hypernasality; nasal.

hyponymy /haɪ'pɒnəmi:/ A semantic relationship between specific and general lexical items, such that the former is included in the latter; for example, *dog* is a **hyponym** of *animal*, and *animal* is a **hypernym** of *dog*. The lexical items which are included within the same superordinate term are said to be **co-hyponyms** – *dog*, *cat*, *cow*, etc., with reference to *animal*. ➤➤incompatibility; lexeme; sense.

hypostatize /haɪ'pɒstətaɪz/ ➤personification.

hypotactic /haɪpə'taktɪk/ Descriptive of a dependent grammatical relationship, especially one where the constituents are linked by subordinating conjunctions. A contrast is drawn with **paratactic** constructions, where the linkage, between constituents of equal status, is conveyed solely by juxtaposition and punctuation/ intonation. *The butcher, whose name is Mr Jones, has got married* illustrates **hypotaxis**;

The butcher, Mr Jones, has got married illustrates **parataxis**. ➤coordination; subordination.

hypothetical ➤conditional.

Hz An abbreviation of **hertz**.

I

iamb /'aɪam/ ►foot.

Iberian /aɪ'bɪərɪən/ A non-Indo-European language spoken in parts of southern and south-eastern Spain, especially around the Ebro River, in pre-Roman times. It may formerly have been used throughout a much wider area of western Europe. It is known mainly through inscriptions on stones and artefacts, few of which have been interpreted. Its 28-letter script showed the influence of both the Greek and the Phoenician alphabets. Some scholars have argued that Basque is a descendant of Iberian, but the limited evidence is not strong. ►Basque; Indo-European; Isolate.

Ibibio /ɪbə'bi:əʊ/ ►Efik.

Ibo ►Igbo.

IC An abbreviation of **immediate constituent.**

ICAME /'aɪkeɪm/ An abbreviation of **International Computer Archive of Modern English**.

ICE ►International Corpus of English.

Iceland (population in 1995 estimated at 268,000) The official language is Icelandic, spoken by the whole population. English is the language used for international purposes. ►Icelandic.

Icelandic A North Germanic language, a member of the West Scandinavian group, spoken by over 260,000 people in Iceland, where it is the official language, with a further *c.*15,000 in Canada and the USA. **Old Icelandic** (the literary language of medieval Iceland) came from Norway in the 9th century, and is best known as the language of the medieval sagas, and of the two 13th century poetry and prose compilations called the *Edda*. The modern language has retained many of the features of the older period, so that Icelanders today can still read the ancient sagas with little difficulty (unlike the situation in English, where special training is needed to read the texts of early Middle or Old English). It is written in the Roman alphabet. ►Iceland; Scandinavian.

iconicity /aɪkə'nɪsɪti:/ A close physical relationship between a linguistic sign (typically, a word) and the entity or process in the world to which it refers. A particularly clear example is a map, where the signs represent real-world features in a one-to-one way. Iconicity is not a central feature of speech or writing, though instances of iconic relationships do occur, as in the case of sound symbolism. ➤➤onomatopoeia; sign 1; sound symbolism.

ictus /'ɪktʊs/ The stressed syllable in a metrical unit. In *The curfew tolls the knell . . .* , there is an ictus on *cur*, *tolls*, and *knell*. ➤➤foot; metrics.

ideation /aɪdi:'eɪʃn/ The cognitive process of forming ideas and relationships of meaning, prior to their formulation in language. **Ideational meaning** is often contrasted with other types of meaning (e.g. emotive meaning), in semantic analysis. ➤➤referential language.

ideogram /'ɪdi:əʊgram/ A symbol used in a writing system to represent a whole word or concept; also called an **ideograph**. Ideographic writing is usually distinguished as a later development from pictographic. Ideograms have an abstract or conventional meaning, no longer displaying a clear pictorial link with external reality. Examples include a foot shape representing 'go' or a sun symbol representing 'wisdom'. ➤➤logogram; pictogram; p. 156.

ideograph /'ɪdi:əʊgraf/ ➤ideogram.

idioglossia /ɪdi:əʊ'glɒsɪə/ An invented form of speech whose meaning is known only to the inventor(s); also called **autonomous speech** or **cryptophasia**. An example is the idiosyncratic form of communication which sometimes emerges spontaneously between twins – though 'twin language' is not usually consciously invented, being generally only a deviant form of the local mother-tongue. ➤➤glossolalia.

idiolect /'ɪdi:əʊlekt/ The linguistic system of an individual speaker. Idiolects are 'personal dialects', arising from the way people have learned slightly different usages in pronunciation, grammar, vocabulary, and style. ➤➤dialect; lect.

idiom A sequence of words which is semantically and often syntactically restricted, so that it functions as a single unit. The meanings of the individual words cannot be combined to produce the meaning of the idiomatic expression as a whole. For example, the meanings of *go*, *fly*, and *kite* cannot account for the use of the sentence *Go fly a kite!*, in its sense of 'Go away' or Don't be silly'. ➤➤lexeme; set expression; stereotype 1.

Ido /'i:dəʊ/ An artificial language created in 1907 by either French Esperantist Louis de Beaufront or French philosopher Louis Couturat. It is a modified version of Esperanto; its name means 'derived from' in Esperanto. ➤➤artificial language.

Igbo /'i:bəʊ/ A language spoken by *c*.17 million people in south-east Nigeria; also spelled **Ibo**. It has official status in the area, and is written with the Roman alphabet. Since the 1970s it has been increasingly used as a second language. Recent research has proposed that, along with other former Eastern Kwa languages, it be placed within the Benue-Congo group. ➤➤Benue-Congo; Kwa; Nigeria.

Ideographic symbols in Hittite. Uncertain interpretations are marked with a question-mark. ➤➤ideogram.

Ijaw ➤Ijo.

Ijo /'iːdʒɔː/ A language spoken by c.1.7 million people in south-east Nigeria, in the area of the Niger River delta; also spelled **Ijaw**. It has official status in the region, and is written in the Roman alphabet. Formerly classified as a Kwa language, it is now considered to be a separate cluster of languages, **Ijoid**, within the Niger-Congo family. ➤➤Kwa; Niger-Congo.

Ijoid ➤Ijo.

ill-formed ➤grammatical.

illiteracy ➤literacy.

illocutionary act A speech act which is performed by a speaker by virtue of the utterance having been made; for example, promising, commanding, or arresting. As soon as someone says *I promise . . .* , a promise has been made. As soon as someone with the right kind of status says *I baptize you . . .* , a person is baptized. The **illocutionary force** of such acts contrasts with the function of **locutionary acts**, where there is no such consequence – as in the sentences of the present entry, which are simply meaningful utterances. A further contrast can be drawn with **perlocutionary acts**, where the acts are defined with reference to the effects they have on the hearer. A perlocutionary effect can be seen in the example of an utterance intended simply to state a fact (e.g. *There have been a lot of burglaries round here recently*), which actually results in the listener becoming frightened. ➤➤performative; speech act.

Ilocano or **Ilokano** /ɪləˈkɑːnəʊ/ An Austronesian language spoken by *c.*8 million people in the Philippines, with a few in the USA; also called **Iloko**. It is written in the Roman alphabet, and has some use as a lingua franca in the north of the country. ➤➤Austronesian; Philippines.

imagery Words or sentences which produce clear or vivid mental pictures; concrete nouns, for example, are highly imageable, whereas abstract nouns are not. In the context of language teaching, high imageability may be a desirable feature of sentences being presented to the learner, as there is some evidence that they are easier to remember. In the context of literature, the term generally has a much more restricted meaning, referring to the use of metaphors, similes, and other figures of speech. ➤➤figurative language.

imitation In the context of language, the copying of a linguistic form or pattern while learning a language. The notion is important both in first language acquisition by children and in learning a foreign language, where the ability to imitate is seen to be rather different from the ability to use the language spontaneously. ➤➤language learning.

immediate constituent ➤constituent.

immersion Descriptive of a bilingual programme where children who speak only one language enter a school in which the foreign language is the only medium of instruction. The children are 'immersed' in the new language for a particular period of time – **total** immersion, if the language is used throughout the school day, **partial** immersion if it is for only part of the day. The advantages of this method have often been claimed (such as in French-speaking Canada), but the approach has its critics. ➤➤bilingualism.

impediment (of speech) ➤speech defect.

imperative A grammatical mood recognized in languages where the verb is inflected, used in the expression of commands. Different sets of endings distinguished imperative from indicative and subjunctive moods in Latin, for example. In English, the imperative form of the verb, as in *Look!*, contrasts with the indicative form, which permits an *-s* ending in the 3rd person singular (*looks*). The term is used in the description of sentence and clause types as well as of verb forms. ➤mood.

imperfect In some languages, a tense form which expresses such meanings as duration or continuity in past time. Latin had an imperfect tense: *amabam* 'I was loving/used to love'. ➤past tense; perfect.

imperfective ➤perfect.

impersonal Descriptive of a construction or verb with an unspecified agent, such as *It's raining*. The notion was prominent in Latin grammar, which recognized such constructions as *Miseret me* (literally, 'it pities me' – that is, 'I pity') and *Eis licet hoc facere* (literally, 'To them it is pleasing this to do' – that is, 'They are pleased to do this'). Impersonal verbs could be used only in the 3rd person singular and in the infinitive, and never with a personal subject. ➤agent; verb.

implicational universal ➤universal.

implicature An implication or suggestion deduced from the form of an utterance. A **conversational implicature** uses the cooperative principles which govern the efficiency of conversations; for example, if someone says *Look, the train!*, while approaching a railway station, the implication is 'We must hurry', and not, say, 'What a lovely colour it has'. A **conventional implicature** is simply attached by convention to particular expressions, as when *What's yours?*, said at a bar, implies 'I'm buying you a drink'. ➤cooperative principle.

implosive Descriptive of a type of consonant produced with the glottalic airstream mechanism. A closure is made in the vocal tract while the vocal folds are brought together. The glottis is then lowered, reducing air pressure in the tract. When the closure is released, an ingressive airstream results, producing a range of sounds, typically voiced, which can be heard for example in Ibo and several other African languages. ➤glottalic.

impressionistic transcription ➤transcription.

inanimate ➤animate.

inceptive /ɪnˈseptɪv/ A type of aspect, referring to a verb in which an inflection is used to express the meaning of 'beginning of an action', 'be on the point of'. Latin, for example, had a verb ending *-escere* which expressed this meaning. ➤aspect.

inclusive Descriptive of a first person dual or plural pronoun where the addressee, as well as the speaker, is included (e.g. *we*, meaning 'I and you'). An **exclusive** pronoun does not include the person being addressed. The contrast can be seen clearly in the pidgin language, Tok Pisin, where *yumi* ('you + me') is inclusive and *mipela* ('me + fellow') is exclusive. ➤➤disjunction; pidgin; pronoun.

inclusive language Language which attempts to avoid a bias towards a particular sex, race, or other section of society in its forms of expression. The notion has been especially found in relation to the modern concern to avoid sexual stereotypes, where it is often referred to as **nonsexist language**. For example, since the 1970s many speakers and writers of English have tried to find alternatives for the generic use of *him* in such contexts as *If there's a doctor in the village, would you ask him to call?* – perhaps by using *him/her* or *her/him*, or by rephrasing the whole construction to avoid the issue. Inclusive lexical items (e.g. *salesman* becoming *sales assistant*) are now commonplace, and often legally obligatory – in advertisements, for example, where equality of opportunity is critical. New publications using inclusive language have continued to appear in the 1990s, though often accompanied by controversy (notably when traditional prayers or forms of worship are reinterpreted). Although not all the proposals for a new inclusive language have met with acceptance (e.g. the invention of new sex-neutral 3rd-person pronouns, such as *hesh* or *sho*), a genuine sensitivity about the issue is now evident, at least in educated usage, in many countries. ➤➤sexist language.

inclusive *or* ➤disjunction.

incompatibility A sense relation between a set of lexical items, where the choice of one item excludes the use of all the other items from that set; for example, *This piece of fruit is a banana* excludes *apple, orange, plum*, and other items from the class of fruit. We may not say *This piece of fruit is a banana and an apple*. The items in the set are incompatible with each other. On the other hand, we may say *This piece of fruit is a banana and a gift* – the items *gift* and *banana* are compatible. ➤➤hyponymy.

incorporating language ➤typology of language.

indefinite ➤definiteness.

indefinite vowel ➤shwa.

indentation ➤indention.

indention /ɪnˈdenʃn/ Beginning a line of writing or print further in from the margin than the rest of the passage; also called **indentation**. It is an important device for showing the beginning of a paragraph. In some page designs, **reverse** or **hanging indention** is employed, where most of the passage is indented – a common device in dictionaries and encyclopedias, where there is a need to make the headwords stand out. ➤➤paragraph.

independent clause ➤clause.

indexical features A feature of speech or writing which reveals the personal characteristics of a language user, such as age, personality, or sex; examples include voice quality and handwriting. In a more general sense, the term refers to any membership-identifying characteristic of a social group, such as a distinctive tone of voice or set of lexical expressions. ►idiolect.

indexicality ►deixis.

India (population in 1995 estimated at 944,157,000) The official union languages are Hindi (spoken as a first or second language by nearly half the population) and English (spoken as a second language by c.3%). English is used for international purposes. Fourteen other languages have official status in certain regions (states in parentheses): Assamese (c.14.5 million, Assam), Bengali (c.67 million, West Bengal), Gujarati (c.43 million, Gujarat), Kannada (c.34 million, Karnataka), Kashmiri (c.4 million, Kashmir), Malayalam (c.34 million, Kerala), Marathi (c.65 million, Maharashtra), Oriya (c.30 million, Orissa), Panjabi (West and East, c.60 million, Panjab), Sindhi (c.2.7 million), Tamil (c.60 million, Tamil Nadu), Telugu (c.67 million, Andhra Pradesh), Urdu (c.46 million), and Sanskrit. Over 1600 languages are officially recognized as being spoken in India, though only about half of these are in regular daily use, and only c.400 are native to India. The language families represented are mainly Indo-European (c.500 million) and Dravidian (c.160 million), with some Tibeto-Burman, Mon-Khmer, and Munda languages. With such linguistic diversity, Hindi/Urdu has come to be widely used as a lingua franca. ►►Devanagari; English; Hindi; lingua franca; Sanskrit.

Indic ►Indo-Aryan.

indicative A type of mood recognized in languages where the verb is inflected, used in the expression of statements and questions; for example, the indicative mood in Latin contrasts with the imperative and the subjunctive. The term may be used with reference to verb forms or to clause and sentence types. ►►mood.

indirect object ►object.

indirect speech ►direct speech.

indirect speech act An utterance whose linguistic form does not directly reflect its communicative purpose. In a classroom, for example, the utterance addressed by a teacher to a child *There's a book on the floor*, which is in the form of a statement, would normally need to be interpreted as a command or request to pick the book up. ►►speech act.

Indo-Aryan A group of over 200 Indo-European languages, forming a branch of the Indo-Iranian family, spoken by c.825 million people in the northern and central parts of the Indian subcontinent; also called **Indic**. On a geographical basis, they may be divided into a Midland group, including Hindi/Urdu, Bihari, and Rajasthani (sometimes classed as a separate group); an Eastern group, which includes Assamese, Bengali, and Oriya; Western and South-western groups, which include Konkani, Maldivian, Marathi, and Sinhalese; and a North-western group, which includes

Panjabi, Sindhi, Lahnda, the Dardic languages (sometimes classified as a separate group), and the Pahari languages. Romani is also a member of this family. The early forms of Indo-Aryan, dating from *c*.1000 BC, are collectively referred to as Sanskrit. Later forms, the Prakrits, were the medium of Buddhist and Jain literature for a thousand years. ➤➤Assamese; Bengali; Bihari; Dardic; Hindi; Indo-Iranian; Konkani; Lahnda; Maldivian; Marathi; Oriya; Pahari; Panjabi; Prakrit; Rajasthani; Romani; Sanskrit; Sindhi; Sinhalese; Urdu.

Indo-European A major family of nearly 400 languages which spread throughout Europe and southern Asia in the fourth millennium BC, and which is now found, as a result of colonialism, all over the world. The parent language, **Proto-Indo-European**, is traditionally thought to have been spoken in many dialects by a seminomadic population living in the steppe region to the north of the Black Sea. These people moved west to Europe, and east to Iran and India, around the beginning of the Bronze Age, the different daughter languages being well established by 1000 BC, when Greek, Anatolian, and Indo-Iranian languages are in evidence. The family has 10 branches, though in the case of Albanian, Armenian, Greek, and Tocharian, the branches are represented by a single language. The total number of speakers is over 2500 million. The existence of Proto-Indo-European was postulated at the end of the 18th century, following a comparison of Sanskrit and European languages. In the 1980s, a controversial alternative view about the Indo-European homeland was proposed by British archeologist Colin Renfrew, who argued for a much earlier point of origin (*c*.7000 BC) in Anatolia (Asia Minor). ➤➤Albanian; Anatolian; Armenian; Balto-Slavic; Celtic; Germanic; Greek; Indo-Iranian; Italic; Tocharian.

Indo-Iranian A group of languages which make up the easternmost branch of the Indo-European language family. It comprises two smaller groups, known as **Indo-Aryan** (or **Indic**) and **Iranian**. ➤➤Indo-Aryan; Indo-European; Iranian.

Indonesia (population in 1995 estimated at 194,956,000) The official language is Indonesian (Bahasa Indonesia), spoken by over 20 million as a first language, but by *c*.70% of the population as a second language. Over 700 languages are found, most with very small numbers; many, moreover, are of uncertain status (as languages or dialects). Among the major languages of the country are Achinese, Balinese, Batak, Buginese, Chinese, Javanese, Madurese, Malay, and Sundanese. In such a linguistically diverse region, lingua francas are critical, Indonesian and Malay being the most widely used in this function. English is the chief language for international purposes. ➤➤lingua franca; Malay.

Indonesian ➤Malay.

Indo-Pacific A family of *c*.750 languages spoken by *c*.3.5 million people in the island of New Guinea and the islands to the immediate east and west; also called **Papuan**. Two other small groups of languages are sometimes included within this family, despite their geographical distance from the main group: Andamanese, spoken by a few hundred people in the Andaman Islands in the Bay of Bengal, and Tasmanian, formerly spoken in the island of Tasmania to the south of Australia, which died out towards the end of the 19th century. There is still a great deal of ignorance about the number and type of languages in this family, as little is known about the many tribes who live in the more inaccessible areas of New Guinea. There is nowhere to compare with the multilingual diversity of this island, which has a geographical area of only *c*.300,000 square miles, yet contains between 700 and 800 languages from this and the Austronesian family. ➤➤Austronesian.

infelicitous utterance ➤felicity conditions.

inferior ➤subscript.

infinitive The nonfinite form of the verb which in many languages is cited as the verb's basic form (e.g. *go, walk*). In English, this form may be used alone (the **bare** or **zero infinitive**) or with the particle *to* (the ***to-infinitive***). Different verbs make use of these alternatives: compare *The policeman saw the man leave* and *The policeman told the man to leave*. Inserting an adverb between *to* and the infinitive (the **split infinitive**) is frowned upon by purists, though this construction has a long history in written English, and is often the most acceptable rhythmical alternative in speech (as in the famous *to boldly go* example from the TV series *Star Trek*). ➤➤finite; purism; verb.

infix ➤affix.

inflected/inflecting/inflectional language ➤typology of language.

inflection 1. An affix whose function is to signal a grammatical relationship, such as plural, past tense, or 3rd person; in European languages, typically encountered as **word endings**. It does not alter the word class of the stem to which it is attached. The study of inflections is a major branch of the study of word structure (**inflectional morphology**). ➤➤affix; case; derivation 1; morphology; typology of language; word class. **2.** A popular term for the melody of speech, in linguistics generally referred to as **intonation**. ➤➤intonation.

informality ➤formality.

informant A native speaker of a language who acts as a source of linguistic data. It is now often replaced by the term **consultant**, which suggests greater equality of status between native speaker and researcher. ➤➤elicitation; intuition.

information structure A proposed analysis of sentences into information units. In speech these units are usually distinguished by intonational criteria, the **information focus** being conveyed by nuclear tone. For example, in the sentence *Mary bought a RED car*, the intonational emphasis on *red* conveys that this is new information in the sentence, while *Mary, bought* and *car* are part of the 'given' information. A different information structure would be suggested by *MARY bought a red car.* ➤➤focus; given; intonation; theme.

-*ing* form In English grammar, the form of the verb ending in *-ing*, such as *running, jumping*. The term has proved to be a popular alternative to the use of Latinate expressions, which do not work comfortably in the description of English. The same verb form is used in *I am running, I was running* and *I shall be running*, for example, which makes it difficult to use a term such as 'present participle' for all three. ➤➤participle.

ingressive /ɪŋˈgresɪv/ ➤egressive.

initial ➤medial 1.

initialism ➤acronym.

Initial Teaching Alphabet ➤i.t.a.

initiator The vocal organs which are the source of an airstream for speech. The usual initiator is the lungs – a pulmonic initiation. ➤➤glottalic; velaric.

innateness hypothesis The view that a child is born with a biological predisposition to learn language, and a knowledge of at least some of the universal structural principles which characterize language; also called the **nativist** hypothesis. The view emerged as part of the mentalistic approach to language espoused by generative linguistics in the 1960s, and has proved controversial, with scholars arguing over exactly which principles might plausibly be said to be innate, and what evidence might bear on the matter. ➤➤generative grammar; Language Acquisition Device; universal.

inner speech The mental use of words to express a sequence of thoughts – according to some psychologists, an essential characteristic of the ability to think at all. The notion is particularly associated with the views of the Russian psychologist, Lev Semenovich Vygotsky (1896–1934). It contrasts with **external speech** – the use of normal speech (or its written form). ➤➤psycholinguistics.

institutional linguistics A developing branch of linguistics which studies the use of language in professional contexts – in such 'institutions' as law, medicine, education, and business. It also includes such topics as language planning, where policies governing the use of languages need to be worked out at national level. ➤➤language planning; linguistics.

instrumental case One of the ways in which an inflected language makes a word (typically a single noun or pronoun) change its form, expressing the meaning 'by means of'. For example, in the sentence *I opened the door with the key, the key* might be said to have an instrumental function, and in some languages (e.g. Russian, Kannada) this function would be expressed with an inflection. ➤➤case; inflection 1.

'Bob will be taking notes. He's doing an anthology of cocktail party chit-chat.'
(**interactional sociolinguistics**)

instrumental phonetics ➤experimental phonetics.

intensifier A word (adverbial or adjectival in function) which has a typically heightening effect on the meaning of another element in a sentence; for example, *very* increases the strength of the meaning of the following word in *The book was very interesting*. The term is also sometimes used to refer to words which intensify 'downwards', reducing the meaning of the associated element; for example, *hardly* decreases the force of the following word in *The food was hardly sufficient*. ➤➤adjective; adverb.

intensity ➤loudness.

intensive ➤extensive.

interactional sociolinguistics The study of the role of language in mediating face-to-face interaction. It examines the way social factors influence how people speak to each other in particular types of communication – for example, how they take their leave of each other. Particular attention is paid to the transcription of recorded interactions. ➤➤address, forms of; sociolinguistics; T/V forms; *cartoon*, p. 164.

interchangeability A suggested defining property of human language, which refers to the system's ability to be mutually transmitted and received by members of the same species. This situation does not always obtain in the animal kingdom, for example, where male and female members of a species may use different kinds of call. ➤➤language 1; zoösemiotics.

interdental ➤dental.

interference The introduction of errors into one language as a result of contact with another language; also called **negative transfer**. It typically occurs while people are learning a foreign language or living in a multilingual situation. Foreigners who say *I live here since three years* are probably displaying interference from their mother-tongue. ➤➤contrastive analysis; error analysis; transfer.

Interglossa A language invented by Lancelot Hogben in 1943, but published only in draft form. A modified version was later developed (1981) by Wendy Ashby and Ross Clark, called **Glosa**. Glosa contains a basic 1000-word vocabulary, derived from Latin and Greek roots. ➤➤artificial language.

interjection In the traditional classification of parts of speech, an item whose function is purely emotive, such as *Gosh!*, *Phew*, or *Tut tut*. Such items do not enter into syntactic relationships with other word classes. ➤➤word class.

interlanguage A language system created by someone who is in the process of learning a foreign language. This intermediate state contains properties of both the first and the second language, and varies according to the learner's evolving system of rules. ➤➤foreign language; language learning.

Interlingua A language devised in 1951 by the International Auxiliary Language Association (a body formed in New York in 1924). It uses a Romance-based grammar, with a standardized vocabulary based on the main western European languages. ➤➤artificial language.

interlocutor Someone who is actively engaged in a conversation, as opposed to those who are passive observers. A dialogue normally consists of two interlocutors, but several people may be simultaneously active in a conversation. ➤➤conversation analysis; turn.

internal evidence Linguistic features in a text which indicate when or where the work was written, or who the author was. Handwriting, idiosyncratic spellings, and other graphic features play an important role, as do favourite patterns of vocabulary and grammar. A contrast is intended with **external evidence**, such as might come from historical records or archeological findings. ➤➤paleography; philology.

internalization In generative linguistics, the acquiring of knowledge about the structure of a language, primarily in the context of child language acquisition. A child who learns a grammatical rule, such as the addition of *-s* to make a plural in English, is said to have 'internalized' that rule. ➤➤acquisition; generative grammar.

internal reconstruction ➤reconstruction.

internal rhyme ➤rhyme.

International Computer Archive of Modern English (ICAME) A clearing centre for storing and distributing information on corpus studies in English, based at Bergen University, Norway. Its aims are to compile an archive of English-language material available for computer processing, and to collect and distribute information on research that uses this material. ➤➤corpus.

International Corpus of English (ICE) A computer corpus being compiled from samples of spoken and written English in countries where English is a first or official second language, with the aim of facilitating comparative study of national varieties. Proposed in 1988, the project is based at University College London. Each regional component aims to be a million running words. In addition, there is a specialized corpus being developed, dealing with writing by advanced learners of English. ➤➤corpus; Survey of English Usage.

international language A language which is in widespread use as a medium of communication among different countries. English is the world's chief international language, but French, Spanish, German, Russian, and Chinese are also found in this role in various parts of the world. ➤➤lingua franca.

International Phonetic Alphabet ➤International Phonetic Association.

International Phonetic Association An organization founded in 1886 by a group of European phoneticians to promote the study of phonetics. It devised the **International Phonetic Alphabet**, first published in 1889, and last revised in 1989, which has become the most widely used system for transcribing the sounds of a language. Both organization and alphabet use the abbreviation **IPA**. ➤➤phonetics; p. 167.

interpersonal function The use of language to establish and maintain social relationships. The notion takes its place as part of a classification of language functions, along with aesthetic, scientific, and other uses. ➤➤address, forms of; phatic communion; pragmatics.

interpreting The process of oral translation. In **consecutive interpreting**, the interpreter translates a speaker in short stretches while the speaker pauses. In **simultaneous interpreting**, the interpreter typically works in front of a micro-

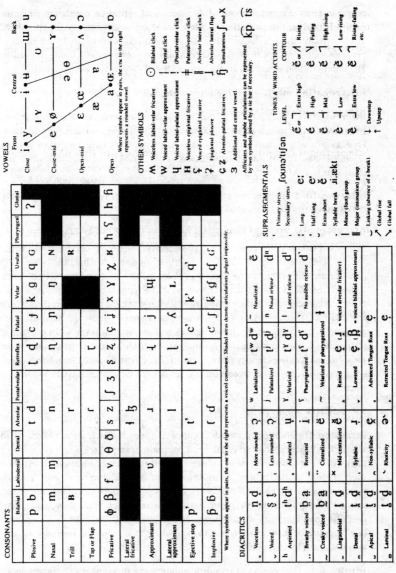

The **International Phonetic Alphabet** (revised to 1989).
Reproduced by courtesy of the International Phonetic Association.

phone in a sound-proofed booth, and carries on a continuous translation while the person is talking; the translation is then passed on to listeners through headsets. The former method is commonly used in person-to-person translation (such as between individual politicians) or with small groups of business people or tourists. The latter method is normal at large international gatherings. ➤➤translatology.

interrogation mark ➤punctuation; question.

interrogative Descriptive of a grammatical category found in verb forms or sentence and clause types, used in the expression of questions; contrasts with **declarative**. Words which mark interrogative constructions are **interrogative words**, often sub-classified as interrogative adjectives (e.g. *which*), adverbs (e.g. *why*), and pronouns (e.g. *who*). ➤➤declarative; question.

intervocalic Descriptive of a consonant used between two vowels, such as the /h/ of *aha* or the /b/ of *about*. ➤➤consonant.

intonation The linguistic functioning of pitch at sentence level, generally analysed in terms of **intonation contours** or **tone units**. The notion contrasts with **tone**, the use of pitch in words or syllables. Sometimes loudness, rhythm, and other tones of voice are considered to be part of intonation. The study of intonation (often called **intonology**) deals with such matters as the types of pitch pattern which can occur in a language (e.g. falling, rising, rising-falling) and the types of meaning which these patterns convey. An intonation pattern can signal an emotional meaning, such as anger, delight, or sarcasm. It can signal a grammatical meaning, as in the case of statement vs. question (compare *It's ready* vs. *It's ready?*). And it can signal a social meaning, such as the identity of a profession (e.g. sergeant major, preacher, football commentator) or type of interaction (e.g. formal speech, informal chat). ➤➤contour; pitch; tone.

intransitive ➤transitivity.

intrusion The addition of sounds in connected speech which are not heard when words or syllables are said in isolation. A common example in English is the use of intrusive /r/ as a linking sound between vowels in Received Pronunciation when there is no *r* in the spelling, as in *Africa(r) and Asia* or *law(r) and order*. Though intrusive sounds are a natural means of increasing the smoothness of utterance flow, they are strongly criticized in English by those with a purist attitude towards language use. The term contrasts with **elision**, and is often classified into different types (e.g. epenthesis, prothesis), depending on where in a word the intrusion occurs. ➤➤epenthesis; linking; purism.

intuition In the context of linguistic enquiry, the judgement of speakers about their language; also called **tacit knowledge** or **Sprachgefühl**. People appeal to their intuition when they have to decide whether a sentence is acceptable or not, or what relationship of meaning exists between a pair of sentences (such as active and passive). ➤➤informant.

Inuit /'ɪnjuːɪt/ ➤Eskimo.

Inupiaq or **Inupik** /ɪ'nuːpɪək, ɪ'nuːpɪk/ ➤Eskimo.

invariable word A type of word which never undergoes change in its internal structure, such as *under* and *the*; also called an **invariant word**. A contrast is intended with **variable words**, such as *house* and *go*, which can be inflected. ➤➤inflection 1; morphology.

inversion The process or result of a syntactic change in which a particular sequence of constituents is seen as the reverse of another. In English, for example, the subject and auxiliary verb invert in order to make questions from statements: *It is ready* becomes *Is it ready?*. Inversion also follows such words as *hardly* and *scarcely* at the beginning of a sentence: *Hardly had I left when the taxi arrived.* ➤➤syntax; word order.

inverted commas ➤quotation marks.

IPA ➤International Phonetic Association.

Iran (population in 1995 estimated at 65,127,000) The official language is Persian (Farsi), spoken by about half the population. There are *c.*60 other languages, including Arabic, Armenian, Azerbaijani (*c.*20% of the population), Baluchi, Kurdish, and Luri. English is widely used for international purposes. ➤➤Persian.

Iranian A group of *c.*70 Indo-European languages, forming a branch of the Indo-Iranian family, spoken by over 75 million people in Iran, Afghanistan, and parts of nearby countries. The oldest forms are Old Persian and Avestan (used for the Avesta, the sacred text of the Zoroastrians), both of which have texts dating from the 6th century BC. The modern languages include Persian, Tadzhik, Pashto, Ossetic, Kurdish, and Baluchi. ➤➤Baluchi; Indo-Iranian; Kurdish; Ossetic; Pashto; Persian; Tadzhik.

Iraq (population in 1995 estimated at 20,645,000) The official language is Arabic, spoken in several varieties by *c.*90% of the population. There are *c.*20 other languages, including Armenian, Assyrian, Azerbaijani, and Persian. Kurdish (*c.*18% of the population) has official regional status in Kurdistan. English is widely used for international purposes. ➤➤Arabic.

Ireland (population in 1995 estimated at 3,500,000) The official languages are Irish Gaelic and English. Irish is used as a first language chiefly in the west of the country, but its use is more widespread, according to census returns, with up to a third of the population claiming some knowledge of the language. English is used for international purposes. ➤➤English; Irish Gaelic; Sheldru.

Irish Gaelic /'geɪlɪk, 'galɪk/ A member of the Goidelic branch of the Celtic family of languages, spoken by *c.*30,000 people as a first language, chiefly in western coastal Ireland in an area known as the Gaeltacht; also called simply **Irish** or **Gaelic**, and also **Erse**. It is an official language in the Irish Republic (along with English), used in government publications, and has been taught in schools since 1922. There has also been a movement to reform the complex spelling system. Irish is written in the Roman alphabet, sometimes using a traditional semi-uncial form of medieval writing ('Gaelic script'). Written evidence dates from the ogham inscriptions of the 5th century, with literary remains from the 8th century, by which time Irish had come to be widely used as a religious medium. There is an extensive medieval literature, and an active literary renaissance is found at the end of the 19th century. Ireland was wholly Gaelic-speaking until the 17th century, but the dominance of English and the effects of 19th century emigration led to a sharp decline, which continued in the 20th century. There is a strong revivalist movement, and *c.*1 million people now make some use of it. ➻Celtic; Ireland; ogham; uncial.

irony Language which expresses a meaning other than that literally conveyed by the words, usually for humorous or dramatic effect. A contrast is often drawn with **sarcasm**, where the intention is to ridicule or wound. Everyday conversation provides many examples of ironic speech – such as the enthusiastic comment following a bad pun. ➻figurative language.

Iroquoian /ɪrəˈkwɔɪən/ ➤Macro-Siouan.

irregular Descriptive of a linguistic form which is an exception to the pattern stated by a rule; opposed to **regular**. In English, *took* is an irregular verb because it fails to conform to the rule which forms past tense by adding *-ed*. The irregular verbs of European languages have long been the bane of foreign language learners' lives. There are far fewer irregular nouns and adjectives. In English there are over 300 irregular verbs, but only a few dozen irregular nouns. ➻normative; rule 1.

isochrony /aɪˈsɒkrəniː/ A type of linguistic rhythm where the stressed syllables fall at roughly regular intervals throughout an utterance; English is an example of an isochronous language. It contrasts with a rhythm where all syllables occur at regular intervals of time (**isosyllabicity**), French (which to English ears gives the impression of a 'machine-gun-like' rhythm) is an isosyllabic language. Isochronous languages are often called **stress-timed**; isosyllabic languages **syllable-timed**. The languages of the world do not fall neatly into these two types of rhythm, however. Both English and German would be called stress-timed languages, but their rhythms are by no means the same. ➻rhythm; stress; syllable.

isogloss /ˈaɪsəglɒs/ A line on a map showing the boundary of an area in which a linguistic feature (e.g. a sound, word, or grammatical form) is used. The **iso-** prefix is used throughout dialect study as part of the labelling of the types of information which can be displayed on maps; for example, an **isophone** shows the distribution of a sound; an **isolex** shows the distribution of a lexical item. ➻dialect.

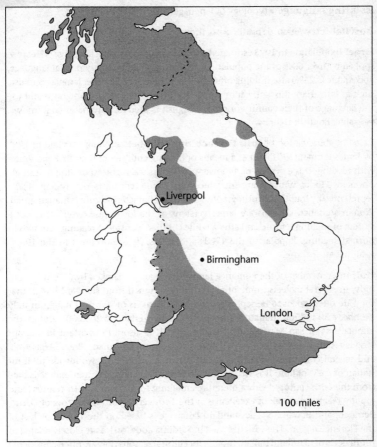

Isoglosses marking those parts of England and Wales which pronounce the /r/ in such words as *car* – the *rhotic* areas. The information is based on the relatively conservative speech of rural people, collected by the English Dialect Survey.

isolate A language with little or no structural or historical relationship to any other language; also called an **isolated language** or a **language isolate**. Many such cases have been noted. They include languages which remain undeciphered, languages where there is insufficient material available to establish a family relationship, and languages where, despite a great deal of data, the relationship is undetermined. ➤Ainu; Basque; Burushaski; Elamite; Etruscan; family of languages; Gilyak; Iberian; Japanese; Korean; Mohenjo-Daro; Salish; Sumerian.

isolating language ►typology of language.

isosyllabicity /aɪsəʊsɪləˈbɪsɪtiː/ ►isochrony.

Israel (population in 1995 estimated at 5,843,000) The official language is Hebrew, spoken by over 60% of the population, with English an auxiliary official language, and Arabic (*c*.25%) also holding official status. There are *c*.20 other languages in use, such as Bulgarian, Russian, Ladino, and Yiddish (*c*.5%). Many immigrants still use the language of their country of origin. English is used for international purposes. ►►Arabic; English; Hebrew.

i.t.a An abbreviation of **Initial Teaching Alphabet**, a scheme devised in 1959 by James Pitman (1901–85) as a means of helping children in their first encounter with reading. It is a system of 44 lower-case letters, each corresponding to a single phoneme. Extra symbols are introduced to handle contrasts not systematically represented by traditional orthography – hence its characterization as an 'augmented' Roman alphabet. Capitals are larger versions of the lower-case letters. It is not a system of spelling reform, and after a while children transfer to reading materials in normal spelling. Popular in the 1960s and 1970s, its use declined in the 1980s. ►►alphabet; spelling.

Italian A member of the Romance family of languages, spoken by *c*.57 million in Italy, in several dialects, some of which differ so much from standard Italian that they are often taken to be separate languages; speakers of standard Italian in Italy number *c*.30 million. Italian is also spoken in Switzerland (*c*.200,000), and by the populations of San Marino and Vatican City. It is also an important immigrant language in many countries, especially the USA, Australia, Canada, Brazil, Argentina, and several countries in north and east Africa, resulting in a worldwide total for Italian of *c*.63 million. It is written in the Roman alphabet. Written materials date from the 10th century, with a literature emerging from the late 12th century, and rapidly reaching a peak of excellence in the 14th century in the writing of Dante, Petrarch, and Boccaccio. The standard language is based on the Tuscan dialect of the Florence region. The varieties used in Sardinia and Corsica are closely related to the dialects of mainland Italian, though for cultural reasons they are often considered to be separate languages. ►►Corsican; Italy; Romance; San Marino; Sardinian; Vatican City.

Italic A family of Indo-European languages, preserved in inscriptions from the 6th century BC, and chiefly known through Latin. Other languages of the group include Faliscan, Oscan, Umbrian, and Venetic, spoken in an area corresponding roughly to modern Italy. From the spoken form of Latin developed the Romance languages. ►►Indo-European; Latin; Romance.

italic A form of sloped cursive lettering, developed by the Italian scribe Niccolò Niccoli in the early 15th century. It eventually led to the development of *italic letters* (**italics**) in printing. The italic typeface is used in print for a wide range of functions, such as titles of works, emphasis, cited forms, and foreign words. In traditional typewritten materials, italics have to be replaced by underlining; and in certain types of software the contrast cannot be shown directly on the screen, but needs to be signalled using codes. ➤letter; typography.

Italy (population in 1995 estimated at 57,333,000) The official language is Italian, though perhaps as many as half the population do not speak the standard language, but one or other of the major regional varieties, some of which are mutually unintelligible – Aquilano, Lombard, Molisano, Neapolitan, Piemontese, Pugliese, Sardinian, Sicilian, Venetian. German is an official regional language in Trentino-Alto Adige, and French in the Aosta Valley. There are *c.*15 other languages in use, such as Albanian, Friulian, Greek, Occitan (Provençal), Romani, and Slovene. Italian, French, and English are all used for international trade and tourism. ➤Italian.

iterative /ˈɪtərətɪv/ Descriptive of a form which expresses the meaning of 'repeated action'. Iterative meaning may be expressed through verb constructions, as part of the system of aspect, or through other word classes, especially adverbs (*frequently*, *regularly*). ➤adverb; aspect.

Ivory Coast ➤Côte d'Ivoire.

J

Jamaica (population in 1995 estimated at 2,519,000) The official language is English. Over 90% of the population speak an English-based creole (Jamaican Creole, or Patwa), which is gaining in prestige. ➤creole; English; Patwa.

Japan (population in 1995 estimated at 124,641,000) The official language is Japanese, spoken by *c*.98% of the population. There are a few other languages, such as Korean (*c*.670,000), and the Ryukyuan languages used in the Ryukyu Islands (*c*.900,000), which are historically related to Japanese. English is used for international purposes. ➤Ainu; Japanese.

Japanese A language spoken by *c*.122 million people in Japan, and by many immigrants (*c*.3 million) in Brazil, the USA, Peru, and several other countries. There is no clear relationship with other languages, though some linguists consider it to be a member of the Altaic family, and some relate it to Korean. There are major dialect differences, the southern dialects of the Ryukyu Islands being markedly different from the standard language based on the Tokyo dialect, and often considered to be separate languages. Written records date from the 8th century, using Chinese characters (kanji). In addition, Japanese makes use of three other writing systems – two syllabaries (hiragana and katakana) and a romanized script (Romaji). Old Japanese (used before the 8th century) is followed by a period of Late Old Japanese (9th–11th centuries), Middle Japanese (12th–16th centuries), and Modern Japanese thereafter. There are many Chinese loan words, and in modern times English borrowings are much in evidence. The language is noted for its careful representation of social structure, with distinctive male and female varieties, and several hierarchical levels of honorific style. ➤Altaic; honorific; Japan; kana; kanji; Korean; Romaji; Roman alphabet.

jargon 1. Technical terms and expressions used by a group of specialists, which are not known or understood by the speech community as a whole. Every subject has its jargon, which can contribute to economy of communication and precision of thought among those who belong to the group. Objections arise when practitioners use jargon unthinkingly or excessively, in contexts where outsiders feel they have a right to comprehension, such as in relation to medicine, law, and the civil service. ➤slang; terminology. **2**. The unintelligible word creations which accompany certain kinds of language breakdown, notably in aphasia. ➤aphasia. **3**. In the normal development of young children, the unintelligible continuous stretches of babbling, with sentence-like intonation, heard in many children around the end of the first year. ➤➤babbling.

Javanese A member of the Austronesian family of languages, spoken by *c.*75 million people chiefly in Java and nearby islands in Indonesia, with some in Malaysia. It has many more speakers than any other Austronesian language. It is traditionally written in the Javanese alphabet, derived from southern India, but the Roman alphabet is now much in use. It has a strong literary tradition, with records dating from the 8th century, but this has been largely eclipsed in recent years because of the dominance of the standard language, Bahasa Indonesia. ➤➤Austronesian; Malay.

Jonesian Adjective derived from Daniel Jones (1881–1967), the leading British phonetician in the first half of the century. He was professor of phonetics at the University of London from 1921 to 1949. ➤➤cardinal vowels; phonetics.

Jordan (population in 1995 estimated at 4,565,000) The official language is Arabic, spoken by most of the population. A few other languages are found, such as Adygey and Armenian. English is used for international purposes. ➤➤Arabic.

Judaeo-German ➤Yiddish.

Judaeo-Spanish ➤Ladino 1.

Jugoslavia ➤Yugoslavia.

Jula ➤Dyula.

juncture A feature of a language's sound system which demarcates grammatical units, signalled by silence, pitch, stress, length, or a variety of phonetic features. Different junctural features need to be recognized when considering the ways in which syllable boundaries can be identified within words, word boundaries within phrases, and clause boundaries within sentences. Several classifications of juncture types have been proposed, and a great deal of effort has been devoted to investigating whether such written contrasts as *ice-cream* and *I scream* are acoustically real. ➤➤prosody.

justification The spacing of words and letters within a line of printed text so that all full lines in a column have an even margin to both left and right; **justified** text contrasts with **unjustified** text. The present book uses a justified setting (though the blurb on the back cover does not). ➤➤typography.

K

Kabardian /kə'bɑ:dɪən/ A member of the Abkhazo-Adyghian group of Caucasian languages, spoken by *c*.350,000 people, chiefly in the Kabardino-Balkar region of Russia, in the northern part of the Greater Caucasus Mountains; also called **Circassian**. At first written in the Roman alphabet, the language has used Cyrillic since 1936. ➤Abkhazo-Adyghian.

Kabyle /kə'baɪl/ A member of the Berber branch of the Afro-Asiatic family of languages, spoken chiefly by *c*.2.5 million people in Algeria, and by a further half a million or more in France. The name comes from the Arabic word for 'tribesman'. It is written in the Arabic alphabet. ➤Berber.

Kaffir /'kafɪə/ ➤Xhosa.

KAL An abbreviation of **knowledge about language**.

Kalenjin ➤Nandi.

Kampuchea ➤Cambodia.

kana /'kɑ:nə/ A writing system in use in Japan, in which each graphic symbol represents a syllable. Historically derived from the 6th century AD from the Chinese kanji characters used in Japan, two kana systems developed in due course. The system known as **hiragana** ('common kana') was a simplification of the cursive style of writing kanji used chiefly by women in the imperial court. The **katakana** ('partial kana') system developed as a method of shorthand used by priests to aid the reading of Chinese texts (by marking Japanese affixes and particles, which had no equivalent in Chinese grammar). The two systems came to be used for different purposes, with hiragana becoming the medium of everyday use and of literature, and katakana the medium of scholarship. A distinction is still present in modern Japanese, where the writing system in common use is a mixture of kanji and hiragana, katakana being restricted to the transcription of foreign words and a few specialized contexts. Each kana contains 75 graphemes representing such syllables as /ka/, /ga/, /shi/, /ji/, /so/, and /go/, some of which enter into further combinations (e.g. /byo/, /pyo/). Kana spellings are now based on modern word pronunciations. ➤Chinese; Japanese; kanji; syllabary.

Kanarese /kanə'ri:z/ ➤Kannada.

kanji /'kandʒi:/ A graphic symbol used in the writing of Japanese – a Japanese word meaning 'Chinese characters'. Kanji are usually used for writing lexical words;

The development of **kana** symbols from Chinese characters: (a) katakana, (b) hiragana. The top line shows the Chinese characters relating to the 15 kana symbols shown in the bottom line. The middle line(s) show earlier forms in Japanese.

grammatical elements and indications of pronunciation are shown by the use of hiragana symbols. ➤➤Chinese; grammatical word; Japanese; kana.

Kannada /ˈkanədə/ A member of the Dravidian family of languages, spoken by *c*.34 million people as a first language in south-west India, chiefly in the state of Karnataka (where it is the official state language), and by a further 10 million as a second language; also called **Kanarese**. It is written in the Kannada alphabet, with inscriptions dating from the late 6th century AD, and a literary tradition from the 9th century. The language has two main varieties, which are in a diglossic relationship. ➤➤diglossia; Dravidian.

Kanuri /kəˈnʊriː/ A Saharan language spoken by over 3 million people mainly in north-east Nigeria, with some speakers in south-east Niger and Chad. It is written in the Roman alphabet. ➤➤Saharan.

Kartvelian /kɑːtˈviːlɪən/ A group of Caucasian languages found in the south of the Caucasus region; also called **South Caucasian**. They include Georgian (the chief language of the region), Zan, Mingrelian, Laz, and Svan, though there is some dispute as to whether these are all distinct languages. Only Georgian has a written form. ➤➤Caucasian; Georgian.

Kashmiri /kaʃˈmiːriː/ A member of the Dardic group of Indo-Iranian languages, spoken by *c*.4 million people in Kashmir, India (where it is an official regional language), and in nearby parts of Pakistan. It is written by Muslims in the Arabic alphabet, while Hindus use a special system (the Sarada alphabet), dating from the

8th century AD. This alphabet is a close relative of Devanagari, which is used for published literature in Kashmiri. ➤➤Dardic; Devanagari; Indo-Iranian.

katakana /ˈkatəkɑːnə/ ➤kana.

Kazakh or **Kazak** /kəˈzak/ A member of the Turkic branch of the Altaic family of languages, spoken by *c*.8 million people, chiefly in Kazakhstan (where it is an official language), with some in China, Mongolia, Iran, Turkey, Afghanistan, and Germany. Formerly written in the Arabic alphabet, it now uses Cyrillic in Kazakhstan, and the Roman alphabet elsewhere. ➤➤Kazakhstan; Turkic.

Kazakhstan (population in 1995 estimated at 17,155,000) The official languages are Kazakh (spoken by *c*.40% of the population), and Russian (spoken by *c*.40%). Other languages include Chinese, Chechen, German, Romani, Uighur, and Ukrainian. ➤➤Kazakh; Russian.

Kenya (population in 1995 estimated at 29,520,000) The official language is Swahili, widely used (by *c*.12 million) as a lingua franca. There are *c*.50 local languages, notably Kikuyu (Gikuyu, spoken by *c*.20% of the population), Luo (*c*.12%), Luya (*c*.12%), and Kamba (*c*.10%). English was the official language after independence, and still retains considerable status as a second language. ➤➤English; lingua franca; Swahili.

kernel A basic type of sentence structure, as used in early generative grammar. It referred to a simple, active, declarative, indicative sentence (e.g. *The cat chased the mouse*), which could be transformed into other kinds of sentence (such as negative, question, passive) through the use of a basic set of transformational rules. ➤➤generative grammar.

key The tone, manner, or spirit in which a speech act is carried out (e.g. mock vs. serious). The term is also used with reference to levels of formality, such as intimate, casual, and formal. ➤➤formality; speech act; style.

key words Terms which capture the semantic identity of a text, group, or period. An abstract of an article, for example, may conclude with a list of key words which summarize what the article is about, and these may be used for the compilation of an index or other reference work. Key words for the present book would include *language, linguistics, communication*, and a few others. Rather more difficult is to identify the key words for a social group or time period, such as 'advertisers' or 'the 1990s'. ➤➤abstract 1.

Khalkha /ˈkalkə/ ➤Mongol.

Khanty /ˈkantiː/ A member of the Ugric group of the Finno-Ugric family of languages, spoken by *c*.13,000 people in the Khanty-Mansi region of western Siberia, Russia, where it has official regional status; previously known as **Ostyak**. It is written in the Cyrillic alphabet. ➤➤Finno-Ugric.

Khmer /kmɛə/ A member of the Mon-Khmer family of languages, spoken by *c*.7 million people, chiefly in Cambodia (where it is the official language), Vietnam, and

Thailand; also called **Cambodian**. It is written in the Khmer alphabet, and records date from the 7th century AD. ➤Cambodia; Mon-Khmer.

Khoisan /ˈkɔɪsan/ A group of less than 40 languages spoken in the southern part of Africa by *c.*300,000 people, mainly in an area around the Kalahari Desert from Angola to South Africa. The smallest of the four main language families of Africa, it is famous for its use of click consonants. The name is a compound deriving from the name of the largest Hottentot group (the Khoi-Khoin) and that of the Bushmen in the Nama region of Namibia (the San). Few of these languages have more than 1000 speakers, and numbers everywhere are diminishing. Only Kwadi (Angola, *c.*10,000) and Sandawe (Tanzania, *c.*50,000) have substantial numbers. About half of the languages have been written down, mainly by missionaries. Several languages of the family have become extinct in recent years. ➤Africa; click.

Kikongo /kiːˈkɒŋgəʊ/ ➤Kongo.

kinesics /kaɪˈniːzɪks/ The systematic use of facial expression and body gesture to communicate meaning. The notion relates especially to the way language is used – for example, a shrug of the shoulders to replace or accompany the utterance 'I've no idea'. Kinesic analysis is carried out using a linguistic frame of reference, recognizing such units as **kinemes** (on analogy with phonemes) – minimal units of meaningful visual expression. ➤body language; phoneme; paralanguage; semiotics; p. 180.

kinesthetic feedback, also spelled **kinaesthetic** /kɪnəsˈθetɪk/ The internal process which enables speakers to be aware of the movements and positions of their vocal organs during speech; also called **kin(a)esthesia** or **kin(a)esthesis**. People sense movement or strain in their muscles, tendons, and joints, and unconsciously use this information to monitor what takes place when they speak. Interference with this process (following a dental anesthetic, for example) can severely hinder a person's ability to talk normally. ➤articulation.

Kingman Report ➤knowledge about language.

kinship terms The system of lexical items used in a language to express personal relationships within the family (whether in a narrow or an extended sense). This semantic topic has attracted particular interest among linguists because of the way languages make different lexical distinctions within what is a clearly defined biological domain. Unlike English, other languages may have separate lexical items for male and female cousins, or for maternal and paternal aunts, or there may be no lexical contrast between brothers and cousins, or between father and uncles. ➤componential analysis; gap; semantics.

Kirghiz, Kirgiz or **Kyrgyz** /ˈkɪəgɪz/ A member of the Turkish branch of the Altaic family of languages, spoken by *c.*2.5 million people, chiefly in Kyrgyzstan (where it is an official language) and also in nearby parts of Afghanistan, Turkey, and China.

—⬭—	Blank faced	⬭	Out of the side of the mouth (left)
—⌒	Single raised brow indicates brow raised	⬭	Out of the side of the mouth (right)
—⌣	Lowered brow	⌣	Set jaw
\/	Medial brow contraction	⌣	Smile tight — loose o
∴∴	Medial brow nods		
⌒⌒	Raised brows	⊢⊣	Mouth in repose lax o tense —
o o	Wide eyed		
— o	Wink	⌐	Droopy mouth
> <	Lateral squint	ꝫ	Tongue in cheek
><><	Full squint	⌒	Pout
A	Shut eyes (with A-closed pause 2 count,	⊓⊓	Clenched teeth
ᴍ ᴍ or	Blink	⊌	Toothy smile
B	B-closed pause 5 plus count) :)	⊞⊞⊞	Square smile
⊙ ⊙	Sidewise look	◎	Open mouth
ꙍ ꙍ	Focus on auditor	s◎ʟ	Slow lick—lips
⊕ ⊕	Stare	ꞯ◎ʟ	Quick lick—lips
◉◉	Rolled eyes	∞	Moistening lips
≨ ≨	Slitted eyes	⊜	Lip biting
⊖ ⊖	Eyes upward	⌣	Whistle
—⊖ ⊖—	Shifty eyes	⟩○⟨	Pursed lips
⊙ ⊙ʼ	Glare	⟩○⟨	Retreating lips
⊝ ⊙	Inferior lateral orbit contraction	⟩○⟨⊣	Peck
		⟩○⟨ !	Smack
△ₛ	Curled nostril	⊞⊞	Lax mouth
ₛ△ₛ	Flaring nostrils	⊌	Chin protruding
⸲△‹	Pinched nostrils	⊍	'Dropped' jaw
⬠	Bunny nose	⊢×⊣	Chewing
▲	Nose wrinkle	⌢	Temples tightened
⌒	Left sneer	ꞓ ꞓ	Ear 'wiggle'
~	Right sneer	⇄	Total scalp movement

Kinesics. Some of the symbols, or *kinegraphs*, which have been used in order to transcribe the various movements of face and body. Different sets of symbols have been devised for different areas of the body, such as the arms, fingers, and head. The symbols above illustrate the set of facial activities.

Formerly written in the Arabic alphabet, it now uses Cyrillic in Kyrgyzstan and Roman elsewhere. ➤➤Kyrgyzstan; Turkic.

Kiribati (population in 1995 estimated at 79,700) The official language is English. About 97% of the population speak Ikiribati (Gilbertese), an Austronesian language. ➤➤English.

Kituba /kɪˈtuːbə/ ➤Kongo.

knowledge about language (KAL) A goal of educational linguistic strategy in the UK since the late 1980s. It involves the fostering of an increased awareness of the structure and function of spoken and written language by children as they move through the school curriculum. Although an essential element in linguistic approaches to language study for many years, the contemporary popularity of the notion (and the new acronym) came from the report published by the Committee of Inquiry into English Language Teaching (known as the Kingman Report) in 1988, and the subsequent development of the country's National Curriculum in English, in which a range of targets for developing language awareness is specified. ➤➤educational linguistics; language awareness; Language in the National Curriculum.

koine /ˈkɔɪneɪ/ The spoken language of a locality which has become a standard language or lingua franca. The term is specifically used for the Greek language used throughout the eastern Mediterranean countries during the Hellenistic and Roman periods. ➤➤Greek; lingua franca; standard.

Koman /ˈkəʊmən/ A small group of Nilo-Saharan languages spoken in adjoining regions of Ethiopia and Sudan. It includes Gumuz, Koma, and Mao. ➤➤Nilo-Saharan.

Komi /ˈkəʊmiː/ A member of the Finnic group of the Finno-Ugric family of languages, spoken by c.400,000 people, in two main varieties, chiefly in the Komi region of north European Russia (where it has official status); formerly called **Zyryan**. It is written in the Cyrillic alphabet. ➤➤Finno-Ugric.

Kongo /ˈkɒŋɡəʊ/ A Bantu language spoken by c.3 million people, mainly in the Democratic Republic of Congo and Angola, with some in Congo; also called **Congo** or **Kikongo**. It is written in the Roman alphabet, and there is a well-developed oral literature. Many people (c.4 million) use a creolized form of the language, known as **Kituba**. ➤➤Bantu; creole.

Konkani /ˈkɒŋkəniː/ A language belonging to the Western group of Indo-Aryan languages, spoken by c.2 million people in Goa, western India, and nearby. It is written in both the Devanagari and Roman alphabets. ➤➤Indo-Aryan.

Korea, North (population in 1995 estimated at 23,518,000) The official language is Korean, spoken by nearly the whole population. English is used for international purposes. ➤➤Korean.

Korea, South (population in 1995 estimated at 44,853,000) The official language is Korean, spoken by nearly the whole population. English is used for international purposes. ➤➤Korean.

Korean A language spoken by *c*.75 million people, chiefly in South Korea (*c*.44 million) and North Korea (*c*.25 million), by others in China (*c*.2 million), Japan (*c*.670,000), Uzbekistan, and Kazakhstan, and by immigrants in several countries (notably the USA). Its genetic relationship to other languages is unclear, though some linguists place it within the Altaic family, and some relate it to Japanese. It has been much influenced by Chinese, with more than half its vocabulary of Chinese origin. The earliest records of the language, dating from before the 12th century, are in Chinese characters. A native Korean alphabet of 28 letters was introduced in the 15th century, and is still used in modified form (known as *Hankul*). A mixed style of writing is also in use, in which Chinese loan words are written in their original characters. ➤➤Altaic; Chinese; Japanese; Korea, North/South.

Krio /ˈkriːəʊ/ An English-based creole language spoken by *c*.470,000 people as a first language in and around Freetown, Sierra Leone (where *c*.4 million use it as a lingua franca), and in nearby parts of Gambia and Equatorial Guinea. Another variety is also found in Liberia. It is written in the Roman alphabet. ➤➤creole; lingua franca.

Kurdish A member of the Iranian group of languages, spoken by an uncertain number of people (perhaps as many as 10 million), chiefly in Turkey, Iran, and Iraq, with others in nearby parts of adjoining countries; also called **Kurdi** (southern) and **Kurmanji** (northern). There are northern, central, and southern dialect groupings, the central dialects being the basis of the modern literary language, which developed only in the 20th century. Its writing system depends on the locality – Arabic, Cyrillic, and (to a lesser extent) Roman are all found. ➤➤Iranian.

Kurmanji ➤Kurdish.

Kuwait (population in 1995 estimated at 1,019,000) The official language is Arabic, spoken by most of the population. Several languages are in use by groups of immigrant workers (e.g. English, Hindi). English is used for international purposes. ➤➤Arabic.

Kwa A group of *c*.75 Niger-Congo languages spoken by *c*.14 million people along the Atlantic coast in the southern part of the bulge of West Africa. In such a complex linguistic area, several pidgin and creole languages have developed, as an aid to inter-group communication; also, English or French are official languages in the area. Languages formerly classified as Eastern Kwa (e.g. Igbo) are now placed within the Benue-Congo family, with Ijo and related languages recognized as a separate branch. ➤➤Akan; creole; Ewe; Niger-Congo; pidgin.

kymograph ➤electrokymograph.

Kyrgyzstan (population in 1995 estimated at 4,694,000) The official languages are Kirghiz (spoken by over half of the population) and Russian (*c*.16%). Other languages include Uzbek (*c*.10%), Chinese, Mongol, and Uighur. ➤➤Kirghiz; Russian.

L

L ➤diglossia.

labial Descriptive of a speech sound made with the active use of one or both lips. In **labio-dental** sounds (such as [f]), the lower lip is in contact with (or approaches very close to) the upper teeth. In **labio-velar** sounds (such as [w]), a sound made at the velum is accompanied by simultaneous lip-rounding. Sounds which involve both lips include the **bilabial** consonants (e.g. [b], [m]) and rounded vowels (e.g. [u]). **Labialization** occurs when a sound which is not normally rounded is articulated with some degree of lip rounding, such as happens to the [s] in *Sue* (because of the influence of the following [u]). ➤➤rounding; velar.

labio-dental ➤labial.

LAD An abbreviation of **Language Acquisition Device**.

Ladino /laˈdiːnəʊ/ **1.** A variety of Romance, spoken by an uncertain number of Sephardic Jews (perhaps over 150,000) in the Balkans, Turkey, Israel, and parts of the Middle East, and through immigration in a few other countries, especially the USA; also called **Judaeo-Spanish**. It began in Spain in the Middle Ages, and was spread by the Jews who were exiled from that country in 1492. It is usually written in the Hebrew alphabet, though the Roman alphabet is used in Turkey. There is a substantial body of literature in the language. ➤➤Romance. **2.** A name sometimes given to Rhaetian, or to one of its dialects; also called **Ladin**. ➤➤Rhaetian.

Lahnda /ˈlɑːndə/ ➤Panjabi.

la-la theory The name of one of the speculative theories about the origins of language (also called the **sing-song theory**): it argues that speech originated in song, play, and other aspects of the romantic side of life. The intonation system provides some evidence, but the gap between the emotional and the rational aspects of speech expression remains to be explained. ➤➤origins of language.

laminal /ˈlamɪnl/ Descriptive of a consonant made by the blade (or **lamina**) of the tongue articulating with the upper incisor teeth or alveolar ridge. Examples include [ʃ] and [tʃ]. ➤➤blade; tongue.

Lancaster–Oslo/Bergen Corpus of British English (LOB) A corpus compiled by linguists at the Universities of Lancaster and Oslo, and prepared for computer analysis at the Norwegian Computing Centre for the Humanities in Bergen. It is the

British equivalent of the Brown Corpus. ►►Brown University Corpus of American English; corpus.

Landsmål /'lantsmɔːl/ ►Norwegian.

langage /lɑ̃'gaːʒ/ A French term introduced by Ferdinand de Saussure to refer to the human biological faculty of speech. It is distinguished in his approach from **langue**, the language system of a speech community. ►►language 1; langue; Saussure, Ferdinand de.

Lango /'laŋgəʊ/ A Nilotic language spoken by nearly a million people in north Uganda; closely related to Acholi. It is written in the Roman alphabet. ►►Acholi; Nilotic.

language 1. The systematic, conventional use of sounds, signs, or written symbols in a human society for communication and self-expression. Within this broad definition, it is possible to distinguish several uses, operating at different levels of abstraction. In particular, linguists distinguish between language viewed as an act of speaking, writing, or signing, in a given situation (often referred to by the French term *parole*, or as linguistic **performance**), the linguistic system underlying an individual's use of speech, writing, or sign (often referred to as **competence**), and the abstract system underlying the spoken, written, or signed behaviour of a whole community (often referred to by the French term *langue*). Particular levels of speech, writing, or sign may also be described as 'language' (e.g. 'scientific language', 'bad language'). And the term may be used in a still more general way, to characterize one of the defining features of human behaviour – the biological faculty which enables individuals to learn and use speech, writing, or sign (sometimes referred to by the French term *langage*). Estimates of the number of languages (in the everyday sense) in the world vary greatly – chiefly because of the difficulty of distinguishing languages from dialects – but are usually between 5000 and 7000. ►►competence; dialect; displacement; duality of structure; endangered languages; interchangeability; *langue*; linguistics; productivity; typology of language; Universal Declaration of Linguistic Rights; variety. **2**. An artificially constructed system used to expound a conceptual area or to facilitate communication; contrasts with **natural language**. This sense includes the notion of a **computer language**, a specially devised system of symbols and rules for programming and interacting with computers. It also includes the idea of an **artificial language**, such as Esperanto, or those sign languages which have been invented for use with deaf people. ►►artificial/natural/ sign language. **3**. In the traditional study of speech pathology, the meaningful or symbolic aspect of language, to be distinguished from the sounds which convey that meaning. In this sense, therapists often talk about disorders of 'speech and language'. The distinction is controversial, with many professionals now preferring to use the more general term 'language' to subsume all disorders of speaking, listening, reading and writing (i.e. including the phonetic kinds). ►►language pathology. **4**. The means animals use to communicate, more precisely referred to as 'animal communication'. This is one of several figurative applications of the term 'language' to aspects of behaviour which, because they lack the creativity and complexity of structure that can be found in speech, writing, and sign, are more properly described as types of 'communication'. Other loose or metaphorical applications include such expressions as 'body language' and 'the language of music'. ►►communication; semiotics; zoösemiotics.

language acquisition ►acquisition.

Language Acquisition Device (LAD) A model of first language learning, encountered especially in generative linguistics, in which the infant is credited with an innate predisposition to acquire linguistic structure. The notion has proved controversial, with debate focusing on the extent to which the LAD can be given a specifically linguistic (as opposed to a cognitive) definition, and on the kinds of linguistic evidence (in particular, universals of early language behaviour) which can be adduced in its support. ►►innateness hypothesis; universal.

language aptitude Natural ability to learn a language. The concept is independent of such other notions as intelligence, motivation, and opportunity. Various specific factors seem to be involved, such as the ability to infer grammatical rules from samples of data, to remember vocabulary, to distinguish sound qualities, and to imitate prosodic patterns. A **language aptitude test** (also called a **prognostic test**) aims to measure this ability, and to identify those who are most likely to succeed in learning a language. ►►language learning.

language areas The areas of the brain which seem to be most closely implicated in speaking, listening, reading, writing, and signing, mainly located at or around the Sylvian and Rolandic fissures; also called the **language centres**. For example, an area in the lower back part of the frontal lobe is primarily involved in the encoding of speech (Broca's area); an area in the upper back part of the temporal lobe, extending upwards into the parietal lobe, is important in the comprehension of speech (Wernicke's area). Other areas are involved in speech perception, visual perception, and the motor control of speaking, writing, and signing. ►►Broca's aphasia; neurolinguistics; Wernicke's aphasia; p. 186.

language arts The areas of an educational curriculum which involve the mastery of skills related to language – chiefly speaking, listening, reading, and writing, as well as related notions such as spelling and nonverbal communication. The notion is often encountered in mother-tongue education, where the emphasis is on an integrated programme of linguistic development, and not on the acquisition of separate skills. ►►educational linguistics; language learning.

Language Assessment, Remediation and Screening Procedure (LARSP) A profile of grammatical development used in the study of language disability. It was devised in the 1970s by a group of linguists at the University of Reading, based on a synthesis of findings from the study of normal language acquisition. It was the

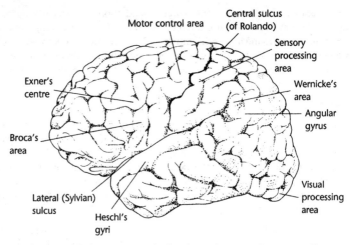

The areas of the brain most involved in the production and reception of language. © 1979 Scientific American Inc. All rights reserved. (**language areas**)

first in a series of linguistic profiles which then emerged, investigating a number of areas of language structure within a clinical perspective. ➤clinical linguistics; profile.

language attitudes The feelings people have about their own language or the language(s) of others. These may be positive or negative: someone may particularly value a foreign language (e.g. because of its literary history) or think that a language is especially difficult to learn (e.g. because the script is off-putting); rural accents generally receive a positive evaluation, whereas urban accents are thought of in negative terms. Knowing about attitudes is an important aspect of evaluating the likely success of a language teaching programme or a piece of language planning. ➤language learning/planning; peace linguistics.

language attrition ➤language death.

language awareness An informed, sensitive, and critical response to the use of language by oneself and others. Although the promotion of language awareness has always been a goal of linguistics (and specifically of educational linguistics), a particular impetus was given to this process at the end of the 1980s in Britain, following the publication of government reports on the teaching of the English language in schools, and the development of a new National Curriculum in English. ➤ecolinguistics; educational linguistics; knowledge about language; metalanguage.

language barrier The difficulties faced by people who do not have the same mother tongue when they attempt to communicate with each other. Many ways of breaking down this barrier have been proposed, such as translation and interpreting, foreign language teaching, and the use of various artificial and auxiliary languages. The phrase is also sometimes used to refer to the difficulties of communication faced by people who *do* have the same language background. ➤artificial/auxiliary language; language teaching; miscommunication; translatology.

language centres (UK) or **centers** (US) ➤language areas.

language change Change within a language over a period of time – a universal and unstoppable process. The phenomenon was first systematically investigated by comparative philologists at the end of the 18th century, and in the present century by historical linguists and sociolinguists. All aspects of language are involved, though most attention has been paid to the areas of pronunciation and vocabulary, where change is most noticeable and frequent. ➤analogy 2; archaism; convergence 2; language shift; overt prestige; philology; purism; sound change; variable; vowel shift.

language contact A situation of geographical continuity or close social proximity between languages or dialects, so that a degree of bilingualism comes to exist within a community. The languages (also called **contact vernaculars**) then begin to influence each other, such as by introducing loan words or making changes in pronunciation. The most dramatic examples of new languages arising out of contact situations are pidgins. ➤bilingualism; pidgin; substrate.

language death The situation which arises when a language ceases to be used by a community; also called **language loss** or **obsolescence**, especially when referring to the loss of language ability in an individual. The term **language attrition** is sometimes used when the loss is gradual rather than sudden. ➤dead language; endangered languages; language revitalization programme.

language delay The failure of a child to learn language (or an aspect of language) at a normal rate. The concept is most commonly applied to speech, and especially to the slow learning of pronunciation, grammar, and vocabulary. The extent of the delay may be mild (a few months), moderate, or severe (several years). In most cases, the problem has no clear physical cause. Children with delayed language are sometimes called **aphasic** or **dysphasic** – though this label is controversial, being used historically to describe the linguistic symptoms of people with known brain damage. ➤aphasia; language disorder/pathology.

language diffusion ➤diffusion.

language disorder A serious abnormality in the system underlying the use of spoken, written, or signed language. Many language disorders are the consequence of damage to an area of the brain responsible for linguistic processing (notably, aphasia), but some have no clear physical cause. Most cases of child language delay involve an element of disordered language, though the reason for the condition is often unclear. ➤aphasia; deviance; language areas/delay/pathology; speech therapy.

language dominance A situation in a multilingual community where one language is held to be more important than others. This situation may arise because the language has more speakers, has a more prestigious history, or has been given an influential role by the government. Similarly, within a bilingual individual, we may speak of one language being the dominant language – the person knows it better or uses it more often. This is usually a person's mother-tongue, but it need not always be so: many of the people who left continental Europe for the USA in the 1930s ended up with English as their dominant language. ➤➤bilingualism; ecolinguistics.

language engineering ➤language planning.

language experience approach A method used in teaching a child to read which emphasizes the recent experience of the child as an essential part of the learning process. For example, a recent excursion may become the focus of a lesson, and the sentences produced by the child in talking about it are written down and read. Reading materials are based on the child's own level of language ability. ➤➤reading.

language family ➤family of languages.

Language(s) for Special Purposes, also **Language(s) for Specific Purposes (LSP)** An area of enquiry and practice in the development of language teaching programmes for people who need a language (or a variety of a language) to meet a predictable range of communicative needs. Examples include courses for scientists, doctors, lawyers, and air traffic controllers. ➤➤English for Special Purposes (ESP).

language game ➤play language.

language generation The production of spoken, written, or signed messages by people or computers. The term is chiefly used for the computational composition of printed text. ➤➤computational linguistics; natural language.

Language in the National Curriculum (LINC) A three-year in-service project in the UK, whose aim was to acquaint teachers with the model of language presented in the Report of the Committee of Inquiry into English Language Teaching (the Kingman Report, 1988). The training took place between 1989 and 1992, and was funded (at a cost of £21 million) by the Department of Education and Science and the local education authorities of England and Wales. A wide range of materials was produced to assist teachers directly. Controversy surfaced in mid-1991 when it was announced that ministers would not permit official HMSO publication of the LINC training materials nor waive Crown Copyright (thus precluding their publication elsewhere). Criticisms included the claims that much of the illustrative children's work was of questionable quality, that there was bias in the way controversial topics were discussed (such as the relationship between language and power), that much of the linguistic terminology was excessively complex, and that dialect forms were being emphasized at the expense of the standard language. There was no restriction on the use of the materials in in-service training courses. A vigorous defence of the project's policy and practice was presented, but the ban remained. However, despite (or perhaps because of) the ban there was widespread circulation of the materials in unpublished form. ➤➤bidialectism; knowledge about language; language arts/awareness.

language in use An approach to the development of a child's linguistic awareness and skills which focuses on the way spoken and written language is used in real situations. The aim is to find contexts which are meaningful and motivating (e.g. advertising, news reporting, operating instructions), so that children can develop their awareness of what language is and how it is used. Popular in the 1970s as an alternative to the parsing techniques previously widespread, the approach tends now to be part of a broader approach which includes a descriptive structural apparatus. ➤➤educational linguistics; knowledge about language; parsing.

language isolate ➤isolate.

language laboratory or **language lab** A classroom which uses booths containing audio or video recorders which enable students to listen and respond to foreign utterances through an individual headset. The recorders have listening, recording, and playback facilities. A teacher sitting at a control desk can monitor or talk to individual students. Students work intensively at their own rate. ➤➤audiolingual method; language teaching.

language learning The process of internalizing a language – either a mother tongue or a foreign language. The factors which affect this process (such as the individual's intelligence, memory, and motivation to learn) are seen as separate from those involved in the task of language teaching. ➤➤acquisition; contrastive analysis (CA); expansion 2; interlanguage; language aptitude/teaching; monitor model; natural order hypothesis; reading; Washoe.

language loss 1. The loss of language by an individual as a result of some trauma, such as brain damage or shock. The loss may be permanent or temporary, and varies in the severity with which it affects different aspects of language structure. Some forms of loss respond well to treatment; others do not. ➤➤aphasia; apraxia; dysarthria; dysphonia; language pathology. **2**. ➤language death.

language loyalty A concern to preserve the use of a language or the traditional form of a language, when that language is perceived to be under threat. For example, many first-generation immigrants to a country are extremely loyal to their first language, but attitudes vary in the second generation. ➤➤language attitudes/death/maintenance/shift.

language maintenance The extent to which people continue to use a language, once they are part of a multilingual area. For example, immigrant groups may continue with their language, out of a sense of loyalty, despite the dominance of the language of their host country (as has often happened in the USA); or a com-

189

munity may try to maintain its language successfully in the face of a conquering nation (as happened with English after the Norman Conquest). ➤➤endangered languages; language dominance/loyalty/shift.

language minority ➤minority.

language pathology The study of all forms of involuntary, abnormal linguistic behaviour, especially when associated with medical conditions; a practitioner is a **language pathologist**, commonly known as a **speech therapist** (UK) or **speech pathologist** (US), with **speech and language therapist** now the official name in the UK. The subject includes disorders of speaking, listening, reading, and writing, and applies both to developmental abnormalities in children and to acquired abnormalities in children or adults. Any recognized area of linguistic structure and use is covered by the term, especially disorders of grammar, semantics, phonology, and pragmatics. The term is broader in its implications than the analogous term **speech pathology**, though in practice the subject-matter and professional expertise referred to by the two domains are similar. However, disorders of a primarily phonetic nature (such as dysarthria and dysphonia) are traditionally described as being disorders of 'speech' (in a narrow sense) as opposed to 'language', on the grounds that they lack any meaningful or symbolic function; and disorders of reading and writing are often excluded or marginalized in the study of speech pathology. The term 'pathology' is itself controversial, because of its medical connotations: therapists are often unhappy about using it to refer to disorders (e.g. stuttering) which lack a clear medical cause. ➤➤acquired language disorder; agnosia; aphasia; communication disorder; dysarthria; dysfluency; dyslexia; dysphonia; dysprosody; language 3; mutism; speech defect/ therapy.

language pedagogy ➤educational linguistics.

language planning A deliberate, systematic, and theory-based attempt to solve the communication problems of a community by studying its various languages or dialects, and developing an official **language policy** concerning their selection and use; also sometimes called **language engineering** or **language treatment**. **Corpus planning** deals with the selection and codification of norms, as in the writing of grammars and the standardization of spelling. **Status planning** deals with the initial choice of language, including attitudes towards alternative languages and the political implications of various choices. ➤➤ecolinguistics; sociolinguistics; standard.

language policy ➤language planning.

language revitalization programme A programme of support or teaching designed to improve the use of a language which is in danger of dying out. Several such programmes are to be found around the world, generally focusing on minority languages, as in the case of various American Indian languages, Irish Gaelic, and Welsh. ➤➤language death; minority.

language rights ➤Universal Declaration of Linguistic Rights.

language shift The gradual or sudden move from the use of one language to another, either by an individual or by a group. It is particularly found among second- and third-generation immigrants, who often lose their attachment to their ancestral language, faced with the pressure to communicate in the language of the host country. Language shift may also be actively encouraged by the government policy of the host country. ➤➤endangered languages; language loyalty/planning.

language socialization The gradual development in children of patterns of language use which reproduce the adult system of social order. For example, adult expectations of politeness (e.g. 'Say please', 'Don't say *she*') are explicitly introduced into conversations with children from around age 3. ➤➤acquisition.

language teaching The process of instructing students in a language – either their mother tongue (e.g. the teaching of reading, speech therapy) or a foreign language. The way in which this is best done is highly controversial, and many teaching methods and theories have been proposed. ➤➤communicative approach; computer-assisted language learning; direct method; drill; grammar-translation method; immersion; Language for Special Purposes; language laboratory/learning; Linguapax; look-and-say; natural approach; notional syllabus; phonics; remedial language teaching.

language therapist ➤speech therapy.

language treatment ➤language planning; speech therapy.

language universal ➤universal.

langue /lãg/ The language system shared by a community of speakers; contrasts with *parole* /pa'rɒl/, the act of speaking in actual situations by an individual. Both terms were introduced by Ferdinand de Saussure, and came to exercise considerable influence on the development of linguistic thought. ➤➤competence; language 1; performance 1; Saussurian.

Languedoc /lã'dɒk/ ➤Occitan.

langue d'oïl/d'oc /lã 'dɔil, 'dɒk/ ➤French.

Lao /laʊ/ A member of the Tai family of languages, spoken by over 3 million people chiefly in Thailand and Laos (where it is the official language); also called **Laotian**. It is written in the Laotian alphabet, a derivative of Cambodian. Its literature is closely linked to both Buddhist and Hindu traditions. There is a dialect continuum linking Lao to Northeastern Tai, yielding a combined total of over 20 million speakers. ➤➤dialect continuum; Laos; Tai.

Laos (population in 1995 estimated at 4,791,000) The official language is Lao (Laotian), spoken by *c.*65% of the population. There are *c.*80 local languages, including Miao, Vietnamese, and several varieties of Thai. French is used for international purposes. ➤➤Lao.

Laotian /ˈlaʊʃn/ ➤Lao.

Lapp(ish) ➤Same.

LARSP An abbreviation of **Language Assessment, Remediation and Screening Procedure**.

laryngealization ➤creaky voice.

laryngectomy /larɪnˈdʒektəmiː/ The surgical removal of some or all of the larynx, usually following an irreversible laryngeal cancer; the patient is a **laryngectomee**. The pathway from the pharynx to the lungs is surgically closed, and breathing takes place through an alternative opening made at the front of the neck. Many people learn to use the upper part of their pharynx and esophagus to initiate vibration, resulting in an esophageal voice quality. Alternatively they may use an artificial larynx to provide a source of vibration. ➤➤artificial larynx; esophageal; vocal tract.

laryngology /larɪŋˈgɒlədʒiː/ The study of the anatomy, physiology, and diseases of the larynx. Its practitioners (**laryngologists**) are doctors who have specialized in ENT (ear, nose, and throat) medicine. ➤➤larynx.

larynx The interconnecting cartilages in the throat which enclose the vocal folds;

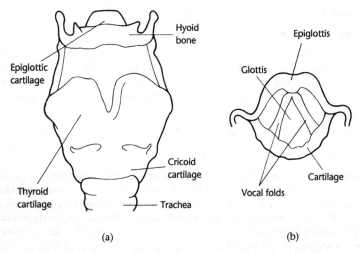

(a) (b)

(a) A front view of the structure of the **larynx**. The vocal folds lie behind the thyroid cartilage (or 'Adam's apple'). (b) A view of the larynx from above, as seen with a laryngoscope.

known popularly as the 'voice box'. Sounds made in the larynx are sometimes called **laryngeals**, especially in studies of language pre-history. **Laryngealization** refers to variations in the mode of vibration of the vocal folds, such as creaky voice. The **laryngograph** (or **electrolaryngograph**) is a device for recording vocal-fold vibrations visually on a cathode-ray screen, using electrodes placed against the appropriate part of the neck. A **laryngoscope** is a long-handled small mirror inserted into the mouth to enable the doctor to see the larynx. ➤creaky voice; vocal folds.

lateral Descriptive of a type of consonant where there is an obstruction to the airstream in the middle of the vocal tract, so that air passes through an incomplete closure at one or both sides. The different kinds of *l* sound are all laterals. ➤clear l; consonant.

Latin The parent language of the Romance family, spoken during the first millennium BC in Rome and the surrounding provinces, then rising and declining in Europe, the Middle East, and Africa along with the fortunes of the Roman Empire. It is preserved in inscriptions from the 6th century BC, and in literature from the 3rd century BC (**Classical Latin**). Major figures include the poet Virgil, the orator Cicero, and the historian Livy, all active in or around the 1st century BC. The **Vulgar Latin** used from around the 3rd century AD in everyday speech throughout the Roman Empire gave rise to the Romance family of languages. A Christian Latin style also emerged, culminating in St Jerome's translation of the Bible (the Vulgate). This proved to be highly influential in the Middle Ages, with Latin the official language of the Roman Catholic Church (a status it retains today) as well as the language of administration, scholarship, education, science, and literature for most of Europe. A **Renaissance Latin** is associated with Dante, Petrarch, and others in the 14th century. As the chief language of education, Latin later exercised considerable influence on the way grammar was taught in schools; Latin grammatical categories came to be routinely used in the description of modern European languages, resulting in a frame of reference whose artificiality has come to be appreciated only in the 20th century. ➤Italic; Latinate; prescriptivism; Romance.

Latin alphabet ➤Roman alphabet.

Latinate Descriptive of any grammar based on the terms and categories used in Classical Latin grammar. Examples include the use of a case system (nominative, vocative, accusative, etc.) to describe the properties of nouns, or the use of an array of tenses (future, future perfect, pluperfect, etc.) to describe verbs. The term usually carries a pejorative implication, especially when it refers to languages where linguists consider the use of Latin-based categories to be inappropriate. ➤case; Latin; prescriptivism; tense 1.

Latvia (population in 1995 estimated at 2,620,000) The official languages are Latvian (spoken by *c.*56% of the population) and Russian (*c.*34%). Romani and Yiddish are also important. ➤Latvian; Russian.

Latvian A Baltic language spoken by over 1.5 million people, chiefly in Latvia (*c*.1.4 million), and also in Lithuania, Ukraine, Estonia, and Belarus, and through emigration in the USA, Australia, and a few other countries; also known as **Lettish**. Its earliest texts (in Gothic script) date from the 16th century. A Roman alphabet was adopted in 1922, with the addition of diacritics to represent palatal consonants. ➤➤Baltic; Latvia.

law An abbreviated statement of the predictable relationships between different languages or the states of a language. The notion has been primarily used with reference to the development of pronunciation (**sound laws**), especially as studied in the 19th-century, where the laws are named after the people who thought them up (e.g. Grimm, Verner). ➤➤Grimm's law; Neogrammarians; philology; sound change; Verner's law.

lax ➤tension.

leading /'ledɪŋ/ The white space between lines of type on a page. The term derives from the thin strips of lead, less than the height of the surrounding type, which were formerly used to separate lines of type when typesetting text. Placing a number of these strips side by side would increase the amount of space between lines. Different methods are used in modern typesetting, but the term continues in use. ➤➤typography.

Lebanon (population in 1995 estimated at 2,919,000) The official language is Arabic, spoken by *c*.93% of the population. Other languages are Armenian, Kurdish, and Aramaic. French is used for international purposes. ➤➤Arabic.

lect Any variety of a language which can be identified in a speech community. The term was introduced as a general notion under which could be subsumed regional, social, personal, occupational, and other kinds of linguistic variation. Grammars which take lectal variation into account are said to be **polylectal** or **panlectal**. ➤➤creole; dialect; idiolect; variety.

Lekhitic /le'kɪtɪk/ A name sometimes given to a group of West Slavic languages originally spoken along the Baltic between the Vistula and the Oder. It included Polish, Kashubian, Polabian (which died out in the 18th century), and Slovincian. ➤➤Polish; Slavic.

lemma ➤headword.

length In phonetics, the physical duration of a sound or utterance, measured in seconds or fractions of a second. In phonology, the term has a less obvious meaning, as it refers to the relative duration of sounds and syllables when these are linguistically contrastive; also called **quantity**, and contrasting with **quality**, which is the kind of articulation involved in a sound, regardless of its duration. A language may have 'long' vs. 'short' vowels, or 'long' vs. 'short' consonants. Long vowels in English include /iː/ (as in *see*) and /uː/ (as in *shoe*); short vowels include /ɪ/ (as in *sit*) and /ʊ/ (as in *put*). ➤➤consonant; duration; Estonian; mora; vowel.

lenis /'liːnɪs/ ➤fortis.

lenition ➤fortis.

lento Descriptive of speech produced slowly or with careful articulation; contrasts with **allegro**, where the speech is faster than usual. Several other music-derived terms have been appropriated for the study of speech prosody, such as **crescendo**. ➤➤prosody.

Lesotho (population in 1995 estimated at 2,017,000) The official languages are English and Sotho (Sesotho). Sotho is spoken by *c*.85% of the population, the other local language being Zulu (*c*.15%). English is used for international purposes. ➤➤English; Sotho.

letter A symbol used in an alphabetic system of writing to represent one or more speech sounds. In many modern writing systems, a distinction is drawn between large letters all the same height (**capital letters** or **upper-case letters**) and smaller letters whose height varies (**lower-case letters**). Capitals have several functions, marking the beginning of a sentence, proper nouns, and abbreviations, and also being used in cases of general emphasis (*HURRY UP PLEASE IT'S TIME*) and special emphasis (*She Who Must Be Obeyed*). Small capitals (of a similar height to lower-case letters) may be distinguished from large ('full') capitals in certain typefaces (e.g. CAPITAL vs. CAPITAL), though this contrast is not available in typewriter setting. The relationship between letters and sounds is the basis of a language's spelling system. ➤➤alphabet; black letter writing; cursive; italic; ligature; majuscule; spelling; uncial; writing.

Lëtzebuergesch /'letsəbuəgeʃ/ A West Germanic language, spoken by *c*.350,000 people, chiefly in Luxembourg (where it is widespread as a language of local identity), with some in Belgium and Germany, and through immigration in the USA; also known as **Luxemb(o)urgish** or **Luxembourgeois**. It is written in the Roman alphabet. ➤➤Germanic; Luxembourg.

level 1. A major dimension of the structural organization of language, which can be independently studied. The major levels are phonology, grammar, and semantics, but certain other domains have also been called 'levels', such as phonetics, morphology, and pragmatics. ➤➤duality of structure. **2**. In generative linguistics, a type of representation encountered within the derivation of a sentence. An influential case is the distinction between deep and surface levels of structure. ➤➤deep structure. **3**. A structural layer within a hierarchy, such as clause, phrase, or word; also called **rank**. A particular syntactic process might be said to operate 'at clause level', for example. ➤➤hierarchy. **4**. A degree of pitch height or loudness; syllables might be pronounced at high, mid, or low levels. A pitch height which does not vary can also be called 'level' (e.g. a 'level tone'), as can a stress pattern where the constituents are equal (a 'level stress'). ➤➤prosody. **5**. A model of expression felt to be appropriate to a type of social situation (a stylistic level), such as formal or intimate. This sense can be illustrated from the way people sometimes talk about 'lowering the level of the conversation'. ➤➤stylistics.

level tone ➤➤falling tone.

lexeme /'leksi:m/ The smallest distinctive unit in the lexicon of a language; also called a **lexical item**. The term was introduced to avoid the ambiguity in the term 'word', when discussing vocabulary. A lexeme may consist of a single word (e.g. *table*) or more than one word (e.g. phrasal verbs, such as *switch off*). Also, a lexeme is an abstract notion, subsuming a range of variant forms (each of which is a word): *go*, for example, subsumes *gone, went, going*, and *goes*. ➤➤idiom; lexicon.

lexical density A measure of the difficulty of a text, using the ratio of the number of different words in a text (the 'word types') to the total number of words in the text (the 'word tokens'); also called the **type–token ratio (TTR)**. It is calculated by dividing the number of different words by the total number of words and multiplying by 100. The result is given as a percentage. The assumption is that increasing the number of different words (i.e. a higher TTR) increases textual difficulty. ➤➤statistical linguistics.

lexical field ➤semantic field theory.

lexical-functional grammar (LFG) A grammatical theory in which the role of the lexicon is seen as central, and syntactic functions (such as subject and object) are seen as basic notions ('primitive terms') within the grammar. This approach developed in the 1980s as an alternative to earlier models of generative grammar, which emphasized syntactic forms rather than functions, and where syntactic structure was thought to be central. ➤➤form 1; function 1; generative grammar.

lexical item ➤lexeme; lexicon.

lexical morphology ➤morphology.

lexical phonology A theory about the organization of grammar in which all morphological rules, and many phonological ones, are placed in the lexicon. The phonological rules are divided into **lexical rules**, which may interact with morphological rules, and **postlexical rules**, which may not. ➤➤lexicon; morphology; phonology; rule 1.

lexical verb A verb which expresses an action, event, or state; also called a **main verb** or **full verb**. The contrast is with the auxiliary verb system, which expresses attitudinal and grammatical contrasts. ➤➤verb.

lexical word ➤grammatical word.

lexicography The art and science of dictionary making. A dictionary is a reference book which lists the words of one or more languages, usually in alphabetical order, along with information about their spelling, pronunciation, grammatical status, meaning, history, and use. Dictionaries vary greatly in size, from unabridged works of several thousand pages to the small concise or pocket books of just a few hundred pages. These days, a strictly linguistic approach, in which information is given only about the properties of the lexical items (the traditional approach in British lexicography), is being replaced by one which adds certain kinds of encyclopedic information (traditional in American and many Continental dictionaries). As a consequence, new ways of describing language reference works are now being devised – as illustrated by the title of the present book. ➤citation form; defining vocabulary; glossary; headword; lexicon; term bank; thesaurus.

lexicology ➤lexicon.

lexicon The vocabulary of a language (technically, its **lexical items** or **lexemes**), especially when these are listed in a dictionary as a set of **lexical entries**; also called **lexis**. The study of a language's lexicon is **lexicology**. A network of semantically related lexical items, such as the words for colour or fruit, is a **lexical field** (or **semantic field**). In generative grammar, the lexicon is the component containing all the information about the structural properties of lexical items. **Lexical syntax**

'Big hairy thing with horns overboard!'

is an approach which incorporates syntactic rules within the lexicon; **lexical phonology** is an approach where some of the phonological rules are transferred to the lexicon. In psycholinguistics, the stored mental representation of what people know about their language is called the **mental lexicon**, and the study of the psychology of word meanings is sometimes called **psycholexicology**. ➤component 2; lexeme; lexicography; semantic field theory; semantics.

lexicostatistics ➤glottochronology.

Lezghian or **Lezgian** /'lezgɪən/ A member of the Dagestanian group of Caucasian languages, spoken by c.450,000 people, chiefly in the Dagestan region of Russia and in Azerbaijan. It is written in the Cyrillic alphabet. The name is also used for a group of related languages spoken in this area. ➤Nakho-Dagestanian.

LFG An abbreviation of **lexical-functional grammar**.

liaison The introduction of a sound at the end of a word in certain phonological contexts. For example, a final consonant may be introduced before a following vowel, as in French *nous avons*, where the *-s* of *nous* is pronounced (compare *nous voulons*, where it is not). ➤linking; transition 1.

Liberia (population in 1995 estimated at 3,029,000) The official language is English. An English-based pidgin (Liberian English) is used by over half the population. There are in addition c.30 local languages, notably Kru and Kpelle. ➤English; pidgin.

Libya (population in 1995 estimated at 4,848,000) The official language is Arabic, spoken by most of the population. There are a few other local languages, such as Tamashek and Teda. English is used for international purposes. ➤Arabic.

Liechtenstein (population in 1995 estimated at 31,000) The official language is German, which is used by the whole population. English is also used for international purposes. ➤German.

ligature /'lɪɡətʃʊə/ A written or printed symbol in which two or more letters have been joined together; examples include Æ and œ. The term is also used for a stroke or bar which connects two or more letters, as in *fi*. ➤graphology 1.

LINC An abbreviation of **Language in the National Curriculum**.

linear In the history of writing systems, descriptive of scripts which use a sequence of simply drawn characters instead of pictorial writing. The earliest examples are known as Linear A and Linear B. Linearity is a feature of most modern writing, though direction varies (e.g. left–right, right–left, downwards), and the physical limitations of the page force an interrupted linearity on to the text, in the form of **line-breaks**. ➤Linear A; writing.

Linear A A script used in Crete in the middle of the 2nd millennium BC. It has not been deciphered, though some scholars believe the language it represents to be

Minoan. The name refers to the way the script is written in lines, probably from right to left – a contrast with previous hieroglyphic writing. The label 'A' distinguishes the script from **Linear B**, which was used to write Greek on the island later in the same millennium. ➤➤Greek; hieroglyphic.

Linear B ➤Greek; Linear A.

line-break ➤linear.

lingua franca An auxiliary language used to permit routine communication between groups of people who speak different native languages. The term means 'Frankish tongue', which was used as a common language in the Mediterranean area in the Middle Ages. Lingua francas are very common in heavily multilingual regions, such as West and East Africa. ➤➤auxiliary language; Bislama; Hausa; Hindi; koine; Krio; Malay; Russian; Sango; Swahili.

lingual/linguo- Descriptive of a sound made with the tongue. For example, a **lingual trill** is the trilled [r], heard in many Welsh and Scots speakers, made with the tip of the tongue against the alveolar ridge. ➤➤tongue.

Linguapax An international programme, initiated by UNESCO in 1987, whose aim is to use language education in general, and language teaching in particular, as a means of promoting increased understanding between nations – 'peace through language diversity and plurilingualism'. First languages, national languages, and foreign languages are all viewed as ways through which a specifically linguistic contribution can be made to foster peace, democracy, and human rights – for example, by introducing materials to do with peace and cultural diversity into language teaching syllabuses. ➤➤peace linguistics.

linguist A term used in two related senses: (1) a student or practitioner of linguistics, sometimes also called a **linguistician** (but not usually by people working in linguistics); (2) a person proficient in more than one language. It is usually necessary to clarify which sense is intended, when describing someone as 'a linguist'. ➤➤bilingualism; linguistics.

linguistic An ambiguous term, which therefore needs to be used with care: (1) descriptive of language, or a feature of language, in such phrases as *linguistic minority*; (2) descriptive of linguistics, referring to an approach or concept which derives from this field, as in *This point is of linguistic importance*. ➤➤linguistics.

linguistic anthropology ➤anthropological linguistics.

linguistic atlas ➤dialect atlas.

linguistic change ➤language change.

linguistic determinism ➤Sapir–Whorf hypothesis.

linguistic geography ➤geolinguistics.

linguistician ➤linguist.

linguistic method An approach to the teaching of reading which claimed to be based on the principles of linguistics, especially on those espoused by structuralist linguists of the 1940s and 1950s (such as Leonard Bloomfield). The approach emphasized the relationship between spoken and written language, the importance of identifying regular patterns, and the need to attack spelling problems in a systematic way. Given the enormous variety of modern linguistic theories and models, the term is no longer appropriate or fashionable. ➤➤Bloomfieldian; reading; structural.

linguistic minority ➤minority.

linguistic philosophy ➤philosophical linguistics.

linguistic relativity ➤➤Sapir–Whorf hypothesis.

linguistic rights ➤Universal Declaration of Linguistic Rights.

linguistics The scientific study of language; also called **linguistic science** – or, when phonetics is seen as a distinct area of study, **linguistic sciences**. Several branches of the subject have been recognized. The study of a language at any given point in time is known as **synchronic** or **descriptive linguistics**; **diachronic** or **historical linguistics** is the study of language change. **Comparative linguistics** studies language history by investigating languages thought to be related. **General** or **theoretical linguistics** aims to establish universal principles for the study of languages, and to determine the characteristics of human language as a phenomenon. **Contrastive linguistics** focuses on the differences between languages, especially in the context of language teaching. **Typological linguistics** aims to identify the common characteristics of different languages or language families. **Structural linguistics** refers to any approach which focuses on the patterned characteristics of language, but is especially used for the approaches to syntax and phonology which were current in the 1940s and 1950s, with their emphasis on providing discovery procedures for the analysis of surface structure. Linguistics is sometimes contrasted with philology, a more specifically historical field. ➤➤anthropological/ applied / bio- / clinical / comparative / computational / critical / educational / ethno- / mathematical/neuro-/philosophical/psycho-/socio-/statistical linguistics; language 1; philology; structural; typology of language.

linguistic science(s) ➤linguistics.

linguistic variable ➤variable.

linking Descriptive of a sound which is introduced between linguistic units, usually for ease of pronunciation; for example, French *il a* 'he has' becomes *a-t-il* 'has he'. Sounds which have no correlation in spelling can attract the criticism of purist language commentators, as in the case of *law(r) and order*. ➤➤intrusion; liaison; purism.

linking verb ➤copula; extensive.

lipogram /'lɪpəʊgram/ A text from which a specific letter has been omitted throughout. An early master of the genre was the 5th-century BC poet Tryphiodorus, who wrote an epic of 24 books, each omitting a different letter of the Greek alphabet. The difficulty comes in attempting to write a text which leaves out the most frequent letters of the alphabet, such as (in English) *e* or *t*.➤➤univocalic; word game.

lip reading ➤speech reading.

lip rounding ➤labial; rounding.

liquid Descriptive of sonorant consonants other than nasals and approximants. It typically includes sounds made with the apex of the tongue against the alveolar ridge, notably /l/ and /r/. ➤➤sonorant.

lisp An abnormal articulation of a sibilant consonant, especially [s]. The commonest problem is that the tongue tip is placed against or between the teeth (a **frontal, lingual** or **interdental** lisp), but several auditory qualities of lisp can be heard, depending on exactly how the tongue is configured. ➤➤sibilant; speech defect.

literacy The ability to read and write; contrasts with **illiteracy**, the two poles now being seen to demarcate a continuum of ability. Discussion of the problem, either within a country or on a world scale, is complicated by the difficulty of measuring the extent of illiteracy in individuals. The notion of **functional literacy** was introduced in the 1940s, in an attempt to identify minimal levels of reading/writing efficiency in a society, such as being able to write one's name; but defining even minimal levels is difficult, especially today, with increasing demands being made on people to be literate in a wider range of contexts. Current world estimates suggest that about 900 million adults are illiterate to some extent. In the UK, figures were being cited in the 1990s of about 2 million illiterate people (3.5% of the population). In the USA, estimates have varied between 10% and 20%. In some Third World countries, the figure may be as high as 80%. National literacy campaigns in several countries have raised public awareness, and standards are slowly rising. **Biliteracy** is the ability to read and write in more than one language. The term 'literacy' is also now often used in a broader sense, referring to the ability to understand a technical or cultural domain, as in *computer literacy* and *graphic literacy*. ➤➤dyslexia; reading; writing.

literal ➤figurative language; typo.

literary pragmatics The study of the relationship of the production and reception of literary texts to their use of linguistic forms. The area of research involves an interaction between linguistics, literary theory, and the philosophy of language. Topics which can be studied from this point of view include the use of regional dialect, obscenity, or blasphemy in drama, especially viewed in relation to their effect on the attitudes and sensibilities of a reader or audience. ➤➤narrative; pragmatics.

literary stylistics ➤stylistics.

Lithuania (population in 1995 estimated at 3,775,000)   The official languages are Lithuanian (spoken by *c*.80% of the population) and Russian (*c*.9%). Polish, Ukrainian, and Romani are among the other languages spoken. ➤Lithuanian.

Lithuanian A Baltic language spoken by *c*.4 million people, chiefly in Lithuania, with many immigrants in several other countries (e.g. USA, Russia, Brazil, Argentina). Written texts date from the 16th century. The modern language is written in a 32-letter Latin alphabet. ➤➤Baltic; Lithuania.

litotes /laɪˈtəʊtiːz, ˈlaɪtətiːz/ A figure of speech where something is understated; the word comes from Greek 'simple, meagre'. An everyday example is *Not bad*, said of something which the speaker feels to be very good. ➤➤figurative language; hyperbole.

living language ➤dead language.

loan blend/shift/word ➤borrowing.

loan translation ➤calque.

LOB corpus ➤Lancaster–Oslo/Bergen Corpus of British English.

locative case One of the common ways in which inflected languages make a word (usually a noun or pronoun) change its form, in order to show a grammatical relationship with other parts of the sentence. The locative case typically expresses the idea of a place of a state or action. Structures which express locational meaning may also be referred to as locative; for example, *in the street* could be called a **locative phrase**. ➤➤inflection 1.

locutionary act ➤illocutionary act.

logical subject ➤subject.

logocentrism A language- or word-centred view of literature or other behaviour. In literary stylistics, the notion is associated with the structuralist approach to analysis, which focused on the study of the language of a text to the exclusion of the author's individuality, the social context, and the historical situation. A reaction to this view in the late 1960s came to be called **post-structuralism**. Here, language is seen as a system whose values shift in response to nonlinguistic factors. A range of viewpoints drew attention to the multiple meanings of words, stressing the role of mental processes in interpreting linguistic relationships, and denying the possibility of objectivity in textual interpretation. In particular, the methods of **deconstruction**, developed by Jacques Derrida (1930–   ), aimed to show the inherent contradictions and paradoxes in logocentric approaches. ➤➤structural; stylistics.

logogram A written or printed symbol which represents a word (or morpheme) in a language; also called a **logograph** or (in the case of Oriental languages) a **character**. The best-known examples of a logographic system are Chinese and its derivative script, Japanese kanji. The term must be used with care, as it suggests that only words are represented by the symbols, whereas meaningful parts of words (e.g. affixes, roots) are also included in the notion. Several thousand graphemes are used in a logographic system, though in modern languages basic literacy requires a command of only *c*.2000. Logograms in European languages include the numerals (1, 2, etc.) and many mathematical and scientific symbols. ➤➤ideogram; morpheme; pasigraphy; writing.

$$\times \quad \div \quad = \quad \pm \quad \simeq \quad \neq$$

$$\leq \quad \geq \quad \sqrt{} \quad ° \quad \infty \quad ©$$

$$\% \quad \& \quad £ \quad \$ \quad ‰ \quad ''$$

$$♠ \quad ♣ \quad ♭ \quad \# \quad 𝄞 \quad 𝄢$$

Examples of modern **logograms**.

logograph ➤logogram.

logogriph A word puzzle using anagrams; the term derives from Greek 'word + reed basket, riddle'. The clues are often given in verse form. ➤➤anagram.

logopedics or **logopaedics** /lɒgəʊˈpiːdɪks/ A term used primarily on the European mainland for the study of language (especially speech) disorders in children; its practitioners are **logopedists**. ➤➤language pathology.

logorrhoea /lɒgəˈriːə/ Excessive, uncontrolled, incoherent speech. The term is often used in an insulting way about anyone who (in the opinion of the listener) is talking too much. It does not have technical status in linguistics.

London–Lund Corpus of Spoken English A corpus of educated spoken British English, consisting of the spoken material collected as part of the Survey of English Usage in London. The texts (of 5000 words each) were transferred to computer tape in the 1970s at the Survey of Spoken English, University of Lund, and are also partly available in printed form. A lexical concordance has also been compiled. ➤➤corpus; Survey of English Usage.

Longman–Lancaster English Language Corpus A corpus of spoken and written English being compiled by Longman Group UK, under the direction of Della Summers, in collaboration with Geoffrey Leech of Lancaster University. Established in 1991, it aims to provide a corpus of between 30 and 50 million words of 20th-century spoken and written English – predominantly British (50%) and American (40%), with some inclusion of other varieties. ➤➤corpus.

long sound ➤length.

look-and-say A method of teaching reading which focuses on the recognition of whole words; also called the **whole word** approach. It assumes that readers can make use of their language knowledge and general experience to identify critical letters or words in a section of text, and thus begin building up a basic sight vocabulary. This initial sampling gives them an expectation about the way a text should be read, and they use their background awareness to 'guess' the remainder of the text and fill in the gaps, gradually increasing the range of their reading vocabulary. ➤➤phonics; reading; sight vocabulary.

loudness The attribute of auditory sensation in terms of which a sound may be ordered on a scale from low to high volume. It corresponds to some degree with the acoustic feature of **intensity**, reflecting the size of the vibrations of the vocal folds. The linguistic use of loudness is studied under the heading of a language's prosodic features. ➤➤prosody; stress.

lower case ➤letter; majuscule.

low tone ➤tone.

low variety ➤diglossia.

low vowel ➤high vowel.

LSP An abbreviation of **Language for Specific Purposes**.

ludic language /'luːdɪk/ Language whose primary function is to be part of play, as in the nonsense, repetitive rhythms, and rhymes heard in children's games all over the world. Adults, too, may play with language, such as by adopting silly tones of voice or by twisting words into unorthodox shapes to create a humorous effect. ➤➤figurative/play/referential language; verbal play; word game.

Luo /ləˈwəʊ/ A Nilotic language spoken by *c*.3 million people, mainly in Kenya, with some speakers in Uganda and Tanzania. It is written in the Roman alphabet. ➤➤Nilotic.

Luorawetlan /ləwɒrəˈwetln/ A family of languages generally placed within the Paleosiberian grouping, spoken in north-eastern Siberia. It includes Chukchi and Koryak, both with several thousand speakers, and Kamchadal, Aliutor, and Kerek, which have only a few hundred. ➤➤Chukchi.

Lusatian /luːˈseɪʃn/ ➤Sorbian.

Luxembourg (population in 1995 estimated at 402,000) The official language is French, with German widely used as a lingua franca, and Lëtzebuergesch being the first language of most people. The language of government administration and in general professional use is French, with both French and German (and increasingly, Lëtzebuergesch) being used in literature. English is also used for international trade and tourism. ➤➤French; German; Lëtzebuergesch.

Luxembourgish ➤Lëtzebuergesch.

M

Maban /'maban/ A small group of Nilo-Saharan languages, spoken in the Central African Republic, Chad, and Sudan. It includes Masalit, Mimi, and Maba. ➤Nilo-Saharan.

Macao (population in 1995 estimated at 470,000) The official language (pending the return to Chinese rule in 1999) is Portuguese. Yue Chinese (Cantonese) is the first language of most of the population. The indigenous Portuguese-based creole, Macanese, is no longer found in the province. English is used for international purposes. ➤Portuguese.

macaronic /makə'rɒnɪk/ Descriptive of a type of speech or writing which mixes two languages – the term is, indeed, from *macaroni*. The label is usually applied to a kind of language (often a verse form) where Latin is mixed with vernacular words, which are sometimes given Latin endings – but any mixture of languages can be so described. *Comez over ici, if you plait. Lots of goodorum gruborum in the fridgibus.* The genre has been known since the 15th century, and will still be encountered both in public-school humour and in literature (e.g. the character of Salvatore in Umberto Eco's *The Name of the Rose*, 1980). A related effect is obtained by constructing a sentence in a foreign language using words which sound like the words in a different language, and which make sense only in that other language. A long-standing schoolboy example is *Caesar adsum jam forte*, read aloud as 'Caesar had some jam for tea'. ➤verbal play.

Macedonia (Former Yugoslav Republic of) (population in 1995 estimated at 1,950,000) Macedonian is spoken by *c.*75% of the population. There are also several speakers of Albanian (*c.*250,000), Romanian, Turkish, Romani, and varieties of Serbo-Croatian. ➤Macedonian.

Macedonian A member of the South Slavic group of languages, spoken by *c.*2 million people chiefly in the republic of Macedonia, where it is the official language, and also in nearby parts of Bulgaria, Greece, and Albania. It is written in the Cyrillic alphabet. Texts with Macedonian features date from the 10th century, but a literature reflecting modern standard Macedonian is found only from the late 18th century. ➤Bulgarian; Slavic.

machine translation (MT) The automatic production of a translation using a computer; also called **automatic translation**. The main aim has been to produce systems of analysis which allow for grammatical and semantic complexity. Automatic procedures (algorithms) have been developed for parsing syntactic structure, and artificial intelligence techniques are beginning to simulate human processes of thought and interaction. Increasing use is being made of interactive systems of MT, in which humans pre-edit or post-edit a text processed by the computer. In **pre-editing**, a natural language source text is rewritten, using a controlled syntax and vocabulary, to produce a version which the computer can handle with relative ease. In **post-editing**, raw machine-produced data in the target language is edited into an error-free text. Also emerging is the field of **machine-aided translation**, which introduces the use of peripheral hardware (e.g. word-processors) and software (e.g. spelling-checkers), as well as the availability of on-line access to technical term banks to speed up the search for the best lexical equivalents. ➤➤computational linguistics; morphology; parsing; syntax; term bank.

Macro-Algonkian ➤Algonkian.

Macro-Chibchan /makrəʊˈtʃɪbtʃən/ A widespread group of *c*.50 Amerindian languages, spoken in Central America, Colombia, and Venezuela, and south into Bolivia and Brazil. Only a few – Guaymí, Cuna (Kuna), Epera (Catío), Páez – have substantial numbers of speakers, in the tens of thousands, and several are on the verge of extinction. Several of the languages have been written down (using the Roman alphabet) as a part of missionary activity in the region. ➤➤Amerindian.

Macro-Gê ➤Gê-Pano-Carib.

macrolinguistics An extremely broad conception of linguistic enquiry, promoted especially in the 1950s; language is seen in its overall relation to extralinguistic experience and to physical phonetic/graphetic properties. A contrast is drawn with **microlinguistics**, the analysis of linguistic data involving maximum depth of detail. ➤➤linguistics.

macron A diacritic which typically indicates syllable or vowel length, as in Latin *favēre* 'to favour'. It will often be seen in a dictionary transcription of pronunciation: ā, for example, might be used for a 'long a', as in *car*. ➤➤diacritic; length.

Macro-Panoan ➤Gê-Pano-Carib.

Macro-Penutian ➤Penutian.

Macro-Siouan /makrəʊˈsuːən/ A group of 26 Amerindian languages spoken in a broad swathe from Canada down through central USA, and in two areas further east. They are usually classified into five families: Siouan (12 languages), Catawba, Iroquoian (8 languages), Caddoan, and Yuchi. The best-known members are Cherokee and Dakota (Sioux), both with *c*.20,000 speakers, Crow and Mohawk, both with less than 5000. The languages use the Roman alphabet when written down. An interesting early exception was the 85-symbol Cherokee syllabary, devised by a half-Cherokee Indian named Sequoya in 1821. ➤➤Amerindian.

Madagascar (population in 1995 estimated at 13,456,000) The official languages are Malagasy and French. Malagasy, in several varieties, is the first language of almost the whole population. French is used for international purposes. ➤French; Malagasy.

Madeira (population in 1995 estimated at 260,000) The official language is Portuguese, spoken by almost everyone. English is also used for international trade and tourism. ➤Portuguese.

Madura ➤Madurese.

Madurese /madə'riːz/ A member of the Austronesian family of languages, spoken in Indonesia by *c*.10 million people in the island of Madura, along the coast of northern Java, and in other nearby islands; also called **Madura**. It is written in both the Roman and Javanese alphabets. ➤Austronesian.

Magahi /'magəhiː/ ➤Bihari.

Magyar /'magjɑː, 'mɒdʒɜː/ ➤Hungarian.

main clause ➤clause.

main verb ➤lexical verb.

Maithili /'maɪdəli/ ➤Bihari.

majority ➤minority.

major sentence A type of sentence which is highly productive in a language, such as subject + predicate; contrasts with **minor sentence**, where there is limited productivity, or where the structure lacks some of the constituents found in the major type. The sentence you are reading now is a major sentence type. The next one is not. No way. ➤productivity; sentence.

majuscule /'madʒəskjuːl/ A form of writing consisting of letters broadly contained within a single pair of horizontal lines; usually called **capital letters**. The Greek and Latin alphabets were originally written in this way. The contrast is with **minuscule** /'mɪnəskjuːl/, where the writing consists of letters whose parts may extend above and below a pair of horizontal lines; usually called 'small' (or **lower-case**) letters. Minuscule writing was a gradual development, in regular use for Greek by the 7th–8th centuries AD. The use of both kinds of letters in a single system is known as the **dual alphabet**, which dates from the time of Emperor Charlemagne (742–814). ➤letter; writing; p. 208.

Makua /mə'kwɑː/ A Bantu language spoken in the northern part of Mozambique by *c*.6 million people, and also in nearby parts of Malawi and Tanzania by over a million; sometimes listed as **Kua**. It is written in the Roman alphabet. ➤Bantu.

Malagasy /malə'gasiː,malə'gaʃ/ A member of the Austronesian family of languages, spoken in several varieties by over 13 million people in Madagascar, where it is an

(a) # A B C D E F G

(b) ## abcdefghijklm

(c) ## HILMNOPQRSTUXY FELICESOPERUMQUIN

(d) exuberib:caprarum·aurou: torum manupraeffif·Long

Majuscule and **minuscule**. (a) A modern majuscule. (b) A modern minuscule. (c) Roman rustic capitals – an early majuscule. (d) Late eighth-century Carolingian minuscule.

official language (along with French). It is written in the Roman alphabet. Brought to the island by Indonesian traders during the 1st millennium AD, various dialects are now used on the islands in the surrounding area. The standard language is based on the dialect of the largest ethnic group, the Merina, a plateau people who were the dominant kingdom in the 19th century. There is a large written literature, as well as a strong oral tradition, notable for its proverbs and ritual speech-making. ➤Austronesian; Madagascar.

malapropism /'maləprəpɪzm/ The inappropriate replacement of a word or phrase by other words with a similar sound but wrong meaning; also called **catachresis**. The user of a malapropism has not fully understood a long word, but makes a shot at it, substituting a word which 'sounds right'. The term comes from the name of Mrs Malaprop, a character in Richard Brinsley Sheridan's *The Rivals* – the name itself comes from French, *mal à propos* ('not to the purpose'). *Illiterate him, I say, quite from your memory*, is one of Mrs Malaprop's substitutions (for *obliterate*). ➤slip of the tongue.

Malawi /mə'lɑːwiː/ (population in 1995 estimated at 10,753,000) The official languages are Nyanja (Chewa) and English. Nyanja is spoken as a first language by about a third of the population, and is widely used as a lingua franca. There are *c.*10 other languages, including Makua (Lomwe), Yao, and Zulu. English is used for international purposes. ➤English; lingua franca; Nyanja.

Malay /mə'leɪ/ A member of the Austronesian family of languages, spoken by *c.*18

million people as a first language chiefly in Indonesia (*c*.10 million) and Malaysia (*c*.7 million), and also in Singapore and Brunei. It is an official language in Malaysia, Singapore, and Brunei, and is widely used throughout Indonesia as a lingua franca. The dialect of the south Malay Peninsula has become the standard language, under the name of **Bahasa Indonesia**, official in Indonesia since 1949, and often referred to simply as **Indonesian**. It is written in both the Roman and (among Islamic communities) Arabic alphabets. A pidginized variety, **Bazaar Malay** is widely used as a lingua franca throughout the Indonesian archipelago. Another form, known as **Baba Malay**, is used by Chinese communities in Malaysia. Other varieties of Malay are found in the region, notably in Thailand (Pattani Malay, *c*.2.4 million). Written records date from the 7th century AD, with a literary tradition dating from the arrival of Islam in the 15th century. The modern written language is now somewhat different from Classical Malay, following the introduction of spelling reforms earlier this century. ➤➤Austronesian; Indonesia; Malaysia.

Malayalam /maləˈjɑːləm/ A member of the Dravidian family of languages, spoken by *c*.34 million people in south-west India, chiefly in Kerala (where it is the official state language). It is written in the Malayalam alphabet, with records dating from the 9th century, and a literary tradition from the 13th century. The language has two main varieties, in a diglossic relationship. ➤➤diglossia; Dravidian.

Malayo-Polynesian ➤Austronesian.

Malaysia (population in 1995 estimated at 20,000,000) The official language is Malay, which is a first language for nearly half the people. English is the chief language of instruction in secondary education, and is widespread as a lingua franca; it is also used for international purposes. There are *c*.130 other languages, including several varieties of Chinese (*c*.4.5 million total), Buginese, Dayak, Javanese, and Tamil. Bazaar Malay is widely used as a contact language, and is a lingua franca in Sabah. ➤➤lingua franca; Malay.

Maldives (population in 1995 estimated at 251,000) The official language is Maldivian, spoken by most people on the islands. There are also some speakers of Sinhalese, Arabic, and various Indian languages. English is used for international trade and tourism. ➤➤Maldivian.

Maldivian A language belonging to the Western group of Indo-Aryan languages, spoken by about 90% of the people living in the Maldive Islands, south-west of India; known locally as **Divehi** or **Dhivehi**. There are also a few thousand speakers in India. It is written in the Maldivian alphabet (*Thaana*), written from right to left, the orthography showing the influence of both South Asian and Arabic scripts. ➤➤Indo-Aryan; Maldives.

Mali (population in 1995 estimated at 10,173,000) The official language is French. Bambara (*c*.2.7 million) is used as a lingua franca by most of the people, and is important in education and the media. There are *c*.30 other languages, notably

Arabic, Fulfulde, Malinke, Senufo, Songhai, Soninke, and Tamashek. French is used for international purposes. ➤➤Bambara; French; lingua franca.

Malinke /mə'lıŋkeı/ A Mande language spoken by *c*.3 million people in Guinea, Mali, and several other areas in the west of the West African bulge; also known by other names, in different parts of the region, such as **Maninka** (sometimes distinguished as a separate language) and **Mandingo**. It is an important lingua franca, and is written in the Roman alphabet. ➤➤Mande.

Malta (population in 1995 estimated at 370,000) The official languages are Maltese and English. Over 80% of the people speak Maltese. English is used for international trade and tourism. ➤➤English; Maltese.

Maltese A Semitic language spoken by *c*.330,000 people in the island of Malta, where it is an official language (along with English), and through immigration in a few other countries, such as Italy, Tunisia, USA, and UK. A development of an Arabic dialect, it now has many loan words from Italian, English, French, and other languages. It is the only variety of Arabic to be written in the Roman alphabet. In recent decades there has been an active campaign to promote the language, especially in broadcasting and the press. ➤➤Arabic; Malta; Semitic.

Manchu /man'ʧuː/ A member of the Manchu-Tungus group of the Altaic family of languages, spoken now by less than a thousand of the Manchu population (of *c*.10 million) in north-east China, but formerly an official language of China and a major lingua franca between China and the outside world for over 200 years. It is written in the Manchu alphabet (an adaptation of Mongolian script), with a literary tradition dating from the 17th century. However, the cultural and linguistic dominance of the Chinese has caused a steady decline in numbers since the 19th century. ➤➤Chinese; lingua franca; Manchu-Tungus.

Manchu-Tungus /man'ʧuː tʊŋ'guːz/ A group of *c*.12 languages within the Altaic family, spoken by *c*.50,000 people in a wide area across south-east Asia and northern China. They include Evenki, Nanai, and Manchu (the only member with a literary history). ➤➤Evenki; Manchu.

Mandarin /'mandərın/ ➤Chinese.

Mande /'mandeı/ A group of *c*.45 languages belonging to the Niger-Congo family, spoken by over 12 million people in the western part of the bulge of Africa, between Guinea and Nigeria. Its main members are Bambara, Malinke, Dyula, and Mende, all found in the western part of the region. ➤➤Bambara; Dyula; Malinke; Mende; Niger-Congo.

manner of articulation The nature of the chief articulatory constriction during the production of a consonant sound. It refers especially to the degree of the constriction and the way it is made. There may be a complete articulatory closure (as in the case of stops); an oral closure, with the soft palate lowered (nasals); a close approximation of the two articulators (fricatives); an open approximation of the two articulators (approximants); a central closure only (laterals); or a vibration (trills, taps, and flaps). ➤➤articulation; consonant.

manual alphabet ➤finger spelling.

manualism An approach which concentrates on the teaching of sign language to the deaf, to the exclusion of speech; contrasts with **oralism**, where the focus is exclusively on the use of spoken language. **Total communication** is a system which involves the simultaneous use of both manual and oral methods. ➤➤sign language.

Manx A member of the Goidelic branch of the Celtic family of languages, spoken now only by a few hundred people who have learned it as adults as part of the modern revivalist movement, and by a handful who claim to have learned it as a first language from their grandparents. It is used officially in the Isle of Man, where laws are written in Manx as well as English, using the Roman alphabet. Manx developed out of Irish Gaelic, and is closely related to nearby dialects in both Ireland and Scotland. Written records date from the early 17th century. The island was wholly Manx-speaking until the 18th century, and there were still some 5000 speakers at the beginning of the 20th century; but by the 1940s the language was no longer in use as a medium of daily interaction. ➤➤Celtic.

Maori /'maʊriː/ A member of the Austronesian family of languages, spoken by *c*.60,000 people in New Zealand, and understood to some degree by perhaps as many as 100,000. The Maori population steadily increased in the 20th century, after a period of massive decline. There has been a marked improvement in social standards, and this has influenced the status of the language, which is now taught as an optional second language in schools. Maori is regularly used in songs, in oratory, and on official occasions, and is developing a modern literature. An increasing number of Maori words have come to be used in contemporary New Zealand English. ➤➤Austronesian.

Marathi /məˈrɑːtiː/ A language belonging to the Western group of Indo-Aryan languages, spoken by *c*.65 million people chiefly in the state of Maharashtra, north-west India (where it is an official regional language), and in nearby areas. It is written in the Devanagari alphabet. ➤➤Devanagari; Indo-Aryan.

Mari /'mɑːriː/ A member of the Finnic group of the Finno-Ugric family of languages, spoken by *c*.535,000 people, chiefly in the Mari region of Russia (where it has official status), and nearby areas along the Volga valley; formerly called **Cheremis**. It is written in the Cyrillic alphabet. ➤➤Finno-Ugric.

Mariana Islands, Northern (population in 1995 estimated at 51,000). The official language is English. Over half the population speak an Austronesian language,

Chamorro. Other languages include Chinese, Korean, and various Philippines languages. ➤➤English.

markedness An analytic principle in linguistics, whereby pairs of linguistic features, seen as oppositions, are given values of positive (**marked**) or negative/neutral (**unmarked**). In its most general sense, this distinction relates simply to the presence or absence of a particular characteristic; for example, a voiced sound might be said to be 'marked for voice', or a plural noun in English to be 'marked for number' (a plural ending having been added to the unmarked singular form, as in *boys* vs. *boy*). There are several other interpretations of markedness; for example, using a semantic criterion, the more specific of a pair of items would be called marked, as in the case of *dog* (unmarked) vs. *bitch* (marked). In recent generative grammar, **markedness theory** deals with the tendencies of linguistic properties to be found in all languages: an unmarked property is one which accords with these tendencies, whereas a marked property goes against them. ➤➤contrast; generative grammar; number; semantics; voicing.

Marshall Islands (population in 1995 estimated at 56,600) The official language is English. Most of the population speak an Austronesian language, Marshallese. ➤➤English.

Martinique (population in 1995 estimated at 385,000) The official language is French. Almost everyone speaks a French-based creole (Patwa) widespread throughout the Lesser Antilles. ➤➤creole; French; Patwa.

Masai /məˈsaɪ/ A Nilotic (or, in some classifications, Nilo-Hamitic) language spoken by *c*.880,000 people, especially in the Great Rift Valley of Kenya and Tanzania. It is written in the Roman alphabet. ➤➤Nilotic.

masculine ➤gender.

mass noun ➤countability.

mathematical linguistics A branch of linguistics which studies the mathematical properties of language. It includes such areas as the statistical properties of texts, the algebraic study of string sets, the study of the formal properties of grammatical rule patterns, and the exploration of parsing algorithms in computing. ➤➤computational linguistics; linguistics.

matronymic /matrəˈnɪmɪk/ ➤patronymic.

Mauritania (population in 1995 estimated at 2,295,000) The official language is Arabic, spoken by *c*.66% of the people. French is still important within the country, and is also used for international purposes. About 7% of the population speak the West Atlantic language, Toucouleur, a variety of Fulfulde. ➤➤Arabic; Fulfulde.

Mauritius (population in 1995 estimated at 1,141,000) The official language is English. About half the population speak a French-based creole (Morisyen, Kreole), widely used as a lingua franca. About 70% of the population is from India, many speaking Bihari, Hindi, Tamil, or Urdu. Both English and French are used for international purposes. ➤➤creole; English; lingua franca.

maxims of conversation General principles thought to underlie the efficient use of language, and which together identify a general **cooperative principle**. Four basic maxims have been recognized: the **maxim of quality** states that speakers' contributions should be genuine, and not spurious (e.g. deliberately misleading); the **maxim of quantity** states that contributors should give no more and no less information than is required to make the message clear to the addressee; the **maxim of relevance** states that contributions should be related to the purpose of the exchange; and the **maxim of manner** states that contributions should be clear and concise, avoiding obscurity and ambiguity. The notion of relevance has been developed into a major principle which purports to explain the nature of cognition (**relevance theory**). In this approach, all communicative acts are viewed as carrying a guarantee of optimal relevance, and are interpreted in the light of this guarantee. ➤➤conversation analysis; cooperative principle; *carton below.*

Mayan /ˈmaɪən/ A family of Amerindian languages spoken in Mexico and Central America. The chief languages are Yucatec (or Maya, *c.*700,000), Quekchi (*c.*350,000), and several varieties of Mam (*c.*450,000), Quiché (*c.*650,000), and Cakchiquel

'*Let's get one thing clear: is this discussion going to be conducted in vague generalities or specific generalities?*'

(*c*.440,000). The Mayans are best known for their early history, developing a system of hieroglyphic writing from about the 3rd century AD, which continued in use until after the Spanish invasions. After many fruitless attempts, considerable progress has now been made in decipherment. However, evidence is limited, as most literary work was considered to be pagan, and destroyed after the Spanish conquest. ➤Amerindian; hieroglyphic.

meaning A basic notion used in language study in two main ways. First, determining the signification of a message is the chief end of linguistic enquiry: above all, language is concerned with the communication of meaning. Secondly, meaning is used as a way of analysing the structure of language, through such notions as contrastiveness and distinctiveness. For example, the criterion of meaning is used in order to establish the set of phonemes in a language: *pit* is different from *bit* in meaning, and therefore /p/ and /b/ are different phonemes. A traditional focus of enquiry recognizes the existence of several different kinds of meaning. Terms such as **referential**, **descriptive**, **denotative**, **extensional**, **factual**, and **objective meaning** are used when the emphasis is on the relationship of language to extralinguistic entities, events, or states of affairs. **Attitudinal**, **affective**, **connotative**, **emotive**, and **expressive meaning** are the chief terms used when the emphasis is on the relationship between language and the personal, emotional state of a speaker; and **cognitive** and **ideational meaning** focus on a person's intellectual state. **Contextual**, **functional**, **interpersonal**, **social**, and **situational meaning** express the way variations in the extralinguistic situation affect the understanding and interpretation of language. **Contextual** and **textual** meaning refer to those factors which affect the interpretation of a sentence, deriving from the rest of the discourse in which the sentence occurs. Within linguistics, the role each linguistic level plays in the total interpretation of a sentence is often referred to as the 'meaning' of that level, notably **lexical meaning** and **grammatical** or **structural** meaning. The science of meaning is **semantics**. ➤affective meaning; ambiguous; connotation; reference 1; semantics; sense.

mean length of utterance (MLU) A measure introduced into child language studies by American psychologist Roger Brown (1925–), as a means of monitoring increasing complexity. Rules are given to compute the length of a child's utterance in terms of morphemes. ➤acquisition.

mechanical translation ➤machine translation.

medial 1. Descriptive of sounds or syllables occurring in the middle of a word, or of words occurring within a sentence or other grammatical unit; contrasts with **initial** items (which occur at the beginning of the unit) and **final** items (which occur at the end). For example, the /n/ of *final* is in medial position, as is the adverb *quickly* in the clause *They quickly walked home*. ➤position 1. **2**. Descriptive of sounds occurring in the middle of the vocal tract, neither very far forward or very far back, nor of vowels where the tongue is neither fully high nor fully low. ➤➤central/front sound; high vowel.

medial vowel ➤high vowel.

medium The means of transmission of a message; also sometimes called **mode** or **modality.** Drawing, music, painting, sculpture, nonverbal communication, and other 'media' are all relevant, but in language study the term refers specifically to the transmission of a linguistic message by speech, writing, or sign. In language teaching, the **medium of instruction** is the language which a country has chosen for use in its educational system. This is usually the standard variety, though in multilingual countries (such as Belgium), the language of instruction may vary among localities. ➤➤communication; language planning; semiotics.

Melanesian /melə'niːʒn/ ➤Austronesian.

Mende /'mendeɪ/ A Mande language spoken by c.1.5 million people in Sierra Leone, with a few in Liberia. It is written in the Roman alphabet. ➤➤Mande.

Mennonite German ➤German.

merger ➤convergence 2.

Meso-American /'mezəʊ ə'merɪkn/ ➤Amerindian.

mesolect /'mezəlekt/ ➤creole.

metalanguage A language for describing an object of study, such as the technical language of chemistry, engineering, or law. The headwords in the present book constitute a linguistic metalanguage, and contribute towards the development of our **metalinguistic** abilities or awareness. ➤➤language awareness.

metanalysis /metə'nalɪsɪs/ The formation of a new lexical item through a wrong analysis of an existing word boundary; for example, in Old English, *a naddre* was heard in the popular mind as *an adder*, which has become the modern form. It is a kind of folk etymology. ➤➤etymology.

metaphor A semantic mapping from one conceptual domain to another, often using anomalous or deviant language. Several kinds of metaphor have been recognized. A **conventional metaphor** is one which forms a part of our everyday understanding of experience, and is processed without effort, such as *to lose the thread of an argument.* A **poetic metaphor** extends or combines everyday metaphors, especially for literary purposes – and this is how the term is traditionally understood, in the context of poetry. **Conceptual metaphors** are those functions in speakers' minds which implicitly condition their thought processes – for example, the notion that 'Argument is war' underlies such expressed metaphors as *I attacked his views.* The term **mixed metaphor** is used for a combination of unrelated or incompatible metaphors in a single sentence, such as *This is a virgin field pregnant with possibilities*. ➤➤figurative language.

metathesis /mə'taθəsɪs/ An alteration in the normal sequence of elements in a sentence – usually of sounds, but sometimes of syllables, words, or other units. The effect may be heard in everyday speech (as when people say *aks* for *ask*), but it is also a noticeable feature of language history: Old English *hros* became Modern English *horse*, for example. ➤➤sound change.

method In the context of pedagogical linguistics, a specific way of teaching a language. A three-fold terminological distinction has grown up, though the terms are not always used consistently. Methods are seen as based on a theoretical view (an **approach**) which takes into account the nature of language and language learning; examples include the aural-oral approach and the communicative approach. Methods then make use of a variety of classroom activities (**techniques**); examples include sentence repetition drills and role playing. The analysis and evaluation of methods is known as **methodology**, a subject which is broadly interpreted to include the investigation of the whole range of principles and practices used in language teaching. ➤➤audiolingual method; communicative approach; composition; direct method; drill; educational linguistics; grammar–translation method; language teaching.

metonymy /mɪ'tɒnəmiː/ A figure of speech in which the name of an attribute of an entity is used in place of the entity itself. People are using **metonyms** when they talk about *the bottle* to mean 'drinking' or *the press* to mean 'newspapers'. ➤➤figurative language.

metre ➤metrics.

metrics Traditionally, the study of versification, usually called **scansion**; in linguistics, the analysis of metrical structure, using the whole range of linguistic techniques, especially those belonging to segmental and suprasegmental phonology. The linguistic approach would pay attention to such factors as intonation in analysing a line's underlying prosodic structure and dramatic performance, and use a more sophisticated analysis of rhythm than is found in the traditional method of counting the length of lines in terms of a fixed set of feet. The traditional measures include the **monometer** (/mə'nɒmɪtə/, a line containing a single foot), **dimeter** (/'dɪmɪtə/, two feet), **trimeter** (/'trɪmɪtə/, three feet), **tetrameter** (/te'tramɪtə, four feet), **pentameter** (/pen'tamɪtə/, five feet), and **hexameter** (/hek'samɪtə/, six feet). ➤➤alexandrine; foot; phonology; prosody; rhythm; stylistics.

metronymic /metrə'nɪmɪk/ ➤patronymic.

Mexico (population in 1995 estimated at 89,872,000) The official language is Spanish, spoken by *c.*90% of the people. There are over 250 Amerindian languages, spoken by *c.*8% of a mainly bilingual Indian population – notably Nahuatl (*c.*1.6

million in total), Maya, Mixteco, Otomí, and Zapotec, all represented by several varieties. Spanish and English are both used for international purposes. ➤Spanish.

Miao-Yao /'miːaʊ 'jaʊ/ A small group of *c*.15 languages spoken in southern China and nearby parts of south-east Asia, especially northern Laos, Thailand, and Vietnam. The two chief languages, which give the group its name, are Miao (also called Hmong), spoken by *c*.4.4 million people, and Yao (Iu Mien), spoken by *c*.1 million. Both are written in the Roman alphabet. The group's status as a separate language family is controversial, and links have been suggested with several other families in the region, notably with Sino-Tibetan. ➤Sino-Tibetan.

microlinguistics ➤macrolinguistics.

Micronesia, Federated States of (population in 1995 estimated at 119,000) The official language is English, but most people speak one of 17 Austronesian languages, such as Ponape, Truk, and Yap. ➤English.

Micronesian /maɪkrəˈniːʒn/ ➤Austronesian.

Middle English ➤English.

middle voice ➤voice 1.

mid vowel ➤high vowel.

mim–mem method ➤audiolingual method.

minimal free form The smallest linguistic form which can stand on its own as an utterance. This is a useful attempt at a precise definition of the notion of a **word**, but it does not solve all problems; for example, words such as *the* and *a*, or *y* and *je* in French, cannot normally be used in isolation as meaningful utterances. ➤clitic; morpheme; word.

minimal pair Two words which differ in meaning when only one sound is changed, enabling linguists to determine whether the sounds belong to different phonemes. For example, the contrast between *sat* and *fat* would warrant the setting up of /s/ and /f/ as different phonemes in English; the contrast between the distinct *l*-sounds of *leap* and *peel*, however, would not, as to replace one quality of *l* by the other would not cause a change in meaning. ➤phoneme.

minority From a linguistic point of view, a group of people who speak a language other than the dominant (or **majority**) language of the country in which they live. **Linguistic minorities** (also called **language minorities** or **minority languages**) are found in most countries. Britain, for example, has over 100 such languages, including both 'native' minorities (such as Welsh) and immigrant minorities (such as Italian, Polish, Hindi, and Greek). ➤language dominance.

minor sentence ➤major sentence.

minuscule /ˈmɪnəskjuːl/ ➤majuscule.

misarticulation The articulation of a vowel or consonant which deviates from what is normal for the speech community to which the speaker belongs. It is common in several clinical conditions, especially those where the vocal organs have been affected as a result of delayed development, brain damage, or other physical or psychological causes; but it may also be heard in everyday speech, as in slips of the tongue. ➤➤apraxia; dysarthria; slip of the tongue.

miscommunication A misunderstanding between participants in an interaction caused by differences in their ways of using language. The problem is particularly marked when communicative exchanges cross cultural boundaries, but it can apply anywhere and to anyone. The notion covers many kinds of difficulty, such as inadvertent ambiguity, taking points for granted, and talking at cross purposes. ➤➤communication; cooperative principle; language barrier; pragmatics.

miscue analysis The analysis of the errors made when children read aloud, as part of the process of learning to read. A miscue is an unexpected response, such as the insertion of a word which is not present in the text, or the use of a word which is visually related to one present in the text; for example, a child might read *He saw the fish in the water* instead of *He saw the fin in the water.* ➤➤reading.

mismatch ➤overextension.

mistake (in language learning) ➤error analysis.

MIT An abbreviation of **Massachusetts Institute of Technology**, associated with the school of linguistic thought launched by Noam Chomsky. The phrase 'MIT linguistics' is synonymous with generative linguistics. ➤➤Chomskyan; generative grammar.

mixed metaphor ➤metaphor.

mixing ➤code mixing.

MLU An abbreviation of **mean length of utterance**.

mnemonic /nəˈmɒnɪk/ A strategy or device intended to assist the memory, often linguistic in character. Rhymes and rhythms are commonly used in this way, as in the verse to remember the number of days in each month: *Thirty days hath September* . . .

Moabite /ˈməʊəbaɪt/ A Semitic language spoken in the Transjordan area of Palestine probably from around the 14th to the 6th century BC, known from various inscriptions. The Moabites are referred to several times in the Old Testament of the Bible. The Moabite Stone was discovered in 1868 at Dibon, near the Dead Sea, containing a 34-line inscription relating to Mesha, king of Moab – one of the earliest examples of alphabetic writing. It is now in the Louvre. ➤➤alphabet; Semitic.

modality ➤medium; mood.

modals ➤mood.

mode ➤medium.

Modern Greek ➤Greek.

modification 1. The structural dependence of one grammatical unit upon another, especially within endocentric constructions. Dependent items which precede the head of a phrase (**premodification**) are distinguished from those following the head of a phrase (**postmodification**). In traditional grammar, the notion is restricted to the relationship between adjective and noun or adverb and verb. In systemic grammar, the term is reserved for premodifying structures only, postmodifying structures being labelled **qualification**. ➤dependent; endocentric construction; head; postmodification; premodification. **2**. In phonetics, any factor which influences the air flow in the vocal tract, such as movement of the soft palate, or the degree of closure of the glottis. The term is also used for any factor which alters the typical actions of the vocal organs in producing the phonemes of a language, such as extra lip rounding. ➤articulation; secondary articulation.

modular ➤government and binding theory.

Mohenjo-Daro /məʊˈhendʒəʊ ˈdarəʊ/ An undeciphered script found in the remains of the ancient city of Mohenjo-Daro, on the banks of the Indus River in Pakistan, where excavations have been continuing since the 1920s. The writing system was probably used throughout the Indus Valley Civilization, which flourished in an area of about half a million square miles around the Indus c.2300–1750 BC. ➤isolate.

Moldavian /mɒlˈdeɪvɪən/ A member of the Romance family of languages, spoken by c.3 million speakers in Moldova. As a result of its period of influence under Soviet rule, the language is written in the Cyrillic alphabet. There is little linguistic difference between Moldavian and Romanian, the most noticeable feature being the use of different writing systems. Moldavian also shows the influence of Russian in its loan words. ➤Moldova; Romance; Romanian.

Moldova (population in 1995 estimated at 4,367,000) The official languages are Moldavian (spoken by c.70% of the population), and Russian (c.12%). Other languages include Ukrainian (c.14%), Gagauz, and several of those spoken further in the west, such as Polish, German, and Bulgarian. ➤Moldavian; Russian.

Mon /məʊn/ A member of the Mon-Khmer family of languages, spoken by c.900,000 people, chiefly in Myanmar (Burma), with some in Thailand; also called **Talaing**. It is written in the Burmese alphabet, and records date from the 6th century AD. ➤Mon-Khmer.

Monaco (population in 1995 estimated at 30,600) The official language is French, spoken by *c*.60% of the population. The remainder speak either Ligurian (Italian) or Provençal. ➤French.

Mongol /'mɒŋgl/ The chief member of the Mongolian group of the Altaic family of languages, spoken in two main varieties by *c*.5 million people in the Inner Mongolian region of China (*c*.3 million) and in Mongolia; also called **Khalkha**. In China the language uses the 26-letter Mongolian alphabet, which is written downwards. The Cyrillic alphabet is now used in Mongolia. ➤Mongolia; Mongolian.

Mongolia (population in 1995 estimated at 2,302,000) The official language is Mongol, spoken by *c*.90% of the population. A few other languages are in use, notably Buryat, Chinese, and Kazakh. Russian is important in education, and is used for international purposes along with English. ➤Mongol; Mongolian.

Mongolian A group of languages within the Altaic family, spoken by over 5 million people in Mongolia and nearby China and Russia. The group inludes Buryat, Mongol, and Kalmyk. Classical Mongolian refers to the written language of the Mongols, attested since the 13th century. ➤Altaic; Buryat; Mongol; Mongolia.

monitor model A theory of the relationship between acquisition and learning, propounded by American linguist Stephen Krashen (1941–   ). This account recognizes a subconscious natural process ('acquisition') which is the primary force behind foreign language fluency. 'Learning' is seen as a conscious process which edits ('monitors') the progress of acquisition, and guides the performance of the speaker. ➤acquisition; language learning.

Mon-Khmer /məʊn 'kmɛə/ The largest group of languages within the Austro-Asiatic family, spoken by over 70 million people throughout the south-east Asian mainland, mainly in Vietnam, Laos, and Cambodia, and parts of Myanmar (Burma) and Malaysia. Its main languages are Vietnamese, Mon, and Khmer. Membership of the group is uncertain; for example, some scholars include Nicobarese, and some exclude Vietnamese. ➤Austro-Asiatic; Khmer; Mon; Vietnamese.

monogenesis /mɒnə'dʒenɪsɪs/ The hypothesis that all human languages originate from a single source; contrasts with **polygenesis**. The terms are also used in discussing the similarities among pidgins and creoles: monogenetic theories assume the diffusion of a single pidgin to other areas via migration; polygenetic theories assume that the development of a pidgin in one community is independent of the development of a pidgin in another. ➤creole; diffusion; pidgin; p. 221.

monoglot ➤bilingualism.

monolingualism ➤bilingualism; multilingualism.

monologue Speech or writing by a single person, as in a lecture or commentary; opposed to **dialogue**, where two people are participants in the interaction. The

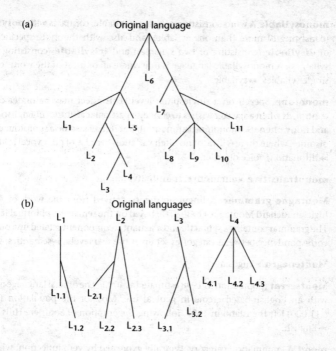

(a) Original language

(b) Original languages

Monogenesis and **polygenesis**. (a) The monogenetic view: all languages have diverged from a common source. (b) The polygenetic view: language emerged more or less spontaneously in several places.

latter term is often used to apply to situations where there are more than two participants, but **multilogue** or **polylogue** are also available for such cases. A **soliloquy** is a literary monologue uttered by a speaker who thinks no one else is present. ➤discourse analysis.

monometer ➤metrics.

monophthong /ˈmɒnəfθɒŋ/ A vowel with a single perceived auditory quality, produced by a movement of the articulators towards one position in the vocal tract; also called a **pure vowel**; contrasts with **diphthong**, where the auditory impression is of two vowel qualities, and **triphthong**, where three qualities can be perceived. When a diphthong becomes a monophthong, as in some cases of historical or dialect change, the sound is said to be **monophthongized**; conversely, when a monophthong becomes a diphthong, the sound is said to be **diphthongized**. ➤diphthong; triphthong; vowel.

monosyllable A word consisting of a single syllable; contrasts with **polysyllable** (consisting of more than one syllable), and also with the more specific notions of **disyllable** (consisting of two syllables) and **trisyllable** (consisting of three syllables). A monosyllabic language is one where all or most of the words consist of single syllables. ➤➤syllable.

monotone Speech on a single pitch level. This effect may be under conscious control, as when a speaker wishes to convey a particular attitude (in English, sarcasm and irony often use monotone intonation); but it may also be a symptom of a voice disorder, where there is little or no pitch variation because of poor vocal fold control. ➤➤intonation; voice disorder.

monotransitive ➤ditransitive; transitivity.

Montague grammar A linguistic theory derived from the work of American logician Richard Montague (1930–70); based on the semantics of formal languages. The grammar contains a syntactic and a semantic component related by a one-to-one correspondence between categories set up at the two levels. ➤➤semantics; syntax.

Montenegro ➤Yugoslavia.

Montserrat (population in 1998 estimated at 4000) The official language is English, with an English-based creole in general use. Most of the population (formerly *c*.11,000) left the island in 1997, following the eruption of Soufrière Hills volcano. ➤➤English.

mood A grammatical category, typically expressed by verb inflection, which indicates what the speaker is doing with a proposition in a particular discourse situation. Mood normally identifies the status of an utterance; for example, an utterance may be **indicative** (the usual form), **imperative** (a command), **hortative** (an exhortation), or **subjunctive** (a subordination). Mood is also referred to as **modality** or **mode**, especially when inflectional forms are not involved. **Modal auxiliaries** are verb-like words which typically express speakers' attitudes towards the factual content of an utterance, such as uncertainty, possibility, and necessity (*may, could, ought*, etc.). ➤➤auxiliary verb; imperative; indicative; optative; subjunctive.

Mòoré ➤More.

mora /'mɔːrə/ In traditional metrics, a minimal unit of metrical time, equivalent to a short syllable. It is now widely used in phonological theory (especially in metrical phonology) as a unit of phonological length. ➤➤length; metrics; phonology.

Mordvin /'mɔːdvɪn/ A member of the Finnic group of the Finno-Ugric family of languages, spoken by *c*.1 million people in the Mordvin region of Russia (where it has official status), and in surrounding areas. It is written in the Cyrillic alphabet. The third largest Uralic language (after Hungarian and Finnish), it has two major dialects, Erzya and Moksha, both in official use, and sometimes listed as separate languages. ►►Finno-Ugric.

More /mə'reɪ/ A Voltaic language spoken by *c*.4.5 million people in Burkina Faso and a further 2 million in Ghana; also called **Mòoré**. The language of the Mossi people (and sometimes called **Mossi**, as a consequence), it is written in the Roman alphabet. ►►Voltaic.

Morocco (population in 1995 estimated at 28,010,000) The official language is Arabic, spoken by *c*.65% of the people. Most of the remainder speak varieties of Berber. French is used for international purposes. ►►Arabic.

morph ►►morpheme.

morpheme /'mɔ:fi:m/ The minimal distinctive unit of grammar, commonly classified into **free forms** (which can occur as separate words) and **bound forms** (which cannot so occur – mainly affixes). Morphemes are the central concern of *morphology*, also sometimes called **morphemics**. They are abstract units, realized in speech as discrete items (**morphs**). Morphemic variants are **allomorphs**; for example, there are three chief allomorphs of the past tense morpheme in English, represented by the /t/ ending of *jumped*, the /d/ ending of *bombed*, and the /ɪd/ ending of *faded*. ►►affix; bound form; free form; morphology; root 1; word.

morphology The branch of grammar which studies the structure of words. It is generally divided into **inflectional morphology**, the study of inflections, and **lexical** or **derivational morphology**, the study of word formation. Morphology contrasts with **syntax**, the combination of words into sentences. ►►grammar 1; morpheme; sandhi; suppletion; word.

morphophonemics ►►morphophonology.

morphophonology /mɔ:fəʊfə'nɒlədʒi:/ A branch of linguistics which analyses the phonological or grammatical factors that determine the form of phonemes; also called **morphonology**, **morphophonemics**, and **morphonemics**. The basic unit recognized in such an analysis is the **morphophoneme**; for example, the notion of 'plural' in English nouns includes /s/ (as in *cats*), /z/ (as in *dogs*), /ɪz/ (as in *horses*), zero (as in *sheep*), and several other forms. ►►morphology; phonology; sandhi.

morphosyntax /mɔ:fəʊ'sɪntaks/ The study of grammatical categories or properties for whose definition criteria of morphology and syntax both apply. The number category in nouns, for example, may be expressed morphologically (through inflectional endings) and syntactically (through agreement with a verb). Tense, person, and voice are examples of other morphosyntactic categories. ►►morphology; syntax.

motherese The style of speech used by mothers when talking to their babies. It is characterized by such features as short sentences, repetitive discourse, simplified vocabulary, and expressive intonation. Because such patterns can also be found in the speech of fathers, siblings, and others involved in looking after a young child (grandparents, baby-sitters, etc.), the more general terms **caregiver** or **caretaker speech** are now commonly used. ➤➤acquisition; baby talk 1.

mother-in-law languages ➤avoidance languages.

mother tongue ➤first language.

motor theory A theory of speech perception which claims that the listener has specialized neural mechanisms which convert the acoustic waveform into distinct articulatory targets, or gestures. In other words, speech is perceived in terms of how it is produced. ➤➤speech perception.

Motu /'məʊtuː/ A member of the Austronesian family of languages, spoken by *c.*10,000 in the central part of Papua New Guinea. A pidginized variety, **Hiri Motu**, developed as a trade language between speakers of Austronesian and Indo-Pacific languages; formerly called **Police Motu**. It is an English-based language, spoken by *c.*150,000 people in the Port Moresby area of Papua New Guinea, where it has official status. ➤➤Austronesian; Papua New Guinea; pidgin.

Mozambique (population in 1995 estimated at 18,138,000) The official language is Portuguese. There are *c.*20 other languages, notably Makua (several varieties, *c.*6 million), Lomwe, Nyanja, Shona, Tsonga, and Yao. Swahili is a lingua franca in the north. French and English are widely known among educated people. Portuguese and English are used for international purposes. ➤➤Portuguese.

multilingualism A situation where a speech community (or an individual) makes use of several languages, as in Switzerland or Belgium; sometimes called **plurilingualism** or **polyglottism**. The term may subsume **bilingualism** (strictly, the use of two languages), but is often contrasted with it, by emphasizing the use of more than two languages (as is the case with the everyday word **polyglot**). ➤➤bilingualism.

multilogue ➤monologue.

Munda /'mʊndə/ A small group of *c.*25 languages within the Austro-Asiatic family, chiefly spoken in several parts of north-east India. The most widely used languages are Santali (*c.*5.7 million) and Mundari (*c.*1.5 million). Northern, southern, and western Munda subgroups have been recognized, with nearly 90% of the speakers belonging to the northern subgroup. They use the Bengali and Devanagari alphabets. ➤➤Austro-Asiatic.

murmur ➤breathy voice.

Muskogean /məs'kəʊgɪən/ ➤Algonkian.

mutation 1. A change in the quality of a sound because of the influence of adjacent morphemes or words. There are several types of initial consonant mutation in Welsh, for example, such as *pen* 'head' becoming *mhen* 'my head'. Initial mutations are a particular problem for foreign learners, as they hide the underlying phonological identity of a word, and make it difficult to find an unfamiliar word in a dictionary. ➤➤inflection 1; morphology; phonology. **2.** ➤voice mutation.

mutism /'mju:tɪzm/ In clinical contexts, the involuntary inability to speak – a pathological condition in which oral expression is absent or minimal, though comprehension of language remains normal. It may result from organic damage to the central nervous system or be associated with psychological problems. In a broader sense, mutism can refer to any instance where speech is suppressed, whether deliberate, semi-deliberate, or involuntary. ➤➤language pathology.

mutual intelligibility A criterion used in linguistic analysis, referring to the ability of people to understand each other. If two varieties of speech are mutually intelligible, they are strictly dialects of the same language; if they are mutually unintelligible, they are different languages. The criterion seems simple, but there are many problem cases. Two varieties may be partially intelligible – for example, because they share some vocabulary. Also, cultural or political factors may intervene, causing two mutually intelligible varieties to be treated as different languages (such as Swedish and Danish) or two mutually unintelligible varieties to be treated as the same language (such as the varieties of Chinese). ➤➤dialect; language 1; variety.

Myanmar (Burma) (population in 1995 estimated at 46,398,000) The official language is Burmese, spoken by nearly 60% of the population. There are *c.*100 other local languages, notably several varieties of Karen (*c.*3 million) and Shan (*c.*3 million). Smaller languages include Arakan, Chin (in many varieties), Jingpo, Lü, and Parauk. English is increasingly used for international trade and tourism. ➤➤Burmese.

Mycenaean Greek /maɪsə'nɪən/ ➤Greek.

N

N An abbreviation of **noun**.

Na-Dene or **Na-Déné** /nəˈdeɪneɪ/ A group of over 50 languages spoken in Alaska and north-west Canada, and in south-west-central USA. (The term derives from the name of an Athabaskan tribe, the Déné; *na* is an Indian word meaning 'dwelling' or 'people'.) Most of the languages belong to the Athabaskan family, spoken in the Northwest Territory and the Yukon, Alaska, and parts of the US Pacific coast. Its best-known member is Navajo (Navaho), spoken by nearly 150,000 speakers in Arizona and New Mexico. The various dialects of Apache and Chipewyan are also in this family. The other main branches are Haida (in south-east Alaska) and Tlingit (in British Columbia), each consisting of a single language. These languages use the Roman alphabet, when written. ➤Amerindian.

Nagari /ˈnagəriː/ ➤Devanagari.

Nahua /ˈnɑːwə/ ➤Nahuatl.

Nahuatl /ˈnɑːwətl/ A member of the Aztec-Tanoan group of languages (specifically, of the Uto-Aztecan family), spoken by *c*.1.4 million people in central and western Mexico; also called **Aztec**. Different pronunciations of the name in the main dialect divisions give rise to the alternative spellings of **Nahual** and **Nahuat**, and the use of **Nahua** as a label for the language as a whole. Classical Nahuatl was the language of the Toltecs (10th–12th centuries) and Aztecs (15th–16th centuries), and there is an extensive Aztec literature from the 16th century, using an orthography devised by Spanish missionaries. The modern language uses the Roman alphabet. Many hieroglyphic inscriptions have been discovered from Classical times. ➤Aztec-Tanoan; hieroglyphic.

Nakho-Dagestanian /ˈnakəʊ dagəˈsteɪnɪən/ A group of Caucasian languages found in the north-east of the Caucasus region; also called **North-east Caucasian**. Most of the languages belong to the Dagestanian branch, notably Avar, Lezghian, Dargwa, Lakk, and Tabasaran. The Nakh branch comprises Chechen, Ingush, and Bats (the latter found in a single village in Georgia). ➤Avar; Chechen; Lezghian.

name ➤alias; ananym; aptronym; byname; eponym; nickname; onomastics; patronymic; proper noun/name; pseudonym; stage name.

Namibia (population in 1995 estimated at 2,156,000) The official language is English, spoken as a first or second language by *c*.5% of the people. About 7% speak

Afrikaans, and there are still speakers of German (*c*.20,000). About 20 local languages belong to the Benue-Congo and Khoisan families. ➤➤English.

Nandi /'nandi:/ A Nilotic (or, in some classifications, Nilo-Hamitic) language spoken by *c*.2.5 million people in Kenya, with some speakers in adjoining Uganda and Tanzania; also called **Kalenjin**. Several major dialects are recognized, some of which have been proposed as different languages. It is written in the Roman alphabet. Nandi is also the name of another language spoken by *c*.1 million people in the Democratic Republic of Congo. ➤➤Nilotic.

narrative A discourse recounting a real or fictional sequence of events. It is a major topic in literary pragmatics, dealing with the temporal and logical structure of a story, spoken or written, especially as encountered in fiction. The structural study of narrative is **narratology**, and the narrative properties of a text constitute its **narrativity**. ➤➤discourse analysis; literary pragmatics; script 2.

narrowing In historical linguistics, a type of change in which a word becomes more specialized in meaning. In Old English, for example, *mete* referred to food in general, whereas it now refers to only one kind of food. ➤➤extension 2.

narrow transcription ➤transcription.

nasal Descriptive of a type of consonant involving a complete closure of the oral tract at the same time as the pathway between soft palate and pharynx is opened; examples include [m] and [n]. **Nasalization** is the perceived nasal resonance heard on sounds (typically, vowels) where the soft palate is lowered during articulation. **Nasalized vowels** usually occur in the immediate environment of nasal consonants, as in [man]. Sounds with reduced nasal resonance are said to be **denasalized** or **hyponasal**. Sounds with excessive nasal resonance are **hypernasal**. ➤➤denasal; hypernasality; palate; vocal tract.

national language A language which is considered to be the chief language of a nation state; for example, French is the national language of France, and also the country's **official language** – used in such public domains as the law courts, government, and broadcasting. In many countries, there is no difference between the national and the official language. However, in a multilingual country, such as Belgium, Singapore, or Ghana, there may be no uncontroversial candidate for a national language, and one or more of the languages used in the area may be designated official. Several countries have two or more official languages, representing the interests of their chief population groupings. ➤➤bilingualism; standard.

native language/speaker ➤first language.

nativist hypothesis ➤innateness hypothesis.

natural approach Any approach to foreign language teaching which claims to follow the principles used by children in learning their first language, emphasizing the primary role of speaking and listening, and the use of everyday objects and activities. It is a reaction against the highly formal and artificial methods used in traditional approaches to language teaching, common since the 19th-century. Several types of natural approach have been proposed. ➤direct method; language learning/teaching.

natural gender ➤gender.

natural language A language used in ordinary human communication, as opposed to a theoretical or artificial system. **Natural language processing (NLP)** is a branch of computational linguistics which deals with the computational processing of textual materials in natural languages. Its applications include such areas as machine translation and literary text analysis. ➤computational linguistics.

natural order hypothesis The view that people follow essentially the same path in learning a foreign language that they used when learning their mother tongue. The motivation for the hypothesis comes from observing the way many learners make similar errors (e.g. *I going*), regardless of their language background. It is suggested that a universal creative process is at work, learners following a natural 'internal syllabus' (as opposed to the 'external' syllabus of the classroom). Because several of the errors closely resemble those made by children learning their first language, a parallel is proposed between the natural order of first language acquisition and the way people acquire a foreign language. ➤language learning.

Nauru (population in 1995 estimated at 9900) The official languages are Nauruan and English. About half the people speak Nauruan, an Austronesian language. Other local languages include Ikiribati, Chinese, and Tuvaluan. English is used for international trade and tourism. ➤English.

Navajo or **Navaho** /ˈnavəhəʊ/ ➤Na-Dene.

Ndebele /ndəˈbeliː, ndəˈbiːliː/ A member of the Bantu group of Benue-Congo languages, spoken chiefly by c.1.5 million people in Zimbabwe and, in a different variety, by c.600,000 in the Transvaal region of South Africa, where it is one of the 11 official languages. It is written in the Roman alphabet. ➤Benue-Congo.

negation A process or construction which typically expresses the contradiction of some or all of the meaning of a sentence. In English, negation is primarily expressed by the use of the **negative particle** *not* or the **contracted negative** *n't*. Items which have **negative polarity** are those words or phrases which are especially found in negative environments in a sentence; *any*, for example, typically occurs in such contexts as *I don't have any* and not *I have any*. ➤affirmative; polarity.

negative transfer ➤interference; transfer.

Nenets /ˈnenets/ A member of the Samoyedic branch of the Uralic family of languages, spoken by c.25,000 people in the Nenets region of Russia (where it has official regional status); formerly known as **Yurak**. It is the chief language of its group, and is written in the Roman alphabet. ⟫Samoyedic.

neo-Firthian ➤Firthian linguistics.

Neogrammarians A group of philologists, based at the University of Leipzig in the 1870s, and dubbed the *Junggrammatiker* ('young grammarians') because of the aggressive way in which they asserted their chief hypothesis, that sound laws admitted no exceptions (the **neogrammarian hypothesis**). They included August Leskien (1840–1916) and Karl Brugmann (1849–1919). ⟫law; philology; sound change.

neologism /ni:ˈɒlədʒɪzm/ The creation of a new lexical item, as a response to changed circumstances in the external world, which achieves some currency within a speech community; also called **coinage**. Examples in the 1990s include many new words which include the prefix *Euro-*, referring to the emerging role of the European Community, such as *Eurofighter, Euromeasure,* and *Eurothuggery*. Only some neologisms will become permanent features of the language, but it is never possible to predict which will stay and which will die out. ⟫cliché; coinage; hybrid; nonce word; word formation.

Nepal (population in 1995 estimated at 20,827,000) The official language is Nepali, spoken by *c.*60% of the people. There are *c.*120 other languages, notably Maithili (*c.*11%), Bhojpuri (*c.*8%), Murmi, Newari, and Magar. English is used for international purposes. ⟫Nepali.

Nepali /nəˈpɔːliː/ A member of the Pahari group of Indo-Aryan languages, spoken by *c.*10 million people in Nepal, and a further million in nearby parts of India; also called **Gurkhali** ('Gurkha language'), after the name of the Gurkha tribe, which conquered Nepal in the 18th century. It is written in the Devanagari alphabet. ⟫Devanagari; Indo-Aryan; Nepal; Pahari.

Netherlandic-German ➤Germanic.

Netherlands, The (population in 1995 estimated at 15,449,000) The official language is Dutch, spoken by almost the whole population. Frisian (*c.*700,000) is an official regional language in Friesland. Low Saxon is spoken by *c.*1.5 million people in the north-east of the country, most of whom use Dutch as a second language. Immigrant minority languages include Arabic, Chinese, Malay, Papiamentu, Sranan, and Turkish, and there are several Romani groups. English is used for international purposes. ⟫Dutch; Frisian.

Netherlands Antilles (population in 1995 estimated at 192,000) The official language is Dutch. On the Leeward Islands (Bonaire, Curaçao, and the self-governing island of Aruba), representing *c.*85% of the population, most people speak a Portuguese-based creole, Papiamentu – with English and Spanish used for international purposes. On the Windward Islands (St Maarten, St Eustatius, Saba), an English-based creole (Sranan) is spoken, and English is used for international purposes. ➤➤creole; Dutch.

neurolinguistics The branch of linguistics which studies the basis in the human nervous system for language development and use; also called **neurological linguistics**. It specifically aims to construct a model of the brain's control over the processes of speaking, listening, reading, writing, and signing. ➤➤clinical linguistics; language areas; linguistics.

neuter ➤gender.

neutral 1. Descriptive of the visual appearance of the lips when they are held in a relaxed position, with no rounding. ➤➤rounding. **2**. Descriptive of a lax vowel made in the centre of the vowel articulation area. ➤➤shwa.

new ➤given.

New Caledonia (population in 1995 estimated at 186,000) The official language is French, spoken by *c*.35% of the people. There are *c*.35 local Austronesian languages, and speakers of Vietnamese, Bislama, and a local variety of Javanese. Bislama and French are both used as lingua francas. ➤➤creole; French; lingua franca.

New Englishes The name often given to the national varieties of English which have emerged around the globe, especially since the 1960s in those countries which opted to make English an official language upon independence. Regionally distinctive use of vocabulary, pronunciation, and (to a much lesser extent) grammar is found in all such countries, but often only on a very limited scale. The term is really applicable only when there has been considerable linguistic development away from the traditional standards of British and American English, with some degree of local standardization (e.g. in the press), as has happened in India, Ghana, and Singapore, and perhaps a dozen other countries where English is used as a second language. It has thus also come to be applied to first-language situations, such as in Canada, Australia, and South Africa, as well as in areas where creole or pidgin Englishes are important, such as the Caribbean and Papua New Guinea – even though in these cases the Englishes in question have a considerable history behind them. ➤➤creole; English; pidgin; standard English; variety.

New Guinea ➤Indo-Pacific.

New Zealand (population in 1995 estimated at 3,560,000) The official language is English, spoken by *c*.90% of the people. Maori is used by *c*.2%. Immigrant languages include Chinese, Hindi, and several from the Pacific islands, such as Samoan (*c*.50,000), Fijian, Niuean, Rarotongan, and Tongan. ➤➤English; Maori.

Nguni /əŋˈguːniː/ ➤Xhosa; Zulu.

Nicaragua (population in 1995 estimated at 4,553,000) The official language is Spanish, spoken by *c*.95% of the people. About 20% of the coastal population speak an English-based creole used throughout the western Caribbean. There are a few Amerindian languages spoken by small numbers. Spanish and English are used for international purposes. ➤creole; Spanish.

nickname An unofficial extra name given to someone or something. The word derives from earlier English *an eke name*, where *eke* meant 'also' or 'additional'. Nicknames may be pleasant (*Richard Lionheart*) or unpleasant (*Fatty Smith, Scarface Pete*), and apply not only to people, but also to places (*the Pool* for *Liverpool*), and all kinds of objects and creations (e.g. Beethoven's *Pastoral*). ➤onomastics.

Nicobarese A tiny group of languages within the Austro-Asiatic family, spoken by *c*.10,000 people in the Nicobar Islands in the Bay of Bengal. Some scholars consider Nicobarese to belong to the Mon-Khmer group. Inscriptions are found from the 11th century. ➤Austro-Asiatic.

Niger (population in 1995 estimated at 9,050,000) The official language is French. There are *c*.15 other languages, including Hausa (spoken by about half the population, and widely used as a lingua franca), Dyerma (Zarma, *c*.23%), Fulfulde (*c*.15%), Arabic, Kanuri, and Tamashek. French is used for international purposes. ➤French; lingua franca.

Niger-Congo The largest language family in Africa, containing *c*.1350 languages and an indefinite number of varieties whose status as languages or dialects is difficult to determine. It spreads across the whole of sub-Saharan Africa, west of the River Nile, and extends along the eastern half of the continent as far north as the Horn of Africa. It is usually divided into six groups of languages (see cross-references). Among the important Niger-Congo languages are Igbo, Swahili, Wolof, Yoruba, and Zulu. ➤Adamawa-Eastern; Africa; Benue-Congo; Kwa; Mande; Voltaic; West Atlantic.

Nigeria (population in 1995 estimated at 96,171,000) The official language is English. Official regional languages are Hausa (spoken by *c*.20 million in the north), Igbo (spoken by *c*.17 million in the south-east), and Yoruba (spoken by *c*.19 million in the south-west). There are *c*.450 other languages, some with very small numbers. A few of the larger languages have some degree of official status in a locality (notably in broadcasting), such as Edo, Efik, Fulfulde, Idoma, and Kanuri. Several languages are used as lingua francas, such as Efik, Hausa and Nigerian Pidgin English. English is used for international purposes. ➤English; lingua franca; pidgin.

Nilo-Hamitic /ˈnaɪləʊ haˈmɪtɪk/ A group of Nilo-Saharan languages sometimes proposed as a separate family, but often grouped as an eastern branch of the Nilotic family. They are spoken in southern Sudan, Uganda, Kenya, and northern Tanzania, and include Nandi, Bari, and Masai. The suggested relationship with the Hamitic group of languages is disputed. ➤Bari; Masai; Nandi; Nilo-Saharan; Nilotic.

Nilo-Saharan /ˈnaɪləʊ səˈhɑːrən/ A group of *c*.180 languages spoken in two areas around the upper parts of the Chari and Nile Rivers, most of which can be placed in a single family, known as **Chari-Nile**. The overall area extends north–south from Egypt to Tanzania and east–west from Mali to Ethiopia. The sub-classification of the languages in the group is a source of argument. A western branch, known as Nilotic, is often recognized; it includes such languages as Luo, Dinka, Acholi, and Lango. Some studies distinguish an eastern branch, known as Nilo-Hamitic, which includes Nandi, Bari, and Masai. Several other languages have been placed within this family, notably Songhai and Fur, as well as the Saharan, Maban, and Koman groups of languages. But the exact relationship of many of these languages to each other is controversial. ⇒Africa; Fur; Hamito-Semitic; Koman; Maban; Nilo-Hamitic; Nilotic; Nubian; Saharan; Songhai.

Nilotic /naɪˈlɒtɪk/ A proposed group of languages within the Nilo-Saharan family, spoken in Uganda, Kenya, and parts of Sudan and Tanzania. The relationship between the languages has been controversial, and they have been variously sub-classified. One important classification recognizes a western group (which includes Luo and Nuer), an eastern group (which includes Masai), and a southern group (which includes Nandi). The eastern and southern groups are sometimes classified under the separate heading of Nilo-Hamitic. ⇒Acholi; Dinka; Lango; Luo; Masai; Nandi; Nilo-Saharan; Nuer.

Niue (population in 1995 estimated at 2100) The official language is English, with most of the population speaking **Niuean** /njuːˈeɪən/, an Austronesian language. ⇒English.

Nivkhi /ˈnɪvkiː/ ➤Gilyak.

NLP An abbreviation of **natural language processing**.

nodule ➤vocal nodule.

nomenclature A list of names, or terms, arranged in a hierarchy so as to provide a classification, as in the case of botanical or zoological terms. The list can then act as a standard of usage to guide those working within a subject or learning about it. ⇒lexicon; term bank.

nominal Characteristic of a noun; in some linguistic approaches used as a substitute for 'noun' in certain technical terms (e.g. **nominal group** is equivalent to 'noun phrase'). The term may also be used as a label for words that have some of the properties of nouns, but not all, as in *the rich, the Chinese*: such words are sometimes called nominals, rather than nouns, to indicate their grammatical individuality. The process or result of forming a noun from some other word class is called **nominalization** (e.g. *good + ness*). ⇒noun.

nominal aphasia ➤aphasia.

nominal group ➤noun; phrase.

nominalism In the philosophy of language, the view that the forms of words have no inherent connection with the objects to which they refer, but are related arbitrarily, the result of customary usage by a community. This was one of two conflicting views argued at length by the Greeks, the other being **naturalism**, that there is an intrinsic connection between words and things. The arbitrariness of the relationship between words and things has been a tenet of modern linguistics since the work of Saussure, though there is considerable interest in those aspects of language which seem to support a naturalistic view, such as onomatopoeia. ➤arbitrariness; philosophical linguistics; Saussurian; sound symbolism.

nominative case One of the ways in which an inflected language makes a word change its form, in order to show its grammatical relationship to other parts of the sentence. The nominative is the case typically taken by a noun phrase (often a single noun or pronoun) when it is the subject of a verb; for example, in German, the sentence *Der Mann seht den Mann* ('The man sees the man') illustrates the nominative form of the definite article, *der*, and the accusative form, *den*. In Latin and related languages, the nominative case is used as the identifying or basic form of a noun – the form under which the noun is given in grammars and dictionaries. ➤case; inflection 1.

nonce word A word which a speaker consciously invents or accidentally uses on a single occasion, in order to solve an immediate problem of communication; also called a **nonce form(ation)**. For example, in order to describe the way a dog on a lead tends to walk round a tree on the opposite side to the way its owner wants it to go, someone invented the word *circumtreeviation*. Lewis Carroll introduced several nonce words into 'Jabberwocky', such as *brillig* and *slithy*. The term *nonce* is an Elizabethan English form of 'once', suggesting that such words are introduced for use on a single occasion, with no intention that they should be remembered for future use. It would be unusual for a nonce word to be widely used, and to be recognized as a dictionary form. If it were, it would be more properly called a neologism. ➤neologism.

noncount(able) noun ➤countability.

nondefining ➤restrictiveness.

nondefinite ➤definiteness.

nondiscrete ➤discrete.

nonfinite ➤finite.

nonfluency ➤dysfluency.

non-native varieties Varieties of a language which have emerged in speech communities where most of the speakers do not have the language as a mother tongue. The notion has been chiefly used with reference to English, and specifically

233

in relation to the kind of English which has grown up in India, Singapore, and many of the countries of Africa. ➤➤English as an international language.

nonproductive ➤productivity.

nonrestrictive ➤restrictiveness.

nonsexist language ➤inclusive language; sexist language.

nonstandard ➤standard.

non-U ➤U and non-U.

nonverbal communication ➤body language; *cartoon below*.

Norfolk Island (population in 1995 estimated at 2100, with 56 on Pitcairn) The official language is English. Some (*c*.600) still speak an English-based creole, Pitcairn-Norfolk. ➤➤creole; English.

normative Descriptive of a linguistic rule which is considered to set a socially approved standard of correctness (or 'norm') for language use. Examples from English include the recommendation to avoid a split infinitive, or to use *whom* (as opposed

to *who*) in such contexts as *The lady – I asked.* . . A systematic collection of such rules constitutes a **normative grammar**. ➤➤correctness; prescriptivism.

Norn ➤Scandinavian.

Norse ➤Scandinavian.

Norway (population in 1995 estimated at 4,345,000) The official language is Norwegian, spoken by almost the whole population. There are some speakers of Finnish, Same, and Romani. ➤➤Norwegian.

Norwegian A North Germanic language, a member of the West Scandinavian group, spoken by *c*.4 million people in Norway, with some in Denmark, and through immigration especially in the USA and Canada. It began to emerge from common Old Norse after the 11th century, but political unions with other Scandinavian countries halted the development of a distinct Norwegian literature until independence was achieved in the 19th century. There are now two main varieties. **Bokmål** ('book language') or **Riksmål** ('language of the kingdom') is the literary variety, deriving from the written form of Danish introduced during the period when Norway was united with Denmark (1380–1814). **Nynorsk** ('new Norwegian', formerly called **Landsmål**) was devised by a language scholar, Ivar Aasen (1813–96) in the 19th century; he based it on western rural dialects, which he felt better represented a direct connection with Old Norse than did the Danish-influenced Bokmål. Both varieties are written in the Roman alphabet; they are mutually intelligible; and both have national status in government and in schools. However, Bokmål is used by three times as many people, and is the language of literature and the national press. Plans to mould them into a common Norwegian language (**Samnorsk**) are highly controversial. ➤➤Danish; diglossia; Norway; Scandinavian.

Nostratic /nɒˈstratɪk/ A proposed super-family of European and Asiatic languages, including Afro-Asiatic, Indo-European, Dravidian, Uralic, Altaic, and Kartvelian (south Caucasian) families. Originally suggested in 1903 by the Danish linguist Holger Pedersen, the notion attracted renewed interest in the 1980s, especially among Soviet linguists. ➤➤Indo-European; philology.

notation In linguistics, any system of graphic symbols used for the representation of speech, or of the categories needed in order to analyse speech. The alphabet is the most widely used kind of notation. Other examples include the various numerical systems devised for calculation, the prosodic notations devised to write down speech melody and rhythm, and systems of phonetic transcription. ➤➤alphabet; transcription; p. 236.

notional grammar ➤formal grammar; grammar 1.

notional syllabus A type of syllabus which has been developed since the 1970s for use in foreign language teaching, organized on the basis of the sentence meanings and functions which a learner needs in order to communicate – notions such as

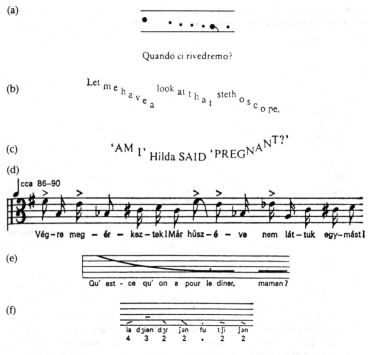

Notation: Six ways of notating intonation (all to be read from left to right): (a) the widely used 'tadpole' notation in which size of dot indicates the relative loudness of syllables (the language is Italian); (b) the typography reflects pitch movement directly; (c) pitch movement and loudness are reflected directly; (d) a musical notation (the language is Hungarian); (e) a semi-musical notation, with an unspecified stave (the language is French); (f) impressionistic pitch levels on an unspecified stave (the language is Chinese).

time, location, and quantity, and functions such as requesting and persuading. A notional syllabus contrasts primarily with the traditional approach, where the basis of organization is a graded series of grammatical structures (a **structural syllabus**). It also contrasts with a **situational syllabus**, where the content is organized into a series of language-using situations, such as the airport, bank, or shops. ➤communicative approach; speech act.

noun A word class, traditionally defined as the 'name of a person, place, or thing', and described linguistically in terms of a set of grammatical properties. These properties include a noun's ability to act as subject or object of a clause, and to be analysed in terms of number, gender, case, and countability. Nouns are generally sub-classified into **common** and **proper** types. A construction with a noun as head is a **noun phrase** (NP). ➤➤case; clause; common noun; countability; gender; nominal; number; phrase.

noun phrase ➤noun.

Novial /'nɒvɪəl/ A language invented by Danish linguist Otto Jespersen in 1928; its name is an acronym of **New International Auxiliary Language**. It was largely based on previous proposals, mainly Ido (1907) and Edgar von Wahl's Occidental (1922). ➤➤artificial language; Ido.

NP An abbreviation of **noun phrase**.

Nubian /'nju:bɪən/ A Nilo-Saharan group of languages spoken by *c*.1 million people in the Sudan and Egypt, chiefly along the banks of the River Nile. There is a long written history (an unusual feature of languages in this region), with manuscripts in a modified Coptic alphabet dating from the 8th to the 14th century AD (Old Nubian); they are largely translations of Greek Christian writings. ➤➤Coptic; Nilo-Saharan.

Nuclear English A proposal to adapt the English language to produce a core system of structure and vocabulary for international use. Suggested by the British linguist Randolph Quirk, it was presented as a possible solution to problems of communication arising from the emergence of international varieties of English. Nuclear English would eliminate all features that were 'dispensable', in the sense that the language has an alternative means available for their expression (e.g. one of the two indirect object constructions, or the range of tag questions). A communicative nucleus would remain, which could be the focus for international purposes. ➤➤common core; English; Quirkian.

nuclear stress/tone ➤nucleus 1.

nucleus 1. The syllable in an intonation unit which has the greatest pitch prominence; also called the **nuclear** or **tonic syllable**. The nucleus carries the **nuclear tone** or **nuclear stress**. In an unemphatic rendition of the sentence *I saw an elephant*, the nucleus would be on the syllable *EL*. ➤➤intonation; syllable; tonicity. **2**. ➤syllable.

Nuer /'nu:ə/ A Nilotic language spoken by *c*.1 million people around the banks of the River Nile in southern Sudan, with some speakers in Ethiopia. It is written in the Roman alphabet. ➤➤Nilotic.

number A grammatical category used for the analysis of word classes, especially nouns, which display such contrasts as **singular**, **dual**, and **plural** – the contrasts of 'one' vs. 'two' vs. 'many', respectively. These contrasts generally correspond to the number of real-world entities referred to, but there is no straightforward one-to-one correlation; for example, the noun *wheat* in English is singular, and *oats* is plural, though there is hardly a difference between the number of stalks in a field in each case. Pronouns and verbs also commonly display contrasts of number. ➤countability; dual; noun.

numbers Words which refer to specific quantities. The two chief linguistic systems are the **cardinal numbers**, which are the numbers used in ordinary counting, answering the question 'How many?' (*one, two*, etc.), and the **ordinal numbers**, which indicate order in a sequence (*first, second*, etc.). The symbols used to represent a number are called **numerals** – such as those used in the Arabic, Roman, and Greek systems. ➤number.

Nyanja /ˈnjandʒə/ A member of the Bantu group of Benue-Congo languages, spoken by *c.*5 million people in Malawi (*c.*3.2 million), where it is an official language (along with English), and parts of Mozambique, Zimbabwe, and Zambia; also called **Chewa**. It is used by a further 5 million people in the region as a second language. It is written in the Roman alphabet. ➤Benue-Congo.

Nynorsk /ˈniːnɔːsk/ ➤Norwegian.

O

O An abbreviation of **object**.

obelisk A typographic symbol (†); also called a **dagger**. Its functions are to mark a cross-reference (e.g. to a footnote or bibliographical item), and alongside someone's name to indicate that the person is dead. ➤typography.

object (O) A major constituent of sentence or clause structure, traditionally associated with the receiver or goal of an action, such as *the ball* in *The boy kicked the ball.* A widely recognized distinction is between **direct** and **indirect object**, as in *The child gave the toy to her mother*, where *the toy* is the direct and *her mother* the indirect object. ➤clause; recipient; subject.

objective case ➤accusative case.

objective genitive ➤subject.

oblique ➤solidus.

obscenity ➤taboo language.

obsolescence 1. In historical linguistics, the gradual loss of a lexical item because changes in the language or in the external world eliminate the opportunity or motivation for its utterance. Examples would be the terms referring to early modern vehicles, such as *landau* or *hansom*. These words have not gone completely out of use, as they will be heard from time to time at vintage rallies and in other specialized settings, but most people would not use them. When a word does go totally out of general use, it would be referred to as **obsolete**. *Traitorly*, for example, is now obsolete: it was used in Elizabethan English, but has since been replaced by *treacherous*. ➤archaism. **2**. The gradual loss of a language, which takes place when its transmission between generations ceases, and the number of its native speakers diminishes. ➤language death.

obsolete ➤obsolescence.

obstruent /ˈɒbstruːənt/ A major division of consonant sounds, in terms of manner of articulation, in which the vocal tract is sufficiently constricted to interfere with free air flow (as is the case with plosives, fricatives, and affricates). A contrast is usually drawn with **approximant** (also **sonorant** or **resonant**), where sounds are produced with a relatively free airflow (as is the case with vowels, liquids, nasals, and laterals). ➤approximant; consonant.

Ob-Ugric /ˈɒbˈjuːgrɪk/ ➤Finno-Ugric.

obviative /ˈɒbvɪətɪv/ A fourth-person form used in some languages (e.g. some of the Algonkian languages of North America). It usually contrasts with the third person pronoun to refer to an entity distinct from that already referred to – the notion of 'someone or something else'. ➤➤person; pronoun.

Occitan /ɒksɪˈtan/ A Romance language, spoken in south-east France, Italy, and Monaco by an uncertain number of people (perhaps 10 million), generally heard mixed with colloquial French; also called **langue d'oc**. The name derives from the name of the geographical region, Occitania. Closely related to Catalan, Occitan has several dialects, notably Provençal, spoken east of the Rhône chiefly in the Provence region. Old or Classical Provençal can be traced back to the 10th century. It was the language of the medieval troubadours, and became a standard language in France and northern Spain until the 14th century; there were literary revivals in the 19th and the 20th centuries. It is written in the Roman alphabet. ➤➤French; Romance.

occlusion The duration of the closure made while a plosive is being articulated. A plosive is sometimes referred to as an **occlusive**. ➤➤plosive.

occupational dialect ➤dialect.

oesophageal ➤esophageal.

off-glide ➤glide.

official language ➤national language.

ogham or **ogam** /ˈɒgəm/ An alphabetic script dating from the 4th century AD, found in about 500 inscriptions in Irish and Pictish. Its origins are unknown. The alphabet has 20 letters, divided into four sets of five. The letters were simple strokes

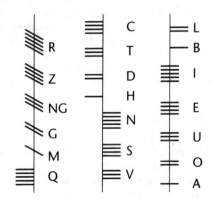

The **ogham** alphabet.

or notches cut into the edges of a stone (or possibly wood). They are usually read from bottom to top, or from right to left. **►►**alphabet; Irish Gaelic.

Old Church Slavonic ►Slavic.

Old English ►English.

Old Norse ►Scandinavian.

Oman (population in 1995 estimated at 1,845,000) The official language is Arabic, spoken by *c.*70% of the population. Other languages are Baluchi, Farsi (Persian), Mahri, Swahili, and Urdu. English is used for international purposes. There are over half a million expatriates in the country. **►►**Arabic.

Omotic /əʊ'mɒtɪk/ A branch of the Afro-Asiatic family of languages, spoken by nearly 3 million people in western Ethiopia and northern Kenya. About half of these are speakers of Walamo. There are about 20 other languages in the group, which is sometimes classified as a western branch of Cushitic. **►►**Afro-Asiatic; Cushitic.

on-glide ►glide.

onomasiology /ɒnəmasi:'ɒlədʒi:/ The study of sets of associated concepts in relation to the linguistic forms which designate them; for example, the study of the ways lexical items can be organized conceptually in a section of an encyclopedia. This direction of study, from concepts to items (as in a typical thesaurus) is sometimes contrasted with **semasiology**, where the direction of study is from items to concepts. **►►**semantics; thesaurus.

onomastics /ɒnə'mastɪks/ A branch of semantics which studies the etymology of proper names; also called **onomatology** (the word comes from Greek *onoma* 'name'). Its subdivisions include **anthroponymy**, the study of the names of people, and **toponymy** (or **toponomastics**), the study of the names of places. **►►**etymology; hydronymy; name; patronymic; semantics; teknonymy.

onomatology /ɒnəmə'tɒlədʒi:/ ►onomastics.

onomatopoeia /ɒnəmatə'pi:ə/ ►sound symbolism.

onset ►syllable.

ontogeny /ɒn'tɒdʒəni:/ The chronological acquisition, development, and decay of language in the individual, from birth to death; chiefly used for the study of language acquisition in children. The corresponding study applied to the speech community as a whole is **phylogeny** – the subject-matter of philology and historical linguistics. **►►**acquisition.

open 1. Descriptive of the lips when they are held relatively wide apart, but without noticeable rounding. The body of the tongue is held low in the mouth. **►►**close vowel; rounding. **2**. Descriptive of a syllable which ends in a vowel; contrasts with a **closed** syllable, which ends in a consonant. ➤➤syllable. **3.** In one approach to early language acquisition, descriptive of the variable item at the 2-element stage of sentence development, the other being referred to as the **pivot**. For example, such utterances as *see there, go there, cat there*, are analysed as having a pivotal item, *there*, in association with an item from a relatively open set. ➤➤acquisition; closed class.

open class ➤closed class.

operator In some approaches to English grammar, the first auxiliary verb to be used in a verb phrase. It is so called because it performs an 'operation' on the clause, such as marking the change from statement to question. In *He was leaving, was* is the operator (cf. *Was he leaving?*). In *She has been telling me, has* is the operator (cf. *Has she been telling me?*). ➤➤auxiliary verb.

oppositeness ➤antonymy; complementarity; converseness.

opposition ➤contrast.

optative /ˈɒptətɪv/ A grammatical category of mood which expresses a desire, hope, or wish. It is chiefly known from Classical Greek. Optative expressions in English use the modal verbs or the subjunctive: *May they get home safely, Heaven help us!*. ➤➤mood.

Oracle ➤teletext.

oracy /ˈɔːrəsiː/ Ability in speech fluency and listening comprehension; a term coined on analogy with **literacy**. The notion is chiefly encountered in relation to the development of spoken language skills in mother-tongue education. ➤➤educational linguistics; literacy.

oral ➤cavity; nasal.

oralism ➤manualism.

oral tradition The spoken expression of a culture, as found in sagas, myths, folk tales, folk poetry, and other texts transmitted from generation to generation without use of written records. The tradition is especially encountered in cultures which have little or no history of literacy, but a living oral tradition may be found anywhere. ➤➤anthropological linguistics.

order The pattern of relationships within a linear sequence of linguistic units. The notion is chiefly encountered with reference to **word order** (e.g. whether an adjective precedes or follows the noun in a noun phrase), but it is also found in discussion of the order of phrases and other elements of sentence structure (e.g. the distinction between languages which use a subject–verb–object order, and those which do not). ➤➤position 1; syntax; typology of language; word order.

order of mention In psycholinguistics, a use of language where the order of events in the outside world is paralleled by the order in the sequence of semantic units within the corresponding utterance. For example, order of mention is preserved in the sentence *After Mary left, Jane went home* – the first thing to be said is the first thing to happen. By contrast, order of mention is lost in the sentence *Jane went home after Mary left* – the first thing to be said is the last thing to happen. This kind of distinction proves to be important in identifying levels of difficulty in learning sentences, especially by young children. ➤➤psycholinguistics.

ordinal number ➤numeral.

organs of speech ➤vocal organs.

origins of language The topic of where, when, and how human speech first developed. The question has attracted a vast amount of speculation, but none of the theories produces much evidence in support. Scientific investigations of the fossil record, to determine whether primitive humans had the physiological capacity to speak, have produced intriguing but inconclusive results. There is an enormous gap between the time period when speech may have begun to develop (perhaps 35,000 – 70,000 years ago) and the earliest recorded evidence of language (written inscriptions of less than 10,000 years ago). ➤➤bow-wow/ding-dong/la-la/pooh-pooh/yo-he-ho theory; glossogenetics; philology.

Oriya /ɒ'ri:jə/ A language belonging to the Eastern group of Indo-Aryan languages, spoken by *c*.30 million people, chiefly in the state of Orissa, eastern India, where it is an official regional language. It is written in an alphabet derived from an early Brahmi script. The earliest known inscriptions date from the 14th century. ➤Brahmi; Indo-Aryan.

Oromo /'ɒrəməʊ/ A member of the Cushitic language family, spoken by *c*.10 million people in two main varieties, chiefly in Ethiopia, with some in nearby parts of Kenya; formerly called **Gallinya**. It is written in the Amharic alphabet. ➤Cushitic.

orthoepy /ɔ:'θəʊəpi:/ The study of correct pronunciation, especially as practised in the 17th and 18th centuries. Among the leading orthoepists of the period were Bishop John Wilkins (1614–72) and the mathematician John Wallis (1616–1703). Several works provide detailed descriptions of the sounds of contemporary English. ➤pronunciation; spelling.

orthography A standardized system for writing a specific language. The notion includes a prescribed system of spelling and punctuation. ➤graphology 1; script 1.

Ossetic /ɒ'setɪk/ A member of the Iranian group of languages, spoken by *c*.500,000 people in the northern Caucasus. It is written in the Cyrillic alphabet. There is a well-established oral epic literature, and a written literary language has developed since the 19th century. ➤Iranian.

Ostrogothic /'ɒstrəgɒθɪk/ ➤Gothic.

Oto-Manguean /əʊtə'maŋɡeɪən/ A family of Amerindian languages spoken in Central America, in a small area centred on the state of Oaxaca, Mexico. The main languages are Otomí, Mixteco, and Zapotec, each with *c*.250,000 people. The modern languages are written in the Roman alphabet. ➤Amerindian.

overcorrection ➤hypercorrection.

overextension A relationship between child and adult meaning in a lexical item, where the child's item has a wider range of application than the equivalent adult term. An example is the use of *cat* to refer to other animals as well as cats. The notion contrasts with **underextension**, where the child's item has a more restricted range than that found in adult language, as when *cat* is used to refer to only one kind of cat (such as the one living in the child's house). A contrast may also be drawn with lexical **mismatch**, where there is no evident overlap at all with the adult meaning, as when *cat* might be used to refer to a biscuit. ➤acquisition; semantics.

overgeneralization ➤generalization.

overt prestige In sociolinguistics, a type of prestige attached to the use of a language or variety which follows the norms set by influential members of society. Someone may use (consciously or unconsciously) the forms of the standard language, for example, because this will convey an educated or cultured impression. The notion contrasts with **covert prestige**, where a positive value is associated with the use of vernacular forms, emphasizing solidarity and local identity. In such a case, speakers may use (again, consciously or unconsciously) nonstandard slang or local dialect forms to show that they 'belong'. ➤➤language change; sociolinguistics.

Oxford English ➤standard English.

oxymoron, plural **oxymora** /ɒksiːˈmɔːrən/ A figure of speech which combines words of incongruous or contradictory meaning. Oxymora are usually identified in literary contexts, such as Milton's *living death* (in *Samson Agonistes*), but they are often to be heard in everyday conversation – for example, describing a toddler as *a piece of charming wickedness*. ➤➤figurative language.

P

P An abbreviation of **phrase**, **predicator**, **preposition**, or **particle**.

paedography /piːˈdɒɡrəfiː/ A writing system which has been devised in order to help children learn to read. An example is the initial teaching alphabet. ➤i.t.a.

page proof ➤proof.

Paget–Gorman Sign System A sign language devised by Sir Richard Paget in the 1950s and developed after his death (1955) by Pierre Gorman, librarian at the Royal National Institute of the Deaf in London. It contains *c*.3000 signs, representing the words and morphemes of spoken English. Sentences are signed following English word order. ➤sign language.

Pahari /pəˈhɑːriː/ A group of languages belonging to the North-western group of Indo-Aryan, spoken in the lower Himalayas. They include Nepali, Garhwali, and Kumauni. ➤Indo-Aryan; Nepali.

Pahlavi /ˈpɑːləviː/ ➤Persian.

Pakhto /ˈpaktəʊ/ ➤Pashto.

Pakistan (population in 1995 estimated at 141,783,000) The official language is Urdu, spoken by *c*.11 million as a first language, and by most others as a second or third language. English is an associated official language. Panjabi (spoken by *c*.40% of the population, chiefly in Panjab) and Sindhi (by *c*.12%, chiefly in Sindh) are official regional languages. There are *c*.60 other languages, notably Pashto (*c*.10 million) and Baluchi (three main varieties, *c*.5 million). English is used for international purposes. ➤Urdu.

palatal ➤palate.

palate The arched structure that forms the roof of the mouth, much used for the articulation of speech sounds. It is divided into the **hard palate**, the immobile bony area immediately behind the alveolar ridge, and the **soft palate** or **velum**, the mobile fleshy continuation which culminates in the uvula. **Palatal** consonants are made when the front of the tongue articulates with the hard palate (as in German *ich* 'I'); this term is also sometimes used with reference to high front vowels, which are made approaching the palate. **Palatalization** refers to any articulation involving a movement towards the hard palate. **Palatography** is the instrumental study of articulation in the palatal area, which produces displays known as **palatograms**. ➤electropalatograph; palato-alveolar; uvular; vocal organs.

palato-alveolar /ˈpalətəʊ alviːˈəʊlə/ Descriptive of a consonant sound made by the blade of the tongue against the alveolar ridge while the front of the tongue is raised towards the hard palate. The initial sound of English *ship* is one example; the initial sound of French *je* 'I' is another. ➤alveolar; palate.

palatography ➤electropalatography; palate.

Palau ➤Belau.

paleography or **palaeography** The study of ancient and medieval writings and inscriptions, in order to establish the provenance, date, and correct form of a text. The subject chiefly involves the study of writing on papyrus, parchment (vellum), or paper, though it does not exclude other forms (e.g. graffiti). Most paleographic research has been into manuscripts within the Greek/Latin tradition. ➤holograph; internal evidence; writing.

Paleosiberian or **Palaeosiberian** A grouping of languages now represented by a few thousand people scattered throughout north-eastern Siberia. They comprise four genetically-unrelated groups, studied together since the 19th century: Luorawetlan in the far north-east, Yukaghir in the west, Yeniseyan on the River Yenisey, and the single language Gilyak in the south. Since the early part of the present century, each of these languages has been written down, using the Cyrillic alphabet. ➤Gilyak; Luorawetlan; Yeniseyan; Yukaghir.

Pali /ˈpɑːliː/ A member of the Indo-Aryan family of languages, known because of its status as the sacred language of the Theravada Buddhist canon; the name means '(canonical) text'. Its use derives from Buddha's wish to use vernacular languages for his teaching (as opposed to Sanskrit, a scholarly language). The oral tradition which ensued was eventually transcribed in the 1st century BC. The language contains many archaisms and mixed dialect features, and cannot be identified with any single vernacular. ➤Indo-Aryan; Prakrit.

palilalia /palɪˈleɪlɪə/ Involuntary repetition of words and phrases. The term has been used only in a clinical context, where it characterizes the symptoms of several types of disorder, notably aphasia. ➤echolalia.

palilology /palɪˈlɒlədʒiː/ In the study of rhetoric, word repetition for emphasis, as in *I am dying, Egypt, dying* (*Antony and Cleopatra*, IV, xvi), or *O villain, villain, smiling, damned villain* (*Hamlet*, I, v). The notion is common in colloquial contexts, too, as in *That was a splendid, splendid performance*. The term is not current in linguistics. ➤rhetoric.

palindrome /ˈpalɪndrəʊm/ A word or expression which reads the same backwards or forwards. Simple examples are such words as *Ada* and *madam*; more complex ones are *Able was I ere I saw Elba*. Two palindromic language names are *Malayalam* and *Nauruan*. Palindromes of several thousand letters have been constructed, presumably for fun. ➤➤word game.

Panama (population in 1995 estimated at 2,669,000) The official language is Spanish. There are *c*.10 Amerindian languages, as well as some speakers of Chinese, and an English-based creole (spoken by *c*.14%) used in other parts of the western Caribbean. Spanish and English are used for international purposes. ➤➤creole; Spanish.

pangram A meaningful sentence which contains every letter of the alphabet – ideally, a single instance of each letter. The typist's sentence *The quick brown fox jumps over the lazy dog* is a pangram, but an imperfect one, as there are several duplications. A 26-letter pangram devised in 1984 (with genuine words, all listed in the large *Oxford English Dictionary*) is: *Veldt jynx grimps Waqf zho buck*. ➤➤word game.

Panini /'pɑːniːniː/ An Indian grammarian, the first to produce an authoritative text on the nature of Sanskrit. Written sometime between the 7th and 5th centuries BC, his 'eight books' deal mainly with rules of word formation, and are notable for their detailed phonetic descriptions. ➤➤Sanskrit.

Panjabi also spelled **Punjabi** /pʊnˈdʒɑːbiː/ A language belonging to the North-western group of Indo-Aryan languages, spoken by *c*.50 million people in Pakistan and *c*.23 million in India, and also in several countries as an immigrant language, notably Great Britain. It is an official regional language both in Panjab province, Pakistan, and in Panjab, India. In India it is written in the Gurmukhi alphabet, devised in the 16th century for writing the Sikh scriptures, and now in widespread use; in Pakistan it is written in the Arabic alphabet. Panjabi is the religious language of Sikhism. A western variety, Lahnda, is often classified as a separate language. ➤➤Indo-Aryan.

panlectal grammar ➤lect.

Panoan /pəˈnəʊən/ ➤Gê-Pano-Carib.

Papiamentu or **Papiamento** /papjəˈmentuː/ A Spanish creole, showing considerable Portuguese and Dutch influence, spoken by *c*.200,000 people chiefly in Curaçao and Bonaire (part of the Netherlands Antilles), and Aruba in the Caribbean, with *c*.60,000 in The Netherlands. Some scholars consider the creole to have a Portuguese origin. It is written in the Roman alphabet. ➤➤creole.

Papuan /'papjuːən/ ➤Indo-Pacific.

Papua New Guinea (population in 1995 estimated at 4,093,000) The official language is English, with Tok Pisin and Hiri Motu also given official status. All three are used as lingua francas – essential in a country which has a higher density of languages (over 800, belonging to the Austronesian and Indo-Pacific families) than any other. ➤➤English; Hiri Motu; Tok Pisin.

paradigm The set of substitutional relationships a linguistic unit has with other units in a particular context; for example, in the context ' – will leave', the pronouns *I, you, we,* etc. can substitute for each other, and thus comprise a paradigm. A class of elements related in this way ('paradigmatically') is often referred to as a **system** – the pronoun system, in this case. More narrowly, the term is used for a set of grammatically conditioned forms all derived from a single root or stem, as in the case of Latin, where all the case-forms of a noun are said to be in the same paradigm (*puella, puellam, puellae,* etc.). ➤➤case; substitution; syntagm; system.

paradox A statement which is contradictory or absurd on the surface, and which thus forces the search for a deeper level of meaning. A famous example is Orwell's *War is peace. Freedom is slavery. Ignorance is strength.* ➤➤figurative language.

paragram A play on words by altering some of its letters, especially the first letter. An example is the pun made by the artist who described his picture of a female nude as a 'shescape'. ➤➤pun.

paragrammatism /parə'gramətızm/ A disorder involving specific errors of morphology or syntax in the spoken or written language of someone suffering from aphasia; a clinician might describe a speech sample as 'paragrammatic' – displaying paragrammatism. The term is also used clinically for an instance of such an error – the use of *was been*, for example, could be described as 'a paragrammatism'. Linguists tend to use rather more detailed terminology when discussing grammatical errors. ➤➤agrammatism; aphasia; grammar 2.

paragraph A unit of written discourse between the sentence and the whole text, graphically distinguished either by indention of the first line or by white space preceding and following. The function of a paragraph is to show the reader that the sentences in a particular set are more closely related to each other than to the sentences in adjacent text. There is no simple way of defining the unit of meaning which a paragraph expresses, or its internal structure, though attempts are often made to specify a 'topic' for each paragraph, and to identify 'topic sentences' (sentences which introduce a paragraph's theme). There are clear stylistic trends – for example, the marked tendency for paragraphs to be shorter in popular writing. ➤➤discourse analysis; indention; punctuation; sentence; topic.

Paraguay (population in 1995 estimated at 4,896,000) The official languages are Spanish and Guaraní. About 95% of the people speak Guaraní. There are *c.*15 other Amerindian languages, most spoken by only a few hundred, and *c.*40,000 speakers of German. Spanish and English are used for international purposes. ➤➤Guaraní; Spanish.

paralanguage /'parəlaŋgwɪʤ/ Variations in tone of voice which seem to be less definable and systematic than other aspects of nonsegmental phonology, such as creaky or breathy voice; also called **paralinguistic features**. The term is sometimes broadened to include other features of speech (e.g. pauses, voice quality) and nonverbal features (e.g. kinesic features). Paralinguistic features are often described using other labels, such as 'vocal qualifiers' or 'voice qualifications'. ➤breathy voice; creaky voice; kinesics; pause; phonology.

parallelism A sequence of identical or strikingly similar elements in speaking or writing. The notion is especially used in grammatical description, where whole constructions can be related through their use of parallel syntax; but sounds and words may be used in parallel, too. An example is Hamlet's *Doubt thou the stars are fire; / Doubt that the sun doth move; / Doubt truth to be a liar; / But never doubt I love* (II, ii). ➤style; syntax.

parameter In linguistics, a specification of the variations that a principle of grammar shows among different languages. A **head parameter**, for example, would specify the possible positions of heads within phrases. Determining the values of parameters for given languages is called **parameter-setting**. The notion was introduced in the mid-1980s as part of government and binding theory. ➤government and binding theory; head.

parametric phonetics An approach to phonetics that analyses speech as a single physiological system in which the range of articulatory variables (**parameters**, such as voicing, tongue movement, and soft palate movement) is seen to be continually in operation. These parameters interact along the time dimension to produce a continuum of sound which listeners segment according to the rules of the language. The approach is a reaction against the traditional view of speech as a sequence of self-contained phonetic segments – [b] + [e] + [t], etc – now seen to be a serious oversimplification. ➤coarticulation; phonetics.

paraphasia In the study of anomia and related disorders, an involuntary error in the production of words or phrases. **Phonological paraphasia** is a type of incorrect response in which phonemic elements are absent, distorted, or misplaced within an otherwise recognizable word; also known as **literal paraphasia**. Examples include *bandona* for *banana*, and *larding* for *loading*. In **semantic paraphasia** the error relates in meaning or category to the desired name, such as *soldier* for *policeman*, or *siren* for *ambulance*; also known as **verbal paraphasia**. These terms have currency within language pathology, not in linguistics. ➤anomia; language pathology; phonology.

paraphrase The process or result of producing alternative versions of a sentence or text without changing its meaning. A similar notion has long been used in school language classes, where a student might be asked to paraphrase a passage: here the new text has to preserve the 'core' meaning of the old, or be a close approximation to it. The linguistic use of the term usually involves a stricter sense, requiring that the two texts have the *same* meaning – thus, *John caught the ball* and *The ball was* *caught by John* are said to be syntactic paraphrases of each other. ➤➤transformation.

pararhyme /ˈparəraɪm/ Repetition of the same initial and final consonants in different accented words, or of the final consonant(s) only; also known as **half-rhyme**. An example, from Wilfred Owen's 'Strange Meeting' (which uses pararhyme throughout) is: *And by his smile I knew that sullen hall, / By his dead smile I knew we stood in Hell.* ➤➤rhyme.

paratactic /ˈparətaktɪk/ ➤hypotactic.

parenthesis 1. In punctuation, either or both of a pair of round brackets (**parentheses**) to signal an optional, included element of meaning; also called **brackets** in British English. The preceding sentence contains an illustration. ➤➤punctuation.
2. In speech, any construction which can be considered an optional, included element of a sentence. If it is genuinely parenthetic, the construction can be removed without this affecting the grammatical structure of the rest of the sentence. Comment clauses (e.g. *you see, to be honest, frankly speaking*) provide good examples: *That car, to be honest, is an expensive failure.* ➤➤comment clause.

parent language ➤family of languages.

parole ➤*langue*.

paronomasia /parɒnəˈmeɪzə/ ➤pun.

paronymy /pəˈrɒnəmiː/ The semantic relationship which exists between words derived from the same root. The notion is especially used for the formation of a word which changes only slightly from a word in another language, such as French *pont* 'bridge' from Latin *pons*, but words such as *boyhood* and *boyish* could also be called paronyms. ➤➤etymology.

parsing In traditional grammar, the pedagogical exercise of analysing and labelling

The old man called me a crazy inventor.

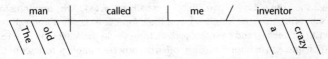

A diagrammatical method of **parsing**. A system of vertical and slant lines represent the syntactic relationships within a sentence – commonly used in American schools. The representations are often called 'Reed and Kellogg' diagrams, after the authors of a nineteenth-century English textbook. A long vertical line marks the subject–predicate boundary; a short vertical line divides verb and object; and a short slanting line marks off a complement. Other items are written in underneath.

the grammatical elements of single sentences; also, especially in the USA, called **diagramming**. A sentence on a blackboard, such as *The cat sat on the dog*, would be parsed into Subject + Predicate, the Predicate parsed into Verb + Adverbial, and the type of Adverbial recognized (of Place). The mechanical nature of the exercise (in which, for example, the several types of adverbial phrase might be learned by rote), and the use of examples which seemed to bear little or no relationship to the linguistic experience of the student, led to this approach going out of fashion in the late 1950s. In linguistics, the analysis of sentences is not generally called 'parsing', therefore, to avoid confusion with the traditional approach; but in any case, linguists are not so much concerned with the labelling of elements as with the criteria which lead to the identification of these elements. However, in recent years, the term has come back into fashion, being widely used for the general process of sentence analysis employed in computational linguistics. ➤computational/educational linguistics; grammar 2; language in use; machine translation.

participant roles 1. The functions that can be ascribed to people taking part in a linguistic interaction. Participants may have such roles as speaker, addressee, and message source (i.e. someone other than the speaker). ➤discourse analysis. **2**. The semantic functions attached to clause elements, such as agent and recipient. In this sense, the roles are participating in the meaning of a sentence, rather than in the dynamics of an interaction. ➤agent; clause; patient; recipient.

participle In traditional grammar, a word derived from a verb and used as an adjective, as in *shining example* and *parked car*. The name comes from the way such a word 'participates' in the characteristics of both verb and adjective. There are two related notions in Latin grammar, and these were carried through into the description of many modern languages (though often without any real regard to differences between the grammar of those languages and that of Latin, with the result that the distinction was generally misunderstood or ignored). A **gerund** is a noun derived from a verb (a 'verbal noun'), such as *amandum* 'loving'; two such forms are illustrated in *Seeing is believing*. A **gerundive** is an adjective derived from a verb (a 'verbal adjective'), such as *amandus* 'lovable'; an English example would be *crumbling ruin*. In linguistics, the notion of participle is generally restricted to the nonfinite forms of a verb (other than the infinitive), and these forms are classified into two types: **present** (e.g. *shining*) and **past** (e.g. *parked*). However, as participles can refer to any time (past, present, or future), linguists often use other terminology to describe them – in English, **-ing forms** and **-en forms**, respectively. ➤adjective; finite; grammar 2; *-ing* form; verb.

particle An invariable item with a grammatical function. The term is especially used for a form which does not readily fit into a standard classification of parts of speech. The *to* in front of an English infinitive (*to see*) is often described as a particle, as is French *y* in such forms as *Il y a* 'There is/are'. ➤infinitive; word class.

partitive A form which refers to a part or quantity, such as *piece*, *ounce*, and *bar* (of soap). Some partitive forms are very general, occurring with almost any quantifiable lexical item (e.g. *some*); others are restricted to a single lexical item, or a very small set (e.g. *blade* – of grass, *flock* – of sheep, birds). ➤➤quantifier.

part of speech ➤word class.

Pashto /'paʃtəʊ/ A member of the Iranian group of languages, spoken by *c*.11 million people in Pakistan, and by *c*.8 million in Afghanistan (where it is an official language, along with Persian); also spelled **Pakhto** (reflecting a northern dialect pronunciation) and sometimes called **Afghan**. It is written in the Arabic alphabet, and has a literary tradition from the 16th century. It was declared the national language of Afghanistan in 1936, and there is a Pashto Academy. ➤➤Afghanistan; Iranian.

pasigraphy /pə'sɪgrəfiː/ The use of a system of symbols which can be understood between different languages. Several such systems have been proposed, some using current signs and symbols in current use (e.g. +, &, 2, £), others using batteries of artificially constructed forms. ➤➤logogram.

passive knowledge ➤active knowledge.

passive voice ➤voice 1.

past anterior A tense form used in some languages to express the rapid completion of a past action. In French, for example, it is chiefly used instead of the pluperfect in past narrative after temporal conjunctions or when the main verb is in the past historic. It is formed by combining the past historic tense of an auxiliary verb with the past participle of a lexical verb: *Dès qu'elle eut mangé, elle sortit* 'As soon as she had eaten, she left'. ➤➤past historic; pluperfect; tense.

past definite ➤past historic.

past historic A past tense form of a verb, used in some languages to refer to a completed action; also sometimes called the **past definite**. In French, for example, it is used in the written language as part of past narrative description as well as in the reporting of completed past events: *Hier, Marie se leva et sortit* 'Yesterday, Marie got up and went out'. ➤➤past tense.

past participle ➤participle.

past perfect ➤perfect.

past tense A tense form which refers to a time of action prior to the moment of utterance. Languages make different distinctions within this period, such as whether the reference is recent or distant, or whether the action is completed or not. French, for example, recognizes imperfect, past historic, perfect, pluperfect, and past anterior tenses, as well as future and conditional perfect forms. English also traditionally recognizes a range of past tense forms, following the influence of Latin grammar, though only a single past tense form is represented inflectionally (*I walked*), other past time reference using auxiliary verbs (*I have walked*, etc.). ➤imperfect; inflection 1; past anterior/historic; perfect; preterite; tense.

pathologist (of speech or language) ➤language pathology.

patient In some grammatical analyses of a sentence, the entity that is affected by the action of the verb. The typical example is the object of a transitive verb, as in *Mary drove **the car***, but the subject of certain kinds of construction may also be described as the patient, as in ***The cat** was chased by the dog.* ➤participant roles; recipient.

Patois /'patwɑː/ ➤Patwa.

patois /'patwɑː/ A popular label for a provincial dialect, especially one spoken by people considered to be primitive, illiterate, or outside society in some way (e.g. rustics, gypsies). It usually carries a disparaging connotation, and is not used in dialectology. ➤dialect.

patronymic /patrə'nɪmɪk/ A name given to someone based on the name of the person's father, such as *Johnson* or *Johanson*. This is a fairly common event in the name histories of different countries. In Russian, for example, people have three names: first name, patronymic, and surname – as illustrated by *Ivan Nikolayevich Gogol*. Much less common is the use of a **matronymic** (or **metronymic**), based on the name of a person's mother, as in *Marjorison*. Spanish is an example of a language where a surname may contain both a father's and a mother's surname, as in *(Gabriel) García Márquez.* ➤onomastics.

pattern drill ➤drill.

Patwa or **Patois** /'patwɑː/ The name given to several varieties of creole French spoken by over a million people in several parts of the Caribbean and French Guiana, notably Saint Lucia, Dominica, Guadeloupe, and Martinique. It is regularly used in broadcasting and the press. The name is also used for the variety of creole English spoken in Jamaica. With a small *p*, the term *patois* is widely used in a general (and usually disparaging) way to refer to any provincial dialect in a region; this usage has no standing in linguistics. ➤creole; Dominica; French Guiana; Guadeloupe; Jamaica; Martinique; Saint Lucia.

pause A temporary break in the flow of speech, often classified into **silent pause**, where there is no vocalization, and **filled pause**, where a hesitation noise is introduced (e.g. *erm, ah*). In grammar, the criterion of **potential pause** is sometimes used as a method for establishing the words in a language, since pauses are more likely at word boundaries than within words. ➤hesitation; paralanguage.

peace linguistics A climate of opinion which emerged during the 1990s among many linguists and language teachers, in which linguistic principles, methods, findings, and applications were seen as a means of promoting peace and human rights at a global level. The approach emphasizes the value of linguistic diversity and multilingualism, both internationally and intranationally, and asserts the need to foster language attitudes which respect the dignity of individual speakers and speech communities. ➤➤ecolinguistics; language attitudes/awareness/planning/teaching; Linguapax.

pedagogical grammar A grammatical account of a language whose purpose is to facilitate the teaching and learning of that language; also called a **pedagogic grammar**. Such a grammar is especially found in foreign language teaching, where it contrasts with such notions as descriptive grammar and theoretical grammar. ➤➤educational linguistics; grammar 1.

pedagogical linguistics ➤educational linguistics.

pejoration /piːʤəˈreɪʃn/ A change of meaning in which a word develops a sense of disapproval. An example is *notorious*, which formerly meant 'widely known', but now means 'widely and unfavourably known'. ➤➤amelioration.

pejorative /prˈʤɒrətɪv, ˈpiːʤərətɪv/ Descriptive of a linguistic form which expresses a disparaging meaning. Examples include *goodish, a youth*, and (see above) *patois*. ➤➤connotation.

pen name ➤pseudonym.

Pennsylvanian Dutch ➤German.

pentameter ➤metrics.

Penutian /pəˈnuːʃn/ A group of over 60 Amerindian languages spoken from south-west Canada down through the western states of the USA, Mexico, and Central America, and into south-west South America. In its broadest interpretation (as **Macro-Penutian**), this grouping thus provides the main linguistic bridge between North, Central, and South America. (A narrower interpretation uses the term for just the 20 or so North American languages involved.) The Penutian languages with most speakers belong to the Mayan family, spoken in Mexico and Central America. The main South American language is Mapudungan (also called Araucanian or Mapuche), spoken by *c*.250,000 people chiefly in Chile, with some in Argentina. All these languages now use the Roman alphabet when written down. Maya developed a sophisticated hieroglyphic system. ➤➤Amerindian; Mayan.

perception ➤speech perception.

perfect (perf.) A grammatical category of a temporal or durative kind, typically applying to verb forms, sometimes handled under the heading of **tense** and some-times under **aspect**; for example, *I go* vs. *I have gone*, or *I have gone* vs. *I had gone* (the latter traditionally called the **pluperfect**, or **past perfect**). In **perfect** contexts, an event in the past is seen as having some present relevance; for example, *I've hurt my knee* implies that the knee is currently sore (whereas in *I hurt my knee (last week)*, the knee may be quite well again). In **perfective aspect**, a contrast is typically seen as a whole, regardless of the time contrasts that may be a part of it; **imperfective** or **nonperfective aspect** typically draws attention to the internal time-structuring of the situation. This last type of contrast is important in Slavic languages. ➤➤aspect; imperfect; tense 1; verb.

perfective ➤perfect.

performance 1. Language seen as a set of specific utterances produced by speakers; contrasts with **competence**. Performance, in this view, includes all the nonfluencies and other limitations (e.g. of memory and attention) which are a normal part of speech production. The notion was introduced by Noam Chomsky in the 1960s, and is analogous to the Saussurian concept of *parole*. A grammar which takes into account the various biological and psychological processes involved in speech is a **performance grammar**. ➤➤Chomskyan; competence; *parole*; speech production. **2**. ➤ear training.

performance grammar ➤grammar 1.

performative A type of sentence or verb where an action is performed by virtue of the sentence having been uttered. Simply by saying *I apologize*, an apology is made ('performed'). To say *I promise* is a sign that a promise has been made. Performative utterances are an important part of a theory of speech acts. ➤➤illocutionary act; speech act.

period A punctuation mark which signals the end of an orthographic sentence in statement form; also called a **full-stop** in British English. It contrasts with the other sentence-final marks (the question and exclamation marks), and also with the mark of sentence-incompletion (usually a triple dot, . . .). ➤➤punctuation.

periphrasis /pəˈrɪfrəsɪs/ The use of separate words instead of inflectional affixes to express the same grammatical relationship. For example, the comparison of adjectives in English involves both inflectional forms (e.g. *bigger*) and **periphrastic** forms (e.g. *more interesting*). ➤➤adjective; circumlocution; inflection 1.

perlocutionary act/effect /pɜːləˈkjuːʃnəriː/ ➤illocutionary act.

perseveration /pɜːsevəˈreɪʃn/ An involuntary tendency to continue an activity, whether it is appropriate to do so or not; in the context of this book, the continuous use of a linguistic form or pattern. The term is chiefly used in clinical contexts, where it identifies a symptom noticeable in aphasia and certain other disorders. In one sequence, an aphasic patient, having described a picture (correctly) as 'The man is sweeping the floor', went on to describe the next picture (of a man cleaning a car) as 'The man is sweeping the car', and then proceeded to perseverate on *sweep* for several more utterances. Perseveration (on sounds) is also a noticeable feature of stuttering. ➤➤aphasia; stuttering.

Persian A member of the Iranian group of languages, spoken by *c*.25 million people in Iran (where it is the official language), with a further 7 million speaking an eastern variety chiefly in Afghanistan (where it has official status along with Pashto); also called **Farsi** (in Iran) and **Dari** (in Afghanistan). It is written in the Arabic alphabet. Written forms of the language date from cuneiform inscriptions in Old Persian during the first millennium BC. Middle Persian (Pahlavi) was spoken from the 3rd century BC to the 9th century AD; it was the basis of the modern language, which has been much influenced by Arabic. ➤➤Afghanistan; cuneiform; Iran; Iranian.

person A grammatical category referring to the number and nature of the participants in a situation. Speakers use **first person** pronouns to refer to themselves, or to a group including themselves (*I, we*); they use **second person** pronouns to refer to the person(s) they are addressing (*you*); and they use **third person** pronouns to refer to other people, animals, things, etc (*he, she, it, they*). Some languages recognize a **fourth person** or **obviative**. Verb constructions which lack a person contrast, usually appearing in the third person, are called **impersonal** (e.g. *it seems to me* . . .). ➤➤inclusive; obviative; pronoun; T/V forms.

personification A type of metaphor in which human qualities are ascribed to nonhuman entities or notions. This kind of figurative expression is common in poetry (e.g. *The mountains spoke of ancient wars*), but there are many everyday examples (e.g. *The town slept*). A related term is **hypostatize** – to speak of an abstract quality as if it were human. ➤➤figurative language.

Peru (population in 1995 estimated at 23,407,000) The official language is Spanish, spoken by *c*.85% of the people. There are *c*.65 Amerindian languages, notably Quechua, spoken in over 30 varieties (by *c*.15% in total), and Aymará. Spanish and English are used for international purposes. ➤➤Spanish.

petroglyph /ˈpetrəglɪf/ An ancient stone inscription; also called a **petrogram**. The earliest petroglyphs made use of primitive pictures and signs (e.g. human figures, geometric shapes). Though there are certain resemblances to writing, they lack the systemicness which is found in a writing system. ➤➤epigraph 1; writing.

petrogram ➤petroglyph.

pharyngeal /fəˈrɪndʒɪəl, farɪnˈdʒɪəl/ Descriptive of a consonant sound made by the root of the tongue with the back wall of the pharynx. Arabic is a language which uses this articulation, and has both voiceless and voiced forms. Any articulation involving a constriction of the pharynx is said to be **pharyngealized**. A 'stage whisper' typically involves a great deal of pharyngeal constriction. ➤➤consonant; pharynx; vocal organs.

pharynx /ˈfarɪŋks/ The part of the vocal tract above the larynx which connects the mouth and nose to the esophagus. It is important in providing resonance for speech sounds, and is actively involved in the production of certain voice qualities and consonants. ➤pharyngeal; vocal tract.

phatic communion /'fatɪk/ The social function of language, used to show rapport between people, or to establish a pleasant atmosphere. A typical British example is a comment about the weather or a passing enquiry about someone's health. The term derives from Greek *phatos*, 'spoken'. ➤referential language.

Philippines, The (population in 1995 estimated at 67,900,000) The official languages are Pilipino (spoken as a first language by *c.*60% of the population, and as a second language by a further 35%) and English (spoken by *c.*50% as a second language). There are over 100 local languages, several spoken in many varieties, including Cebuano (*c.*25%), Ilocano (*c.*11%), Hiligaynon (*c.*10%), and Bicolano (*c.*7%). Over 250,000 speak a Spanish-based creole (Spanish was formerly an official language), such as Chavacano (Zamboangueño), and Chinese is also spoken (over 500,000). Pilipino and English are lingua francas. English is used for international purposes. ➤Cebuano; creole; English; Ilocano; lingua franca; Pilipino.

philology Traditionally, the study of language history, sometimes including the historical study of literary texts; also called **comparative philology** when the emphasis is on the comparison of the historical states of different languages. The subject overlaps substantially with **historical linguistics**, but there are several differences of emphasis, both in training and in subject-matter. The philological tradition is one of painstaking textual analysis, often related to literary history, and using a fairly traditional descriptive framework. The newer, linguistic approach tends to study historical data more selectively, as part of the discussion of broader issues in linguistic theory, such as the nature of language change. ➤diachronic linguistics; internal evidence; law; reconstruction.

philosophical linguistics A branch of linguistics which studies the role of language in relation to the understanding and elucidation of philosophical concepts, as well as the philosophical status of linguistic theories, methods, and observations. Within philosophy, this interaction is often referred to as **linguistic philosophy** or the **philosophy of language**. ➤linguistics.

Phoenician /fəˈniːʃn/ A Semitic language spoken in an area corresponding to modern Lebanon and parts of nearby Syria and Israel, as well as in those parts of the Mediterranean coast colonized by the Phoenicians. Inscriptions in the language date from the 11th century BC, and there is evidence of its use in Phoenicia for about a millennium. It is written from right to left, using a 22-letter alphabet which does not represent vowels. A derivative of the North Semitic alphabet, it is probably the ancestor of the Greek alphabet, which in turn gave rise to all Western alphabets. Several variant forms of the alphabet exist. An important later development of both the language and the alphabet, known as **Punic**, came to be used throughout the Carthaginian Empire, and continued in use until around the 5th century AD. ➤➤alphabet; Greek; Semitic.

phonation The use of the vocal folds to produce the range of voiced sounds in speech, as well as certain other laryngeal effects, such as creaky and breathy voice. These effects are often called **phonation types**. ➤➤breathy voice; creaky voice; larynx; setting; vocal folds.

phone In phonetics, the smallest perceptible discrete segment of sound in a stream of speech. From a phonological point of view, the term has a similar application, referring to the physical realization of a phoneme. ➤➤discrete; phoneme; phonetics.

phoneme The smallest unit in the sound system of a language, according to the traditional phonological theory called **phonemics** or **phonemic phonology**. In this approach, units such as /p/ and /b/ are established on the grounds that substitution of one for the other can cause a change in meaning (as in *pit* vs. *bit*). A complete analysis in these terms displays a language's phonemic system. Phonemic units are transcribed within slashes, to distinguish them from the physical sounds of speech, which appear within square brackets. Thus, the phoneme /l/ in English can appear in speech as a 'clear' [l] (as in *lead*), a 'dark' [ɫ] (as in *fool*), and voiceless (as in *please*). These variant forms of a phoneme are called **allophones**. ➤➤allo-; clear *l*; minimal pair; phonological feature theory; phonology; transcription; *table below*.

phonemic transcription ➤transcription.

phonesthenia or **phonaesthenia** /fɒnəsˈθiːnɪə/ An abnormally weak voice quality. The term is found only in clinical contexts, where the problem (often caused

Consonants				Vowels			
	%		%		%		%
n	7.58	b	1.97	ə	10.74	ʊ	0.86
t	6.42	f	1.79	ɪ	8.33	ɑː	0.79
d	5.14	p	1.78	e	2.97	aʊ	0.61
s	4.81	h	1.46	aɪ	1.83	ɜː	0.52
l	3.66	ŋ	1.15	ʌ	1.75	ɛə	0.34
ð	3.56	g	1.05	eɪ	1.71	ɪə	0.21
r	3.51	ʃ	0.96	iː	1.65	ɔɪ	0.14
m	3.22	j	0.88	əʊ	1.51	ʊə	0.06
k	3.09	ʤ	0.60	a	1.45		
w	2.81	ʧ	0.41	ɒ	1.37		
z	2.46	θ	0.37	ɔː	1.24		
v	2.00	ʒ	0.10	uː	1.13		

The **phonemes** of southern British English, with an indication of their frequency in conversation. From D. Fry, *Archives Néerlandaises de Phonétique Experimentale* 20, 1974.

by inadequate respiratory pressure from the lungs) is an important contributory factor in some types of voice disorder. ➤➤voice disorder/quality.

phonesthetics or **phonaesthetics** /fɒnəsˈθetɪks/ The study of the aesthetic properties of sound, especially of the symbolism attributed to individual sounds, sound clusters, or sound types. Examples include the implication of smallness in the close vowels of such words as *teeny weeny*, and the unpleasant associations of the consonant cluster /sl-/ in such words as *slime*, *slug*, and *slush*. Direct sound/meaning correspondence is also called **phon(a)esthesia** or **syn(a)esthesia**, and the postulated sound units are sometimes analysed as **phon(a)esthemes**. A direct linguistic imitation of a sound in nature is traditionally referred to as **onomatopoeia**. ➤➤sound symbolism.

phonetically consistent forms (PCFs) The first recognizably recurrent, meaningful units of speech produced by a child; also called **protowords**. The forms are phonetically less controlled than the corresponding forms in adult speech. ➤➤acquisition; babbling.

phonetic alphabet ➤transcription.

phonetician ➤phonetics.

phonetics The study of the characteristics of human sound-making, especially of those sounds used in speech; generally divided into **articulatory**, **acoustic**, and **auditory** branches. **Instrumental phonetics** is the study of any of these aspects using physical apparatus. The use of scientific methodology is reflected in the term **experimental phonetics**. **General phonetics** emphasizes the aim of discovering universal principles governing the nature and use of speech sounds. A student or scholar of phonetics is a **phonetician**. ➤➤acoustic phonetics; articulation; auditory phonetics; parametric phonetics; sonority.

phonetic spelling A spelling system which represents speech sounds in a one-to-one way; strictly, the term should be 'phonemic spelling', as it is the phonemes of the language which are being represented, but the popular usage is 'phonetic'. The most ambitious attempt at such a spelling system is the International Phonetic Alphabet. The alphabets of some languages come close to being consistently phonemic (e.g. Spanish, Finnish); English is one of several languages which does not. ➤➤International Phonetic Alphabet; phoneme; spelling.

phonetic transcription ➤transcription.

phoniatrics /fəʊniːˈatrɪks/ The study of pathologies affecting voice quality and pronunciation. The phoniatrist /fəˈnaɪətrɪst/ is especially concerned with the diagnosis and treatment of voice disorders. ➤➤voice disorder/quality.

phonics A method of teaching reading which trains recognition of the sound values of individual letters; also sometimes called the **phonetic method**. Syllables and words are then built up in a linear way. ➤➤look-and-say; reading.

phonic substance Speech regarded as a set of physical properties; also called **phonetic substance**. It can be defined in acoustic or articulatory terms. ➤➤phonetics.

phonogram A symbol in a writing system representing a speech sound. A contrast is intended with the logogram, where symbols represent words. Any writing system which represents individual speech sounds (as in the alphabet and syllabary) is a **phonography**. ➤➤alphabet; logogram; syllabary.

phonological feature theory An analysis of vowels and consonants in terms of a set of additive components within a single phonetic framework. The sounds are classified using a hierarchical arrangement of binary features, such as voiced [+ voice] vs. unvoiced [– voice], or high [+ high] vs. low [– high]. Features can be grouped into four main classes, relating to place of articulation, type of stricture, the oral/nasal process, and laryngeal activity. However, several different approaches have been devised, and terms vary. ➤➤distinctive; phoneme; phonology.

phonology The study of the sound systems of languages, and of the general or universal properties displayed by these systems. In linguistic theory, it is seen either as a level of linguistic organization, contrasted with phonetics, grammar, and semantics, or as a component of a generative grammar, i.e. the **phonological component**, contrasted with the syntactic and semantic components. **Segmental phonology** analyses speech into discrete segments, such as phonemes; **suprasegmental phonology**, also called **nonsegmental** or **plurisegmental phonology**, analyses features which extend over more than one segment, such as intonation contours. The student or scholar of phonology is a **phonologist**. ➤➤intonation; phoneme; phonetics; phonotactics; prosody; syllable.

phonostylistics ➤stylistics.

phonotactics The sequential arrangements of phonological units that are possible in a language. In English, for example, initial /spr-/ is a possible phonotactic sequence, whereas /spm-/ is not. ➤➤distribution; phonology; position 1; postvocalic; syllable.

phrasal verb A type of verb consisting of a sequence of a lexical element plus one or more particles, such as *come in, sit down*. There are many such verbs in English. Subtypes may be distinguished on syntactic or semantic grounds, and 'phrasal' is sometimes used in a narrower sense to refer to one or other of these subtypes. ➤➤verb.

phrase (P) An element of structure typically containing more than one word, but lacking the subject–predicate structure usually found in a clause. Phrases are traditionally classified into functional types related to word class, such as **noun phrases** (e.g. *the big car*) and **verb phrases** (e.g. *has been walking*). The equivalent notion in systemic grammar is **group** – for example, a noun phrase is described as a 'nominal group'. In generative grammar, the term has a broader sense as part of a general characterization of the first stage of sentence analysis – the **phrase-structure** part of a grammar. In this approach, several traditional terms are used differently; in particular, the term 'verb phrase' is used to subsume everything except the subject of a sentence. ➤clause; generative grammar; grammar 2; phrase-marker; phrase-structure grammar; systemic grammar.

phrase-marker (PM) In generative grammar, the structural representation of a sentence in terms of a labelled bracketing, as assigned by the rules of the grammar. For example, the first steps in the analysis of the sentence *the cat chased the dog* can be represented as ((the cat)$_{NP}$ (chased the dog)$_{VP}$)$_S$. Such analyses are usually presented in the form of a tree diagram. ➤generative grammar; tree.

phrase-structure grammar (PSG) A type of grammar containing rules, called **phrase-structure rules** (**PS rules**), capable not only of generating strings of linguistic elements, but also of providing a constituent analysis of the strings. The **phrase-structure component** of a transformational grammar specifies the hierarchical structure of a sentence, the linear sequence of its constituents, and indirectly some types of syntactic relation. Several approaches to syntax have been developed that are equivalent to PSGs, but do not employ PS-rules, such as Generalized Phrase Structure Grammar. ➤constituent; generative grammar; phrase; rewrite rule; syntax.

Phrygian /ˈfrɪʤɪən/ ➤Anatolian.

phylogeny /faɪˈlɒʤəniː/ ➤ontogeny.

phylum /ˈfaɪləm/ The highest level recognized in genetic linguistic classification, representing a group of languages where the genetic relationship has not been fully demonstrated. The term contrasts with **family**, which is used for established levels of classification (though sometimes 'family' is used loosely for both kinds of grouping). For example, the Andean and Equatorial groups of languages spoken in parts of South America are sometimes placed together in a single Andean-Equatorial phylum. ➤family of languages; genetic classification.

physiological phonetics ➤articulation.

pictogram A symbol used in picture writing; also called a **pictograph**. **Pictography** is the study of pictorial systems, or an instance of such a system. The pictograms provide a recognizable representation of entities as they exist in the world (e.g. wavy lines representing sea). They have been discovered in Egypt and Mesopotamia dating from *c*.3000 BC (see illustration at **cuneiform**). Modern pictograms are widespread, such as those used in present-day road signs (e.g. crossroads ahead). ➤hieroglyphic; ideogram; p. 263.

pictograph ➤pictogram.

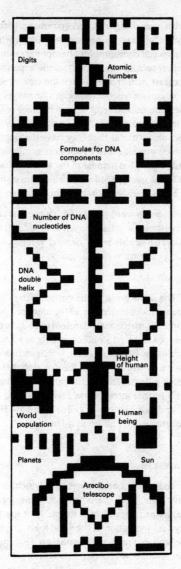

Modern **pictograms**. The pictographic message transmitted into space by the Arecibo radio telescope in Puerto Rico in 1974, aimed at the M13 star cluster. The radio pulses, arranged pictographically, represent data on the chemical basis of life on earth, the human form, and the solar system. © 1975 Scientific American Inc. All rights reserved.

pidgin A language with a markedly reduced grammatical structure, lexicon, and stylistic range. The native language of no one, it emerges when members of two mutually unintelligible speech communities attempt to communicate; often called a **trade language**, when seen in the context of the expansionist era of colonial economies. Pidgins contrast with creoles, which are created when pidgins acquire native speakers. Many pidgins are based on European languages, reflecting the history of colonialism, but there are undoubtedly a large number of unstudied pidgins in the many situations of language contact in Africa, south-east Asia, and South America. Some pidgins have become so useful that they have developed a role as auxiliary languages, and been given official status by the community (e.g. Tok Pisin). These cases are called **expanded pidgins** because of the way they have added extra forms to cope with the needs of the users. ➤➤Bislama; Cameroon; creole; language contact; Liberia; monogenesis; Motu; relexification hypothesis; Sango; Tok Pisin; Zambia.

Pig Latin A type of children's word-play in which the first consonants of a word are put at the end, and a nonsense syllable (such as *ay*) added. An example is *ontday oselay isthay ookbay* 'Don't lose this book'. Several variants exist, in which other letters are placed in odd positions. ➤➤play language.

Pike, Kenneth ➤tagmemics.

Pilipino /pɪlɪ'piːnəʊ/ The name given to the national language of the Philippines, when the country became independent in 1946, now spoken by over 40 million people (*c*.60% of the population). It is a standardized form of **Tagalog**, an indigenous Austronesian language spoken by *c*.15 million people as a first language in central and south-western parts of the island of Luzon, which includes the capital, Manila, and parts of Mindanao. It is written in the Roman alphabet. It is now taught in schools, and has become a lingua franca throughout the Philippines (along with English). In the 1970s a further attempt was made to create a national language, based less on Tagalog, and this came to be called **Filipino**. However, this has not replaced Pilipino. ➤➤Austronesian; Philippines, The.

pinyin ➤Chinese.

Pitcairn Island ➤Norfolk Island.

pitch The attribute of auditory sensation in terms of which a sound may be ordered on a scale from 'low' to 'high'. Pitch corresponds to some degree with the acoustic feature of fundamental frequency, which in the study of speech is based upon the number of complete cycles of vibration of the vocal folds. The linguistic use of pitch in words is called **tone**, and in sentences **intonation**. Pitch forms part of the study of a language's prosodic features. ➤➤contour; intonation; prosody; tone; vocal folds.

pivot ➤open 3.

place of articulation The location of the chief articulatory constriction during the production of a consonant sound. The main places of articulation involve the action of the lips (labial, bilabial); the tip or blade of the tongue and the upper teeth or teeth ridge (dental, alveolar); the blade or front of the tongue and the hard palate (palato-alveolar, palatal); the back of the tongue and the soft palate or uvula (velar, uvular); and the root of the tongue and the back wall of the pharynx (pharyngeal). ➤➤articulation; consonant; phonetics.

Plain English Campaign A campaign which began in the late 1970s to promote the use of clear spoken and written English in all specialized contexts. The campaigners attack the use of unnecessarily complex or obscure language ('gobbledegook') by governments, businesses, and other authorities whose role puts them in linguistic contact with the general public. Annual awards are given to those individuals or organizations which, in the views of the campaigning body, have produced the clearest documents, and booby prizes (the Golden Bull Awards in the UK, the Doublespeak Awards in the USA) to those guilty of excessively complex, misleading, confusing, or evasive language. ➤➤English.

play language A linguistic code, usually devised for jocular purposes, which manipulates some of the rules of normal speech or writing in an unconventional way; also called a **language game**. The notion includes the many forms of children's game (Pig Latin, talking backwards, etc.), secret codes, and speech disguises, and may involve serious as well as playful purposes (as with thieves' rhyming slang). ➤➤ludic language; Pig Latin; rhyming slang; verbal play.

pleonasm /'pliːənazm/ An unnecessary use of words, often taken to be an indication of careless speech or writing. Examples include *in this present day and age* and *in the future which is to come*. Not all instances are as clear-cut as these, however, and often expressions are condemned as pleonastic which in fact actually contain important nuances of meaning or add stylistic emphasis. In the preceding sentence, for example, some readers might consider it pleonastic to use both *in fact* and *actually*, which overlap in meaning; this view the author would vigorously oppose. ➤➤solecism; tautology.

plosive /'pləʊsɪv, 'pləʊzɪv/ A consonant sound made when a complete closure in the vocal tract is suddenly released (e.g. [p], [d]). The outward movement of air upon release is called **plosion**. ➤➤consonant; occlusion.

pluperfect ➤perfect.

plural ➤number.

plurilingualism ➤multilingualism.

plurisegmental ➤phonology.

PM An abbreviation of **phrase-marker**.

pneumotachograph /njuːməʊˈtakəgraf/ An instrument which measures air flow from nose and mouth independently and simultaneously. A face mask is placed over the nose and mouth, and separate meters monitor the air flow. ➤➤aerometry; experimental phonetics.

poetics The study of those aspects of linguistic structure which make a verbal message a work of art, and which thus identify the aesthetic function of language in literary texts. The analysts involved are sometimes called **poeticians**. ➤➤phonesthetics; stylistics.

point size The size of a printed letter. The notion derives from the method of sizing pieces of type in printing, where the 'point' was equal to 1/72 of an inch (*c*.0.35 mm). The system is now also used as a reference measure in desk-top-publishing software. ➤➤typography.

12 13 14 16 18 20 22 24 30 36
42 48 60 72

A selection of **point sizes**.

Poland (population in 1995 estimated at 39,000,000) The official language is Polish, spoken by *c*.98% of the population. Other languages include Belorussian (*c*.230,000), German (*c*.1.5 million), Ukrainian (*c*.1.5 million), and an uncertain number of Romani speakers. English and Russian are used for international purposes. ➤➤Polish.

polarity The system of positive/negative contrastivity found in a language. It may be expressed syntactically (e.g. *It was there* vs. *It was not there*), morphologically (e.g. *wise* vs. *unwise*), or lexically (e.g. *fat* vs. *thin*). ➤➤negation.

Police Motu ➤Motu.

Police Speak ➤Seaspeak.

Polish A member of the West Slavic group of languages, spoken by *c*.44 million people, chiefly in Poland, and also in nearby parts of the republics of the former USSR. It is an important immigrant language in the UK, USA, Australia, and several other countries. Traces of the language can be found in the 12th century, but the modern literary language dates from the 16th century, based on the dialect of the Poznań area. Polish is closely related to Sorbian, Czech, and Slovak. It is written in the Roman alphabet, with the addition of diacritics, notably for the nasalized vowels ą and ę – the latter heard (but not usually printed) in English transcripts of the surname of former President Lech Walesa. ➤➤Poland; Slavic.

politeness phenomena Features of language which serve to mediate norms of social behaviour, in terms of such notions as courtesy, rapport, deference, and distance. Such features include the use of special sentence markers (e.g. *please*), appropriate tones of voice, and acceptable forms of address (e.g. choice of intimate vs. distant pronouns, or of first vs. last names). ➤➤address, forms of; honorific; T/V forms.

polyalphabetic ➤cipher.

polygenesis /ˌpɒliˈdʒenɪsɪs/ ➤monogenesis.

polylectal grammar ➤lect.

polylogue ➤monologue.

Polynesian /ˌpɒləˈniːʒn/ ➤Austronesian.

polysemy /ˈpɒliːsiːmiː, pəˈlɪsəmiː/ The association of one lexical item with a range of different meanings, such as the various senses of *plain* ('clear, ordinary', etc.); also called **polysemia**. A large proportion of a language's vocabulary is **polysemic** or **polysemous**. ➤➤homonymy; lexicon.

polysyllable ➤monosyllable.

polysynthetic language ➤typology of language.

polysystemicism ➤Firthian linguistics.

pooh-pooh theory The name of one of the speculative theories of the origins of language: it argues that speech arose through people making instinctive sounds, caused by pain, anger, or other emotions. The main evidence is the use of interjections, but no language contains many of these. ➤➤origins of language.

popular etymology ➤etymology.

Portugal (population in 1995 estimated at 9,793,000) The official language is Portuguese, spoken by the whole population. There is also an uncertain number of Romani speakers. English and French are used along with Portuguese for international trade and tourism. ➤➤Portuguese.

Portuguese A member of the Romance family of languages, spoken by *c.*175 million people as a first language, chiefly in Brazil (*c.*163 million) and Portugal (*c.*10 million), with others in the former colonies in Africa. It is also an official language in Angola, Mozambique, Guinea-Bissau, São Tomé and Principe, and Cape Verde, and also has special status in Macao (along with Chinese). It is an important immigrant language in many countries, and there are several Portuguese-based creoles in former colonial areas. At least 12 million people use it as a second language. Galician, spoken by *c.*3

million people in parts of north-west Spain (where it is an official regional language) is closely related to Portuguese, and is being given increasing recognition in its own right. There is a dialect continuum with Spanish in the border areas, with several varieties of the two languages being mutually intelligible. The standard language is based on the dialect of Lisbon. It is written in the Roman alphabet. Written materials date from the 12th century, with a literature emerging a century later in the form of troubadour songs. The national epic, *Os Lusíadas* ('The Lusciads') by Luís de Camões, was published in 1572. ➤creole; Romance.

position 1. A functionally contrastive place within a linguistic unit; for example, initial, medial, or final position of a sound within a word, or of a word within a sentence. Some sounds are restricted to certain positions, such as English /h/, which cannot occur at the end of a word. Also, the meaning or syntactic function of a word may be affected by its position: compare *Naturally, he walked* and *He walked naturally*. ➤order; phonotactics. **2**. In phonetics, the location of the vocal organs during the articulation of a sound. In order to articulate the sound [u], for example, the position of the back of the tongue needs to be high, and the position of the lips needs to be rounded. ➤articulation.

positive ➤affirmative; degree; polarity.

positive transfer ➤transfer.

possessive A linguistic form which indicates possession. English examples include both words (**possessive adjectives** such as *my* and *your*, and **possessive pronouns** such as *mine* and *theirs*) and inflections (the **possessive case**, or genitive, as in *John's*). ➤genitive case.

postalveolar ➤alveolar.

post-creole continuum ➤creole.

postdeterminer A type of word which occurs after the determiner and before an adjective in a noun phrase. Several quantifying words hold this position, such as *first, other*, and the numerals (e.g. *the three big chairs, the other leading participants*). ➤determiner.

post-editing ➤machine translation.

postlingual deafness ➤deafness.

postmodification The part of a construction that follows the head of an endocentric phrase. In *The car by the house is John's*, *by the house* postmodifies *car*. Several types of unit may be strung together as part of the postmodification, such as *John's is the car in the street with a bald tyre and a broken headlight*. ➤endocentric construction; modification 1.

postmodifying genitive ➤genitive.

postposition A word that follows a noun phrase (often a single noun or pronoun) to form a structural constituent, often of adverbial function. The notion is analogous to the use of a preposition in front of a noun phrase. Several languages use postpositions (e.g. Panjabi, Japanese). In Japanese, for example, the phrase 'from X to Y' would appear as *X kara Y made*. ➤preposition.

post-structuralism ➤logocentrism; structural.

postvocalic /pəʊstvəʊˈkalɪk/ Descriptive of a sound which follows a vowel; for example, /t/ is postvocalic in the word *cat*. 'Postvocalic *r*' refers to the use of an *r* quality after vowels in certain accents (e.g. in Scotland and most parts of the USA). There is a contrast with **prevocalic**, referring to a sound which precedes a vowel – /k/ in the word *cat*, for example. Some consonants are restricted to one position or the other: in English syllables, /h/ occurs only prevocalically, as in *hot*, and /ŋ/ only postvocalically, as in *sing*. ➤phonotactics; vowel.

potential pause ➤pause.

pragmalinguistics The study of language use from the viewpoint of the language's structural resources. It contrasts with an approach to pragmatic studies (sometimes called **sociopragmatics**) which examines the conditions on language use deriving from the social situation. The former approach might begin with the pronoun system of a language, and examine the way in which people choose different forms to express a range of attitudes and relationships (such as deference and intimacy). The latter approach might begin with the social backgrounds of the participants in an interaction, and examine the way in which different factors (such as age, sex, class) lead people to choose particular pronouns. ➤pragmatics.

pragmatic competence ➤competence.

pragmatics The study of language from the point of view of the users – especially of the choices they make, the constraints they encounter in using language in social interaction, and the effects their use of language has on the other participants in an act of communication. The study of the principles governing the communicative use of language, especially as encountered in conversations, is sometimes called **general pragmatics**. The study of verbal interaction in such domains as counselling, medical interviews, language teaching, and judicial sessions, where problems of communication are of critical importance, is the domain of **applied pragmatics**. ➤conversation analysis; literary pragmatics; pragmalinguistics; presupposition; speech act; *cartoon*, p. 270.

Prague School The name given to the Linguistic Circle of Prague, and the scholars it influenced. The Circle was founded in 1926 by Vilèm Mathesius (1882–1946). Its main emphasis was on the analysis of language as a system of functionally related units (showing the influence of Ferdinand de Saussure), and led to important develop-

(pragmatics)

ments in phonology. Prague School ideas are still practised, especially among Czech linguists. ➤functional; Saussurian.

Prakrit /ˈprɑːkrɪt/ The name given to a group of Indo-Aryan vernacular varieties which developed into literary styles in India in the Middle Ages – the name means 'ordinary, natural'. Used by Hindu, Jain, and Buddhist writers, the Prakrits provided the basis for the modern Indian languages. ➤Indo-Aryan; Pali.

predeterminer An item that occurs before the **determiner** in a noun phrase. In English, *all* in *all the people* is a predeterminer. Other such items include *both* and *half*. ➤determiner.

predicate A major constituent of sentence structure, in which all obligatory constituents other than the subject are considered together. **Primary predication** is the relationship between a predicate and its subject, as illustrated by *the cat* and *chased the ball*. **Secondary predication** is the relationship between an adjunct complement of a noun phrase in a clause which already contains a primary predication (e.g. the relationship between *Mary* and *happy* in *Mary returned home happy*). At a more detailed level, distinctions are often drawn between **predicative** and

nonpredicative functions of words, such as the use of adjectives in predicative (post-verbal) and attributive (pre-noun) positions in English: *the child is happy* vs. *the happy child*. ➤adjective; constituent; sentence; subject.

predicative ➤adjective; predicate.

pre-editing ➤machine translation.

prefabricated language ➤formula.

preface ➤foreword.

prefix ➤affix.

prelims /ˈpriːlɪmz/ ➤end matter.

prelingual deafness ➤deafness.

prelinguistic 1. Descriptive of the hypothetical stages in speech production which precede those involved with the structural organization of language. The term presupposes the existence of various kinds of cognitive function (e.g. processes of attention and memory) which need to be identified as part of a complete explanation of linguistic behaviour. ➤psycholinguistics; speech production. **2**. In language acquisition, descriptive of the period immediately preceding the emergence of linguistic patterning in children's vocalization, usually towards the end of the first year. In a broader usage, this prelinguistic stage can be thought of as stretching back to birth (or even beyond, if studies of fetal response to sound are taken into account). ➤acquisition; babbling.

premodification The part of a construction which precedes the head of an endocentric phrase. For example, *both the new red* premodifies the head *cars* in the phrase *both the new red cars*. ➤endocentric construction; modification 1.

prep. An abbreviation of **preposition**.

preposing Moving a constituent to a position earlier in the sentence (e.g. saying *Today I went to town* instead of the unemphatic *I went to town today*). The term is chiefly used in generative grammar. ➤constituent; generative grammar.

preposition (P, pr., prep.) An item that typically precedes a noun phrase to form a single constituent of structure – a **prepositional phrase** or **prepositional group** – often used as an adverbial. Examples include *in* the garden and *on* my bike. Prepositions may also combine with certain other kinds of construction, such as clauses: *by* leaving the door open... Constructions of the type *in accordance with* are sometimes called **complex prepositions**, because they can be analysed as a sequence of two prepositions surrounding a noun, the whole construction then being used with a following noun phrase: *in accordance with your instructions*. ➤adverbial; noun phrase; postposition; stranded.

prescriptivism The view that one variety of language has an inherently higher value than others, and that this ought to be imposed on the whole of the speech community. It is an authoritarian view, propounded especially in relation to usage in grammar and vocabulary, and often with reference to pronunciation. The favoured variety is usually a version of the standard written language, especially as encountered in literature, or in the formal spoken language which most closely reflects literary style. Those who speak or write in this variety are said to be using language 'correctly'; those who do not are said to be using it 'incorrectly'. An example of a **prescriptive rule** in English is the recommendation to use *whom*, and not *who*, in such sentences as – *did you speak to?*. Some authors distinguish rules of this kind, which recommend usages that are acceptable, from **proscriptive** rules, which identify usages that should be avoided (such as 'Never end a sentence with a preposition'). Linguists avoid both prescriptive and proscriptive attitudes, concentrating instead on the task of description and explanation. ➤➤appropriateness; correctness; description; grammar 1; Latinate; normative; purism; solecism.

present participle ➤participle.

present tense A tense form which typically refers to a time of action contemporaneous with the time of utterance; widely used in descriptions of ongoing events (as in sports commentary) and accounts of mental states (*I know, I remember*). In practice, the form is often used as part of a reference to other durations and aspects of time: in particular, it may be used with adverbials of frequency, to convey a 'habitual' sense (*I go often*); with time-specific adverbials, to convey future or past time (*I'm going tomorrow, Three weeks ago I'm walking down this street . . .*); and in newspaper headlines, to convey a 'recent past' interpretation (*Minister dies*). ➤➤adverbial; tense.

pressure stop ➤stop.

Prestel ➤viewdata.

presupposition What a speaker assumes in saying a particular sentence, as opposed to what is actually asserted. The invitation *Have you time for a drink?*, said by one man to another while leaving work, presupposes, for example, that the speaker knows somewhere which will provide a drink, and that he has the wherewithal to pay for it. ➤➤pragmatics; speech act.

preterite /'pretərɪt/ The simple past tense form of a verb, seen in *I saw* or *I jumped*. The term is chiefly used in traditional grammar. ➤➤tense; traditional grammar.

prevarication A suggested defining property of human language, referring to the way languages can be used to misinform. Lying, irony, the half-truth, and conscious ambiguity are some of the ways in which we can prevaricate. ➤➤language 1; zoösemiotics.

prevocalic /priːvəʊ'kalɪk/ ➤postvocalic.

primary stress ➤stress.

primary vowel ➤cardinal vowels.

primitive In the context of language, a term popularly used to describe languages thought to have a very simple grammar and a vocabulary of only a few dozen or hundred words, and where the speakers have to compensate for the deficiencies by relying on gestures. No such languages have ever been discovered, and it is a tenet of linguistics that no such languages exist. Although a community may be 'primitive' in anthropological terms, it uses a fully developed language, with a complexity quite comparable to those of the so-called 'civilized' nations. ➤➤pidgin.

principal parts The forms of a verb required to determine which conjugation it belongs to. The notion was important in Latin grammars, where the principal parts of *amo*, for example, included the first person form of the present indicative (*amo*), the infinitive (*amare*), the first person form of the perfect indicative (*amavi*), and the supine (*amatum*), which was a type of verbal noun. Verbs like *amo* ('first conjugation verbs') could thus be quickly distinguished from verbs belonging to other conjugations. ➤➤conjugation; verb.

principles and parameters ➤government and binding theory.

proclitic /prəʊˈklɪtɪk/ ➤enclitic.

production The active use of language, whether spoken, written, or signed. The notion usually contrasts with **comprehension** and with **perception**. ➤➤speech production.

productivity The capacity of language users to produce and understand an indefinitely large number of sentences; also referred to as **creativity**, and sometimes suggested as a defining property of human language. In a narrower sense, a pattern is **productive** if it is repeatedly used to produce further instances of the same type, such as the use of *-s* to form plural nouns in English. This contrasts with **nonproductive** or **unproductive** patterns, which lack any such potential, such as the plural formation involved in *mouse/mice*. The term also contrasts with **semi-productive** forms, where there is limited or occasional productivity, such as the use of *un-* to form lexical opposites – *unhappy, unqualified, uninformed*, but not **unsad*. ➤➤language 1; stereotype 1; zoösemiotics.

profanity ➤taboo language.

proficiency test ➤achievement test.

profile In some areas of language study, a chart which describes an aspect of a person's spoken or written language in such a way that distinctive patterns of achievement readily emerge. Profiles permit a more detailed impression of the range of structures used than can be obtained from a test, and enable the analyst to plot emerging strengths and weaknesses in several areas simultaneously. The concept has been used in several domains, such as language pathology, foreign language teaching, and stylistics. Specific profiles have now been devised relating to the main linguistic levels (grammar, semantics, etc.), and are used in research, teaching, and therapy. ➤➤Language Assessment, Remediation and Screening Procedure.

pro-form /ˈprəʊfɔːm/ An item in a sentence which substitutes for another item or construction, such as *it* (*I saw it in the garden*) and *so* (*He did so too*). The central class of examples (which gave rise to the general term) is the **pronoun**, which substitutes for a noun phrase. Analogous terms include **pro-constituent**, **pro-NP**, and simply **pro**. ➤➤pronoun; substitution.

prog. An abbreviation of **progressive**.

prognostic test ➤language aptitude.

progressive (prog.) A grammatical category, typically applied to verbs, showing a contrast of a temporal or durative kind, sometimes handled under **tense** and sometimes under **aspect**. A **progressive** or **continuous** form, which emphasizes the duration or frequency of an action (e.g. *I was kicking*) contrasts with the **nonprogressive** or **simple** form (e.g. *I kicked*), where these emphases are lacking. ➤➤aspect; tense 1; verb.

prolongation The abnormal lengthening of a sound in stuttering. The effect may be unanticipated, as when an initial [m] is held for several seconds while the stutterer tries to release the word *man*; or it may be controlled, as part of a therapeutic technique (known as 'slowed speech') in which the stutterer is taught to articulate sounds in a deliberately slow manner. ➤➤slowed speech; stuttering.

prominence In auditory phonetics, the degree to which a sound or syllable stands out from others in its environment. In the word *interpretation*, the most prominent syllable is *ta*; in the sentence *It was Mary who paid*, the most prominent word would usually be *Mary*. ➤➤accent 2; auditory phonetics.

pronoun An item that can substitute for a noun phrase (or single noun); sometimes referred to as a **pronominal**. Several types of pronouns are distinguished in grammars. They include: **personal pronouns** (e.g. *I, you*), **possessive pronouns** (e.g. *my, mine*), **demonstrative pronouns** (e.g. *this, that*), **interrogative pronouns** (e.g. *who, which*, as in *Who did you see?*), **reciprocal pronouns** (e.g. *each other*), **reflexive pronouns** (e.g. *myself, yourself*), **indefinite pronouns** (e.g. *anyone, nobody*), and **relative pronouns** (e.g. *who, whom*, as in *the girl who left*). Some linguists also recognize a **resumptive** or **shadow pronoun**, such as the use of *him* in *John, I know him*. ➤➤person; T/V forms.

pronunciation The way in which speakers articulate speech sounds. This word is the most general way of describing what we hear when people speak, but it is rather too vague for it to have achieved a technical status in linguistics. In particular, it fails to distinguish between the phonetic and the phonological aspects of speech production, or between segmental and nonsegmental features. ➤orthoepy; phonetics; phonology; segment.

proof A trial printing of a text, made for checking and correction. Two stages of proofing are commonly used in book preparation (but there may be more). A **galley proof** presents the text on long strips of paper, with no division into pages (a **galley** is a flat tray used for holding metal type, in the days when text was typeset by hand). After the galleys are corrected, **page proofs** present the text divided into the pages as they will appear in the book. With textual material which is unlikely to need much realignment, the galley stage is often omitted, as an economy. ➤stet; typography; p. 276.

prop A meaningless element introduced into a structure to ensure its grammaticality (e.g. the *it* in *It's a nice day*). Substitute words (e.g. *one* in *I've found one*) are also sometimes described in this way. ➤grammatical; syntax.

proper noun/name ➤common noun.

proposition The unit of meaning which constitutes the subject matter of a statement, and which is asserted to be true or false. It takes the form of a simple declarative sentence, such as *The car is outside*. ➤declarative.

propositional language ➤referential language.

proscriptive ➤prescriptivism.

prose Written language which typically lacks the grammatical compression, figurative focus, and linear discipline of poetry (specifically, its metrical and verse form). This negative definition is rather more useful than the one which looks towards etymology, where Latin *prosa* can be glossed as 'straightforward discourse'. While much prose is indeed straightforward, in that it lacks the artistic shaping and adornment characteristic of poetry, a great deal of imaginative prose is highly poetic, and hybrid notions (such as 'poetic prose' and 'prose poem') have been recognized in literary criticism. For example, a great deal of the first narrator's part in Dylan Thomas's *Under Milk Wood* could be called poetic prose: *in bonnet and brooch and bombazine black, butterfly choker and bootlace bow, coughing like nanny-goats, sucking mintoes, forty-winking hallelujah . . .* ➤figurative language; metrics.

prose poem ➤found poem.

prosody Variation in pitch, loudness, tempo, and rhythm, as encountered in any use of spoken language; also called **prosodic features**, and studied as part of nonsegmental phonology. The notion subsumes the traditional sense of the term, referring to the metrical features of versification. ➤juncture; lento; loudness; metrics; phonology; pitch; rhythm; tempo.

prothesis /prəˈθiːsɪs/ ➤epenthesis.

	In text	In margin
To substitute	ma~~k~~e	*d*
OR	they ~~bond~~ letters	*give*
To transpose	~~list~~	*list*
OR	to⌐boldly⌐go	⌐ ⌐
To delete	pur~~p~~le	∂
OR	he also cared ~~tod~~	∂
To insert	t⌃t	*g⋏*
OR	they⌃gone	*had* ⋏
To close up	over‿reach	‿
To insert space	self⌃knowledge	Ƴ
To change to italic	<u>self</u> knowledge	⊔⊔
To change italic to upright type	(*self*)knowledge	↳↲
To change to bold	the vector r̰	∿
To change capital to lower case	the Ⓢtate	≢
To change lower case to capital	the s̲tate	≡
To start a new paragraph	ends here ⌐In the next	⌐
OR	the discussion ends here. ⌐In the next lecture Johns	⌐
To run on	ends here⌐ ⌐In the next lecture	⌐ ⌐
OR	the discussion ends here. ⟻In the next lecture	⌐
To insert space between lines	⟩the discussion ends here. ⟋In the next lecture Johns	
To close up space between lines	the cavalry ⟨the paratroops ⟨the gunners	
To substitute or insert note indicator or superior	According to Johns⌃this	⅔
To substitute or insert inferior	the formula H₂O is	⅃₂
To stet (if you make a mistake and want to restore the original)	the ~~saints~~ were important	~~bishops~~ ⊘

To make punctuation changes

Text mark   to substitute   OR   ⋏   to insert

Margin mark	⊙	⊙	;	,	�ʼ ʼ	( )	⊢⊣	⊢⊣	⑦
	full stop	colon	semi-colon	comma	quotation marks	paren-theses	hyphen	dash	oblique stroke

Put / after each correction that does not already end in a caret (omission sign). This is especially important when two or more correction marks are required on one line.

Example **d** / ⊙ / ≡ /

The chief **proof**-correcting conventions.

proto- 1. Descriptive of a linguistic form or state of a language said to be the ancestor of an attested form or language. The term is widely used as part of the language names of prehistory (**proto-languages**), such as Proto-Indo-European or Proto-Germanic. ➤family of languages; reconstruction. **2**. In child language acquisition, descriptive of the emerging linguistic system of the young child. Word-like forms might be described as **proto-words**, and sentence-like forms as **proto-sentences**. ➤acquisition; phonetically consistent forms (PCFs).

Proto-Indo-European ➤Indo-European.

proto-language The common ancestor of the languages of a family, such as Proto-Indo-European. A proto-language implies a **proto-culture** participated in by the speakers of the proto-language. ➤Indo-European; Nostratic.

prototype A typical member of the extension of a referring expression; for example, a sparrow could be a prototype of a bird, whereas an ostrich (because of its atypical

This array of objects for sitting on raises the question of how the **prototype** chair is best defined.

features) would not. **Prototype semantics** holds that word meaning is best analysed in terms of such prototypes, with category membership not absolute: birds display different degrees of 'birdness', which can be analysed along a gradient ranging from most to least prototypical. Several areas of meaning seem to benefit from being analysed in this way; further examples include *chair*, *cup*, and *shrub*. ➤➤extension 1; semantics; stereotype 2.

protowords ➤phonetically consistent forms (PCFs).

Provençal /prɒvən'sal/ ➤Occitan.

proverb A short, pithy, rhythmical saying which expresses a general belief or truth; also referred to as an 'adage', 'maxim', or 'saying'. Many can be divided into two parts which balance each other, often displaying parallel syntax and rhythm, and links of rhyme and alliteration. Examples include *Least said, soonest mended* and Welsh *Cenedl heb iaith, cenedl heb galon* ('A nation without a language is a nation without a heart'). ➤➤aphorism.

proxemics /prɒk'si:mɪks/ The study of variations in posture, interpersonal distance, and tactile contact in human communication. Touching behaviour, for example, has a wide range of functions in a community, expressing such 'meanings' as affection, aggression, sexual attraction, greeting and leave taking, congratulation, and the signalling of attention. Some societies are much more tolerant of touching than others: among the 'contact' societies are the Arabs and Latin Americans; among the 'non-contact' societies are the North Europeans and Indians. The subject forms part of the study of semiotics. ➤➤communication; semiotics.

PS(G) An abbreviation of **phrase structure (grammar)**.

pseudepigraphy /sju:də'pɪgrəfi:/ The false ascription of an author's name to a written work. The notion has been particularly employed in relation to the writings of biblical times, where several of the works traditionally ascribed to Moses or St Paul, for example, are now thought to be by other authors.

pseudonym /'sju:dənɪm/ A fictitious name, especially one used by an author (a **pen name**). The intention is to conceal the writer's true identity, for any of a wide range of personal reasons. Famous examples include the Brontë sisters, who called themselves Currer, Ellis and Acton Bell, and Charles Dodgson, who called himself Lewis Carroll. ➤➤proper name.

psittacism /'sɪtəsɪzm/ Meaningless repetitive ('parrot-like') speech. The term has never had much currency.

psycholinguistics A branch of linguistics which studies the correlation between linguistic behaviour and the mental processes and skills thought to underlie that behaviour; earlier called the **psychology of language**. The study of the acquisition of language by children is often distinguished as **developmental psycholinguist**

ics. When the emphasis is on the use of language as a means of elucidating psychological theories and processes, the term **psychological linguistics** is sometimes used. ➤➤acquisition; cocktail party effect; speech perception/production.

Puerto Rico (population in 1995 estimated at 3,683,000) The official languages are Spanish (spoken by *c*.75% of the population) and English. There are a few speakers of French, German, Italian, and local creoles. ➤➤English; Spanish.

pulmonic /pʊl'mɒnɪk/ Descriptive of any activity associated with the lungs, especially in the context of speech sound production. Speech typically uses a pulmonic airstream, a flow of air from the lungs under relatively constant pressure. The normal direction of the air flow is outwards, though inwards-flowing pulmonic air is also sometimes used. ➤➤airstream; egressive.

pun A witticism which relies for its effect on playing with the different meanings of a word, or bringing together two words with the same or similar form but different meanings. Notwithstanding the contempt poured on the poor pun ('the lowest and most grovelling form of wit', according to the English poet, John Dryden), they have a respectable and long-standing literary history (illustrated by the many puns to be found in Shakespeare). Most puns are auditory, a feature of informal conversation or special speech settings, such as drama or advertising (e.g. the adhesive slogan, *Our word is your bond*). Some are visual, illustrated by a Spanish author's description of some girls he knew as *senoreaters*. Punning is technically called **paronomasia**. ➤➤verbal play.

punctual ➤durative.

punctuation A set of graphic signs used in written language to signal certain important grammatical and attitudinal contrasts. Its three main functions are: to separate units in a linear sequence (e.g. a space separates words, a period separates sentences); to indicate when one unit is included within another (e.g. a parenthesis, quotation marks, or a pair of commas); and to mark a specific grammatical or attitudinal function, such as a question (question-mark), exclamation (exclamation mark), or the notion of possession (the apostrophe). A further aspect of punctuation is to express something of the prosody of spoken language, though the correlation here is a complex one, and prone to idiosyncrasy, especially in the use of capitalization, the comma, and the dash. Non-English punctuation marks include the use of the inverted question-mark and exclamation-mark in Spanish direct speech. ➤➤apostrophe; brackets; colon; comma; dash; hyphen; paragraph; period; quotation marks; semi-colon; solidus; typography; writing; *cartoon*, p. 280.

Punic /'pjuːnɪk/ ➤Phoenician.

Punjabi ➤Panjabi.

pure vowel ➤monophthong.

'No – stupid boy! Exclamation mark! Doesn't that pratt Bairnswater teach you anything?' (**punctuation**)

purism A school of thought which sees a language as needing preservation from the external processes that might infiltrate it and thus make it change. Purist attitudes are a normal accompaniment to the perception, which each generation represents, that standards of language (as social standards generally) are deteriorating. Purists are conservative in matters of usage, emphasize the importance of prescriptive rules in grammar and pronunciation, and insist on the authority of dictionaries, grammars, and other manuals. ➤academy; language change; linking; prescriptivism.

putonghua /puːtɒŋˈwa/ ➤Chinese.

Q

Q An abbreviation of **question** or **quantifier**.

Qatar (population in 1995 estimated at 597,000) The official language is Arabic, spoken by *c.*56% of the population. The remainder speak Farsi (*c.*23%), Urdu, or other languages from the South Asian subcontinent or the Philippines. English is used for international purposes. ➤Arabic.

qualification A type of structural dependence of one grammatical unit upon another. A **qualifier** is a word or phrase which limits the meaning of another element. The notion is traditionally used for the dependent items (such as adjectives) in a noun phrase: these are said to **qualify** the noun. In systemic grammar, the term is used more narrowly for structures following the head of the noun phrase; this contrasts with **modification**, for structures preceding the head. ➤dependent; modification 1; systemic grammar.

quality 1. In auditory phonetics, the characteristic resonance or timbre of a sound, resulting from the range of frequencies which make up the sound's identity. Single types of sound can be considered in this way (e.g. vowel quality) as can more general notions (e.g. voice quality). A specific contrast is often drawn between quality and **quantity**, or length. ➤length; timbre; voice quality. **2**. ➤maxims of conversation.

quantifier An item which expresses a notion of quantity (e.g. *all, some, both*). In logic, a distinction is drawn between **universal quantification** ('For all X, it is the case that . . .') and **existential quantification** ('For some X, it is the case that . . .'), and this is often used in semantic theory. ➤partitive; semantics.

quantitative linguistics A branch of linguistics which studies the frequency and distribution of linguistic units using statistical techniques. It aims to establish general principles concerning the statistical regularities governing the structure of language, as well as to elucidate linguistic problems (such as authorship identity). ➤linguistics; statistical linguistics.

quantity ➤length; maxims of conversation.

Quechua /ˈketʃwə/ A member of the Quechumaran family of Andean-Equatorial languages, spoken by *c.*8 million people, chiefly in Peru (*c.*3.5 million), Ecuador (*c.*1.5 million), and Bolivia (*c.*2.9 million), and as a lingua franca widely throughout the central Andean region. Quechua was the language of the Inca civilization in the 15th–16th centuries. It is written in the Roman alphabet. Several related languages are placed together in a Quechuan group; all are now losing numbers because of the dominance of Spanish. ➤Amerindian; Andean-Equatorial.

Quechumaran /ˌketʃʊˈmɑːrən/ ➤Andean-Equatorial.

question (Q) A major type of sentence, typically used to elicit information or a response, and defined variously on grammatical, phonological, semantic, or socio-linguistic grounds; contrasts with **statement**, **command**, and **exclamation**. Questions may be marked by a **question word**, such as **_wh_-questions** in English (_what, where_, etc.); these are also called **special questions**. Other types include **_yes-no_** or **general questions** (e.g. _Did she phone?_), **disjunctive questions** (e.g. _Did she phone or did she write?_), and **tag questions** (e.g. _She phoned, didn't she?_). A **rhetorical question** is a question to which no answer is expected (_Whoever heard of such a thing?_). ➤direct speech; echo; interrogative; statement; tag 1.

Quirkian Adjective derived from (Charles) Randolph Quirk, Lord Quirk (1920–), British grammarian and writer on the English language, a major influence on the development of English language studies in the UK since the 1960s. He was professor of English at University College London (1960–81), where he founded and directed the Survey of English Usage. Major grammars in which he has been involved include several co-authored works, notably _A Comprehensive Grammar of the English Language_ (1985) – and it is this series of works which has given rise to the use of the adjective 'Quirkian'. ➤Nuclear English; Survey of English Usage.

quotation marks A punctuation mark which typically signals a piece of direct speech; also called **inverted commas** or, informally, **quotes**. Opening and closing quotation marks are usually distinguished in print, but not in typescript, and often not in handwriting or on the computer screen. Single quotation marks (' ') are generally used in American publishing, and are normal in typescript and handwritten material. Double quotation marks ("") are traditional in British publishing, but there is now a notable tendency towards simplification, and single marks are increasingly the norm. There are also variations between the two dialects about whether other punctuation marks should occur inside or outside the quotation marks. _I told him it was called 'The Fly'._ is typically British usage; _I told him it was called 'The Fly.'_ is typically American. When a quotation is used within a quotation, both varieties agree that it is essential to switch from one convention to the other: _"Who said 'charming' like that", John asked._ ➤direct speech; punctuation.

R

Rajasthani /raʤə'stɑːniː/ Several varieties (considered by some to be separate languages) belonging to the Midland group of Indo-Aryan languages, spoken by *c*.30 million people, chiefly in the state of Rajasthan in India, but also in adjoining states and in Pakistan. The chief variety/language is Marwari, spoken by *c*.12 million. Hindi is the official language in the state. ➤Indo-Aryan.

rank ➤level 3.

rapid reading A technique which teaches people to read more quickly, while retaining understanding; also called **speed reading**. Readers are trained to use more effective eye movements, so that they do not make so many backward glances (regressions) along a line, and to assimilate text in larger chunks, avoiding a 'word by word' approach. Average reading speed for everyday material is between 250 and 500 words per minute (w.p.m.). For careful reading (such as while studying), speed may be as low as 200 w.p.m. or less. While skimming a text, speeds of over 800 w.p.m. can be achieved, though comprehension there is inevitably much reduced. ➤reading.

rate of speech The speed at which people speak, usually measured in number of syllables per minute. A distinction can be drawn with **rate of articulation**, which is the number of syllables per minute less any time devoted to pausing. ➤tempo.

readability The ease with which the written language can be read with understanding. Several approaches have tried to devise measures of readability (**readability formulae**), generally computing the average length of the words and sentences in a passage, and sometimes attempting to deal with lexical novelty (the number of new words found in successive samples from the passage) and grammatical complexity. The formulae are often criticized as primitive and misleading, in that none of them is able to take semantic complexity adequately into account. ➤reading.

reading The recognition and comprehension of written text. The process can take place silently (**silent reading**) or by reading aloud (**oral reading**), and the comprehension of the passage can be evaluated in different ways (e.g. by asking readers questions about it, or asking them to paraphrase or draw inferences from it). Two main theories have been developed to explain what takes place in learning to read. One theory (of 'phonic mediation') argues that a phonological step is an essential feature of the process; on this account, letters are sounded out in a linear way, with larger units gradually being built up ('reading by ear'). The alternative argues that there is a direct relationship between the graphology and the semantics, a phonological bridge being unnecessary; on this account, words are read as wholes, without being broken down into a linear sequence of symbols ('reading by eye'). Several integrated accounts have also been proposed. ➤➤dyslexia; language experience approach; linguistic method; literacy; look-and-say; miscue analysis; phonics; rapid reading; readability.

realization The physical expression of an abstract linguistic unit. Phonemes, for example, are realized in phonic substance as phones. ➤➤phoneme.

rebus /'ri:bəs/ Words and sentences made out of a combination of letters, pictures, or logograms. An everyday example is *IOU* 'I owe you'. More complex items include *XQQ* 'excuse' and *H&* 'hand'. Children's comics and game books often contain rebuses with a strong pictorial element. The notion has also been used in devising systems of simplified communication for people suffering from language disability. ➤➤word game; *illustration below*.

Received Pronunciation (RP) The regionally neutral, educationally prestigious accent in British English. When this accent displays features of regional influence, it is known as **modified RP**. ➤➤accent 1; Estuary English; standard.

receptive aphasia ➤aphasia.

recipient In some grammatical analyses of sentences, the animate being which is passively implicated by the happening or state expressed by the verb; also called

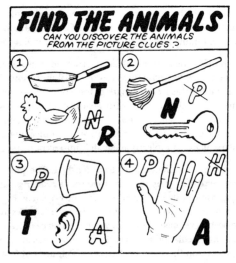

A typical **rebus** game from a children's annual.

patient, **dative**, or **affected**. This is typically the role of the indirect object (e.g. *you* in *I gave you the book*), but other elements may act as recipient. The term is sometimes used in a more general sense to include the role of the direct object. ➤object; participant roles.

reciprocal Descriptive of a grammatical feature expressing the meaning of mutual relationship. The notion is chiefly encountered in **reciprocal pronouns** (e.g. *each other*) and **reciprocal verbs** (e.g. *meet*). ➤pronoun.

reconstruction A method in historical studies of language whereby a hypothetical system of sounds or forms, representing an earlier, non-extant state of a language, is established from an analysis of the attested sounds and forms of extant texts. This is called **internal reconstruction**, if evidence from only one language is used, and **comparative reconstruction**, if evidence from a number of related languages is used. The comparison of forms taken from cognate languages to determine the details of their historical relationships is called the **comparative method**. ➤cognate; philology.

recursive /rɪˈkɜːsɪv/ Descriptive of rules which are capable of repeated application in generating a sentence; also sometimes called **iterative**. For example, a rule for inserting adjectives before a noun applies recursively in English: adjectives can in theory be added indefinitely to 'the small, interesting, expensive . . . book'. The term is further applied to the structures generated in this way, and to the languages characterized by these rules. ➤rule 1.

reduction **1**. In phonology, a process in which a unit loses some of its full phonetic identity. The term is chiefly used with reference to stressed vowels which become unstressed; for example, the stressed vowels in *telegraph* are reduced in the word *telegraphy*. It is also used for the simplification of consonant sequences found in early child speech (e.g. /kl-/ becoming /g-/ would be an instance of **consonant cluster reduction**). ➤phonology; stress. **2**. ➤ellipsis. **3**. ➤contraction.

redundant Descriptive of a feature whose presence is unnecessary in order to identify a linguistic unit or make a linguistic contrast. In English, *The bell rings* displays redundancy, in that *both* subject and verb are marked for singular – the noun lacks a plural ending, and the verb adds a singular ending. ➤contrast.

reduplication Various types of repetition in the structure of a word. In historical linguistics, the term refers to the way a prefix/suffix reflects certain phonological characteristics of a root. In Greek, for example, /luːoː/ is the present tense form, 'I loose'; /leluka/, with a repeated /l/, is the perfect tense form, 'I have loosed'. In English, compound words such as *helter-skelter* are called **reduplicative compounds**. In language acquisition, the term describes the early pronunciation of polysyllabic words when children pronounce the different syllables in the same way (e.g. *water* as /ˈwawa/). ➤prefix; root 1.

reference 1. The relationship between a linguistic expression and the entity in the external world to which it refers; also called the **referential meaning** of the expression. For example, the referent of the word *table* is the object 'table'. Reference is an extra-linguistic notion, therefore, in which aspects of the real world play a part, and contrasts with the intralinguistic notion of **sense**, a property arising from the meaning relations between lexical items and sentences. ➤➤connotation; sense. **2**. In grammatical analysis, a relationship of identity which exists between grammatical units, as when a pronoun refers to a noun phrase. When the reference is to an earlier part of the discourse, it may be called **back-reference**; reference to a later part of the discourse is **forward-reference**. ➤➤anaphora; extension 1; referential language.

reference grammar ➤grammar 1.

referential language Language whose primary function is to communicate ideas, facts, opinions, and other notions of an intellectual kind; also called **propositional** or **ideational language**. It is the kind of language employed whenever people wish to learn from each other. The term was devised to draw a contrast with those functions of language where the communication of information is *not* the main consideration, such as the language of play, social interaction, or social identity, which are relatively neglected areas of linguistic study. ➤➤connotation; emotive language; ideation; ludic language; phatic communion; reference.

referential meaning ➤reference.

reflexive Descriptive of a construction where the subject and the object refer to the same entity, as in *She washed herself*. Such forms as *herself* and *themselves* are known as **reflexive pronouns**. ➤➤pronoun.

regional dialect ➤dialect.

register 1. In phonetics, the voice quality produced by a particular physiological constitution of the larynx (e.g. soprano, tenor, falsetto). The term is also used for the types of phonation that a speaker can use in a controlled manner, such as creaky voice. ➤➤creaky voice; phonation; voice quality. **2**. In stylistics and sociolinguistics, a variety of language defined according to its use in social situations. Examples include the 'scientific register' and the 'formal register'. ➤➤genre; stylistics; variety.

regular ➤irregular.

relational grammar A model of grammar which takes as central the notion of grammatical relations (e.g. subject and object), rather than the categorial terms of standard phrase-markers (e.g. NP, VP). A **relational network** is a formal representation of a sentence, showing the grammatical relations that elements of the sentence bear to each other, and the syntactic level(s) at which these relations hold. ➤➤grammar 1; phrase-marker.

relative Descriptive of various items and constructions which occur as part of the postmodification in a noun phrase. **Relative pronouns** (e.g. *who, which, that*) are used to introduce a postmodifying clause, the **relative clause**. *When* and *where* are sometimes called **relative adverbs** when linking a relative clause to its noun. Types of relative clause include **adnominal** (*The case that I cited is convincing*), **nominal** (*What interests me is his answer*), **sentential** (*The house is for sale, which is absurd*), and **zero** or **contact** (*The book I read is on the table*). **Restrictive** or **defining** relative clauses (where the identity of the head is dependent upon the presence of the clause) are contrasted with **nonrestrictive** or **nondefining** (where the identity of the head is independent of the clause); compare the restrictive character of *The Bible which I own. . .* and the nonrestrictive character of *The Bible, which I often read. . .* In transformational grammar, the process of forming a relative clause is called **relativization**. ➤➤clause; postmodification; pronoun; restrictiveness; *wh*-form.

relative universal ➤universal.

relativity, linguistic ➤Sapir–Whorf hypothesis.

release The type of movement made by the vocal organs away from a point of articulation. The notion is particularly used as part of the description of plosive sounds (e.g. [p]). ➤➤plosive.

relevance ➤maxims of conversation.

relexification hypothesis The hypothesis that pidgin languages are derived from the first widely-used pidgin, which was based on Portuguese. The grammar of this language was retained, but new lexical items were introduced from the other European languages. ➤➤pidgin.

remedial language teaching Instruction designed to increase the achievement of a language learner so that it matches expected norms. The notion is chiefly used in educational and clinical settings, with reference to the needs of language-disadvantaged or language-delayed children, but it may also be found in relation to adult language disorders and foreign language teaching. ➤➤language pathology/teaching.

repair In conversation analysis, the attempt made by participants to make good a real or imagined deficiency in the interaction, such as a mishearing or misunderstanding. A **self-initiated repair** is made by a speaker without prompting from the listener; this is contrasted with an **other-initiated repair**, which is prompted by the listener. Repairs may also be classified as **self-repairs** (made by the speakers themselves) and **other-repairs** (made by listeners). ➤➤conversation analysis.

repertoire The range of languages or language varieties available for someone's use, each of which enables the person to perform a particular social role; sometimes called a **repertory**. The term is also used collectively for the range of linguistic varieties within a speech community. ➤➤variety.

reported speech ➤direct speech.

resonance Vibrations of air movement in the vocal tract which are set in motion by a source of phonation. The main **resonance chambers** are the mouth, nose, and pharynx. ➤➤phonation; vocal tract.

resonant ➤obstruent.

REST An abbreviation of **Revised Extended Standard Theory**.

restricted code ➤elaborated code.

restricted language A highly reduced linguistic system used for a special communicative purpose. Examples include the language of air-traffic control, ship-to-shore communication at sea, heraldry, radio weather reports, and knitting patterns. ➤➤variety.

restrictiveness The semantic relationship of a modifying structure to its accompanying head word. In **restrictive** or **defining modification**, the linguistic identity of the head is dependent upon the accompanying modification; if the modification is inessential to the head's identity, the term **nonrestrictive** or **nondefining** is used. For example, in *I've got a black car*, emphasis on *black* implies that the blackness is crucial to the identity of the car (thus restrictive) – the contrast is with cars of other colours; with no emphasis on *black*, a nonrestrictive interpretation is more likely – I have just the one car, which happens to be black. ➤➤modification 1; relative.

result A clause or clause element whose meaning expresses the notion of consequence or outcome; also called **resultative**, **resulting**, or **resultant**. In English, clauses introduced by *so that* are typically resultative. ➤➤clause.

resumptive pronoun ➤pronoun.

retracted Descriptive of the backward movement of an articulator. It is especially used of the back of the tongue moving towards the velum, as heard in velarization. ➤➤velum.

retroflex Descriptive of a consonant sound made by the tongue tip against the back of the alveolar ridge. **Retroflexed** forms of *t, d,* and *r* are common, and are heard in several languages of India. Retroflex *r* is common in American English. Vowels preceding a retroflexed consonant are said to be *r*-**coloured** or **rhotacized**. ➤➤alveolar; rhotic.

Réunion (population in 1995 estimated at 654,000) The official language is French. A French-based creole is spoken by over 90% of the population. ➤➤creole; French.

reverse indention ➤indention.

Revised Extended Standard Theory (REST) ➤Standard Theory.

rewrite rule In generative grammar, a type of rule which takes the form X → Y; also called a **rewriting rule**. The symbol to the left of the arrow represents a single structural element; the symbol to the right represents a string of one or more elements; and the arrow is an instruction to replace X by Y. So, if the string were VP → V + NP, the rule would replace any verb phrase in the sentence with a sequence of verb and noun phrase. ►►generative grammar; phrase-structure grammar; rule 1.

Rhaetian /'riːʃn/ A member of the Romance family of languages, spoken by c.40,000 people chiefly in Italy, with some in Switzerland; also called **Rhaeto-Romance**, and sometimes **Ladin** or **Ladino**. A western variety is spoken in Switzerland by c.65,000 people, chiefly in the Grisons canton (Graubünden), where it is known as **Romansch** or **Grishun**; this language has national status in Switzerland, and is in official use in the Grisons. It has a literary tradition dating from the 12th century. **Dolomitic** is a central variety spoken in the regions of Trentino–Alto Adige and Veneto, Italy. **Friulian** is an eastern variety, spoken north of Venice in an area extending east as far as Slovenia. The central and eastern varieties display the influence of Italian, whereas Romansch is closer to French. Written Rhaetian varieties all use the Roman alphabet. ►►Romance.

Rhaeto-Romance /'riːtəʊ-/ ►►Rhaetian.

rhetoric The study of effective or persuasive speaking and writing, especially as practised in public oratory. Several hundred **rhetorical figures** were used by classical rhetoricians, classifying the way words could be arranged in order to achieve special stylistic effects. Notions which have continued in use in modern analysis include metaphor, simile, personification, and paradox. ►►figurative language; stylistics.

rhetorical question ►question.

rhinophonia /raɪnəʊ'fəʊnɪə/ Abnormal nasal resonance in speech. The term is restricted to clinical contexts. ►►nasal; voice disorder.

rhopalic /rəʊ'palɪk/ A type of verbal play in which word length increases by a fixed amount (e.g. an extra syllable or letter) as the text proceeds. The effect can be attempted either within poetic lines (rhopalic verse), or in prose. *This sentence illustrates convincingly*. The term comes from Greek *rhopale* 'club' – a device which is thin at one end and gradually gets thicker. ►►verbal play.

rhotacism /'rəʊtəsɪzm/ A phonetically abnormal use of /r/. Particularly noticeable is the 'weak *r*', where the normal articulation is replaced by a semi-vowel of a [w] quality or a uvular sound. The term is chiefly used in clinical contexts. ►►speech defect.

rhotic /'rəʊtɪk/ Descriptive of a dialect or accent where /r/ is pronounced following a vowel, in such words as *car* and *cart*. A geographical area in which this sound is used (such as much of south-west England) is called a **rhotic area**. Varieties which do not have this feature are **non-rhotic**. (➤*illustration at isogloss*.) ➤➤retroflex.

rhyme A correspondence of syllables, especially at the ends of lines in verse; for example, *Hilary* rhymes with *distillery*. **Internal rhyme** is the rhyming of words within a single line of verse. ➤➤pararhyme.

rhyming slang A form of expression, used by Cockney speakers, which hides the identity of a word in a rhyming phrase that has little or no meaningful relationship to it. The expression typically consists of two or three words, the last of which rhymes with the target. Examples include *Cain and Abel* for 'table' and *Hampstead Heath* for 'teeth'. Often the expression is abbreviated, keeping the first word only, so that the rhyme is not apparent, as in *china* from *china plate*, 'mate'. Sometimes, a comic allusion is present, as in *Gawd forbids* for 'kids'. The origins of the genre are obscure. It emerges clearly in the early 19th century, and may have arisen from an earlier criminal argot. ➤➤argot; Cockney; slang.

rhythm The perceived regularity of prominent units in speech. It is stated in terms of such patterns as stressed vs. unstressed syllables (as in English), or long vs. short syllables (as in Latin). Languages vary greatly in their basic rhythmic types. ➤➤foot; isochrony; metrics; prosody.

riddle A traditional utterance intended to mystify or mislead. Objects, animals, people, and events are deliberately described in such a way that their description suggests something quite different. The task of the recipient of the riddle is to resolve the ambiguity and arrive at an appropriate interpretation. In Europe, riddles are common in children's games, generally with humorous intent. They often take the form of a **conundrum** – a riddle whose answer involves a pun (*When is a door not a door? When it's ajar*). In many cultures, however, they are used seriously by adults, often to express a philosophical or spiritual issue or to test a person's wisdom or worthiness. ➤➤enigma; pun; verbal play.

rights ➤Universal Declaration of Linguistic Rights.

Riksmål /ˈrɪksmɔːl/ ➤Norwegian.

rising tone ➤falling tone.

Roget, Peter Mark ➤thesaurus.

roll ➤trill.

Romaji /ˈrɒmajiː/ A script used for writing Japanese in the Roman alphabet, with the addition of Arabic numerals. It is often seen in Japan in such contexts as street signs, train station names, and international company names. Two transliteration systems have been used: one devised by a 19th-century US missionary, James Hepburn (*Hebon-shiki*) and the other introduced by the Japanese government in 1954 (*kunreishiki*), which has replaced the Hepburn system in all but a few international contexts (such as in passports). ➤➤Japanese; Roman alphabet; transliteration.

Roman alphabet An alphabetical system derived from that used in ancient Rome for Latin, and the source of most Western alphabets; also called the **Latin alphabet**. The use of this alphabet to transcribe the signs of non-Latin writing systems is called **romanization**. Chinese is a particularly well-known example of the application of this process. ➤➤alphabet; Chinese; pinyin; Romaji; transliteration.

Romance A group of Indo-European languages descended from the spoken (or 'vulgar') form of Latin used throughout the Roman Empire, and forming the main part of the Italic language family. The chief languages are French, Spanish, Portuguese, Italian, and Romanian. Also within the family are Sardinian, Occitan, Rhaetian, and Catalan. Dalmatian became extinct at the end of the 19th century. Over 650 million people now speak a Romance language, or one of the creoles based on French, Spanish, or Portuguese. ➤➤Catalan; French; Indo-European; Italian; Ladino; Latin; Occitan; Portuguese; Rhaetian; Romanian; Sardinian; Spanish.

Romani, earlier **Romany** A member of the Indo-Aryan group of languages, spoken by an uncertain number of Gypsies (perhaps 5–8 million) in a wide range of dialects worldwide; also called **Gypsy**. Gypsy populations are largest in Europe, especially in Slavic countries (notably Slovenia, Croatia, Bosnia-Herzegovina, Macedonia, Yugoslavia, Romania, Hungary, Bulgaria, and the Czech and Slovak republics), but there are also many in other parts of Europe, the Middle East, the USA, and South America. Regional forms display considerable influence (especially in vocabulary) of the languages with which they are in contact. When written, Romani uses the alphabet of the locality, generally Roman or Cyrillic, but it is essentially a spoken language, with a rich oral literature. It is also widely used as an argot, when Gypsy groups come into contact (and conflict) with local communities. ➤➤argot; Indo-Aryan; language contact.

Romania (population in 1995 estimated at 23,033,000) The official language is Romanian, spoken by *c.*90% of the population. There are *c.*10 other languages, including German (*c.*150,000), Hungarian (*c.*3 million, strongly present in Transylvania), Bulgarian, Gagauz, and Turkish. There may be as many as half a million speakers of Romani. French and English are used for international trade and tourism. ➤➤Romanian.

Romanian or **Rumanian** A member of the Romance family of languages, spoken by *c.*26 million people, chiefly in Romania (over 20 million), with some in nearby parts of Yugoslavia (in Voivodina, where it has official status), Greece, Albania, Bulgaria, and Moldova, with many immigrants in Israel, the USA, Canada, and Australia. It is written in the Roman alphabet, and materials date from the 16th century. Its geographical separation from the other Romance languages has made Romanian very different, with many Slavic loan words and idiosyncratic grammatical features (notably, the suffixation of the definite article to the noun). ➤➤affix; Moldavian; Romance; Romania.

Romansch or **Romansh** /rəʊ'manʃ/ ►Rhaetian.

Romany ►Romani.

root 1. The base form of a word, which cannot be further analysed without loss of the word's identity; alternatively, that part of the word left when all affixes are removed. Roots may be free morphemes (e.g. *go*, *hat*) or bound morphemes (e.g. *-ceive* in *receive*, *conceive*, etc.). A **root-inflected** language is one where the inflections affect the internal phonological structure of the root (e.g. Arabic); this contrasts with a **root-isolating** language, where the root morphemes are invariable (e.g. Chinese). ►►affix; morpheme; stem; typology of language; word. **2**. In phonetics, the furthest back part of the tongue, opposite the pharyngeal wall. ►►tongue. **3**. In generative grammar, the topmost node in a tree diagram. ►►tree. **4**. In historical linguistics, the earliest form of a word. ►►etymology.

root language ►typology of language.

Rosetta Stone /rə'zetə/ The name given to a black basalt stone discovered at Rashid (Rosetta) in Egypt by members of Napoleon's Egyptian expedition in 1799; it is now in the British Museum. The stone, measuring 114 × 72 cm, was carved with three scripts: hieroglyphic, a demotic script, and Greek. Because the Greek version could be translated, the Stone provided the key to the other scripts, which had previously been undeciphered. The full text was published in 1822 by the French Egyptologist Jean-François Champollion (1790–1832). It proved to be part of a commemoration of the accession of Ptolemy V Epiphanes (2nd century BC). ►►demotic; hieroglyphic.

round brackets ►brackets.

rounding The use of lip protrusion for the articulation of vowels and sometimes of consonants. **Rounded** vowels include [u] and [o]; they are opposed to **unrounded** or **spread** vowels, such as [i] and [e]. ►►labial; vowel.

routine ►formula.

RP An abbreviation of **Received Pronunciation**.

Ruanda ►Rwanda.

rule 1. A formal statement of relationship between linguistic elements or structures. In contrast with the traditional use of the term (where it refers to a recommendation for correct usage), no prescriptive or proscriptive implication is present. A **generative rule** is predictive, expressing a hypothesis about the relationships between sentences which hold for a language as a whole, and reflect the speaker's competence. Rules may be classified in terms of the components of the grammar in which they appear, such as 'phonological rules' or 'syntactic rules'. ►►competence; irregular; phrase-structure grammar; prescriptivism; rewrite rule. **2**. In typography, a continuous line, such as would be used to mark the top and foot of a table, or the upper and lower parts of a fraction. ►►typography.

Rumanian ➤Romanian.

Rundi /'rʊndiː/ ➤Rwanda 2.

rune A letter from a type of alphabet used in north-west Europe from around the 3rd century AD. The earliest runic alphabet, used in Scandinavia and southern Germanic areas, consisted of 24 letters, and is usually known as the **older futhark**, a name made up out of the sounds of its first six letters. (The contrast is with the **younger futhark** of 16 letters, used in Scandinavia in the 8th century.) It may have derived from the Roman alphabet. The version used in Britain, usually called the **futhorc**, devised extra symbols to cope with the range of Anglo-Saxon sounds. Runes continued to be used on charms and monuments until the 17th century, and their traditional association with religion and magic continues to provide resonances today. ➤alphabet; writing.

The English **futhorc**.

running head ➤headline.

running text In typography, a piece of continuous text. A contrast is intended with any textual material which is displayed in a special setting, such as equations, footnotes, and tables. ➤typography.

Russia (population in 1995 estimated at 149,900,000) The official language is Russian, spoken by over 80% of the population. There are over 80 other languages, a number with local official status, such as Avar, Bashkir, Buryat, Chechen, Chuvash, Kabardian, Kalmyk, Komi, Mari, Mordvin, Ossetic, Tatar, Tuvin, Udmurt, and Yakut. Several western European languages are in use, such as German, Polish, and Yiddish, and there are many speakers of Romani. ➤Russian.

Russian A member of the East Slavic group of languages, spoken by *c*.290 million people as a first (*c*.170 million) or as a second (*c*.120 million) language, chiefly in Russia (*c*.125 million), with the others mainly in the republics of the former USSR and in nearby countries (such as Afghanistan and China). The language is also widely used as a lingua franca in those parts of eastern Europe which formerly fell under Soviet influence, and has been taken by immigrants to the USA, Canada, and elsewhere. It is written in the Cyrillic alphabet. There are many dialects, broadly grouped into northern, central, and southern divisions, with the modern standard language based on the (central) Moscow dialect. Russian can be traced back to the 11th century. It displays considerable influence of western European languages, especially in vocabulary. Among its interesting linguistic features are its use of palatalized consonants, and its distinction between perfective and imperfective verb aspects. The works of the poet Alexandr Pushkin (1799–1837) are recognized as having had a particular influence on the development of the modern language. ➤aspect; Cyrillic; lingua franca; palate; perfect; Slavic.

Rwanda /ruːˈandə/ **1**. (name of country) (population in 1995 estimated at 8,430,000, but figures are uncertain in the aftermath of the civil war) The official languages are Rwanda (Kinyarwanda, spoken by *c*.98% of the population), English, and French. French is used for international purposes. ➤French. **2**. (name of language) A Bantu language spoken by over 15 million speakers, mainly in Rwanda (*c*.8 million), Burundi (*c*.5 million), and the Democratic Republic of Congo, with smaller numbers in Uganda and Tanzania; also known as **Rwanda-Rundi**, and sometimes spelled **Ruanda**. In Burundi, where it also has official status, the language is called **Rundi**. It is written in the Roman alphabet. Rwanda-Rundi is the Bantu language with the largest number of speakers as a mother tongue. ➤Bantu.

S

S An abbreviation of **sentence** or **subject**.

Saami ➤Same.

Saharan A small group of Nilo-Saharan languages spoken in Chad and adjoining areas of Nigeria, Niger, Libya, and Sudan. It includes Kanuri (its chief member), Tebu, and Zaghawa. ➤➤Nilo-Saharan.

Saint Helena (population in 1995 estimated at 6800, including Ascension and Tristan da Cunha) The official language is English, spoken by the whole population. ➤➤English.

Saint Kitts and Nevis (population in 1995 estimated at 42,800) The official language is English. Most people use an English-based creole widespread throughout the Lesser Antilles. ➤➤creole; English.

Saint Lucia (population in 1995 estimated at 140,000) The official language is English. Most people use a French-based creole (Patwa) found throughout the Lesser Antilles. ➤➤creole; English; Patwa.

Saint Pierre and Miquelon (population in 1995 estimated at 6600) The official language is French, spoken by almost everyone. There are a few speakers of English. ➤➤French.

Saint Vincent and the Grenadines (population in 1995 estimated at 120,000) The official language is English. Most people use an English-based creole widespread throughout the Lesser Antilles. ➤➤creole; English.

Salish /ˈseɪlɪʃ/ A group of *c*.20 Amerindian languages whose relationship to the other language groups of North America has not been determined. They are spoken along the Canadian/US Pacific coastline, with a few found inland. They include Bella Coola, Okanogan, and Squamish. Numbers of speakers are now very small, in the hundreds or less. ➤➤Amerindian; isolate.

Same or **Saami** /ˈsɑːmeɪ/ A member of the Finnic group of the Finno-Ugric family of languages, spoken by *c*.20–50,000 people chiefly in northern Norway, with some in northern Sweden, Finland, and Russia; also called **Lapp** or **Lappish** (but these terms are considered derogatory by Same speakers). It is written in both Roman and Cyrillic alphabets (the latter in Russia). There are three main dialects, sometimes considered to be different languages. Same has no official status, and most if not all speakers use one or other of the national languages of the country where they live. There is now a certain revival of interest in Same language and culture, and increasing concern over the social problems of Same minorities. ➤➤Finno-Ugric.

Samnorsk /'samnɔ:sk/ ➤Norwegian.

Samoa, formerly **Western Samoa** (population in 1995 estimated at 193,000) The official languages are Samoan (spoken by *c*.86% of the population) and English. English is used for international purposes. ➤➤English; Samoan.

Samoa ➤American Samoa.

Samoan /sə'məʊən/ A member of the Austronesian family of languages, spoken by over 360,000 people chiefly (*c*.153,000) in Samoa (where it is an official language, along with English) and the USA, with some in American Samoa, New Zealand, Hawaii, and Fiji. It is written in the Roman alphabet. ➤➤Austronesian.

Samoyedic /samə'jedɪk/ A branch of the Uralic family of languages, spoken by less than 30,000 Samoyeds, scattered across a vast area of Arctic Russia. The most widely spoken language is Nenets; others include Selkup, Nganasan, and Enets. Several Samoyedic languages have very few speakers, and some (e.g. Kamas) have died out in recent years. ➤➤Nenets; Uralic.

sandhi /'sandi:/ The phonological modification of grammatical forms which have been juxtaposed, such as *do* + *not* becoming *don't*, or *je* + *ai* becoming *j'ai* (French). A distinction is sometimes made between **external sandhi**, which operates across word boundaries, and **internal sandhi**, which operates within words. ➤➤morpho-phonology.

Sango /'saŋgəʊ/ A pidginized language spoken by *c*.5 million people, used primarily in the Central African Republic (where it has official status). It is derived from Ngbandi, a member of the Adamawa-Eastern group of African languages, with much influence from French, and is widely used as a lingua franca in the Central African Republic and surrounding areas. It is written in the Roman alphabet. ➤➤Adamawa Ubangi; lingua franca; pidgin.

San Marino (population in 1995 estimated at 24,500) The official language is Italian, spoken by the whole population. Over 80% use a local dialect, Emiliano-Romagnolo. ➤➤Italian.

Sanskrit A member of the Indo-Aryan group of languages, the classical language of the Hindus of India. Dating from the early part of the second millennium BC, it is the language in which the Vedas, the oldest sacred texts, are written – the name itself means 'purified' or 'refined'. Sanskrit was described and codified by the Indian grammarian Panini in the 5th century BC, and is written in the Devanagari alphabet. Classical Sanskrit (dated from *c*.500 BC to *c*.1000 AD) came to be used as the standard language of Hindu scholarship and literature, and in recent years has attracted renewed interest, both as a language for original writing and as a spoken language. Awareness of the structural similarity of Sanskrit to Latin and Greek was a major factor in the development of comparative philology at the end of the 18th century. ➤Devanagari; Indo-Aryan; Panini; philology; Prakrit.

sans serif or **sanserif** ➤serif.

São Tomé and Principe (population in 1995 estimated at 135,000) The official language is Portuguese. Most people (*c*.85%) speak a Portuguese-based creole (Crioulo). English and Portuguese are used for international purposes. ➤creole; Portuguese.

Sapir–Whorf hypothesis /sə'pɪə 'wɔːf/ A view about the relationship between language and thought, proposed by US linguist Edward Sapir (1884–1939) and his pupil Benjamin Lee Whorf (1897–1941). It combines two principles: that language determines the way we think (*linguistic determinism*); and that the distinctions encoded in one language are not found in any other language (*linguistic relativity*). The existence of successful translations argues against the strong form of the hypothesis; but some conceptual differences between speakers of different languages can be shown, and there is clear evidence that language does influence the way we perceive, remember, and perform mental tasks. ➤psycholinguistics.

sarcasm ➤irony.

Sardinian A variety of Romance, closely related to Italian, spoken by an uncertain number (perhaps over a million) on the island of Sardinia. Written materials date from the 11th century, but there has been little literary work, and none of the dialects has emerged as a standard, Italian being the official language. Sardinian is the variety of Romance which is closest to Vulgar Latin. ➤Italian; Latin; Romance.

satem language ➤centum language.

Saudi Arabia (population in 1995 estimated at 17,124,000) The official language is Arabic, spoken by over 80% of the population. There are many immigrants of varying language backgrounds, notably from the Philippines, Iran, and the subcontinent of India. English is used for international purposes. ➤Arabic.

Saussurian /səʊ'sjʊərɪən/ Adjective derived from Ferdinand de Saussure (1857–1913), a Swiss linguist whose theoretical ideas are widely regarded as providing the foundation for the science of linguistics. His thought is summarized in the posthumously published *Cours de linguistique générale* ('Course in general linguistics', 1916), consisting of a reconstruction by two of Saussure's students of his lecture notes and other materials. The **Geneva School** of linguistics continued to develop Saussurian thought. ➤linguistics; Prague school; semiotics; sign 1; structural.

scale and category grammar A linguistic theory developed by Michael Halliday in the early 1960s. The structure of language is seen as an intersecting set of scales (rank, exponence, delicacy) and categories (unit, structure, class, system) operating at different levels. The approach developed into systemic grammar. ➤➤Firthian linguistics; systemic grammar.

Scandinavian A group of languages forming the North Germanic branch of the Germanic family, traditionally divided into East Scandinavian (Swedish and Danish) and West Scandinavian (Norwegian, Icelandic, and Faeroese). A more recent classification distinguishes Mainland Scandinavian (Swedish, Danish, Norwegian) and Insular Scandinavian (Icelandic, Faeroese). The older states of these languages are called **Old Norse** – known especially from the Icelandic sagas. Runic inscriptions from the 3rd century provide the earliest evidence of the group. The differences between the modern languages began to emerge at the end of the 11th century. Today, Norwegian, Swedish, and Danish are largely mutually intelligible (though their status as separate languages is firmly maintained by the different peoples on cultural and historical grounds). Icelandic and Faeroese are grammatically rather different, and not usually comprehensible to speakers of other languages in the group – facts which have motivated the more recent classification referred to above. A variety of West Scandinavian, **Norn**, was spoken on Shetland and Orkney until the 18th century. ➤➤Danish; Faeroese; Germanic; Icelandic; Norwegian; rune; Swedish.

scansion ➤metrics.

schwa ➤shwa.

scope The stretch of language affected by the meaning of a particular form. For example, the **scope of negation** in English normally extends from the negative word to the end of the clause. Compare *She hasn't bought the fridge and the microwave*, where it is the buying of both fridge and microwave that is denied, and *She has bought the fridge and not the microwave*, where only the microwave is denied. ➤➤negation.

Scotland ➤Scottish Gaelic; United Kingdom.

Scottish Gaelic /ˈgeɪlɪk, ˈgalɪk/ A member of the Goidelic branch of the Celtic family of languages, spoken by *c*.80,000 people in Scotland (mainly in the north-west mainland and in the Hebrides); also called **Scots Gaelic** (often referred to simply as **Gaelic**) or **Erse**. It is an official regional language in the Western Isles, and is written in the Roman alphabet. The language developed from Irish Gaelic, which was brought to Scotland by immigrants from the 6th century. A distinction between Irish and Scots Gaelic is clearly in evidence from the 10th century, and a literary tradition emerged. There was a major period of poetic literature in the 18th century, but a standard written language did not develop until the Bible translation of 1801. In the 18th century, many Scots Gaels emigrated to Cape Breton Island, Nova Scotia; there were *c*.30,000 speakers of Cape Breton Gaelic in the 1930s, though the number is tiny today. There has been a steady decline in numbers everywhere during the past century, despite a modern revivialist movement. ➤➤Celtic.

Scouse /skaʊs/ The colloquial name for the variety of English heard in Liverpool. The name derives from a kind of sailor's stew (lobscouse) popular on Merseyside. ➤dialect.

script 1. The graphic form of the units of a writing system (e.g. the Roman vs. the Cyrillic alphabet). The term is used in a general way, to include the properties of different systems: hieroglyphic writing, syllabaries, and alphabets are all scripts. ➤graphology; transcription. **2**. In the study of narrative discourse, an encoding of the relations which typically connect events (e.g. the sequence of events which take place during a visit to a restaurant). The matching of events in a text with events in a script allows inferences to be made about information not explicitly mentioned in the text. ➤discourse analysis; narrative.

Sea Islands Creole English An English-based creole used along the south-eastern coast of the USA; also called **Gullah** (though many find this name demeaning). It has many linguistic features in common with West African varieties. Estimates of the number of speakers vary between 100,000 and 250,000. ➤creole.

Seaspeak A variety of English devised for unambiguous maritime communication. It was introduced in the 1980s through a project called Essential English for International Maritime Use. Its recommendations relate mainly to communication by radio, and include procedures for initiating, maintaining, and terminating conversations, as well as a recommended grammar, vocabulary, and structure for messages on a wide range of maritime subjects. Following the success of this project, other kinds of standardized language system are currently being investigated, notably Police Speak (initially for use by the French and British police forces in relation to the Channel Tunnel) and EmergencySpeak, for the emergency rescue services. ➤English; variety.

secondary articulation A vowel-like articulation which occurs at the same time as a primary consonantal articulation. Cases include palatalization (adding a high front tongue position), velarization (raising the back of the tongue), pharyngealization (narrowing the pharynx), and labialization (adding lip rounding). ➤articulation; coarticulation; consonant; rounding.

second language A language which is not a person's mother tongue, but which is learned in order to meet a communicative need. Immigrants commonly learn the language of their host nation as a second language. Often, a country chooses to give a language official status as a second language, using it as a medium of government, law, education, or the media – a role played, for example, by English or French in many countries of Africa. The developing branch of applied linguistics known as **second language acquisition** studies what goes on in the minds of learners as they develop their control of any language other than their first. ➤first language; Teaching English to Speakers of Other Languages.

second person ➤person.

secondary stress ➤stress.

secondary vowel ➤cardinal vowels.

secret language ➤argot; idioglossia.

segment A minimal discrete unit in the sound system of a language, defined physically or auditorily, and generally classified as a vowel or consonant; an analogous use is found in the study of writing systems. The process of analysing speech into segments is **segmentation**. **Segmental phonology** analyses speech into contrastive units – traditionally, **segmental phonemes**; this contrasts with **suprasegmental**, **nonsegmental**, or **plurisegmental phonology**, where speech is analysed into features that extend over more than one segment (e.g. intonation, vowel harmony). ➤➤consonant; phonology; vowel.

segmentator In instrumental phonetics, a device which plays back a piece of tape-recorded speech a small section at a time, so that it can be analysed in detail. The size of the segment to be replayed can vary from less than a second to several seconds. ➤➤experimental phonetics.

selectional feature In generative grammar, a syntactic feature which specifies restrictions on the permitted combinations of lexical items within a given grammatical context; also called a **selectional restriction** or **selectional rule**. For example, a verb that requires an animate subject noun phrase (e.g. *sleep*) would have the restriction stated as part of its feature specification. ➤➤collocation; generative grammar.

self-repair ➤repair.

semantic component ➤semantic feature.

semantic differential A technique devised by American psychologist Charles Osgood (1916–) and others to find out the emotional reactions of speakers to lexical items. Subjects are asked to rate words in terms of a seven-point scale with opposed adjectives at each end – for example, 'good–bad', 'active–passive', or 'tense–relaxed'. The word *bus*, for instance, might be rated strongly with respect to 'bad', 'active', and 'tense' – by someone who did not take much pleasure from bus-commuting. When the responses of many subjects are obtained, it is possible to draw conclusions about the main affective dimensions in terms of which a language's concepts are organized, and to make comparisons between cultural groups. ➤➤connotation.

semantic feature A minimal contrastive element of a word's meaning; in some approaches called a **semantic component**. *Girl*, for example, might be analysed into such features as 'young', 'female', and 'human'. In child language acquisition, the **semantic feature hypothesis (SFH)** claims that the order of appearance of a child's lexical items is governed by the type and complexity of the semantic features they contain. ➤➤acquisition; component; lexicon.

semantic field theory The view that the vocabulary of a language is a system of interrelated lexical networks, and not an inventory of independent items; also called **lexical field theory**. Examples include the fields of vehicles, fruit, clothing, colour, and parts of the body. Not all aspects of experience neatly divide up into semantic fields, however, and it is always necessary to consider context before assigning a lexical item to a field – for example, *hospital* relates to both the semantic field of health (as in *I was in hospital last week*) and that of buildings (as in *The hospital needs a new roof*). ➤lexicon; semantics.

semantic paraphasia ➤paraphasia.

semantic relations ➤sense.

semantics The study of meaning in language. **Structural semantics** applies the principles of structural linguistics to the study of meaning through the notion of **semantic relations** (also called **sense relations**), such as synonymy and antonymy. In generative grammar, the **semantic component** is a major area of the grammar's organization, assigning a **semantic representation** to sentences, and analysing lexical items in terms of **semantic features**. The theory of **semantic fields** views vocabulary as organized into areas within which words (lexical items) interrelate and define each other. ➤meaning; prototype; semantic feature/field theory/triangle; sense.

semantic triangle A particular model of meaning proposed by C. K. Ogden and I. A. Richards in the 1920s. It claims that meaning is essentially a threefold relationship between linguistic forms, concepts, and referents. ➤meaning; reference 1.

semasiology /sɪmasiˈɒlədʒiː/ ➤onomasiology; semiotics.

semeiology /semiˈɒlədʒiː/ ➤semiotics.

semeiotics ➤semiotics.

semi-auxiliary verb ➤auxiliary verb.

semi-bold ➤bold.

semicolon A punctuation mark whose typical function is to coordinate clauses, in much the same way as does the conjunction *and*. It plays an important contrastive role when commas are used within the same sentence, as it then keeps the different levels of sentence organization apart. *We first went to France, remembering to visit Helen; then to Germany, where we saw Paul; and finally to Spain, where we bumped into Peter.* Intelligibility would be diminished if such a sentence were punctuated only with commas. ➤colon; comma; punctuation.

semiconsonant ➤consonant.

semilingual Descriptive of people who have acquired two or more languages, but who lack a native level of proficiency in any of them. The situation is likely to arise when someone has moved between countries a great deal in their early years. Semilingualism has been little studied, and is controversial, as it suggests that there are people who do not have a true mother tongue; however, many people do claim to be semilingual. ➤bilingualism.

semiology /semiːˈɒlədʒiː/ ➤semiotics.

semiotics /semiːˈɒtɪks/ The study of signs and their use, focusing on the mechanisms and patterns of human communication and on the nature and acquisition of knowledge; also sometimes spelled **semeiotics**, and also called **semiology** or **semeiology** – though these terms have a different intellectual history. 'Semiology' relates primarily to a continental European tradition deriving from Ferdinand de Saussure; 'semiotics', primarily to an Anglo-American tradition deriving from US philosopher Charles Sanders Peirce (1839–1914). Language is viewed in semiotics as one type of sign system, along with such other systems as bodily gestures, clothing, and the arts. Other terms for the field include **semasiology** and **significs**. ➤communication; kinesics; proxemics; Saussurian; sign 1.

semi-productive ➤productivity.

semi-sentence A sentence whose grammaticality is doubtful, but where there is sufficient plausibility of interpretation to disallow a definite judgement of ungrammaticality. An example is *The wall was arrived before by the army.* ➤grammatical.

Semitic A large group of Afro-Asiatic languages, spoken by *c.*170 million people across the whole of North Africa, from the Atlantic to the Red Sea, throughout the Saudi Arabian peninsula, and in parts of Ethiopia. The languages are recorded from the 3rd millennium BC. The chief member of the group is Arabic; other important languages are Hebrew and Amharic. ➤Akkadian; Amorite; Arabic; Aramaic; Maltese; Moabite; Phoenician; Syriac; Tigrinya.

semivowel A sound functioning as a consonant at the margins of a syllable, but lacking the phonetic characteristics normally associated with consonants (such as audible friction); instead, its quality is phonetically that of a vowel, though of shorter duration. Examples include [w] and [j] in English, and [r] in some Slavic languages (e.g. *Trst* = Trieste). The term is often used as an equivalent to **semiconsonant**. ➤consonant; vowel.

Senegal (population in 1995 estimated at 8,314,000) The official language is French. About 35% of the people speak Wolof as a first language, and a further 45% as a second language. There are *c.*30 other local languages, notably Dyola, Fulacunda, Malinke, Serer, and Soninke. French is used for international purposes. ➤French.

sense The meaning of a linguistic expression. **Sense relations** (or **semantic relations**) are the relations of meaning which exist between words, such as sameness or oppositeness of meaning. ≫antonymy; hyponymy; meaning; reference 1; synonymy.

sensorineural ➤deafness.

sentence (S) The largest structural unit in terms of which the grammar of a language is organized. It is an independent unit which can be given both a formal and a functional classification (though with varying terminology). Formal classifications recognize such types as declarative, interrogative, imperative, and exclamative; functional classifications recognize such types as statement, question, and command. Most analyses recognize a classification into **simple** vs. **complex** and **compound sentence** types, in terms of the number and kind of subject–predicate constructions they contain. Another widespread distinction is into **favourite** or **major sentences**, which are the productive patterns in a language, and **minor sentences**, which lack productivity. ≫complex sentence; holophrase; major sentence; productivity.

sentence adverb ➤adverb.

sequence The observable succession of units in an utterance or text. The notion includes both linear relationships (where the dependencies are between successive, adjacent units) and nonlinear relationships, such as agreement between words that are separated. **Sequence of tenses** refers to the dependencies between tense forms in successive clauses: the use of a particular tense form in one clause requires the use of a particular tense form in another, as in *He tells me that he's leaving* vs. *He told me that he was leaving*. In psycholinguistics, **sequencing** refers to the influence that successive structures exercise upon each other. In language teaching, this term refers to the order in which a graded series of items is presented to the learner. ≫language teaching; method; order; psycholinguistics; string; tense.

Serbian The name increasingly being used since the mid-1990s for the Slavic language spoken in Yugoslavia (Serbia and Montenegro) by *c.*7.5 million people; before the civil war, considered a variety of Serbo-Croatian. It is also found in the Serb Republic enclave within Bosnia and Herzegovina, and through emigration in several other European countries. It is written in the Cyrillic alphabet. ≫Serbo-Croatian; Yugoslavia.

Serbo-Croatian The name traditionally given to a member of the South Slavic group of languages, spoken by *c.*20 million people in the republics which formerly (pre-1991) comprised Yugoslavia, with some speakers in adjoining countries; also called **Serbo-Croat** or (less usually) **Croato-Serbian.** Since the civil war, the term has virtually gone out of use in the Balkan states, having been replaced by names which reflect the identities of the individual countries and the growing linguistic differences between them – Serbian, Croatian, and (increasingly) Bosnian. The traditional term will still be encountered in linguistic descriptions outside the Balkans, as it provides a convenient label for the group of languages as a whole (cf. the use of *Scandinavian* for Swedish, Norwegian, etc.) and for identifying varieties which do not fall neatly into one or other of the socio-political categories. Substantial numbers of Serbo-Croatian speakers, in one or other of its varieties, are found in the USA, Canada, Australia, and Germany. The earliest texts date from the 12th century. ►►Bosnian; Croatian; Serbian; Slavic; Slovene; Yugoslavia.

serif /'serɪf/ In typography, a small terminal stroke at the end of the main stroke of a letter. Typefaces which lack this feature are called **sans serif** or **sanserif** /'san 'serɪf/. ►►typography; *figure below*.

Sesotho ►Sotho.

set expression A group of words standing in a fixed association; also called a **fixed**

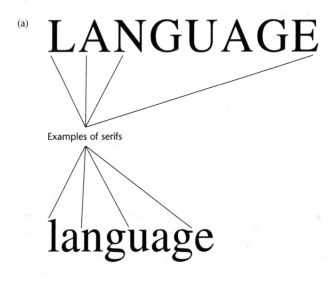

(a) LANGUAGE

Examples of serifs

language

(b) LANGUAGE

language

A **serif** (Times Roman) and sans-serif (Helvetica) typeface.

or **frozen expression**. Examples include restricted collocations (e.g. *run amok*), idioms, catch phrases, proverbs, aphorisms, and other stereotyped forms. ➤catch phrase; formula.

Setswana ➤Tswana.

setting A global configuration of the vocal organs which underlies the articulatory or phonatory performance of a speaker. **Articulatory settings** are reflected in tendencies to habitual articulatory postures, such as marked lip rounding or low tongue-body position. **Phonatory settings** include the habitual use of a whispery or creaky mode of phonation. ➤articulation; creaky voice; phonation; vocal organs.

sexist language Language which reflects and maintains a social attitude towards men or women. The notion applies almost entirely to the perceived linguistic biases which are said to constitute a male-orientated view of the world, fostering unfair sexual discrimination, and leading to a denigration of the role of women in society. The most commonly cited examples of the linguistic features involved are the use of the 3rd person pronoun *he* to refer generically to males and females (*If a student wants a comment, he should* . . .), and the generic use of the suffix *-man*, as in *chairman*. ➤generic; inclusive language.

Seychelles (population in 1995 estimated at 71,100) The official language is Creole French (spoken by *c*.96% of the population), with French and English auxiliary official languages, and used for international purposes. ➤creole; English; French.

SFH An abbreviation of **semantic feature hypothesis**.

SGML An abbreviation of **Standard Generalized Markup Language**.

shadow pronoun ➤pronoun.

Sheldru /'ʃeldruː/ An Anglo-Irish creole, used by Irish travellers and their descendants mainly in Ireland (*c*.6000), England (30,000) and the USA (*c*.50,000); also called **Shelta**. It is based on English grammar, with (often modified) Irish vocabulary. ➤creole.

Shelta /'ʃeltə/ ➤Sheldru.

Shona /'ʃəʊnə/ A member of the Bantu group of Benue-Congo languages, spoken by *c*.7 million people chiefly in eastern Zimbabwe (*c*.6 million), and also in nearby parts of Mozambique and Botswana. Shona is widely used as a lingua franca in the region. It is written in the Roman alphabet. ➤Benue-Congo; lingua franca.

shorthand A system which enables writing to take place at speed; technically known as **brachygraphy** ('short writing'), **tachygraphy** ('quick writing'), or **stenography** ('narrow writing'). Shorthand systems, known since the 1st century BC, use special symbols or abbreviations for the usual letters and words of speech. Famous systems include those of Isaac Pitman (1813–97), widely used in Britain,

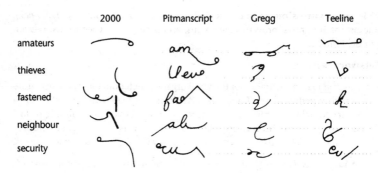

	2000	Pitmanscript	Gregg	Teeline
amateurs				
thieves				
fastened				
neighbour				
security				

Shorthand: Five words transcribed in Pitman 2000, Pitmanscript, Gregg and Teeline.

and John Robert Gregg (1867–1948), mainly used in the USA. It is best known for its use in press reporting and in secretarial work, though in recent years the development of voice-recording equipment has somewhat reduced the demand for professional shorthand skills. ➤➤stenotypy; writing.

shwa /ʃwɑː/ The neutral vowel, [ə], heard in English at the beginning of such words as *amazing*; also spelled **schwa**, and sometimes called the **indefinite vowel**. ➤➤central sound; vowel.

Siamese ➤Thai.

sibilant /'sɪbɪlənt/ A fricative sound made with a narrow, groove-like stricture in the blade of the tongue, while approaching the back part of the alveolar ridge. Sibilance is a particular characteristic of [s] and [z], and is also a feature of [ʃ] and [ʒ]. ➤➤fricative; groove.

Sierra Leone (population in 1995 estimated at 4,719,000) The official language is English. There are *c.*20 local languages, notably Mende and Temne. An English-based creole, Krio, is spoken by most of the population as a second language with *c.*10% using it as a first language. All three are important lingua francas – Mende especially in the south, Temne in central areas, and Krio generally. English is used for international purposes. ➤➤creole; English.

sight translation ➤translation.

sight vocabulary Words which can be recognized as wholes by someone learning to read. Grammatical words, many of which are irregular in spelling (*the, of*, etc.), are commonly presented in this way (often using flash cards) in the early stages of learning to read. ➤➤look-and-say.

sigmatism /'sɪgmətɪzm/ A distinctive use of [s]. The notion is chiefly used in a clinical context, where it refers to an abnormal pronunciation of [s], as in a lisp. It is also sometimes used in poetics, where it refers to a repetitive use of [s] to create a particular effect. ➤➤lisp; poetics; speech defect.

sign 1. A feature of language or behaviour which conveys meaning, especially when used conventionally within a system (such as speech, writing, gesture, dance); also called a **symbol** (but many writers make a distinction between these terms). The term was particularly used by Ferdinand de Saussure to summarize the two-way, arbitrary relationship which exists between a vehicle (a **signifier**, French *signifiant*) and a meaning (a **signified**, French *signifié*). The relationship itself is known as **signification**. ➤➤iconicity; Saussurian. **2**. ➤sign language.

signifiant/signifié /sɪgnɪfiːˈɑ̃, sɪgnɪfiːˈeɪ/ ➤sign 1.

significant ➤contrast; distinctive.

signification ➤sign 1.

significs ➤semiotics.

sign language A system of gestures, made with the hands and other body parts, used to replace speech as a mode of communication on all occasions of interaction. Sign languages which are used within deaf communities, or which permit communication to develop naturally between deaf people and hearing people (as in home sign systems), are sometimes referred to as **primary sign languages**. These are distinguished from the **alternate sign languages** used among hearing people (such as certain religious orders). A further distinction is often drawn between these naturally occurring sign languages and **contrived sign languages** – the sign systems invented by educators to convey spoken language to the deaf. ➤➤American Sign Language; Amer-Ind; cherology; cued speech; deafness; finger spelling; Paget–Gorman Sign System; tick-tack.

silent pause ➤pause.

silent way An approach to language teaching, devised by American educator Caleb Gattegno, that aims to provide an environment which keeps the amount of teaching to a minimum, and encourages learners to develop their own ways of using the language elements introduced. The method uses gesture, mime, charts, visual aids, and other devices (especially Cuisinière rods, of different shapes and colours) to help students to talk to each other. As students say more, the teacher says less (hence the name of the approach). ➤➤humanistic.

simile /ˈsɪməliː/ A figurative expression which makes an explicit comparison, typically using such words as *as* or *like*. Examples include *as tall as a mountain* and *ran like the wind*. ➤➤figurative language.

simple ➤compound; progressive.

simultaneous translation ➤translation.

Sindhi /'sɪndiː/ A language belonging to the North-western group of Indo-Aryan languages, spoken by *c.*17 million people in Pakistan and by *c.*2.5 million in north-west India. An official regional language in Sindh province, Pakistan, it holds a similar regional status in India. It is written in the Persian form of the Arabic alphabet in Pakistan, and in the Devanagari alphabet in India. ➤➤Devanagari; Indo-Aryan.

Singapore (population in 1995 estimated at 2,963,000) The official languages are Malay (spoken by *c.*15% of the population), several varieties of Chinese (*c.*60%), English (*c.*9%) and Tamil (*c.*4%). There are *c.*20 other languages, including Japanese, Korean, Malayalam, Panjabi, and Thai. English is the chief lingua franca, and is used for international purposes. ➤➤Chinese; English; lingua franca; Malay; Tamil.

Singhalese /sɪŋɡə'liːz/ ➤Sinhala.

sing-song theory ➤la-la theory.

singular ➤number.

Sinhala /sɪn'hɑːlə/ A language belonging to the Western group of Indo-Aryan languages, spoken by *c.*13 million people in Sri Lanka, where it is an official language along with Tamil; also called **Sinhalese** or **Singhalese**. It is written in the Sinhala syllabic script. Early inscriptions date from the 3rd century BC, and a substantial Buddhist literature is found from *c.*1000 AD. The language was brought to the island by colonists from northern India (*c.*5th century BC), and its geographical isolation led to its developing along rather different lines from other Indo-Aryan languages – notably due to the influence of Tamil, a Dravidian language. The passing of the Sinhala Only Bill in Ceylon in 1956 resulted in violent riots by the Tamil minority, and led to Tamil being given special status in 1958. ➤➤Dravidian; Indo-Aryan; Tamil.

Sinhalese /sɪnə'liːz/ ➤Sinhala.

Sinitic /sɪ'nɪtɪk/ ➤Sino-Tibetan.

Sino-Tibetan /'saɪnəʊ tɪ'betn/ A family of *c.*270 languages whose classification and membership is controversial, including various languages of China, Tibet, Myanmar (Burma), and nearby territories. Some scholars include the Tai and Miao-Yao groups within the family. The **Sinitic** group of Chinese languages is spoken by over 1140 million people, in China (*c.*1120 million) and Taiwan (*c.*21 million), with many more throughout south-east Asia, and through emigration all over the world. The **Tibeto-Burman** group of *c.*275 languages is widely distributed in Myanmar, Thailand, Vietnam, Laos, China, and India, its chief members being Burmese and Tibetan. It is spoken by *c.*50 million people. ➤➤Burmese; Chinese; Tibetan.

Siouan /'suːən/ ➤Macro-Siouan.

sister language ➤family of languages.

situational context ➤context 2.

situational syllabus ➤notional syllabus.

skimming ➤rapid reading.

slang Informal, nonstandard vocabulary, usually intelligible only to people from a particular region or social group; also, the jargon of a special group, such as doctors, cricketers, or sailors. Its chief function is to mark social identity – to show that one belongs – but it may also be used just to be different, to make an effect, or to be informal. Such 'in-group' language is subject to rapid change. ➤➤argot; back slang; jargon; rhyming slang; standard.

slant ➤solidus.

slash ➤solidus.

Slavic /'slavɪk/ A branch of the Balto-Slavic family of languages, spoken by *c*.300 million people; also called **Slavonic**. It is usually divided into three main groups. **South Slavic** (*c*.30 million speakers), found in Bulgaria, Bosnia-Herzegovina, Croatia, the Former Yugoslav Republic of Macedonia, Yugoslavia, Slovenia, and parts of Greece, includes Bulgarian, Macedonian, Serbian, Croatian and Slovene. **West Slavic** (over 50 million speakers), found in the Czech and Slovak republics, Poland, and the eastern part of Germany, includes Czech, Slovak, Sorbian, and Polish. **East Slavic** (over 200 million mother-tongue speakers, with many more as a second language) includes Russian, Belorussian, and Ukrainian. Old Church Slavonic is found in texts from the 9th century, and its later form (Church Slavonic) is still used as a liturgical language in the Eastern Orthodox Church. The Cyrillic alphabet is used to write all the East Slavic languages, as well as several others in the region (e.g. Bulgarian). Other languages use the Roman alphabet. The choice of alphabet has considerable cultural and political implications; in particular, Serbian is written in the Cyrillic alphabet, and Croatian in the Roman alphabet (with some diacritics), and this helps motivate the nationalist arguments that these are separate languages. ➤➤Balto-Slavic; Belorussian; Bosnian; Bulgarian; Croatian; Cyrillic; Czech; Glagolitic; Lekhitic; Macedonian; Polish; Russian; Serbian; Serbo-Croatian; Slovak; Slovene; Sorbian; Ukrainian.

Slavonic /slə'vɒnɪk/ ➤Slavic.

slip of the tongue An involuntary departure from the speaker's intended production of a sequence of language units – as when someone says /kiːm kreɪks/ for *cream cakes*. Sounds, syllables, morphemes, words, and sometimes larger units of grammar are affected. The kinds of error provide important evidence concerning the underlying neuropsychological processes involved in speech production. ➤➤malapropism; misarticulation; speech production; spoonerism.

slit ➤groove.

Slovak /'sləʊvak/ A member of the West Slavic group of languages, spoken by *c*.5 million people, chiefly in the Slovak Republic, where it is an official language, and in nearby parts of Slovenia, Hungary, and Ukraine. There are also many immigrant speakers in the USA and Canada. It is closely related to Czech, most dialects of the two languages being mutually intelligible. Written in the Roman alphabet, a standard literary language dates from the mid-19th century, though traces of Slovak can be found from as early as the 11th century. ➤Czech; Czechoslovakia; Slavic.

Slovene /'sləʊviːn/ A member of the South Slavic group of languages, spoken by *c*.2.2 million people chiefly in the republic of Slovenia (where it is the official language), and in nearby parts of Austria and Italy; also called **Slovenian**. It is written in the Roman alphabet. Written remains date from the 11th century, but a standard written language emerged only in the 19th century. There is a close relationship with varieties of Serbo-Croatian. ➤Serbo-Croatian; Slavic; Slovenia.

Slovenia (population in 1995 estimated at 2,000,000) The official language is Slovene, spoken by most of the population. Several languages from nearby territories are also spoken in the country, such as German, Hungarian, and Italian. Many people also speak one of the varieties of Serbo-Croatian. English is increasingly being used for international purposes. ➤Serbo-Croatian; Slovene.

Slovenian /slə'viːnɪən/ ➤Slovene.

slowed speech A therapeutic technique used in the treatment of stuttering. Stutterers are taught to pronounce the syllables of words in a smooth and fluent manner, but at a very slow speed (usually *c*.40 syllables a minute, to begin with). They then gradually increase their speed of utterance, while trying to maintain fluency. The technique is generally quite successful, though it forms only one part of an overall approach to fluency therapy. ➤stuttering.

social dialect ➤dialect; social dialectology.

social dialectology The application of dialectological methods to the study of social structure, especially the relationship between linguistic features and such factors as class, sex, age, profession, and ethnicity. The emphasis is on group membership as a determinant of dialectal competence. ➤dialect.

sociohistorical linguistics A branch of linguistics which studies the forms and uses of language in society, and how particular linguistic functions and types of variation develop over time within specific languages, speech communities, social groups, and individuals. ➤linguistics; variety.

sociolect A linguistic variety defined on social (as opposed to regional) grounds, such as a social class or occupational group. It is also called a **class dialect** or **social dialect**. ➤dialect; lect.

sociolinguistics A branch of linguistics which studies the ways in which language is integrated with human society (specifically, with reference to such notions as race, ethnicity, class, sex, and social institutions). The subject is often distinguished from the **sociology of language**, which tends to operate from the viewpoint of sociology, and (especially in Europe) from **sociological linguistics**, which aims to see language as an integral part of sociological theory. ➤interactional sociolinguistics; linguistics; pragmalinguistics; social dialectology; sociohistorical linguistics; variable; *cartoon below*.

sociological linguistics ➤sociolinguistics.

sociology of language ➤sociolinguistics.

sociopragmatics ➤pragmalinguistics.

soft palate ➤palate.

soft sign ➤hard sign.

'No, that's not my name. The National Geographic people gave it to me.'

solecism /ˈsɒləˈsɪzm/ A minor deviation from what is considered to be linguistically correct. English examples include splitting an infinitive (*to boldly go*) and ending a sentence with a preposition (*the person I gave it to*). ➤➤pleonasm; prescriptivism.

solid ➤hyphen.

solidus /ˈsɒlɪdəs/ An oblique stroke typically used to indicate alternatives (as in *either/or*) or certain kinds of abbreviation (as in *c/o* for 'care of '); also called a **slash**, **slant**, **oblique**, or **virgule**. It also has several minor uses, such as in dating (*6/7/41*) and classification (*Section B/36/2*). ➤➤punctuation.

soliloquy ➤monologue.

Solomon Islands (population in 1995 estimated at 367,000) The official language is English. There are *c.*60 local languages belonging to the Austronesian and Indo-Pacific families. Solomon Islands Pidgin (Pijin) is an English-based variety used by about a third of the people. ➤➤English; pidgin.

Somali /səˈmɑːliː/ A member of the Cushitic language family, spoken by *c.*8.5 million people, chiefly in Somalia (where it is an official language, along with Arabic), and also in Kenya, Ethiopia, and Djibouti. It is written in the Roman alphabet. ➤➤Cushitic; Somalia.

Somalia (population in 1995 estimated at 8,565,000) The official languages are Somali (spoken by *c.*70% of the population, *c.*6 million) and Arabic. Italian is still used in parts of the south. There are *c.*10 other African languages, such as Maay and Swahili. English and Arabic are used for international purposes. All speaker estimates in the region are uncertain, following the civil unrest of the 1990s. ➤➤Arabic; Somali.

Songhai or **Songai** /sɒŋˈgaɪ/ A Nilo-Saharan language spoken by *c.*2 million people over a wide area, from Mali to Nigeria, in the area around the River Niger, and not clearly related to any of the other languages in the region. It is written in the Roman alphabet. ➤➤Nilo-Saharan.

sonorant /ˈsɒnərənt/ ➤obstruent.

sonority The overall loudness of a sound, relative to others of the same pitch, stress, and duration. Sounds are said to have an **inherent sonority**, which accounts for the impression of a sound carrying further (see illustration at **decibel**). The centre of a syllable is defined as the place where sonority is greatest – the **sonority peak**. ➤➤phonetics; syllable.

Sorbian /ˈsɔːbɪən/ A member of the West Slavic group of languages, spoken by *c.*70,000 people chiefly in Lusatia, Germany (south-east of Berlin), where it has official status as a regional language; also called **Lusatian** or **Wendish**. It is written in the Roman alphabet, and texts date from the 15th century. High Sorbian is spoken around Bautzen, near the Czech border; Low Sorbian is spoken around Cottbus, near Poland. ➤➤Slavic.

sort A special character of type, such as an individual letter, numeral, or punctuation mark. A **special sort** is a character which cannot be typeset along with the rest of the text, because it is not included in the standard font of type. ➤➤font; typography.

Sotho or **Sesotho** /'su:tu:/ A member of the Bantu group of Benue-Congo languages, spoken by *c*.4 million people, *c*.2.7 million in South Africa (where it is one of the 11 official languages) and also in Lesotho (where it is an official language, along with English). The language is sometimes called **Southern Sotho**, to distinguish it from Northern and Western varieties. Sesotho sa Leboa is also one of South Africa's official languages. It is written in the Roman alphabet. ➤➤Benue-Congo; Lesotho; Tswana.

sound change A change in the phonological system of a language over a period of time. A **sound shift** is a series of related sound changes at a particular stage of a language's history (e.g. the English Great Vowel Shift). In comparative philology, a regular change is called a **sound law**. Many types of sound change have been recognized in comparative philology. ➤➤apocope; assimilation; convergence 2; dissimilation; epenthesis; functional change 2; haplology; law; metathesis; Neogrammarians; philology; phonology; syncope; umlaut; vowel shift.

sound spectrograph ➤spectrograph.

sound symbolism A direct association between the form and meaning of language. This can take place when phonetic sounds reflect sounds in the external world (**onomatopoeia**), as in *cuckoo, murmur*, and *splash*. Other properties, such as size or light, may also be suggested (**phonesthetics**), as in *glitter, slimy*, and *swerve*. ➤➤eurhythmy; phonesthetics.

sound system ➤phonology.

source In translating and interpreting, the language from which a message originates, called the **source language**. There is a contrast with the **target language**, into which the translation takes place. ➤➤interpreting; translatology.

South Africa (population in 1995 estimated at 37,900,000) Eleven languages were recognized as official in the new constitution formulated in 1993: Afrikaans, English, Ndebele, Sesotho sa Leboa, Sesotho, Swati, Xitsonga, Setswana, Tshivenda, Xhosa, and Zulu. About 20 other African or immigrant languages are used in the area, including Tamil, Tsonga, Tswana, and Urdu. There are many immigrants who speak various European languages. English is used for international purposes. ➤➤Afrikaans; English; Ndebele; Tswana; Xhosa; Zulu.

Spain (population in 1995 estimated at 38,734,000) The official language is Spanish, spoken by *c*.73% of the population. Basque (*c*.1.5%, in the Basque Provinces), Catalan (*c*.20%, first and second language speakers in Catalonia), and Galician (*c*.8%, in Galicia) are official regional languages. Other varieties include Aragonese, Asturian, and Extremaduran. There are unclear but large numbers of Romani speakers.

Spanish, English, and French are all used for international trade and tourism. ➤➤Basque; Catalan; Galician; Spanish.

Spanglish ➤Spanish.

Spanish A member of the Romance family of languages, spoken by *c*.270 million people as a first language, chiefly in Mexico and Central America (*c*.82 million), Spain (*c*.28 million), the USA (*c*.22 million), the Caribbean (*c*.18 million, chiefly in Cuba), Argentina (*c*.33 million), Bolivia (*c*.3.5 million), Chile (*c*.14 million), Colombia (*c*.34 million), Ecuador (*c*.12 million), Paraguay (*c*.100,000), Peru (*c*.20 million), Uruguay (*c*.3.1 million), and Venezuala (*c*.21.5 million). A further *c*.80 million speak it as a second language. It is written in the Roman alphabet. Rapidly increasing in numbers and status in the USA, it was probably the world's most rapidly growing language in the 1990s. The earliest written materials date from the 10th century, a Spanish literature emerging in the 12th century with the popular epic *Cantar de Mio Cid* ('Song of my Cid'). The golden age is the 17th century, at its peak in the *Don Quixote* of Miguel de Cervantes. The modern standard language is based on the dialect of Castile, which became the official language of all Spain after the merging of the Spanish kingdoms in the 15th century; and Spanish is often called **Castilian** as a result, especially in Latin America. Several Spanish-based creoles survive in countries which were once colonies of Spain, and several mixed ('Spanglish') varieties exist in locations where Spanish and English are in contact, such as 'Tex-Mex' in south-west USA. ➤➤creole; Judaeo-Spanish; Romance.

speaker recognition A branch of phonetics which investigates the way individuals can be identified or discriminated by analysis of their voices. In **speaker verification**, a sample of a speaker's speech is used to check a claimed identity. ➤➤phonetics; speech recognition; voiceprint.

special language ➤English for Special Purposes; Language(s) for Special Purposes.

spectrograph An instrument which provides a visual representation of the acoustic features making up the sounds of speech; also sometimes called a **sonagraph** (trade name). It uses a three-dimensional record on paper or screen (a **spectrogram**) in which time is displayed horizontally, frequency vertically, and intensity by the density of the marks. ➤➤experimental phonetics.

speech act A communicative activity defined with reference to the intentions of a speaker while speaking and the effects achieved on a listener. In this context, the act itself is called a **locutionary act**; the intentional aspect is the act's **illocutionary force**; and the impact on the listener is the act's **perlocutionary effect**. A wide range of speech acts has been proposed, such as directives (e.g. commanding), commissives (e.g. promising), and expressives (e.g. apologizing). ➤➤felicity conditions; indirect speech act; performative.

speech chain A model of communication in which the communicative act is seen

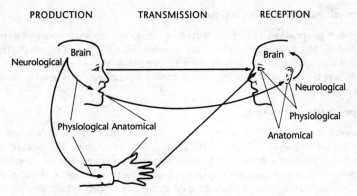

PRODUCTION   TRANSMISSION   RECEPTION

Speech chain: the steps in the communication chain.

as an interrelated sequence of stages between a speaker and a receiver. Three main stages are recognized: speech production – acoustic transmission – speech reception. Within production, it is possible to distinguish a neurological stage (the formulation of speech in the brain and its transmission using the nervous system), a physiological stage (the use of the muscles controlling the vocal organs), and an anatomical stage (the physical structure of the vocal organs themselves). Similarly, under the heading of reception, sounds are transmitted from the ear (anatomy) through the bones of the middle ear and cochlea (physiology) to the acoustic nerve and brain (neurology). ➤➤communication; speech perception/production.

speech community A regionally or socially definable human group, identified by the use of a shared spoken language or language variety. It can vary in size from a tiny cluster of speakers to whole nations or supranational groups (such as the Russian-using speech community in Asia). ➤➤language 1; variety.

speech defect A regular, involuntary deviation from the norms of pronunciation, such as a lisp or a weak [r]; also called a **speech impairment** or **impediment**. A more serious and systematic problem, involving a disruption in the linguistic system which underlies spoken language, would be a **speech disorder**. ➤➤language pathology; lisp; rhotacism; sigmatism.

speech disguise ➤argot.

speech disorder ➤language pathology; speech defect.

speech event A communicative exchange made meaningful by culturally-specific structures of participants, genres, codes, and other elements. Usage in a language is organized through the higher-level patterning of speech events. Examples of highly structured speech events are debates and interviews. Much less structured are conversations. ➤➤ethnography of speaking.

speech pathology ➤language pathology.

speech perception The process whereby a listener extracts a sequence of discrete phonetic and linguistic units from the continuous acoustic signal of speech. The term also applies to the study of the neuropsychological mechanisms governing this ability. ➤➤dichotic listening; motor theory; psycholinguistics; speech chain/ recognition.

speech play ➤verbal play.

speech production The activity of the respiratory, phonatory, and articulatory systems during speech, along with the associated neural programming required for their coordination and use. A contrast is usually drawn with the receptive aspects of spoken communication, such as speech perception and recognition. ➤➤articulation; imitation; neurolinguistics; phonation; slip of the tongue; speech chain/perception/ recognition; timing.

speech rate ➤rate of speech.

speech reading A method of visually interpreting a speaker who cannot be heard, by following the movements of the mouth; also called **lip reading**. It is typically practised in an expert way by deaf people, but everyone can find it necessary to speech-read some words on occasion (e.g. in a noisy environment). ➤➤cued speech; deafness; homophenes.

speech recognition The initial stage of the decoding process in speech perception. In recent years it has developed into a branch of phonetics which uses research in acoustic phonetics and speech perception to develop a computer system capable of responding to a wide range of forms of spoken input; also called **automatic speech recognition (ASR)**. ➤➤phonetics; speaker recognition; speech perception.

speech science The study of all the factors involved in the production, transmission, and reception of speech; also called **speech sciences** or **speech and hearing science**. As well as phonetics, the study includes such subjects as anatomy, physiology, neurology, and acoustics, as applied to speech. ➤➤phonetics.

speech stretcher A device which presents a slowed but undistorted recording of speech. It is helpful in identifying sounds which might otherwise be lost in the speed of normal speech, in studying the transitions between adjacent sounds, and in monitoring such features as intonation. ➤➤experimental phonetics.

speech surrogate A communication system which replaces the use of speech. Examples include drum languages and whistle languages. ➤➤alternative communication system; drum language; whistled speech.

speech synthesis The process of generating artificial speech signals, using a model of the linguistically important acoustic or articulatory properties. **Acoustic domain analogs** or **terminal analogs** replicate the acoustic properties of the vocal tract in terms of its output; **articulatory analogs** replicate the anatomical geometry of the tract between the larynx and the lips. The devices involved are called **speech synthesizers**. ➤➤experimental phonetics; text-to-speech system.

speech therapy The commonly used name of the profession which diagnoses and treats disorders of communication, especially of spoken language. A practitioner in the UK is now officially known as a **speech and language therapist** (though this label has not supplanted the former name of **speech therapist** in popular use); in the USA, the term is **speech (and language) pathologist**. The varying clinical situation in Europe has produced several designations (though they do not all have the same professional responsibilities), such as **orthophonist**, **logopedist**, and **phoniatrist**. ➤➤language disorder/pathology.

speed reading ➤rapid reading.

spelling The rules which govern the way letters are used to write the words of speech; also, a particular sequence of letters in a word. A language where there is a close (one-to-one) correspondence between sounds and letters is said to be spelled phonetically. **A spelling reform** movement is devoted to improving the regularity of the relationship between sound and spelling in a language. ➤➤graphology 1; haplography; phonetic spelling; spelling bee/pronunciation.

spelling bee A pastime which takes the form of a spelling competition. The concept emerged in mid-19th century USA, the term *bee* referring to a social get-together for a specific purpose (e.g. spinning, or, for that matter, making honey). ➤➤spelling; verbal play.

spelling pronunciation The pronunciation of a word based on its spelling. Examples include pronouncing *says* as /seɪz/, instead of the usual /sez/, and pronouncing the /t/ in *often* 'because it's there'. ➤➤spelling.

spirant /'spaɪrənt/ ➤fricative.

split ➤convergence 2.

split infinitive ➤infinitive.

spondee /'spɒndiː/ ➤foot.

spoonerism A slip of the tongue which involves the exchange of (usually initial) sounds to produce an unintentionally humorous or embarrassing result. The term derives from the name of William Archibald Spooner (1844–1930), warden of New College, Oxford, to whom several famous examples are attributed (e.g. *dear old queen* becoming *queer old dean*). ➤➤slip of the tongue.

Sprachbund /'ʃprɑːxbʊnt/ ➤areal linguistics.

Sprachgefühl /'ʃprɑːxgəfyːl/ ➤intuition.

spread ➤rounding.

square brackets ➤brackets.

Sri Lanka (population in 1995 estimated at 18,100,000) The official language is Sinhala (spoken by *c*.72% of the people), with Tamil (*c*.17%) an official regional language. About 50,000 use a Malay-based creole, especially in the cities, and *c*.100,000 have English as a first language. English is used for international purposes. ➤➤creole; Sinhala; Tamil.

stage name A new personal name adopted for public use by someone in the world of entertainment. Famous examples include *Dirk Bogarde* (otherwise *Derek Gentron Gaspart Ulric van den Bogaerde*) and *Greta Garbo* (originally *Greta Gustafsson*). If the concept of 'stage' is suitably extended, the notion includes such examples as *Stalin* ('steel', for *I.V. Dzhugashvili*). ➤➤nickname; onomastics; pseudonym.

stammering ➤stuttering.

standard A prestige variety of language used within a speech community, providing an institutionalized norm for such purposes as the media and language teaching. Linguistic forms or dialects that do not conform to this norm are often called **substandard** or (more usually, within linguistics) **nonstandard. Standardization** is the natural development of a standard language in a speech community, or an attempt by a community to impose one dialect as a standard. ➤➤language planning; national language; standard English.

standard English The variety of English used as a standard throughout the English-speaking world; in Britain often called 'BBC English' or 'Oxford English', though these terms relate more to the use of Received Pronunciation than to the use of grammar and vocabulary. Since the 1960s, particular attention has been paid to the emergence of differing national standards in areas where large numbers of people speak English as a first or second language: there are important regional differences between the UK, the USA, Canada, Australia, South Africa, the West Indies, India, West Africa, and several other parts of the English-speaking world. It remains to be seen how it will be possible to resolve the tension between the demand for mutual intelligibility among these nations and the demand for linguistic distinctiveness as a marker of national identity. ➤➤English; New Englishes; Received Pronunciation; standard.

Standard Generalized Markup Language (SGML) The basis of a scheme currently being developed in literary and linguistic computing for putting texts into machine-readable form, using a single encoding system. The scheme avoids the need for researchers to write special programs to convert texts from one encoding format into another. ➤➤computational linguistics.

Standard Theory The model of generative grammar proposed by Noam Chomsky in *Aspects of the Theory of Syntax* (1965), viewed at the time as the leading statement concerning the aims and form of a transformational grammar. The model was revised in the early 1970s, when it came to be known as the **Extended Standard Theory (EST)** – the extension being primarily in relation to the semantic rules, some of which were allowed to operate with surface structure as input. A further revision in the mid-1970s, following developments in the notion of movement rules, was called the **Revised Extended Standard Theory (REST)**. ➤➤Chomskyan; generative grammar; transformation.

starred form ➤asterisk.

statement A major sentence function, declarative in form, used chiefly to assert or report information. In English it typically contains a subject before a verb, as in *The door is open*. Statements are usually contrasted with **questions**, **commands**, and **exclamations**. ➤➤declarative; indicative; sentence.

state verb ➤dynamic verb.

static verb ➤dynamic verb.

statistical linguistics A branch of linguistics which studies the application of probabilistic techniques in linguistic theory and description. Examples include the analysis of frequency and distribution of linguistic units in texts, and the relationship between word types and tokens. ➤➤lexical density; linguistics; quantitative linguistics; p. 320.

statistical universal ➤universal.

stative verb /'steɪtɪv/ ➤dynamic verb.

status planning ➤language planning.

steganography /stegə'nɒgrəfiː/ The use of techniques to conceal the existence of a message. For example, a message might be reduced in size to a microdot, and hidden in a postage stamp. Such techniques are common in the field of intelligence. ➤➤cryptography.

stem The element of word structure to which inflectional affixes are attached. It may consist solely of a root morpheme (a simple stem, e.g. *girl*), or of two root morphemes (a compound stem, e.g. *blackbird*), or of a root morpheme plus a derivational affix (a complex stem, e.g. *manli* + *ness*). ➤➤morphology; root 1.

stenography /stə'nɒgrəfiː/ ➤shorthand.

stenotypy /'stenətaɪpiː/ A mechanical system for producing a shorthand version of speech. It was invented in 1906 by W.S. Ireland, an American court reporter, and is mainly used to record the verbatim proceedings of law courts and legislative meetings. It has a keyboard of 22 keys which the operator strikes using both hands simultaneously, producing a set of abbreviated words printed without noise on a roll of paper. The left-hand fingers type consonants occurring before vowels, and

Rank	French	German	Written English	Spoken English
1	de	der	the	the
2	le (a.)	die	of	and
3	la (a.)	und	to	I
4	et	in	in	to
5	les	des	and	of
6	des	den	a	a
7	est	zu	for	you
8	un (a.)	das	was	that
9	une (a.)	von	is	in
10	du	für	that	it
11	que (p.)	auf	on	is
12	dans	mit	at	yes
13	il	sich	he	was
14	à	daß	with	this
15	en	dem	by	but
16	ne	sie	be	on
17	on	ist	it	well
18	qui	im	an	he
19	au	eine	as	have
20	se	DDR	his	for

statistical linguistics: The 20 most-frequently occurring words in studies of newspaper writing in English, French and German, and in a corpus of English conversation, using material gathered in the 1960s. (a = article, p = pronoun).

these are printed on the left of the paper; the right-hand fingers type consonants occurring after vowels, and these appear on the right. The thumbs type the vowels, which appear in the centre. ➤shorthand; writing.

stereotype 1. In grammar, a sequence of words which resembles a productive grammatical structure, but which in fact has been learned as a single unit and has little or no productivity; examples include proverbs, quotations, aphorisms, and many idioms. ➤formula; idiom; productivity; set expression. **2**. In semantics, the set of characteristics which describes a **prototype**; for example, a stereotyped feature of cars is that they have four wheels. The theory of **stereotype semantics** holds that word meaning includes a stereotype of the object designated by the word. ➤prototype; semantics.

stet An instruction to a printer or reader that an altered or deleted piece of text is to be retained in its original form. In proof-correction, the convention is to use a row of dots or dashes below the wrongly corrected word(s). The term is from Latin, meaning 'let it stand'. ➤proof; typography.

stop A type of consonant involving a complete closure of the oral tract at some point, such as [p], [t], and [g]. Stops using inward-flowing air are often referred to as **suction stops**; stops using outward-flowing air as **pressure stops**. ➤continuant; manner of articulation; plosive.

stranded Descriptive of an element that is left unattached after a grammatical analysis moves it out of a construction, or after the rest of the construction has been moved. For example, a preposition is commonly left stranded when the noun phrase within the prepositional phrase has been moved, as in *That's the girl you gave it to* (compare *That's the girl to whom you gave it*). ➤preposition; transformation.

stratificational grammar A linguistic theory devised in the 1960s by US linguist Sydney M. Lamb (1929–). It models language as a system of several related layers or **strata** of structure. ➤linguistics.

stress The relative perceived prominence of a unit of spoken language. A **stressed** syllable is usually produced by an increase in articulatory force, increased rate of air flow, and greater muscular tension in the articulators. It is characterized phonetically by greater intensity than is found in adjacent **unstressed** syllables, but higher pitch and longer duration are also typically involved. Several degrees of stress can be recognized, most commonly **primary, secondary**, and **weak stress**, all three heard in the word *antigravity* (where *grav* is primary, *an* is secondary, and the other syllables are weak). A sequence of syllables constituting a rhythm unit, containing one primary stress, is a **stress group**. **Sentence stress** or **contrastive stress** is the use of stress to express a contrast of meaning in a sentence: *The tape ISN'T broken*. Many pairs of words and word sequences can also be distinguished using **lexical stress** or **word stress** (e.g. *record* as noun vs. *record* as verb). A language where the stresses fall at roughly regular intervals within an utterance is a **stress-timed language**. ➤accent 2; isochrony; loudness; strong form; syllable.

stress-timed language ➤isochrony.

stricture An articulation which restricts the airstream to some degree. It can range from a complete closure to a slight narrowing. ➤articulation.

Strine A jocular name for Australian English, derived from the rapid colloquial pronunciation of 'Australian' as /straɪn/. The concept received particular attention in the 1960s, when Afferbeck Lauder's *Let Stalk Strine* was published. Several books in the genre followed, poking fun at other accents. ➤dialect; English; Scouse.

string A linear sequence of elements, displaying a particular length and structure, such as a sentence, phrase, or complex word. A **substring** is any part of a string which is itself a string, such as a phrase within a clause. In formal analysis, a string may also consist of just a single element, or even of no element at all (the **empty** or **null string**). ➤formal grammar; sequence.

strong form One of two possible pronunciations of a word (typically, a grammatical word) in connected speech, which results from the word being stressed. The notion contrasts with a **weak form**, where the word is unstressed (e.g. *and* vs. *'n'*). ➤➤stress.

strong verb A verb which changes its root vowel when changing its tense, as in *sing* vs. *sang*. The term contrasts with **weak verb**, where the past tense is formed by adding an inflection, as in *kick* vs. *kicked*. The distinction is important in the Germanic languages. ➤➤ablaut; root 1.

structural Descriptive of any approach to the analysis of language which pays explicit attention to the way linguistic features can be described in terms of patterned organization (**structure**). **Structuralism** in a broad sense developed out of Ferdinand de Saussure's notion of a language as a system of signs. It led eventually to the theory that any human institution or behaviour (e.g. religion, literature, dance) can be analysed in terms of an underlying network of relationships, with the structural patterns related to basic modes of thought. In a narrow sense, structuralism refers to the emphasis on the processes of segmenting and classifying utterances promoted by Leonard Bloomfield in the 1930s, and to the school of thought which emerged, called **structural** or **structuralist linguistics**. Structuralists saw language primarily as a system of formal patterning, especially in grammar and phonology, and paid little attention to the meaning which the patterns conveyed. The 1960s saw a reaction to this 'logocentric' view. ➤➤Bloomfieldian; linguistics; logocentrism; Saussurian; structure.

structural ambiguity ➤ambiguous.

structuralism ➤structural.

structural semantics ➤semantics.

structural syllabus ➤notional syllabus.

structural word ➤grammatical word.

structure A network of interrelated units, in which the significance of the parts emerges only with reference to the whole. More narrowly, the term is applied to an isolatable section of this network, such as a particular grammatical area – for example, 'the structure of the pronoun system'. More narrowly still, it refers to a sequential pattern of linguistic elements at a given level, as in such notions as 'phonological structure' and 'clause structure'. ➤➤structural.

stuttering A disorder of speech fluency, marked by a lack of ability to communicate easily, rapidly, and continuously; also called **stammering**, especially in the UK. The most widely recognized symptom is the abnormal repetition of sounds and syllables, especially at the beginnings of words, but there is a wide range of other symptoms, such as the abnormal lengthening of sounds, the inability to release a sound which is being articulated (known as 'blocking'), erratic stress and rhythm, and the use of circumlocutions to avoid words which the speaker knows are difficult to pronounce. ➤blocking; feedback 2; prolongation; slowed speech; speech therapy.

style ➤stylistics.

stylistics The study of any situationally distinctive use of language, and of the choices made by individuals and social groups in their use of language; alternatively, the study of the aesthetic use of language, in all linguistic domains. Each of these notions may be referred to as **style**. The study of style is sometimes called **applied stylistics**, especially when there is an emphasis on the use of style in literary and nonliterary texts. In its literary applications, the subject brings together the insights and methods of linguistics and literary criticism; in this context, it has also been called **literary linguistics** or **linguistic criticism**. A contrast is often drawn between **literary stylistics**, the study of the linguistic characteristics of literature as a genre and of the style of authors, and **general stylistics**, the study of the whole range of nondialectal varieties of a language. The quantification of stylistic patterns is the province of **stylostatistics** or **stylometry**. The study of the expressive or aesthetic function of sound is sometimes called **phonostylistics**. ➤diction; metrics; poetics; variety.

stylometry /staɪˈlɒmətriː/ ➤stylistics.

stylostatistics ➤stylistics.

subject (S) A major element of sentence or clause structure, traditionally associated with the 'doer' of an action, as in *The dog chased the cat*, where *the dog* is traditionally described as the **grammatical subject**. A distinction is often drawn between the grammatical and the **logical** or **underlying subject**, illustrated by *the dog* in *The cat was chased by the dog*. In languages which make inflectional distinctions between subject and object, the case of the subject is often called the **subjective**, contrasting with **objective**. A **subjective genitive** occurs when the underlying structure of the genitive construction is that of subject + verb (e.g. *the playing of the footballers* = 'footballers play'). This contrasts with the **objective genitive**, where the underlying structure is verb + object (e.g. *the building of the castle* = 'build the castle'). ➤clause; genitive; object; topic.

subjective genitive ➤subject.

subjunctive A grammatical feature typically found in verb forms, sentences, or clauses, occurring in subordinate clauses to express such attitudes as tentativeness, vagueness, and uncertainty. The term is used in English linguistics in relation to such constructions as *if he were going*, formulae such as *So be it*, and clauses introduced by *that* (especially in American English), such as *I insist that he leave*. ➤mood.

subordinating conjunction ➤conjunction.

subordination The process or result of linking linguistic units so that they have different syntactic status, one being dependent upon the other, and usually being a constituent of the other; **subordinate** is sometimes contrasted with **superordinate**. A **subordinate** or **dependent clause** is illustrated by the *when*-clause in *John left when the bus arrived*; the marker of linkage is *when*, a **subordinator** or **subordinating conjunction**. ⇒clause; coordination.

subscript A small letter, numeral, or other symbol set beside and/ or below the foot of a full-size written character; also called an **inferior**. It contrasts with a **superscript**, which is set beside and/ or above the top of a full-sized character; also called a **superior**. ⇒typography.

substance The undifferentiated raw material out of which language is constructed – the sound waves of speech (**phonic substance**) and the marks of writing (**graphic substance**). This contrasts with **form**, the abstract pattern of relationships imposed on this substance by a language. ⇒form 1; graphetics; phonetics.

substandard ⇒standard.

substantive /'sʌbstəntɪv/ In some descriptive grammars, a word class which includes nouns and noun-like items (e.g. *the rich*). It also sometimes includes pronouns. ⇒noun; word class.

substantive universal ⇒universal.

substitution The process or result of replacing one item by another at a particular place in a structure. In grammar, the structural context in which this replacement occurs is a **substitution frame** (e.g. *The – is outside*), and the set of items which can be used at a given place is a **substitution class**. In language teaching, exercises to improve the ability of learners to carry out this process of replacement are **substitution drills**. ⇒drill; paradigm.

substitution frame ⇒frame.

substrate /'sʌbstreɪt/ A linguistic variety or set of forms which has influenced the structure or use of a socially dominant variety or language within a community; also called a **substrate language** or a **linguistic substrate** or **substratum**. An example is the influence of Celtic on the Latin of ancient Gaul. It contrasts with a **superstrate** or **superstratum**, where the influence is in the other direction (such as the influence of Norman French on Old English). ⇒language contact.

substring ⇒string.

suction stop ⇒stop.

Sudan (population in 1995 estimated at 31,173,000) The official language is Arabic, spoken by over half the population, and widely used as a lingua franca. There are *c.*120 other languages, notably Dinka, Hausa (important as a lingua franca), Nuba, Nuer, and Zande. There is an Arabic-based creole in certain areas. English is used for international purposes. ⇒Arabic; creole; lingua franca.

suffix ➤affix.

suggestopedia or **suggestopaedia** /sədʒestəʊ'piːdɪə/ A method of foreign language teaching developed by a Bulgarian teacher, Georgi Lozanov, in the 1970s, based on *suggestology*, the science of suggestion. The approach takes the view that the brain (especially the right hemisphere) has great unused potential which can be exploited for language learning. Suggestopedia uses music, visual images, and relaxation exercises to put the learner into a state of mind where language learning can take place quickly and effectively. ➤➤humanistic.

Sumerian /suːˈmɪərɪən/ The oldest known language to be preserved in written form, spoken in southern Mesopotamia (part of modern Iraq) until the 2nd millennium BC. Inscriptions date from *c.*3100 BC, written in cuneiform script, and there are several later literary and religious works. It continued in use as a written form long after its spoken form had become extinct (having been supplanted by Akkadian *c.*2000 BC). The existence of Sumerian was not recognized until cuneiform was deciphered in the 19th century. Attempts to relate it to other languages have so far proved unsuccessful. ➤➤Akkadian; cuneiform; isolate.

Sundanese or **Sunda** /ˈsʊndə/ A member of the Austronesian family of languages, spoken by *c.*27 million people in the western part of Java, Indonesia. Written records date from the 14th century, and use the Roman alphabet. ➤➤Austronesian.

superfix A vocal effect which extends over more than one sound segment in an utterance (e.g. pitch, loudness); also called a **suprafix**. The notion is particularly used in the context of a specific grammatical structure, such as a questioning intonation contour. ➤➤intonation.

superior ➤subscript.

superlative ➤degree.

superordinate Descriptive of a linguistic unit higher in a hierarchy than another, **subordinate** unit. For example, in *I know where she went*, the clause *I know* (or *I know X*) is the **superordinate clause**. ➤➤hierarchy; subordination.

superscript ➤subscript.

superstratum /ˈsuːpəstreɪtm/ ➤substrate.

suppletion /sʌˈpliːʃn/ In morphology, a relationship between forms which cannot be accounted for by a general rule, because the forms involved have different roots. An example is the relationship between *go* and *went*. ➤➤morphology; root 1.

suprafix ➤superfix.

supraglottal Descriptive of the entire area of the vocal tract above the glottis. ➤➤glottis.

suprasegmental ➤phonology.

surface structure In transformational grammar, the final stage in the syntactic representation of a sentence, which provides the input to the phonological component of the grammar; contrasts with **deep structure**. The term **surface grammar** is sometimes used informally for the superficial properties of a sentence. ➤➤syntax; transformation.

Suriname or **Surinam** (population in 1995 estimated at 414,000) The official language is Dutch. There are *c.*10 Amerindian languages spoken by small numbers, and three English-based creoles – Guyanese, Saramaccan, and Sranan (the last used by *c.*30% as a first language, and by a further 60% as a second language). Immigrant languages include Hindi (*c.*38% of the population), Javanese (*c.*15%), and Chinese. English is used for international purposes. ➤➤creole; Dutch; lingua franca.

Survey of English Usage A survey of the grammatical repertoire of adult educated native speakers of British English, begun in London in 1960 by Randolph Quirk. The corpus comprises 200 texts of spoken or written material, classified according to stylistic type. The Survey is still housed at University College London, though the research unit there has considerably broadened the scope of its enquiries, including work on computational parsing and international varieties of English. ➤➤corpus; International Corpus of English; London–Lund Corpus of Spoken English; Quirkian; p. 326.

Swahili /swəˈhiːliː/ A Bantu language spoken by *c.*5 million people as a mother tongue, mainly in Tanzania and Kenya; also called **KiSwahili**. It is used as a lingua franca throughout East Africa by *c.*30 million, and has official status in Tanzania and Kenya. It is written in the Roman alphabet, though the oldest preserved writing (from the 18th-century) uses Arabic. The language has been greatly influenced by Arabic, from which it has taken a great deal of vocabulary (the name *swahili* is itself from an Arabic word meaning 'of the coast'). ➤➤Bantu; lingua franca.

Swaziland (population in 1995 estimated at 900,000) The official languages are English and Swati (Swazi), the latter spoken by *c.*90% of the people (and also used as an official language in South Africa). Zulu and Tsonga are also found. English is used for international purposes. ➤➤English.

swearing ➤taboo language.

Sweden (population in 1995 estimated at 8,889,000) The official language is Swedish, spoken by *c.*93% of the population. Other languages include Estonian, Finnish (*c.*5%), Latvian, Romani, Syriac, Turkish, and several varieties of Same (Lappish, *c.*11,000 speakers in total). English is used for international purposes. ➤➤Swedish.

Swedish A North Germanic language, a member of the East Scandinavian group, spoken by *c.*9 million people in Sweden, by *c.*300,000 in Finland, where it is also an

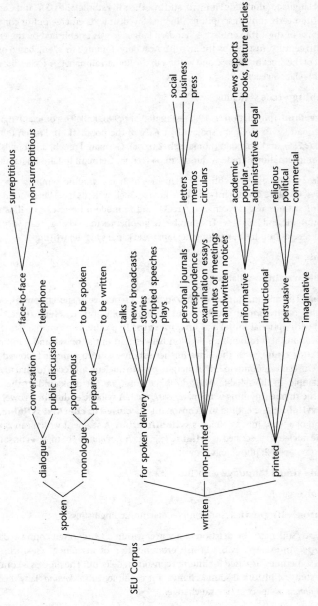

The chief sample categories in the **Survey of English Usage**.

official language (alongside Finnish), and by others in Estonia, the USA, and Canada. Apart from early runic inscriptions, the first Swedish texts emerge out of common Old Norse in the 13th century. A standard language was established by the end of the 18th century, fostered by the Swedish Academy (founded in 1786), based on the dialect of the Stockholm area, and written in the Roman alphabet. ➤➤Icelandic; rune; Scandinavian; Sweden.

switching ➤code switching.

Switzerland (population in 1995 estimated at 6,990,000) The official languages are German (Swiss German, spoken by *c*.64% of the population), French (*c*.19%), Italian (*c*.7%), and Rhaetian (Romansch, *c*.0.6%). German, French, and English are used for international trade and tourism. ➤➤French; German; Italian; Rhaetian.

syllabary /ˈsɪləbəriː/ A writing system in which the graphic symbols represent syllables, usually a consonant–vowel sequence. Such systems have been found from the earliest times (e.g. Mycenaean Greek), and in modern times can be illustrated from Amharic and Japanese. The number of graphemes in a syllabary can vary from *c*.50 to several hundred. ➤➤grapheme; Japanese; kana; syllable; writing.

syllabic ➤syllable.

syllabic writing ➤syllabary.

syllable The minimal unit of organization for a sequence of speech sounds, acting as a unit of rhythm. It usually consists of an obligatory **nucleus** (typically, a vowel) with optional initial and final **margins** (typically, consonants). Structural classifications also recognize a division between an initial **onset** and a following **rhyme** (or **rime**), with the latter further subdivided into a **peak** followed by a **coda**. Onset corresponds to initial margin, peak to nucleus, and coda to final margin. For example, in the syllable /kat/, /k/ is the onset, /a/ the peak, and /t/ the coda; /at/ is the rhyme (rhyming with /pat/, /sat/, etc.). A syllable ending in a vowel is an **open syllable**; one ending in a consonant is a **closed** or **checked syllable**. The division of a word into syllables is **syllabification**. A segment which can act as a syllable nucleus is described as **syllabic** (e.g. the /n/ of *button* /ˈbʌtn/). ➤➤consonant; isochrony; open 2; phonology; vowel.

syllable-timed language ➤isochrony.

symbol ➤sign 1.

synchronic linguistics /sɪŋˈkrɒnɪk/ ➤diachronic linguistics.

syncope /ˈsɪŋkəpiː/ The deletion of a vowel within a word; often contrasted with **apocope**. An example is the British pronunciation of *secretary* as /ˈsekrɪtriː/. The term is sometimes also used for internal consonant deletion. The process is common in the study of historical sound change; for example, Latin *domina* 'lady' became Italian *donna*. ➤➤apocope; sound change.

syncretism /ˈsɪŋkrətɪzm/ The merging of forms following the loss of inflections; more generally, identity between two forms of the same lexical item (e.g. *jumped* as past tense and past participle). ➤➤convergence 2; inflection 1.

syndeton /ˈsɪndətn/ The use of conjunctions to link parts of a syntactic construction, as in *They left hastily and angrily*. It contrasts with **asyndeton** /ˈeɪsɪndətn/, which describes the omission of conjunctions – a type of construction often used to achieve an economical or dramatic form of expression, as in *They left hastily, angrily, sadly*. Both terms come from the Greek rhetorical tradition. ➤➤conjunction; rhetoric.

synecdoche /sɪˈnekdəkiː/ A figure of speech in which the part is used for the whole or the whole is used for the part; the term is from Greek 'taking up together'. An example of the first type is the use of *wheels* for car (*I've got a new set of wheels*); of the second type is the use of *creature* for people (*Those poor creatures*). ➤➤figurative language.

synesthaesia /sɪnəsˈθiːʒə/ ➤phonesthetics.

synesthesia /sɪnəsˈθiːʒə/ ➤phonesthetics.

synonymy /sɪˈnɒnəmiː/ The relationship of sameness of meaning between lexical items. Items are **synonyms** if they are close enough in meaning to allow a choice to be made between them in some contexts, without this affecting the meaning of the sentence as a whole; an example is *a nice range/selection/choice of flowers*. ➤➤antonymy; sense.

syntactic blend ➤blending.

syntactic frame ➤frame.

syntagm /ˈsɪntam/ A string of related constituents, usually in linear order; also called a **syntagma**. The sequential relationships between the constituents at a given level of analysis are **syntagmatic relations**, contrasting with **paradigmatic relations**. ➤➤paradigm; syntax.

syntax The study of the rules governing the way words are combined to form sentences; contrasts with **morphology**, the study of word structure. More generally, the study of the interrelationships between all elements of sentence structure (including morphemes), and of the rules governing the arrangement of sentences in sequences. In generative linguistics, the **syntactic component** contains rules for the generation of **syntactic structures**. These structures are analysable into sequences of **syntactic categories** or **syntactic classes**, established on the basis of the formal relationships that linguistic items have with each other. The study of the field as a whole is **syntactic theory**. ➤➤ellipsis; endocentric construction; formal grammar; generative grammar; grammar 1; morphology; morphosyntax; valency.

synthetic language ➤typology of language.

Syria (population in 1995 estimated at 14,325,000) The official language is Arabic, spoken by *c*.80% of the population. Other languages include Adygey, Aramaic, Armenian (*c*.3%), Azerbaijani, Domari (Romani), Kurdish (*c*.6%), and Syriac. French is used for international purposes. ➤Arabic.

Syriac /'sɪriːak/ A variety of eastern Aramaic, an important Christian liturgical language between the 2nd and 7th centuries AD, spoken at first in south-east Asia Minor, where it developed a scholarly and literary tradition that remained until the 14th century. It was at first chiefly used for the translation of Greek Christian writings, including the Bible, and later for many Greek medical and scientific texts. Written records date from the 1st century, in a distinctive script which eventually developed variant forms (used by different sects). The language is still used in the liturgy of the Syrian Jacobite Church, and also (though to a much lesser extent) in the Syrian Catholic Church. ➤Aramaic.

system A network of patterned relationships which makes up the organization of language. It can be divided into a hierarchically ordered arrangement of sub-systems (finite sets of formally or semantically connected units), such as the tense system, the pronoun system, and the vowel system. A system with a determinate number of members is a **closed system**; new members are not normally created. ➤hierarchy; paradigm; structure.

system architecture A computing term used in computational linguistics, referring to the set of superordinate principles which define the operations of a language processing system. System architectures specify the components of such a system, the structural relations between the components, and the flow of control from one to another component during processing. ➤computational linguistics.

systematic phonemics A level of representation in generative phonology which sets up a single underlying form capable of accounting in a regular way for the phonological variations that relate grammatical structures (e.g. *divine, divinity*). The units in these representations are called **systematic phonemes**, as opposed to the autonomous phonemes of traditional phonemic phonology, which are established without reference to grammatical structure. ➤generative grammar; phoneme; systematic phonetics.

systematic phonetics A level of representation in generative phonology which provides a narrow phonetic transcription of the systematic features of pronunciation (i.e. excluding those attributable to performance factors). ➤performance 1; systematic phonemics; transcription.

systemic grammar A grammatical theory developed by Michael Halliday from scale and category grammar, in which the notion of paradigmatic relationship or **system** is made the central explanatory principle. Grammar is concerned to establish a network of systems of relationships which will account for all the semantically relevant choices in the language. The emphasis of the theory is on the way language functions in the act of communication, and on the choices which speakers make as they interact in speech situations. ➤Firthian linguistics; scale and category grammar; system.

syzygy /'sɪzɪʤiː/ A word game devised by Lewis Carroll, in which one word is worked into another by steps; a type of word-chain. For example, 'Send MAN on ICE' is achieved through MAN–PERMANENT–ENTICE–ICE. ➤word game.

T

T An abbreviation of **transformation**.

taboo language Words which people may not use without causing offence, because they refer to acts, objects, or relationships which are widely felt to be embarrassing, distasteful, or harmful. Verbal taboos are usually related to sex, the supernatural, excretion, and death, but in some cultures they extend to other aspects of domestic life (such as in-laws, private names, and certain animals). Polite society devises alternative forms of language to refer to these areas. Several types of taboo expression can be distinguished. **Profanity** is a relatively mild notion, the choice of language conveying disrespect for what people hold sacred (usually something or someone religious). **Blasphemy** is much more serious, being the expression of gross irreverence towards the divine. **Obscenity** is language which arouses disgust because of its crude reference to sexual functions. All of these are loosely included under the heading of 'swearing' or 'bad language'. The term **expletive** is used in official contexts. ➤➤avoidance languages; circumlocution; euphemism.

tachistoscope /tə'kɪstəskəʊp/ A device used chiefly in reading research which gives a very brief exposure to a visual image, such as a letter. The term comes from the Greek word *tachys* 'brief, swift'. ➤➤reading.

tachygraphy /tə'kɪgrəfiː/ ➤shorthand.

tacit knowledge /'tasɪt/ ➤intuition.

Tadzhik or **Tajik** /'tadʒɪk/ A member of the Iranian group of languages, spoken by *c.*4.4 million people in Tadzhikistan (where it is an official language), Uzbekistan, and nearby territories. The largely Muslim population writes the language in the Arabic alphabet, but Cyrillic is also used in the republics of the former USSR. ➤➤Iranian; Tadzhikistan.

Tadzhikistan (population in 1995 estimated at 5,367,000) The official languages are Tadzhik (spoken by *c.*62% of the population) and Russian (*c.*5%). Other languages include Uzbek (*c.*16%), Farsi, and Pashto. ➤➤Russian; Tadzhik.

tag 1. A structure used in **tag questions**, typically consisting of an auxiliary verb plus a pronoun, attached to the end of a statement in order to convey a negative or positive orientation (e.g. *It's outside, isn't it?*). Some grammarians also recognize **tag statements** (e.g. *That was nice, that was*). ➤➤question. **2.** A grammatical label attached to a word in a computer corpus to indicate its class. The procedure is known as **tagging**. ➤➤corpus; word class.

Tagalog /tə'gɑːləg/ ➤Pilipino.

tagmemics /tag'miːmɪks/ A system of linguistic analysis developed by US linguist Kenneth Pike (1912–), in which language is seen as comprising the three modes of phonology, lexicon, and grammar. The relationship of phonology to phoneme and of lexicon to morpheme is paralleled by grammar to **tagmeme** – a functional slot within a construction frame, where a class of substitutable items can occur. ➤➤frame; morpheme; phoneme; substitution.

Tahitian /tə'hiːʃn/ A member of the Austronesian family of languages, spoken by *c.*125,000 people in the Society Islands, especially Tahiti (where it is an official regional language), New Caledonia, and New Zealand, and widely used as a lingua franca throughout French Polynesia. It is written in the Roman alphabet. ➤➤Austronesian; lingua franca.

Tai /taɪ/ A family of *c.*60 languages found in south-east Asia, in an area centred on Thailand, and extending north-east into Laos, north Vietnam, and China, and north-west into Myanmar (Burma) and India. The spelling 'Tai' is to avoid confusion with the main language of the family, Thai. There are three main groups, spoken in the south-western, central, and northern areas by a total of *c.*75 million people. Most speakers belong to the south-western group. Chief languages include Thai, Lao, Shan, Yuan, Nung, and Tho. The relationship between Tai and other families is unclear: links have been proposed with both the Sino-Tibetan and Austronesian families. Speaker estimates for all languages, in this part of the world, are highly speculative. ➤➤Austronesian; Lao; Sino-Tibetan; Thai.

Taiwan (population in 1995 estimated at 21,419,000) The official language is Chinese, spoken by almost everyone, chiefly Taiwanese (Southern Min, 67%), with Hakka (11%) and Mandarin (20%) also used. There are *c.*20 other (mainly Austronesian) languages, spoken by small numbers. English is used for international purposes. ➤➤Chinese.

Talaing /tə'laɪŋ/ ➤Mon.

tamber/tambre ➤timbre.

Tamil /'tamɪl/ A member of the Dravidian family of languages, spoken by *c.*65 million people, chiefly in India (where *c.*59 million use it as the official state language of Tamil Nadu), Sri Lanka (*c.*3 million), Malaysia, and many parts of the Far East, eastern and southern Africa, and the islands of the Indian and Pacific Oceans. It is written in the Tamil alphabet, found in inscriptions dating from the 3rd century BC, with a literary tradition from the 1st century AD, thus (apart from Sanskrit) providing the oldest literature in India. Present-day Tamil is found written in the Grantha alphabet, used for Sanskrit texts, and in an everyday version called Vaṭṭelluttu ('round script'). The language is found in two main varieties, in a relationship of diglossia. ➤➤diglossia; Dravidian; Sanskrit.

Tanzania (population in 1995 estimated at 31,363,000) The official language is Swahili (spoken by over 90% of the population as a second language). There are over 120 local languages, notably Nyamwezi (*c*.930,000), Makonde (*c*.900,000), Gogo (*c*.1.3 million), Haya (*c*.1.2 million), Sukuma (*c*.5 million), and Chagga (*c*.1 million). Swahili is an important lingua franca. English was a joint official language until 1967. ➤➤English; lingua franca; Swahili.

tap ➤➤flap.

target A hypothetical articulatory state, called a **target articulation**, used as a reference point when describing speech production in dynamic terms. An analogous construct in speech perception is the **auditory target**, proposed to explain the ability of the listener to identify the common factors in different accents and voices. ➤➤articulation; speech perception/production.

target language A language or variety that is the goal of a linguistic operation. Examples include a language into which one is translating, or a language which is being taught to foreigners. ➤➤source.

Tasmanian ➤Indo-Pacific.

Tatar /ˈtɑːtə/ A member of the Turkic branch of the Altaic family of languages, spoken by *c*.8 million people chiefly in Russia (*c*.6 million) in the Tatar region (where it is an official language), and also in parts of Romania, Bulgaria, Turkey, and China. It is written in the Cyrillic alphabet, and there is a literary language based on the dialect of the Kazan area. ➤➤Turkic.

ta-ta theory ➤ding-dong theory.

tautology An unnecessary repetition of a word or idea in speech or writing; repeating something a second or third time without cause. In the philosophy of language, it refers to such self-defining sentences as *A bachelor is an unmarried man*; also called **analytic sentences**. ➤➤pleonasm.

taxonomic linguistics An approach to linguistics which is predominantly or exclusively concerned with procedures of segmentation and classification. In the history of ideas in linguistics, it contrasts with **generative linguistics**, which stresses the role of underlying structure in linguistic analysis. ➤➤generative grammar; linguistics.

Teaching English as a Foreign Language ➤Teaching English to Speakers of Other Languages (TESOL).

Teaching English to Speakers of Other Languages (TESOL) /ˈtiːsɒl/ The teaching of English to anyone who does not have it as a mother tongue; used thus chiefly in American English. Annual TESOL conventions are now a major feature of the English-teaching world in many countries. In British usage, a distinction is widely drawn between two types of situation. (1) English may be taught in countries where it is not the mother tongue, but none the less has a widespread special status within the community (being used for communication in such areas as education, broadcasting, business, law, or government); in this context it is referred to as **Teaching English as a Second Language (TESL)**. There are over 60 such countries, including India, the Philippines, and Ghana. The TESL notion has also been used to describe the teaching of English to immigrant and other groups who live within a country where English is the first language – people who need to speak English at work or in school, but who speak their mother tongue at home. (2) English may be taught in countries where it is not the mother tongue nor does it have any special status, as in Japan, France, Sweden, and most other countries; in this context it is referred to as **Teaching English as a Foreign Language (TEFL)**. ➤English; language teaching.

technique ➤method.

technography A writing system devised for a specialized field. Examples include phonetic transcription, chemical notation, cartographic symbols, and computer machine code. ➤writing.

TEFL (informally /'tefl/) An abbreviation of **Teaching English as a Foreign Language**.

teknonymy /tek'nɒnɪmiː/ The custom of naming a parent after a child, found in certain primitive tribes, such as 'mother of the red-haired one' or 'father of twins'. The term (a **teknonymic**) derives from the Greek word for 'child'. ➤onomastics.

telegrammatic speech Descriptive of an elliptical style of speech in which grammatical words and inflectional endings tend to be omitted; also called **telegraphic speech**. The name derives from the written style used in the days when telegrams were a common method of communication, and people were charged by the word (e.g. *Arriving Monday. Meet train station*). This style is still found in any context where a payment-by-the-word principle applies, such as want-ads in newspapers. The term has also been used as an impressionistic description of the simplified speech used by young children, such as *Man kick ball*. ➤ellipsis.

telestich /tə'lestɪk/ ➤acrostic.

teletext /'teliːtekst/ The transmission of graphic data from a central source to a television screen; also called **teletex**. The approach is known primarily through its use by the broadcasting services, where it deals with such topics as news, weather, and sports results. In Britain, the BBC service is called **Ceefax**, and the ITV service **Oracle**. ➤viewdata.

telic verb /'telɪk/ A verb expressing an event where the activity has a clear terminal point (e.g. *kick*). The contrast is with an **atelic verb**, where the event has no such natural end point (e.g. *play*). ➤aspect; inceptive; verb.

Telugu /'telʊgu:/ A member of the Dravidian family of languages, spoken by *c.*73 million people chiefly (*c.*66 million), in south-east India in Andhra Pradesh (where it is the official state language). It is written in the Telugu alphabet, with records dating from the 7th century, and a literary tradition from about the 11th century. The language is found in two main varieties, in a relationship of diglossia. ➤diglossia; Dravidian.

tempo The linguistic use of speed. There are several contrasts of meaning which can be marked by an increase or decrease in tempo. For example, speakers may speed up while expressing interest or uttering a parenthetic remark; they may slow down while being sarcastic or giving an utterance special emphasis. Contrasts in tempo are analysed in nonsegmental phonology, along with the study of pitch, loudness, and rhythm. ➤prosody; rate of speech; rhythm.

temporal Descriptive of a word or construction which refers to the time of an action or event. Temporal conjunctions include *after* and *when*; temporal adverbials include *then* and *three weeks ago*; and temporal clauses can be illustrated by *when the clock struck four*. ➤adverbial; clause; conjunction.

tense **1**. The grammatical expression of the time of a situation described in a proposition, relative to some other time; traditionally classified into present, past, and future, with other contrasts recognized depending on the language. Tense forms are usually defined as variations in the morphological form of the verb (e.g. *I jump* vs. *I jumped*), but some analyses allow the use of auxiliary verbs to be classified as tenses (e.g. *I have jumped, I will jump*). ➤aorist; aspect; auxiliary verb; future tense; historic present; imperfect; morphology; past/present tense; preterite; verb. **2**. ➤tension.

tension The overall muscular effort used in producing a sound, usually classified into **tense** vs. **lax**, or **fortis** vs. **lenis**. Tense sounds are produced with a relatively strong muscular effort, involving a greater movement of the upper vocal tract away from the position of rest, and a relatively strong spread of acoustic energy; examples include high front or high back vowels. Lax sounds are produced with less muscular effort and movement, and are relatively short and indistinct; examples include centralized vowels. ➤vocal tract; vowel.

term bank A data bank of terminology in a specialized field, compiled to correlate and standardize terms either within a language or between languages. For example, the European Union term bank known as Eurodicautom (European Automatic Dictionary) contains a large number of items in the official languages of the EU. Each term or abbreviation is listed along with a contextual example, equivalent items in other EU languages, a definition, and bibliographical references. ➤lexicography; translation; vocabulary; p. 337.

```
DO TERM
% P001 -DLL V-26
PRESS L FOR TERMINOLOGY OR X FOR ABBREVIATION
*L
TYPE CODE OF SOURCE LANGUAGE
DG GERMAN    DK DANISH      EG ENGLISH     FG FRENCH
IT ITALIAN   NG DUTCH       PT PORTUGUESE  SP SPANISH
*EG
TYPE CODE(S) OF TARGET LANGUAGE(S) WITH SINGLE SPACE BETWEEN
(FOR EXAMPLE: DG NG) OR A FOR ANY LANGUAGES
*A
SOURCE LANGUAGE      :EG
TARGET LANGUAGE(S)   :DG IT FG NG DK SP PT
SUBJECT CODE         :
PRESS Q OR ANOTHER COMMAND
*Q
TYPE YOUR QUESTION
*INFLATION
                                        DOC =  1  PAGE =  1
BE= BIM  TY= TF174  NI= 00381228  DATE = 750220  CF = 4
    CM EC4 EOB
EG VE  INFLATION
   PH  PRICE INFLATION IS MOST LIKELY TO OCCUR WHEN DEMAND
       INCREASES WHILE THE LABOUR SUPPLY IS TIGHT AND THE
       INDUSTRIAL CAPACITY IS FULLY UTILIZED...WHEN SOURCES OF
       SUPPLY DRY UP..
FG VE  INFLATION
   PH  EXCES DE POUVOIR D'ACHAT OU EXCES DES MOYENS DE PAIEMENT.
       ON LA CONFOND SOUVENT...AVEC LA SIMPLE HAUSSE DES PRIX.
       OR CELLE-CI EST LA CONSEQUENCE DE L'INFLATION ET NON DE
       L'INFLATION ELLE-MEME.
       PRESS C TO CONTINUE OR GIVE ANOTHER COMMAND
```

The result of an on-line search for the term *inflation* in the Eurodicautom **term bank**.

terminology The set of technical words used in a particular subject, such as physics, law, cricket – or language study. Terms can be explained in specialized dictionaries (such as this one), term banks, glossaries, and other handbooks. ➤dictionary; jargon; term bank; thesaurus.

TESL An abbreviation of **Teaching English as a Second Language**.

TESOL An abbreviation of **Teaching English to Speakers of Other Languages**.

tetrameter ➤metrics.

Tex-Mex ➤code-mixing; Spanish.

text A piece of naturally occurring spoken, written, or signed discourse identified for purposes of analysis or description. It is often established as a language unit with a definable communicative function, such as a conversation, a poster, or a road sign.

337

Not many men speak only *Esperanto.*

The study of the defining properties of texts – what constitutes their **textuality** or **texture** – is carried on by **textlinguistics**. ➤corpus; discourse analysis.

textlinguistics ➤text.

text retrieval The process of searching a linguistic database for an individual item of text, such as a word, a phrase, or a dictionary entry. The procedure uses indexes especially constructed for the purpose. ➤computational linguistics.

text-to-speech system A system of speech synthesis designed to transform conventional orthographic representations of language into their spoken form. Its applications include information technology and aids for the disabled, such as reading machines for the blind. ➤speech synthesis.

T forms ➤T/V forms.

TG An abbreviation of **transformational grammar**.

Thai /taɪ/ The main member of the Tai family of languages, spoken by *c.*25 million people, chiefly in Thailand, with some in Vietnam, China, and Laos; formerly called **Siamese**. It is written in the Thai alphabet, derived from Devanagari, though the Roman alphabet is used in China. A literary tradition dates from the 13th century. ➤Devanagari; Tai; Thailand.

Thailand (population in 1995 estimated at 60,100,000) The official language is standard Thai, spoken by *c.*40% of the people, with other varieties used by *c.*50%. There are *c.*70 other languages, notably Chinese (chiefly Southern Min, *c.*1 million),

Malay (*c*.2.4 million), and Khmer (*c*.1 million). English is used for international purposes. ➤➤Thai.

***that*-clause** A clause in English which is introduced by the conjunction *that*, or in which *that* is possible, such as *I said (that) it was ready.* ➤➤clause.

theme The first major constituent of a sentence, an important element in the sentence's **thematic structure**. The process of moving an element to the front of the sentence to act as theme is **thematization** or **thematic fronting**. ➤➤fronting; information structure; topic.

theography The study of the language which people use in order to talk about God. The study of religious language in general is sometimes called **theolinguistics**. ➤➤linguistics.

theoretical grammar ➤grammar 1.

thesaurus A book of words and phrases grouped on the basis of their meaning. The most influential and popular work is the *Thesaurus* of Peter Mark Roget (1779–1869), first published in 1852. Roget divided the vocabulary into six main areas: abstract relations, space, matter, intellect, volition, and affections. Each area was then given a detailed and exhaustive sub-classification, resulting in *c*.1000 semantic categories. The semantic information in a thesaurus complements that found in a dictionary: in a dictionary, you know a word and wish to discover its meaning; in a thesaurus, you are aware of a meaning, and wish to discover the relevant word(s). ➤➤lexicography.

third person ➤person.

thorn The name of the runic symbol þ used in Old English and some Middle English manuscripts, corresponding to the sounds of *th* in Modern English. The name is also used in phonetic transcription to represent the voiceless interdental fricative in such words as *thin* – and *thorn*. ➤➤English; fricative.

Tibetan A member of the Tibeto-Burman group of Sino-Tibetan languages, spoken by *c*.1 million people in China, chiefly in the Tibetan region (Xizang), where it has official status, and by *c*.250,000 in other countries, especially India and Nepal. Speaker estimates are highly uncertain, because of the dominant influence of Chinese in the area in recent decades. It is written in the Tibetan alphabet. Written records date from the 7th century, and a predominantly Buddhist literature dates from the 13th century. There are several major dialects, which are sometimes viewed as separate languages. ➤➤Sino-Tibetan.

Tibeto-Burman ➤Sino-Tibetan.

tick-tack A signing system used at dog tracks and racecourses in Britain to circulate information about the way bets are being placed. The signs indicate the amount of a bet, a horse or dog number, and the number of a race. A signer acts as an agent for a group of bookmakers who have bought his 'twist card', on which the dogs and horses are given different numbers to those on the official race card. The same set of tick-tack signs is used by all signers, but only those who have an individual signer's twist card will be able to interpret what a number refers to. ➤➤sign language.

Tigrinya /tɪˈɡrɪnjə/ A member of the Semitic language family, spoken by *c*.3 million people in northern Ethiopia and Eritrea. It is written in the Amharic alphabet. Written texts are of recent origin, and consist largely of missionary and educational materials. ➤➤Amharic; Semitic.

tilde /ˈtɪldə/ A diacritic [~] typically used in phonetic transcription to mark a nasal quality. It is also used in some writing systems, such as Spanish *señor*, where it indicates a palatal quality of *n*. ➤➤palate; transcription.

timbre (also spelled **tamber** or **tambre**) /ˈtambə, ˈtɪmbə/ The attribute of auditory sensation in terms of which a listener can judge the dissimilarity between sounds of otherwise identical pitch, loudness, and length; sometimes called the 'colour' or 'tonal quality' of a sound. For example, an oboe and a clarinet playing the same note with identical loudness and length will still sound distinct, because of their differences in timbre; and the same kind of distinction applies to speech, in such areas as voice quality and vowel description. ➤➤prosody; quality 1; voice quality.

timing Temporal constraints on the articulation and sequencing of sounds in speech production. For example, important matters of timing are involved in the programming of phonotactic sequences or the coordination of musculature. ➤➤articulation; phonotactics; speech production.

tip ➤apical.

Tiv A language spoken around the Benue River in south-eastern Nigeria by *c*.2.2 million people. It is a non-Bantu member of the Benue-Congo language family, and is written in the Roman alphabet. ➤➤Benue-Congo.

Tlingit /ˈtlɪŋɡɪt/ ➤Na-Dene.

Toba Batak /ˈtəʊbə ˈbatak/ ➤Batak.

Tocharian or **Tokharian** /təˈkɛərɪən/ An Indo-European language spoken in the northern part of Chinese Turkistan during the first millennium AD. It is now extinct. Documents dating from the 7th century were discovered only in the 1890s, and translated a decade later. They indicated the existence of two dialect areas – Tocharian A, spoken in the east, and Tocharian B, spoken in the west. The language, written in a syllabic script, is largely preserved in various kinds of commercial document and Buddhist religious text. The relationship between the dialects is unclear, and little has been deduced about the speakers of the language. ➤➤Indo-European; syllabary.

Togo (population in 1995 estimated at 4,074,000) The official language is French. There are *c*.40 other languages, notably Ewe (spoken by *c*.20% of the population as a first language, and widely used as a lingua franca, especially in the south), Kabre, and Gurma. French is used for international purposes. ➤➤French; lingua franca.

***to*-infinitive** ➤infinitive.

Tokelau /'təʊkəlaʊ/ (population in 1995 estimated at 1500) The official language is English. Almost everyone speaks an Austronesian language, Tokelau. ➤➤English.

Tokharian ➤Tocharian.

Tok Pisin /'tɒk 'pɪzɪn/ A pidgin language widely spoken within Papua New Guinea, especially in the north of the country. Many now use it as a mother tongue (c.50,000), and as a lingua franca it may be used by over half the population (c.2 million). It is an English-based pidgin, influenced by local Austronesian languages. ➤➤Austronesian; Papua New Guinea; pidgin.

tone The linguistic functioning of pitch at word level. Tones are usually classified in terms of pitch range and direction into high vs. low, and rising vs. falling vs. level, with more complex sequences (such as rising-falling) often recognized. In a **tone language**, tone is one of the features which determines the lexical meaning of a word. The notion is also used as part of the study of intonation. Here, a **nuclear tone** is the most prominent pitch level in an intonation unit (also called a **tone unit** or **tone group**). The study of the phonetic properties of tone is **tonetics**, and contrastive tones are classified as **tonemes**, the province of **tonemics**. The general study of the forms and uses of tone in language is sometimes called **tonology**. ➤➤contour; falling tone; intonation; pitch.

tonemics ➤tone.

tone of voice. ➤paralanguage.

tonetics ➤tone.

tone unit ➤contour; tone.

Tonga (population in 1995 estimated at 105,000) The official languages are Tongan, spoken by most of the population, and English. English is used for international purposes. ➤➤English; Tongan.

Tongan /'tɒŋgən/ A member of the Austronesian family of languages, spoken by c.103,000 people on Tonga (the Friendly Islands), where it is an official language (along with English) and by c.20,000 more in Hawaii, New Zealand, and other Pacific islands. It is written in the Roman alphabet. ➤➤Austronesian; Tonga.

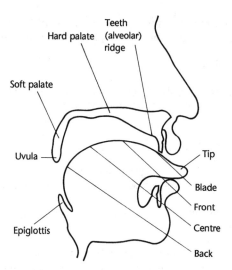

The main parts of the **tongue**, in relation to the roof of the mouth.

tongue The organ of articulation most involved in speech sounds – all the vowels and most of the consonants. Many articulations are classified with reference to the part of the tongue involved: from front to back, the **tip** or **apex**, the **blade** or **front**, the **centre** or **top**, the **back** or **dorsum**, and the **root**. ➤vocal organs; *above*.

tongue slip ➤slip of the tongue.

tongue twister A text made up of words containing the same or similar sounds, which has to be said as rapidly as possible. A familiar English example is *She sells sea-shells by the sea shore*. Tongue twisters provide an example of an unusual kind of word game – one which relates to the spoken medium only. ➤word game.

tonic ➤nucleus; tonicity.

tonicity /təˈnɪsɪtiː/ The place of greatest prominence in an intonation unit, called the **tonic syllable**. The prominence is usually the result of pitch change. For example, in the sentence. *There WAS a cat in the larder*, the word *was* would normally be said with a strong falling tone, and would be the tonic syllable of that tone unit. ➤intonation; tone.

tonology ➤tone.

topic ➤given; paragraph.

toponymy /təˈpɒnɪmiː/ ➤onomastics.

Tosk ➤Albanian.

total communication ➤manualism.

trade language ➤pidgin.

traditional grammar ➤grammar 1.

transcription A method of writing down speech sounds in a systematic and consistent way; also called a **notation**, **script**, or **transcript**. In a **phonetic transcription**, sounds are symbolized on the basis of their articulatory/auditory identity, regardless of their function in a language; this is sometimes called an **impressionistic transcription**. In a **phonemic transcription**, the only units to be symbolized are those which have a linguistic function. In an **allophonic transcription**, phonetic details are added to the phonemic transcription. A phonetic transcription that is relatively detailed is a **narrow transcription**; one less detailed is a **broad transcription**. ➤➤allo-; diacritic; phoneme; phonetics; phonology; transliteration.

transfer The influence of linguistic features of one language upon another, in such contexts as bilingualism and language learning; also called **transference**. Positive transfer makes learning easier, because forms from the native language work correctly in the foreign language. **Negative transfer** (or **interference**) takes place when the use of a native form produces an error in the foreign language. Subject–verb– object word order positively transfers into French, most of the time; but with pronouns, students have to beware that the English pattern (*I saw them*) does not transfer into French (*Je les ai vu*, not **J'ai vu les*). ➤➤contrastive analysis; language learning.

transformation (T) A formal linguistic operation which enables two levels of structural representation to be placed in correspondence. A **transformational rule (T-rule** or **transform)** consists of a sequence of symbols which is rewritten as another sequence, according to certain conventions – for example, English statements and questions can be related by transforming the order of the subject and first auxiliary verb, as in *It's there* vs. *Is it there?*). A grammar which makes use of these notions is a **transformational grammar**; and the term is also applied to the theoretical approach employed. In recent years, transformational grammars have been contrasted with **non-transformational grammars** such as relational grammar and generalized phrase-structure grammar. ➤➤deep structure; generative grammar; standard theory; syntax.

transient ➤transition 2.

transition 1. In phonology, the way adjacent sounds are linked. **Close transitions** involve an articulatory continuity between successive sounds; **open transitions** involve a break in this continuity. ➤➤glide 1; liaison; phonology. **2.** In acoustic phonetics, the acoustic change that takes place as the vocal organs move to and from the articulatory positions of consonants, especially plosives. These **transitional features** or **transients** can be seen on a spectrogram. ➤articulation; formant; plosive; spectrograph.

transitivity A category used in the grammatical analysis of clause/sentence constructions to define the types of relationship between a verb and the presence or absence of object elements. With **transitive** constructions, the verb takes a direct object (e.g. *I saw the book*); with **intransitive** constructions, it does not (e.g. **I arrived the town*). Verbs which take two objects are sometimes called **ditransitive**. Verbs that are marginal to one or the other of these categories are **pseudo-intransitive** (e.g. *The eggs are selling well*). ➤object; unaccusative; verb.

translation The process or result of turning the expressions of one language (the 'source language') into the expressions of another (the 'target language'), so that the meanings correspond. Several levels of translation exist. In a **word-for-word** translation, each word (or morpheme) in the source language is translated by a word (or morpheme) in the target. The result often makes little sense, especially when idioms are involved. In a **literal translation**, the linguistic structure of the source text is followed, but is normalized according to the rules of the target language. In a **free translation**, the linguistic structure of the source language is ignored, and an equivalent is found based on the meaning it conveys. The three levels can be illustrated by French 'translations' of *It's raining cats and dogs: Il est pleuvant chats et chiens* (word-for-word); *Il pleut des chats et des chiens* (literal); *Il pleut à verse* (free). ➤back translation; false friends; interpreting; machine translation; translatology; transliteration.

translatology The study of translation, subsuming both **interpretation** of oral discourse and **translation** (in a narrow sense) of written discourse. The process of transferring an oral message from one language to another at the moment of utterance is variously known as **simultaneous interpretation** or **simultaneous translation**. The oral transference of a written message from one language to another is **sight translation**. ➤interpreting; translation.

transliteration The conversion of one writing system into another. Each character of the source language is given an equivalent character in the target language – as in the representation of Russian names in English. Transliteration is commonly carried out for the names of people, places, institutions, and inventions. Several systems may exist for a single language. Transliteration needs to be distinguished from **transcription**, in which the *sounds* of the source word are conveyed by letters in the target language. ➤kana; Romaji; Roman alphabet; transcription.

tree In generative grammar, a two-dimensional branching diagram used as a means of displaying the internal hierarchical structure of sentences as generated by a set of rules; also called a **tree diagram**. The internal relationships of nodes within

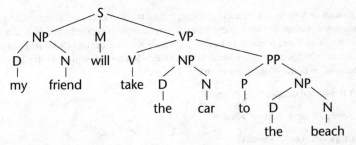

A **tree** diagram showing a possible analysis of a sentence. In the phase, *my friend*, the NP is the mother node of the phrase; D and N are daughter nodes, and are sisters of each other; M refers to a modal element.

the tree are described using 'family tree' terminology (mother, daughter, sister). ➤➤generative grammar; hierarchy; phrase-marker; *above*.

trial ➤dual.

triglossia ➤diglossia.

trigraph /'traɪgraf/ A sequence of three written symbols representing one speech sound. Examples include *manoeuvre*, where the *oeu* represents /u:/, and French *eau* 'water', pronounced /o:/. ➤➤digraph.

trill A type of consonant in which there is a rapid vibration at the point of contact between the articulators; also called a **trilled** or **rolled** consonant. An example is uvular [ʀ]. ➤➤consonant; uvular.

trimeter ➤metrics.

Trinidad and Tobago (population in 1995 estimated at 1,270,000) The official language is English. About 36,000 people on Tobago speak an English-based creole widespread throughout the Lesser Antilles, and there is also a French-based creole used in Trinidad (Trinidadien). There are *c*.50,000 speakers of Hindi on the islands. English is used for international trade and tourism. ➤➤creole; English.

triphthong /'trɪfθɒŋ/ A vowel with two perceptible changes of quality within a single syllable. Examples include some pronunciations of the words *tire* /taɪə/ and *hour* /aʊə/ in English. ➤➤diphthong; monophthong; vowel.

trisyllable A linguistic unit (typically a word) consisting of three syllables. ➤➤syllable.

trochee /'trəʊkiː/ ➤foot.

trope ➤figurative language.

Tswana or **Setswana** /'tswɑːnə/ A member of the Bantu group of Benue-Congo languages, spoken in many dialects by *c.*3.9 million people, chiefly in South Africa (*c.*2.8 million) and Botswana (1 million), where it is one of the official languages. The language is sometimes referred to as **Western Sotho**. It is written in the Roman alphabet. ➤Benue-Congo; Botswana; Sotho.

TTR ➤lexical density.

Tuareg /'twareg, 'tʊəreg/ ➤Berber.

Tungus /tʊŋ'guːz/ ➤Evenki.

Tunisia (population in 1995 estimated at 8,902,000) The official language is Arabic, spoken by *c.*98% of the population. There are a few Berber languages, spoken by unclear numbers, and several thousand speakers of French. French is used for international purposes. ➤Arabic.

Tupian /tuːˈpiːən/ ➤Andean-Equatorial.

Turkey (population in 1995 estimated at 62,964,000) The official language is Turkish, spoken by *c.*90% of the population. There are *c.*30 other languages, notably Adygey, Arabic, Armenian, Azerbaijani, Georgian, Kurdish (*c.*4 million), and Romani. English is used for international purposes. ➤Turkish.

Turkic A group of *c.*40 languages within the Altaic family, spoken in Asia Minor and southern Asia by over 100 million people. Major languages in the south-west include Turkish, Azerbaijani, and Turkmen; in the south-east, Uzbek and Uighur; and in the north-west, Tatar, Kazakh, Kirghiz, and Bashkir. Many of the languages are spoken by small numbers, especially in the north-east. Literary forms date from the 8th century, in the case of the Asian languages. Formerly, the Arabic alphabet was in general use, but in the present century this has been largely replaced by Roman (in Turkey) or Cyrillic alphabets. Linguistically, the distinctive feature of most languages in the family is the use of vowel harmony. ➤Azerbaijani; Bashkir; Chuvash; harmony; Kazakh; Kirghiz; Tatar; Turkish; Turkmen; Uighur; Uzbek; Yakut.

Turkish The chief member of the Turkic group of the Altaic family of languages, spoken by *c.*59 million people, chiefly in Turkey (*c.*55 million), with some in Bulgaria and other nearby countries, including Turkish Cyprus (where it is an official language), and in several European countries as an immigrant language. The language has three periods, distinguished as Old Turkish (13th–15th centuries), Middle Turkish (16th–18th centuries), and Modern Turkish thereafter. The golden age of literature in the language followed the capture of Constantinople (1453). Though Turkish was previously written in the Arabic alphabet, the Roman alphabet was introduced in 1929 as part of Kemal Atatürk's modernization programme in Turkey, which included a movement for language reform. Turkish is well known for its use of vowel harmony: generally, all the vowels of a word must be either front or back, and there are constraints on whether they may be rounded or unrounded. ➤➤harmony; rounding; Turkey; Turkic; vowel.

Turkmen A member of the Turkic branch of the Altaic family of languages, spoken by *c*.5.4 million people, chiefly (*c*.3.4 million) in Turkmenistan (where it is an official language), parts of Kazakhstan and Uzbekistan, and also in Iran, Afghanistan, Pakistan, and Iraq. It has a literary tradition from the 14th century, with a new standard introduced in the present century. It was traditionally written in the Arabic alphabet, but in the present century the Cyrillic alphabet came to be used in the republics of the former Soviet Union, with the Roman alphabet widespread elsewhere. ➤➤Cyrillic; Turkmenistan; Turkic.

Turkmenistan (population in 1995 estimated at 4,322,000) The official languages are Turkmen (spoken by *c*.80% of the population), and Russian (*c*.8%). Other languages include Baluchi and Uzbek. ➤➤Russian; Turkmen.

turn In conversation analysis, a single contribution of a participant in a conversation, preceded and followed by speech from other participants; also called a **conversational turn**. In this framework, **turn-taking** is seen as a coordinated and rule-governed aspect of conversational interaction. ➤➤adjacency pair; conversation analysis.

Tuvalu (population in 1995 estimated at 10,100) The official language is English. Tuvaluan is spoken by almost everyone. ➤➤English.

T/V forms Alternative pronoun forms expressing different kinds of orientation to the addressee. The T forms (so-called from the initial of French *tu*) are typically singular and mark familiarity; the V forms (from French *vous*) are typically plural and mark politeness. Other languages contrast 2nd and 3rd person pronouns in a similar way, such as Spanish *tu* (familiar), *Usted* (polite). A mutual use of T encodes intimacy and social closeness; a mutual use of V encodes respect and social distance. Asymmetrical usage identifies a power or status imbalance. ➤➤address, forms of; pronoun.

twin language ➤idioglossia.

type-token ratio ➤lexical density.

typescript Printed material produced with a typewriter. Traditional typewriters have the advantage over everyday handwriting, in terms of clarity and speed, but they lack the range of typographic contrasts available in printing (such as variations in type size and shape, and the provision of special symbols), and they employ several idiosyncratic conventions (such as the use of underlining for italics). Modern word-processors and electronic typewriters have overcome many of these disadvantages. ➤➤typography; writing.

typo A mistake made by a typist or typesetter when composing a line of print;

technically called a **literal**. The notion usually applies to single letters or very short sequences. ➤➤typography.

typography The study of the selection and organization of letter-forms and other graphic features of the printed page. The subject deals with all matters which affect the appearance of a page, and which contribute to the effectiveness of a printed message. These include the shapes and sizes of letters, diacritics, punctuation marks, and special symbols; the distances between letters and words; the length of lines; the space between lines; the size of margins; the extent and location of illustrations; the use of colour; the selection of headings; and all other factors to do with spatial configuration (or 'layout'). ➤➤ascender; bold; diacritic; font; graphic translatability; headline; italics; indention; leading; letter; ligature; point size; punctuation; serif; sort; subscript; typo; writing.

typological linguistics ➤typology of language.

typology of language A branch of linguistics which studies the structural similiarities between languages, regardless of their history; also called **typological linguistics**. Typological comparison is part of an attempt to establish language relationships especially in cases where there is no historical evidence available to support a classification on genetic grounds. Several notions have been recognized. An **analytic**, **isolating**, or **root** language is one in which the words are invariable, and syntactic relationships are shown by word order, such as Chinese and Vietnamese. This notion contrasts with a **synthetic**, **fusional**, or **inflecting** (also called **inflected** or **inflectional**) language, where the words typically contain more than one morpheme, but there is no one-to-one correspondence between these morphemes and the linear structure of the word. Examples include Latin, Greek, and Arabic. An **agglutinative** or **agglutinating** language is one in which words are built up by stringing forms together, often into quite lengthy sequences. Turkish, Japanese, and Swahili are of this type. An **incorporating** or **polysynthetic** language is one characterized by long, complex word forms, containing a mixture of agglutinative and inflectional features, often functioning as entire sentences. This type (not recognized in all classifications) can be seen in Australian aboriginal languages. ➤➤genetic classification; inflection 1; language 1; morpheme; root 1; word order.

U

U and non-U A distinction which describes the linguistic demarcation that supposedly exists between 'upper-class' (U) and 'other' (non-U) usage in British English. It was introduced in 1954 by British linguist Alan Ross, and popularized by novelist Nancy Mitford soon after. It reflected distinctive pronunciation and vocabulary, as well as written language conventions. Examples include U *luncheon* vs. non-U *dinner*, U *lavatory* vs. non-U *toilet*, and U *sick* vs. non-U *ill*. Although a personal and subjective account, it drew attention to many kinds of usage variation, and has remained in the public consciousness ever since. ➤ variety; *cartoon below*.

UC An abbreviation of **ultimate constituent**.

Udmurt /ˈʊdmʊət/ A member of the Finnic group of the Finno-Ugric family of

'I've been calling the drawing-room a lounge again, Father.'

languages, spoken by *c*.550,000 people, chiefly in the Udmurt region of Russia (where it has official status); formerly called **Votyak**. It is written in the Cyrillic alphabet. ➤➤Finno-Ugric.

Uganda (population in 1995 estimated at 21,368,000) The official language is English. There are *c*.40 other languages, notably Ganda (Luganda, *c*.16% of the population), Nkole (Nyankore, *c*.8%), Teso (*c*.8%), and Rwanda (*c*.6%). Gujarati and Hindi each have *c*.150,000 speakers. Swahili is widely used as a lingua franca, as are English and Ganda. English is used for international purposes. ➤➤English; lingua franca.

Ugaritic /uːɡəˈrɪtɪk/ A Semitic language known from a wide range of clay tablet inscriptions dating from the 15th to the 13th centuries BC, found in 1929 mainly at Ugarit (a city lying in an artificial mound called Ras Shamra, on the coast of modern Syria). The writing system is a previously unknown alphabet, written in a cuneiform script, from left to right, and containing 30 symbols (including three vowel signs). The texts deal mainly with legends and myths of the Canaanite peoples, and have provided a fresh perspective on several of the stories in the Old Testament of the Bible. ➤➤alphabet; cuneiform; Semitic.

Ugric /ˈjuːɡrɪk, ˈuːɡrɪk/ ➤Finno-Ugric.

Uighur /ˈwiːɡʊə/ A member of the Turkic branch of the Altaic family of languages, spoken by over 7.5 million people, chiefly (*c*.7.2 million) in the Xinjiang-Uighur region of China, with some in Uzbekistan, Kazakhstan (*c*.300,000), Kyrgyzstan, and Afghanistan. The language was formerly written in the Arabic alphabet, with the Roman alphabet widespread in China since the 1930s, and Cyrillic now used in the republics of the former Soviet Union. ➤➤Turkic.

Ukraine (population in 1995 estimated at 52,570,000) The official languages are Ukrainian (spoken by *c*.60% of the population) and Russian (*c*.20%). Other languages include several of those spoken in nearby countries, such as German, Belorussian, Romanian, and Bulgarian, and there are a number of speakers of Romani. ➤➤Russian; Ukrainian.

Ukrainian A member of the East Slavic group of languages, spoken by over 40 million people, chiefly (*c*.31 million) in the republic of Ukraine (where it is the official language), with many more in Hungary (*c*.300,000), Kazakhstan (*c*.900,000), Moldova (*c*.600,000), Poland (1.5 million), and other nearby areas. There are also many immigrant speakers, especially in the USA, Canada, and South America. It is written in the Cyrillic alphabet. Traces of Ukrainian date from the 13th century, but the modern standard language did not emerge until the late 18th century. The language contains a large number of Polish loan words. ➤➤Slavic; Ukraine.

ultimate constituent ➤constituent.

umlaut /ˈʌmlaʊt/ A sound change in which a sound is influenced by the vowel in the following syllable. An example is Germanic *gosi*, where the final vowel caused a change of /oː/ to /iː/, resulting in *geese*. ➤➤sound change.

unaccented syllable ➤accent 2.

unacceptable ➤acceptable.

unaccusative Descriptive of an intransitive verb whose subject originates as an object; also sometimes called an **ergative verb**. An example is *The vase broke* (i.e. someone or something broke the vase). ➤➤transitivity; verb.

uncial /'ʌnʃəl/ A form of writing consisting of large, rounded letters. It was especially used in Greek and Latin manuscripts from the 4th to the 8th centuries AD, and a later development (**half-uncial** or **semi-uncial**) prepared the way for modern small letters. The name derives from Latin *uncialis* 'inch-high'. ➤➤letter; writing.

(a)

(b)

An **uncial** script of the fourth centure AD. The Latin reads *Vae autem praegnantibus et lactan*. (b) A half-uncial script from *c.* 500 AD. The Latin reads *proferrem non queror quia [igno]ro sed tamen quaerella fam[osa]*.

uncountable noun ➤countability.

underextension ➤overextension.

underlying Descriptive of an abstract level of representation, postulated to explain the patterns encountered in the empirical data of a language. The notion of **underlying forms** is central to generative grammar, where a stage of underlying structure is recognized in the derivation of a sentence. ➤➤deep structure; generative grammar.

ungradable ➤gradability.

ungrammatical ➤grammatical.

unification An operation in several grammatical theories whereby two categories can be combined as long as they do not contain conflicting information. Theories which permit this operation are known as 'unification-based' approaches. ➤➤grammar 1.

United Arab Emirates (population in 1995 estimated at 2,181,000) The official language is Arabic, spoken by over a third of the population. There are *c.*20 other immigrant languages, including Baluchi, Bengali, English, Farsi, Pashto, Sinhala, Somali, Swahili, Tagalog, and Telugu. English is used for international purposes. ➤Arabic.

United Kingdom (population in 1995 estimated at 58,541,000) The official language is English. Welsh (in Wales) and Scottish Gaelic (in Scotland) have official regional status. Also found within the British Isles are Manx (in the Isle of Man), and French (*c.*15,000 speakers in Jersey and Guernsey). There is some Irish Gaelic in Northern Ireland. There are over 100 immigrant languages, spoken by *c.*2 million people, notably Bengali, Chinese, Greek, Gujarati, Hindi, Italian, Panjabi, Polish, Portuguese, Spanish, Turkish, Ukrainian, Urdu, and Vietnamese. Several Romani varieties are spoken by an uncertain number (perhaps 90,000). ➤English.

United States of America (population in 1995 estimated at 262,693,000) The union language is English. French (Cajun) has official regional status in Louisiana, and Spanish in New Mexico. There are *c.*170 Indian languages spoken. The major immigrant languages are English (*c.*226 million), Spanish (*c.*23 million), Arabic (*c.*3 million), French (*c.*1.7 million), Chinese (*c.*1.6 million), Italian (*c.*1.3 million), and varieties of German (Hutterite, Pennsylvania, Mennonite, *c.*1.5 million) – but there are over 350 languages spoken by significant numbers in the USA today. About 32 million people speak an immigrant language other than (or in addition to) English at home, according to the 1990 census. About 300,000 people still speak one or other of the *c.*170 Amerindian languages (though the number recognized depends on the classification used), and there are *c.*1 million speakers of Romani. Several English-based creoles are in use, especially in the south, along the Atlantic coast (Sea Islands Creole English, formerly often called Gullah, *c.*130,000), and in Hawaii; and there is a French-based creole spoken by *c.*60,000 in Louisiana. ➤American Samoa; Amerindian; creole; English; Guam; Hawaiian Islands; Mariana Islands, Northern; Marshall Islands; Micronesia, Federated States of; Palau; US Virgin Islands.

universal A property claimed to be characteristic of all languages, or a defining property of language; also called a **language universal**. **Universal grammar** aims to specify the possible forms of a human grammar, especially the restrictions on the form such grammars can take. **Statistical universals** are constants of a statistical kind, such as a ratio of use between different structures. **Implicational universals** are generalized statements of the form 'If X occurs in a language, then Y will (or will not) occur in a language'. **Absolute universals** are properties that all languages share, without exception. **Relative universals** are general tendencies in language, with principled exceptions. In generative linguistics, **formal universals** are the necessary conditions which have to be imposed on the construction of grammars in order for them to be able to operate (e.g. types of rule, number of components). **Substantive universals** are the primitive elements in a grammar, required for the analysis of linguistic data (e.g. NP, VP), and classified into phonological, syntactic, and other types. The **Universal Base Hypothesis** states that all languages can be generated by using the same set of basic rules. ➤formalization; generative grammar; grammar 1; statistical linguistics.

Universal Declaration of Linguistic Rights A document drawn up at an international conference in Barcelona in 1996, proclaiming the equality of language rights, seen both collectively (in relation to whole communities) and individually (in relation to the rights of individuals within communities). The document, which takes its place in a series of political statements dating back to the 1948 Universal Declaration of Human Rights, was being seen as an initial step towards the establishment of a United Nations convention on language rights. It drew attention to the need for principles to be found which would guarantee the promotion of and respect for all languages and their social use, highlighted the plight of the world's endangered languages, and emphasized the need for any universal approach to be based on a conception of linguistic and cultural diversity. Its statements of inalienable personal rights included: the right to be recognized as a member of a language community; the right to the use of one's own language both in private and in public; the right to the use of one's own name; the right to interrelate and associate with other members of one's language community of origin; and the right to maintain and develop one's own culture. Its statement of collective rights included: the right for a community's own language and culture to be taught; the right of access to cultural services; the right to an equitable presence of its language and culture in the communications media; and the right to receive attention in its own language from government bodies and in socioeconomic relations. ➤ecolinguistics; endangered languages.

universal grammar ➤grammar 1.

universal language ➤artificial language.

universal quantifier ➤quantifier.

univocalic /juːnɪvəʊˈkalɪk/ A word game in which the aim is to construct a grammatical and meaningful text in which the words contain the same vowel. Short sentences are not too difficult to compose (*We were never seen except when the rest left*), but several lengthy texts have been successfully completed. ➤word game.

unjustified ➤justified.

unmarked ➤markedness.

unproductive ➤productivity.

unrounded ➤rounding.

unvoiced ➤voicing.

upper case ►letter.

Uralic /juːˈralɪk/ A family of *c*.30 languages whose ancestor (Proto-Uralic) was spoken in the region of the north Ural Mountains, Russia, over 7000 years ago. Two main branches of the family are represented today: Finno-Ugric and Samoyedic. Written records date from the 13th century, but there has been a marked decline in many of the languages in the present century, chiefly because of the dominant influence of Russian. About 24 million people now speak Uralic languages. ►►Finno-Ugric; Samoyedic.

urban dialectology ►dialectology.

Urdu /ˈɜːduː/ A member of the Midland group of Indo-Aryan languages, spoken by *c*.56 million people as a first language in India and Pakistan, and by many others as an immigrant language in Great Britain and elsewhere. It is an official language, along with English, in Pakistan (1995 population over 141 million), and a very large number (perhaps as many as 200 million) use it as a religious language (alongside Arabic). Urdu displays very little structural difference with Hindi, but there is a marked cultural difference between them, as Urdu is predominantly the language of Muslims in the area (as opposed to Hindus), displaying the considerable influence of Persian and Arabic vocabulary, and written in a form of the Persian Arabic alphabet. Literary texts are known from the 14th century. ►►Hindi; Indo-Aryan; Pakistan.

Uruguay (population in 1995 estimated at 3,187,000) The official language is Spanish, used by virtually the whole population. English and Spanish are used for international purposes. ►►Spanish.

usage The collective speech and writing habits of a community. The notion is seen especially within the perspective of individuals' preferences for alternative linguistic forms (**divided usage**). One person's usage will always be different from another's, in certain respects. ►►corpus; prescriptivism.

US Virgin Islands (population in 1995 estimated at 113,000) The official language is English. About half the population use an English-based creole widespread throughout the Lesser Antilles, and there are some speakers of a Portuguese-based creole (Papiamentu), and of Spanish. ►►creole; English.

utterance A stretch of speech typically preceded or followed by silence or by a change of speaker. The notion is also used in a loose sense, referring to any stretch of speech about which no assumptions have been made in terms of linguistic theory (thus contrasting with the concept of **sentence**). ►►sentence.

uvular /ˈjuːvjʊlə/ Descriptive of a consonant sound made by the back of the tongue against the back of the soft palate or **uvula**. An example is the *r* sound widely used in French, as at the beginning of *rose*. ►►palate; tongue.

Uzbek /ˈʊzbek/ A member of the Turkic branch of the Altaic family of languages, spoken by over 18 million people, chiefly (16.5 million) in Uzbekistan (where it is an official language), with some in nearby parts of Turkmenistan, Tadzhikistan, Kazakhstan, Afghanistan, and China. It is written in the Cyrillic alphabet in the republics of the former Soviet Union, and in the Arabic alphabet elsewhere. A literary tradition, largely Islamic in character, dates from the 9th century. ➤➤Turkic; Uzbekistan.

Uzbekistan (population in 1995 estimated at 21,669,000) The official languages are Uzbek (spoken by *c.*75% of the population) and Russian (*c.*7%). There are *c.*5 other languages, including Crimean Tatar (Crimean Turkish, *c.*190,000), Karakalpak (*c.*400,000), and Arabic. ➤➤Russian; Uzbek.

V

V An abbreviation of **verb**.

valency /'veɪlənsiː/ The number and type of bonds that syntactic elements may form with each other. A **valency grammar** presents a model of a sentence containing a fundamental element (typically, the verb) and a number of dependent elements or **valents** (also called arguments, expressions, or complements) whose number and type is determined by the valency attributed to the verb. A **monovalent** verb has a valency of 1 (e.g. *vanish* can take only a subject); a **bivalent** verb of 2 (e.g. *scrutinize*); a **trivalent** verb of 3 (e.g. *give*); and a **zero valency** (or **avalent**) verb takes no complements at all (e.g. *rain*). Verbs which differ in these ways belong to different **valency sets**. ➤syntax; verb.

Valentine An expression of love on St Valentine's Day (14 February). The phenomenon is of linguistic interest because of the bizarre language which the usually anonymous lovers employ to convey their message and hide their real names. Several national newspapers now devote space to publishing Valentines. ➤hypocoristic.

Vanuatu (population in 1995 estimated at 167,000) The official languages are English, French, and Bislama (the last widely used as a lingua franca). There are *c*.100 other languages (almost all of them Austronesian) spoken by very small numbers. English and French are used for international purposes. ➤Bislama; English; French; lingua franca.

variable In sociolinguistics, a linguistic unit subject to social or stylistic variation, with reference to such factors as region, social class, age, and sex; also called a **sociolinguistic variable** or **variant**. The results of this variation are stated in the form of **variable rules**, which specify the socio-regional conditions under which they apply. For example, in one New York study, the use of final /r/ (in words like *car*) was found to be affected by socioeconomic group membership: the higher the group, the more likely its members were to use /r/. ➤diffusion; sociolinguistics.

variable word ➤invariable word.

variant ➤variable.

variety Any system of linguistic expression whose use is governed by situational variables, such as regional, occupational, or social class factors. The term is sometimes used more narrowly, referring to a single kind of situationally distinctive language. Varieties of English include scientific, religious, legal, formal, conversational, American, Welsh, and Cockney. ➤➤dialect; diglossia; lect; New Englishes; stylistics.

Vatican City (population in 1998 estimated at 1000) The official language is Italian. Latin has special status as the official language of the Roman Catholic Church. ➤➤Italian; Latin.

velar /'viːlə/ Descriptive of a consonant sound made by the back of the tongue against the soft palate or **velum**, such as [k] and [g]. Any secondary articulation involving a movement towards the velum is called **velarization**. Such **velarized** sounds have a distinctive back (or 'dark') resonance. ➤➤consonant; secondary articulation; tongue.

velaric /viːˈlarɪk/ Descriptive of sounds in which the tongue in contact with the velum initiates an airstream capable of making consonant sounds. An ingressive flow of air results, used in the production of click consonants. ➤➤click; velar.

velum /'viːləm/ ➤palate; velar.

Venezuela (population in 1995 estimated at 21,547,000) The official language is Spanish, spoken by almost all the population. There are *c*.40 other languages, many spoken by tiny numbers. Spanish and English are used for international purposes. ➤➤Spanish.

verb (V) A word class, traditionally defined as a 'doing' or 'action' word, formally identifiable in many languages as an element displaying contrasts of tense, aspect, voice, mood, person, and number. Functionally, it is the element which can be used as the minimal predicate of a sentence, co-occurring with a subject (e.g. *She answered*), and generally dictating the number and nature of other elements in the predicate. Traditionally, a **verb phrase** is a group of verbs which together have the same syntactic function as a single verb (e.g. *He left / may have left*); also called a **verbal group** or **verbal cluster**. In such sequences, one verb is the **main verb** or **lexical verb**; other verbs are subordinate to it – notably, the **auxiliary verbs**. A verb followed by a nonverbal particle is a **phrasal verb**. In generative grammar, the term **verb phrase** has a broader definition, being equivalent to the whole of the predicate of a sentence. ➤➤aspect; catenative; impersonal; mood; number; person; predicate; tense 1; voice 1.

verbal apraxia ➤apraxia.

verbal duelling The competitive use of language, within a gamelike structure, with rules that are known and used by the participants. It is a ritual dialogue in which each speaker attempts to outdo an opponent by producing an utterance of increased verbal ingenuity. An ancient behaviour, it is seen in the ritual cursing and boasting recorded in several early epic texts. In modern times, it has been observed in the trading of insults between street gangs in many parts of the world. ➤➤flyting; verbal play.

verbal group ➤verb.

verbal paraphasia ➤paraphasia.

verbal play The playful manipulation of the elements of language, either in relation to each other, or in relation to the social or cultural contexts of language use; also called **speech play**. Humour is not an essential part of the definition. The notion includes play languages, puns, jokes, verbal duelling, proverbs, and riddles. ➤➤chronogram; macaronic; play language; proverb; pun; rhopalic; riddle; verbal duelling; wellerism.

verbless clause A clause in which the verb is omitted (and often the subject as well). An example is *When ready, we left the house.* ➤➤clause.

verb phrase ➤verb.

vernacular The indigenous language or dialect of a speech community. Pidgin languages are sometimes called **contact vernaculars**. ➤➤Black English Vernacular; pidgin.

Verner's law A sound change, first worked out by the Danish linguist Karl Verner (1846–96), which explained a class of apparent exceptions to Grimm's law. He found that Grimm's law worked well whenever the stress fell on the root syllable of the Sanskrit word; but when it fell on another syllable, the consonants behaved differently. Voiceless plosives then did not stay as voiceless fricatives, but became voiced plosives. ➤➤fricative; Grimm's law; plosive; sound change.

V forms ➤T/V forms.

vibrato /vɪbˈrɑːtəʊ/ A tiny, rapid, controlled rise and fall in the pitch and volume of the voice, usually heard only in singing. Vibrato adds warmth and richness to the voice, and is a noticeable feature of the voice of the professional (as opposed to the amateur) singer. ➤➤voice quality.

Vietnam (population in 1995 estimated at 73,655,000) The official language is Vietnamese, spoken by *c.*87% of the population. There are *c.*70 other languages, including several varieties of Tai (*c.*1 million), Muong (*c.*800,000), Khmer (*c.*800,000), and (Yue) Chinese (*c.*500,000). French is used for international purposes. ➤➤Vietnamese.

Vietnamese The chief language of the Mon-Khmer family, spoken by *c.*65 million people in Vietnam, with perhaps a further million in Cambodia and many thousands in Western countries through refugee movements following the Vietnam War; formerly known as **Annamite**. It is written in the Roman alphabet introduced by missionaries in the 17th century, and known as *Quoc-ngu* ('national language'). Its status in the Mon-Khmer group is a matter of dispute: some scholars see it as a marginal member, while some relate it to the Tai family. Its early history is obscured by the use of Chinese throughout the area, a consequence of rule by China until the 10th century. ➤➤Chinese; Mon-Khmer; Tai; Vietnam.

viewdata The interactive transmission of data between a central source and a local television set. Computer-stored information is sent through the telephone system, but viewers are allowed to return data to the computer, thus permitting a wide range of services, such as shopping and travel booking from home. In Britain, the trade name of this service, started by British Telecom in 1979, is **Prestel**. ➤➤teletext.

Virgin Islands ➤British Virgin Islands; US Virgin Islands.

virgule /ˈvɜːgjuːl/ ➤solidus.

visible speech Any system in which speech is represented other than by the usual writing system (such as the letters of the alphabet). The term is chiefly used for systems of graphic or manual symbols which have been devised for a particular teaching purpose (such as in teaching the deaf or the mentally handicapped). In a 19th-century usage, Scottish educator Alexander Melville Bell devised a system of visible speech for the deaf in which the symbols represented the positions of the vocal organs. The term is also used loosely for the acoustic representation of speech shown in a spectrogram, or for symbols based on this representation. ➤➤spectrograph.

Visigothic /ˈvɪziːɡɒθɪk/ ➤Gothic.

vocabulary The set of lexical items ('words') in a language; also called the **lexicon**. Estimates of vocabulary size, either for a language as a whole or for an individual speaker, are notoriously unreliable, chiefly because there are so many variables which need to be taken into account; the scale of the task, moreover, is daunting. The largest dictionaries of English contain well over half a million words, but do not include a great deal of the regional vocabulary found in local and international dialects, nor much of the vast field of scientific nomenclature (such as in natural history). Estimates of an individual's active vocabulary are also highly variable, as so much depends on interests and educational background. They generally range from 20,000 to 50,000 words, with passive vocabulary estimates tending to be two or three times larger. ➤➤active knowledge; etymology; lexicon; semantics; term bank.

vocal abuse Overuse of the muscles of the larynx and pharynx, resulting in a voice disorder. The problem may arise from excessive shouting, or from straining the voice over a period of time (such as in trying to talk in a noisy environment). ➤➤dysphonia; vocal nodule.

vocal–auditory channel ➤communication; speech chain.

vocal cords ➤vocal folds.

vocal folds Two bands of muscular tissue within the larynx, which vibrate in response to an airstream; also called **vocal cords, vocal bands**, or occasionally **vocal lips**. The vocal folds are important in the production of voiced sounds, variations in pitch, and several voice qualities. ➤➤glottal; larynx; phonation; voice quality; voicing.

vocal fry ➤creaky voice.

vocalization An utterance viewed solely as a sequence of sound, without reference to its internal linguistic structure, if any. For example, **infant vocalization** refers to a prelinguistic period of utterance by very young children. ➤➤babbling.

vocal nodule A small localized swelling on the vocal folds; also called a **vocal node**. Vocal nodules are often found as a result of people overusing their voice (continually shouting in a noisy environment, for example), and result in a hoarse or breathy voice quality which may not disappear without speech therapy or surgical intervention. ➤➤dysphonia; speech therapy.

vocal organs The physiological structures actively involved in the process of speaking; also called the **organs of speech**. They are usually grouped into three systems: the *respiratory system*, containing the lungs and trachea; the *larynx*, enclosing the vocal folds; and the *supralaryngeal system*, comprising the movable organs in the mouth (primarily the tongue, lips, lower jaw, soft palate), the relatively fixed structures in the mouth (primarily the teeth and hard palate), the pharynx, and the nasal cavity. ➤➤larynx; pharynx; tongue; vocal tract; p. 361.

vocal tract The whole of the air passage above the larynx, the shape of which is the main factor affecting the quality of speech sounds; generally divided into the *nasal* and *oral* tracts. The term is sometimes used in a more general way for the whole of the respiratory tract involved in speech sound production (including lungs and larynx). ➤➤cavity; larynx; vocal organs; p. 361.

vocative case One of the ways in which an inflected language makes a word change its form, in order to show its relationship to other words in the sentence. The vocative is the case used when a noun phrase (typically, a single noun or pronoun) is used in the function of direct address. In non-inflecting languages, the term refers to any noun phrase used in this function (often with a distinctive intonation), such as the last item in the sentence *The dog is in the garden, Hilary.* ➤➤case; inflection 1.

voice 1. A category used in grammatical description, chiefly with reference to the verb, to express the way a clause may alter the relationship between subject and object without changing the meaning of the sentence. When the grammatical subject is the actor, in relation to the verb, the clause is said to be **active**; when it is the goal or recipient of the action denoted by the verb, it is said to be **passive**. The transformation of a sentence from an active to a passive is called **passivization**. The term **middle** is sometimes used (especially in grammars of Classical Greek) for actions which seem to fall between these two possibilities, such as 'I hurt myself'. ➤➤clause; verb 2. ➤voicing.

voice box ➤larynx.

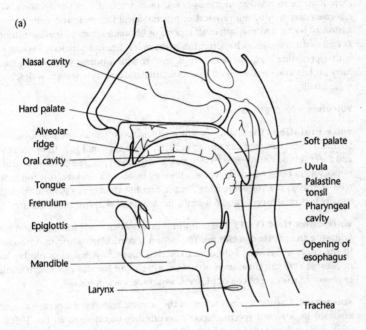

(a)

Nasal cavity

Hard palate

Alveolar ridge

Oral cavity

Tongue

Frenulum

Epiglottis

Mandible

Larynx

Soft palate

Uvula

Palastine tonsil

Pharyngeal cavity

Opening of esophagus

Trachea

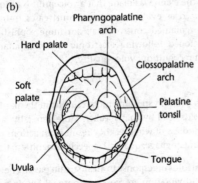

(b)

Pharyngopalatine arch

Hard palate

Glossopalatine arch

Soft palate

Palatine tonsil

Uvula

Tongue

The main features of the **vocal tract**: (a) side view; (b) front view of oral cavity.

voice disorder An involuntary, abnormal voice quality which interferes with communication or draws unfavourable attention to the speaker's voice (e.g. by being inappropriate in relation to the age, sex, or physical size of the speaker). Voice disorders may result from physical or psychological factors (often, from a combination of both), and may affect all aspects of phonation (pitch, loudness, timbre) as well as the resonance characteristics of the voice. Examples include a young man with a persisting high-pitched voice, a teacher with a hoarse voice which fails to carry in class, and someone with an unpleasant nasal quality in speech. ►dysphonia; voice quality.

voiceless ►voicing.

voice mutation The change of voice which accompanies the development of secondary sex characteristics during puberty. There is a rapid growth of the larynx, and the child voice differentiates into male and female types. The effect is particularly noticeable in boys, where the voice is lowered by about an octave. It is common to refer to this as the voice 'breaking', but in fact the change is a gradual transition, usually taking between 3 and 6 months to complete. ►larynx; voice quality.

voice onset time (VOT) The point in time at which vocal fold vibration starts, following the release of a closure. The notion is particularly important in relation to the contrast between voiced and voiceless plosives. A voiceless plosive has a noticeable VOT gap (an average of 0.06 sec. after [p], in one study), which is minimal or absent in the case of voiced plosives. ►plosive; vocal folds.

voiceprint A visual representation of the acoustic features of a person's voice, as analysed by a sound spectrograph. Voiceprinting was devised in the 1960s, on analogy with fingerprinting, and the claim was made that a voiceprint is unique to an individual. Although introduced as evidence in some court cases (primarily in the USA), the technique has remained controversial, but more sophisticated approaches are now being developed following electronic and computational advances. ►spectrograph; speech recognition; voice quality.

voice qualifier ►paralanguage.

voice quality Those aspects of a person's speech which result from the particular mode of vibration of the vocal folds used by that speaker. More generally, all the personal attributes of a voice, regardless of whether they result from actions of the vocal folds or of other organs. ►paralanguage; quality 1; speech recognition; timbre.

voicing The vibration of the vocal folds in response to an airstream passing between them. Sounds which use vocal fold vibration are **voiced**; those which do not are **voiceless** or **unvoiced**. Voiced sounds may be **devoiced** under certain conditions, such as the final /d/ of /dad/ in English. ►devoiced; vocal folds.

Volapük /vɒləˈpyk/ A language invented by Johann Martin Schleyer in 1880; the name means 'world speak'. Based largely on English and German, it was the first large-scale proposal of its kind. ➤➤artificial language.

Voltaic /vɒl'teɪɪk/ A group of *c.*70 languages belonging to the Niger-Congo family, spoken in several countries around the Upper Volta River in West Africa; also called the **Gur** group of languages. They include Bobo, Dagbani, Lobi, Senari, and More (its chief member). ➤➤More; Niger-Congo.

VOT An abbreviation of **voice onset time**.

Votyak /'vəʊteɪak/ ➤Udmurt.

vowel (V) In phonetics, a speech sound produced by a relatively open configuration of the vocal tract, so that there is no audible friction, such as [a] or [i]; in phonology, a unit of the sound system which typically occupies the nucleus of a syllable, as in /kat/ and /si:t/. In both approaches, the term contrasts with **consonant** (as it does when it is used correspondingly with reference to the writing system). ➤➤consonant; diphthong; front sound; high vowel; monophthong; postvocalic; rounding; syllable; triphthong.

vowel gradation ➤ablaut.

vowel harmony ➤harmony.

vowel quadrilateral ➤cardinal vowels.

vowel shift A series of changes in vowel values in the history of a language. A famous example in English (the **English Vowel Shift** or **Great Vowel Shift**) took place soon after 1400, when the six long vowels began to change their values in a systematic way. Chaucer would have pronounced the vowel in the middle of the word *time* like that in modern *team*; *see* would have sounded more like *say*; *fame* like *farm* (without the *r*); *so* like *saw*; *do* like *doe*; and *now* like *noo*. The Great Vowel Shift resulted in a major barrier to intelligibility between Middle and Modern English. Since the 1980s, however, reanalysis of the textual evidence has suggested that several different factors may have been causing the sound changes of this period, and that the notion of a single interlinked 'shift' of vowels may be illusory. ➤➤sound change; vowel.

VP An abbreviation of **verb phrase**.

Vulgar Latin ➤Latin.

W

Wade–Giles ➤Chinese.

Wales ➤United Kingdom; Welsh.

Washoe /'wɒʃəʊ/ A female chimpanzee who was taught to use a selection of signs from American Sign Language in the late 1960s, as part of a series of experiments on the relationship between human language and animal communication. She acquired over 130 signs in just over four years, several of which she began to combine to express a small set of meaning relations. Several other chimpanzees have since been studied in similar ways. Explanations of the behaviour (whether the learning is essentially imitative or cognitive) have proved to be controversial. ➤language learning; *cartoon below.*

weak form ➤strong form.

'First the sign language. Then the knife and fork. Then the toothbrush. Don't you ever know when to stop?'

wellerism A kind of saying derived from a verbal mannerism used by Sam Weller in Dickens's *Pickwick Papers*. It takes the form of a comment followed by an analogy introduced by *as someone/something said* . . . , and generally making use of a pun: *I can see the point, as Macbeth said to his dagger*. ➤verbal play.

well-formed ➤grammatical.

Welsh A member of the Brythonic branch of the Celtic family of languages, spoken by *c*.500,000 people in Wales, where it has official status (along with English). Wales was monoglot until the 16th century, when the Act of Union with England (1536) led to a rapid decline in numbers of Welsh speakers. Revivals in the 18th and 19th centuries led to Welsh being taught in schools, and the present century has seen this revival continue on an unprecedented scale, with some evidence of a reduction in the rate of decline. The majority of first language users come from the north-west quarter of the principality, where some counties operate a bilingual language policy. A Welsh-speaking television channel was introduced in the 1970s. Literary remains date from the 6th century, and there was a renaissance in classical bardic verse in the 18th century, still influential in the literary sections of the modern eisteddfod. The language is written in the Roman alphabet. In 1865 a Welsh settlement was established in Patagonia (Argentina), which led to *c*.3000 speakers by 1900, though the language has all but disappeared today, under the influence of Spanish. ➤Celtic.

Wendish /'wendɪʃ/ ➤Sorbian.

Wernicke's aphasia /'vɜːnɪkə/ A type of aphasia which arises from damage to Wernicke's area, located in the upper part of the temporal lobe of the brain; named after German neurologist Karl Wernicke (1848–1905). It is characterized by difficulty in understanding, and by the use of speech which is fluent but empty of meaning. ➤aphasia; jargon; language areas.

West Atlantic A group of about 60 languages belonging to the Niger-Congo family, spoken in the extreme western part of the bulge of Africa, in Senegal, The Gambia, Guinea-Bissau, Guinea, Sierra Leone, and Liberia. The northern branch includes Dyola, Serer, Wolof, and Fula (*c*.15 million speakers, the most widespread member); the southern branch includes Kissi, Limba, and Temne. ➤Fula; Niger-Congo; Wolof.

Western Samoa ➤Samoa.

wh-form /'dʌblju: 'eɪtʃ fɔ:m/ A class of items in English, generally beginning with *wh*- (e.g. *why, what, where, how*) used in a variety of constructions. ***Wh*-questions** include such sentences as *Why did you do that?* or *What else did you buy?*. ***Wh*-relatives** are found in relative clauses, such as *The bus which was late*. . . ***Wh*-complements** are found in complement clauses, such as *I know what you want*. Several other types of construction also contain *wh*-forms, and any clause which is introduced by a *wh*-word is a ***wh*-clause**. ➤clause; complement; question; relative.

whisper Speech produced without vocal fold vibration. It will be heard in everyday communication in certain contexts (e.g. a conspiratorial whisper, a stage whisper), and is also a feature of certain kinds of voice disorder. ➤dysphonia; vocal folds; voice disorder.

whistled speech A stylized form of communication in which whistling substitutes for normal speech, usually between people who are at a distance from each other. It has been found in several Central and South American tribes, and occasionally elsewhere, and is normally used only by and between males. The whistling patterns closely correspond to the patterns of tone and rhythm in spoken language. Whistled dialogues tend to contain a small number of exchanges, and the utterances are short. ➤speech surrogate; tone.

White Russian ➤Belorussian.

whole word method ➤look-and-say.

Whorf, Benjamin Lee ➤Sapir–Whorf hypothesis.

Wolof /ˈwəʊlɒf/ A West Atlantic language spoken by over 2.6 million people as a first language chiefly in Senegal, with some in nearby Gambia. It is used as a lingua franca throughout the region, and is written in the Roman alphabet. ➤West Atlantic.

word The smallest unit of grammar which can stand alone as a complete utterance. It is a unit of expression in both spoken and written language, with several possible definitions. The **orthographic word** is the unit bounded by spaces in the written language. The **phonological word** is the corresponding unit for speech, bounded by (real or potential) pauses or juncture features. At a more abstract level, a word is a grammatical unit consisting of morphemes (minimally, one free morpheme) and functioning within phrases, clauses, and sentences. ➤lexeme; word class/game/order.

word blindness ➤dyslexia.

word chain A word game in which words are derived from other words through a series of steps. Many techniques have been proposed, such as changing a fixed number of letters or adding extra parts. A common type is to use overlapping elements in compounds, such as *EGGCUP–CUPCAKE–CAKESTAND–STANDPIPE* ... ➤word game.

word class A group of words which share the same syntactic and morphological properties; traditionally called a **part of speech**. The notion can also be included within the broader concept of **form class**. ➤adjective; adverb; article; class; classifier; conjunction; determiner; closed class; form 2; interjection; noun; participle; particle; preposition; verb.

word ending ➤inflection 1.

word-finding problem The inability to retrieve a desired word while speaking. While everyone has a word-finding difficulty, from time to time, the term is chiefly used for the severe difficulty in word retrieval encountered by many people suffering from aphasia. ➤aphasia.

word formation ➤affix; morphology.

word game Any form of game, puzzle, or competition in which an aspect of language provides the basis of the challenge. The task may involve knowledge of or ingenuity with spelling (e.g. Hangman, Scrabble), pronunciation (e.g. tongue twisters), vocabulary (e.g. crosswords), or any combination of linguistic features. Often, other forms of activity are incorporated, such as drawing (rebus) or mime (charades). ➤acrostic; anagram; crossword; doublet 2; grid game; lipogram; palindrome; pangram; rebus; syzygy; tongue twister; univocalic; verbal play; word chain; word square.

word order The sequential arrangement of clause elements or words in a sentence. In English, for example, the normal order of clause elements is Subject–Verb–Object, whereas in Welsh it is Verb–Subject–Object. The six possible options (SVO, VSO, VOS, etc.) provide the basis of an important system of classification in the syntactic typology of languages. At a lower level, many specific grammatical contrasts can be signalled by variations in word order, such as English statement vs. question (*It is raining* vs. *Is it raining?*). Some unusual orders are conventional, not allowing any contrast; an example is the inversion which follows such words as *hardly* and *barely* – *Hardly had she left when . . .* , where the alternative order **Hardly she had left* is ungrammatical. ➤inversion; order; typology of language.

word square A word game in which the aim is to complete a square of letters, using words of equal length, which read in horizontal, vertical, and occasionally diagonal directions. Usually the words read the same in each direction, but in a

```
P R E P A R E
R E M O D E L
E M U L A T E
P O L E M I C
A D A M A N T
R E T I N U E
E L E C T E D
```

A seven-letter **word square**.

'double word square' they read differently. Word squares using words of up to nine letters have been completed. ➤➤word game.

writing The process or result of recording spoken language using a system of visual marks on a surface. The concept includes the particular writing system (or **orthography**) which is available for a language, the choice and mastery of a particular medium of expression (usually handwriting or typing), and the product which emerges (the piece of writing, or composition). An additional sense reflects the profession of someone who writes creatively – a 'writer'. ➤➤alphabet; chirography; cursive; diplomatics; epigraph 1; graphology 1; letter; linear; orthography; paedography; paleography; shorthand; steganography; syllabary; technography.

wynn A letter ƿ used in Old English with a sound value corresponding to Modern English [w]. ➤➤English.

X

X-bar theory A system of generative linguistic analysis developed as an alternative to traditional accounts of phrase-structure and lexical categories. In this approach, the rules of phrase-structure grammar are more constrained, and more phrasal categories are recognized. In particular, within the noun phrase, intermediate categories are established larger than the noun but smaller than the phrase; each level of phrasal expansion is called an **X-bar**, normally written $\bar{X}$ or, for greater typographic ease, X'. ➤generative grammar; phrase-structure grammar.

xenoglossia /zenə'glɒsɪə/ The speaking of a foreign language which has not been previously learned or heard. Xenoglossic claims are sometimes made in the practice of Pentecostal Christianity, though more usually the ability to 'speak in tongues' is not considered to involve a real foreign language. The phenomenon awaits scientific attestation – difficult to achieve, given the problems of eliminating alternative explanations (such as a speaker having heard the foreign language before). ➤glossolalia.

x height In typography, the height of the small letter 'x'. The x-height of a lower-case alphabet is the height of the printing surface of a lower-case x – in other words, a lower-case letter without ascender or descender. The notion is useful in relating the heights of letters to each other. ➤ascender; typography.

Xhosa /'kɔːsə/ A Bantu language spoken by over 6.8 million people in the southeastern part of South Africa; also spelled **Xosa** and formerly known as **Kaffir**. It belongs to the Nguni sub-group of languages, and is written in the Roman alphabet. It is largely mutually intelligible with Zulu, but its speakers consider it to be a separate language. An interesting feature of Xhosa is its use of click consonants, borrowed from the Khoisan languages (one of which is used in local pronunciation of the name, the *Xh* representing a lateral click). It is one of the 11 official languages of South Africa. ➤Bantu; click; Khoisan; Zulu.

Xosa ➤Xhosa.

Y

Yakut /jə'kʊt/ A member of the Turkic branch of the Altaic family of languages, spoken by *c.*360,000 people in the Yakut region of north-east Siberia (where it is an official language). It is written in the Cyrillic alphabet. Because of its geographical isolation, the language displays many differences from other Turkic languages, and is classified as a separate branch of that group. ➤Turkic.

Yao ➤Miao-Yao.

Yemen (population in 1995 estimated at 13,510,000) The official language is Arabic, spoken by over 95% of the people. Other languages include Hindi and Somali. English is used for international purposes. ➤Arabic.

Yeniseyan /jenə'seɪen/ A family of languages generally placed within the Paleosiberian grouping, now represented by only one language, Ket (or Yenisey-Ostyak), spoken by less than 1000 people along the Yenisey River. It is written in the Cyrillic alphabet. Kott, Arin, and Assan, also in this family, are now extinct. ➤Paleosiberian.

yes/no **question** ➤question.

Yiddish A West Germanic language spoken by *c.*3 million people in central and eastern Europe, the USA (*c.*1.2 million), and Israel (*c.*215,000), by most as a second language; sometimes called **Judaeo-German**. It is identified with the Jewish people who emerged in central Europe from around the 9th century (the Ashkenazim), and is linguistically a mixture of Semitic and Germanic, with the addition of other features (Slavic, in particular) as it spread throughout eastern Europe. It has written records from the 12th century. The modern literary language is based on the Eastern Yiddish dialect, and is written in the Hebrew alphabet. It was proclaimed a national Jewish language in 1908, and has become a lingua franca for Jews all over the world. Yiddish literature has flourished in the present century, in both Europe and the USA, despite severe oppression by Germany in the 1940s and the Soviet Union in the 1950s, and in 1978 the American Yiddish writer, Isaac Bashevis Singer (1904–91) won the Nobel Prize for Literature. ➤Germanic; Hebrew.

yogh /jəʊk, jɒg/ A symbol ʒ used in Old and Middle English to represent a range of sounds, such as [g], [j], and [x]. Its values in Middle English, for example, included [j] (as in *year*) and [x] (as in the middle consonant of Scots *nicht*, English *night*). ➤English.

yo-he-ho theory The nickname of one of the speculative theories about the origins of language: it argues that speech arose because, as people worked together, their physical efforts produced communal, rhythmical grunts, which in due course developed into chants, and thus language. The main evidence is the use of universal prosodic features (but these provide only a small part of language structure). ➤➤origins of language.

Yoruba /ˈjɒrəbə/ A Kwa language spoken by *c*.20 million people, chiefly in southwest Nigeria (*c*.18.8 million), where it has official status, with some further speakers in Benin and Togo. There is a large oral literature of poetry, myths, and proverbs. The modern language is written in the Roman alphabet. Formerly classified as a Kwa language, it is now usually placed within Benue-Congo. ➤➤Benue-Congo; Kwa.

Yucatec /ˈjuːkətek/ ➤Mayan.

Yugoslavia (population in 1995 estimated at 10,494,000, for Serbia and Montenegro) The official language is Serbian (formerly considered a variety of Serbo-Croatian), spoken by *c*.75% of the population. Albanian (*c*.1.5 million) has official status in the autonomous province of Kosovo, and Hungarian (*c*.450,000) in Voivodina. There are also considerable numbers speaking Romanian (*c*.250,000), Romani (*c*.150,000), Slovak (*c*.100,000), Turkish (*c*.200,000), and other European languages. English is used for international trade and tourism. ➤➤Bosnian; Croatian; Macedonian; Serbian; Serbo-Croatian; Slovene.

Yukaghir /juːkəˈgɪə/ A family of languages generally placed within the Paleosiberian grouping, now represented by only one language, Yukaghir (or Odul), spoken probably by less than 200 people in the Yakut region of north-east Siberia. It is written in the Cyrillic alphabet. Omok and Chuvan, also in this family, are now extinct. ➤➤Paleosiberian.

Yupik /ˈjuːpɪk/ ➤Eskimo.

Yurak /jəˈrak/ ➤Nenets.

Z

Zaire ►Congo, Democratic Republic of.

Zambia (population in 1995 estimated at 9,846,000) The official language is English. There are *c*.35 other languages, notably Bemba (spoken by *c*.25% of the population), Tonga (*c*.12%), and Nyanja (*c*.12%). A Xhosa-based pidgin, Fanagalo, is widely used in towns and mining areas as a lingua franca, and there is also a Swahili-based pidgin, Settla. English is used for international purposes. ►English; lingua franca; pidgin.

zero An abstract unit with no physical realization in the stream of speech; also called a **null element**. The term is commonly used for the absence of a morpheme in contexts where one would normally occur; for example, in English a **zero article** can be identified where there is no definite or indefinite article before a noun. A **zero morph** is sometimes proposed to handle singular/plural alternations in such nouns as *sheep*, where no change is involved. ►infinitive; morpheme.

zero infinitive ►infinitive.

zeugma /'zjuːɡmə/ A type of figurative language in which a word is made to govern two other elements in such a way that a different sense relationship is obtained in each case. The effect is usually semantically incongruous. An example is *They arrived in a bus and a bad mood*. The term is from Greek, where it meant a 'yoking' or 'bringing together'. ►figurative language.

Zimbabwe (population in 1995 estimated at 11,365,000) The official language is English. There are *c*.20 other languages, notably Shona (spoken by over half the population) and Ndebele (*c*.13%). English is used for international purposes. ►English.

zoösemiotics /zəʊəʊsemiːˈɒtɪks/ The study of the properties of animal communication. The subject developed as part of a comparative zoological approach to communication, with the initial aim of identifying the main points of connection between language and other communicative systems. Several 'design features' of communication were investigated, such as displacement, productivity, and duality of structure. The subject later became a domain in its own right, as a branch of semiotics investigating the diverse methods (e.g. movement, colour, sound, touch, smell) used as communication within different species, such as the 'dancing' of honey bees, the courtship rituals of herring gulls, and the whistle patterns of dolphins.

'Well, dialect jokes, mainly – corgis, alsatians, beagles.'

➤discrete; displacement; duality of structure; feedback 1; interchangeability; prevarication; productivity; semiotics.

Zulu A Bantu language spoken by over 9 million people, chiefly (*c*.8.8 million) in South Africa, especially in the part of Natal formerly known as Zululand (now KwaZulu), with some in nearby countries. It belongs to the Nguni sub-group of languages, and is largely mutually intelligible with Xhosa, but is considered by its speakers to be a separate language. Like Xhosa, it uses click sounds borrowed from the neighbouring Khoisan languages, and its vocabulary shows considerable influence from Afrikaans and English. It is one of the 11 official languages of South Africa, and is written in the Roman alphabet. ➤Bantu; click; Xhosa.

Zyryan /ˈzɪrɪən/ ➤Komi.

INDEX OF LANGUAGES

This index is a listing of all the locations where names of individual languages or varieties are referred to in the book, whether they are treated as separate entries or mentioned within entries. Variant forms and spellings are included. It does not include the names of families of languages, nor of scripts. The list under English does not include those entries where English has been used as the language of illustration. The arrangement of the index is letter-by-letter.

Esperanto: artificial language; Esperanto; Ido; language
Estonian: Estonia; Estonian; Finland; Finno-Ugric; Sweden
Ethiopic: Ethiopia
Etruscan: alphabet; Etruscan
Evenki: Evenki; Manchu-Tungus
Ewe: Ewe; Ghana; Togo
Extramaduran: Spain
Faeroese: Danish; Denmark; Faeroese; Germanic; Scandinavian
Faliscan: Italic
Fanagalo: Zambia
Fang: Cameroon; Equatorial Guinea; Gabon
Fante: Akan
Faroese: Faeroese
Farsi: Bahrain; Iran; Oman; Persian; Qatar; Tadzhikistan; United Arab Emirates
Fijian: Fiji; Fijian; New Zealand
Filipino: Pilipino
Finnish: alphabet; Estonia; Finland; Finnish; Finno-Ugric; Mordvin; Norway; phonetic spelling; Sweden; Swedish
Flemish: Belgium; Dutch; Germanic
Fon: Benin
Fox: Algonkian
Franglais: Franglais
French: Académie française; accent; acute accent; address, forms of; Africa; Algeria; Andorra; auxiliary language; Belgium; Benin; borrowing; Burkina Faso; Burundi; Cambodia; Canada; cedilla; Central African Republic; Chad; circumflex; clitic; cognate; Comoros; concord; conditional; Congo; Congo, Democratic Republic of; contraction; Corsican; Côte d'Ivoire; dental; diglossia; discontinuous construction; Djibouti; double

negative; Dutch; elision; enjambement; false friends; France; Franglais; French; French Guinea; French Polynesia; future tense; Gabon; gender; grave accent; Guadeloupe; Guinea; Haiti; immersion; international language; isochrony; Italy; Kwa; Laos; Lebanon; liaison; linking; Luxembourg; Madagascar; Malagasy; Mali; Maltese; Martinique; Mauritania; Mauritius; minimal free form; Monaco; Morocco; Mozambique; national language; New Caledonia; Niger; palato-alveolar; paronymy; particle; past anterior; past historic; past tense; Portugal; Puerto Rico; Réunion; Rhaetian; Romance; Romania; Rwanda; Saint Pierre and Miquelon; sandhi; Sango; second language; Senegal; Seychelles; sign; Spain; statistical linguistics; Switzerland; Syria; Togo; transfer; translation; trigraph; Tunisia; T/V forms; United Kingdom; United States of America; uvular; Vanuatu; Vietnam
French, creole: Dominica; Dominican Republic; French; French Guinea; Guadeloupe; Haiti; Martinique; Mauritius; Réunion; Romance; Saint Lucia; Seychelles; Trinidad and Tobago; United States of America
Frisian: Frisian; Germanic; Germany; Netherlands, The
Friulian: Italy; Rhaetian
Ful: Fula; Gambia, The
Fula: Fula; Guinea; West Atlantic
Fulacunda: Guinea-Bissau; Senegal
Fulani: Fula
Fulfulde: Benin; Burkina Faso;

Lao: Lao; Laos; Tai
Laotian: Lao; Laos
Lappish: Finland; Finno-Ugric; Same; Sweden
Latin: ablative case; absolute construction; affix; alphabet; analects; assimilation; caesura; case; centum language; chronogram; classical language; cognate; concord; conjugation; copula; cuneiform; dative case; dead language; declension; deponent verb; dissimilation; epenthesis; epicene; extension; government; grammar–translation method; Grimm's law; hybrid; imperative; imperfect; impersonal; inceptive; indicative; Glosa; Italic; Latin; Latinate; macaronic; macron; majuscule; paleography; paronymy; participle; past tense; principal parts; prose; rhythm; Romance; Sanskrit; Sardinian; stet; syncope; typology of language; uncial; Vatican City
Latvian: Baltic; Latvia; Latvian; Sweden
Laz: Kartvelian
Lettish: Latvian
Lëtzebuergesch: Belgium; Lëtzebuergesch; Luxembourg
Lezghian: Lezghian; Nakho-Dagestanian
Libyan, Old: Berber
Ligurian: Monaco
Limba: West Atlantic
Lingala: Congo; Congo, Democratic Republic of
Lithuanian: Baltic; Lithuania; Lithuanian
Lobi: Burkina Faso; Voltaic
Lombard: Italy
Lomwe: Malawi; Mozambique
Low Saxon: Netherlands, The

Lü: Myanmar
Luba: Congo, Democratic Republic of
Luganda: Uganda
Lugbara: Congo, Democratic Republic of
Luo: Kenya; Luo; Nilo-Saharan; Nilotic
Luorawetlan: Paleosiberian
Luri: Iran
Lusatian: Sorbian
Luwian: Anatolian
Luxembourgeois: Lëtzebuergesch
Luxembourgish: Lëtzebuergesch
Luya: Kenya
Lycian: Anatolian
Lydian: Anatolian
Maay: Somalia
Maba: Maban
Mabuyag: Australian
Macanese: Hong Kong; Macao
Macedonian: Albania; Bulgaria; Bulgarian; Greece; Macedonia; Macedonian; Slavic
Madura: Madurese
Madurese: Indonesia; Madurese
Magahi: Bihari
Magar: Nepal
Magyar: Hungarian
Mahri: Oman
Maithili: Bilhari; Nepal
Makonde: Tanzania
Makua: Makua; Malawi; Mozambique
Malagasy: Comoros; Madagascar; Malagasy
Malay; Brunei; Indonesia; Malay; Malaysia; Netherlands, The; Singapore; Sri Lanka; Thailand
Malayalam: Dravidian; India; Malayalam; Singapore
Maldivian: Indo-Aryan; Maldives; Maldivian
Malinke: Gambia, The; Mali; Malinke; Mande; Senegal
Maltese: Malta; Maltese

Malto: Dravidian
Mam: Guatemala; Mayan
Manchu: Manchu; Manchu-Tungus
Mandarin Chinese: China; Chinese;
Taiwan
Mandingo: Malinke
Mandinka: Gambia, The;
Guinea-Bissau
Mandyak: Cape Verde; Guinea-Bissau
Maninka: Guinea; Malinke
Mansi; Finno-Ugric
Manx: Celtic; dead language; Manx;
United Kingdom
Mao: Koman
Maori: Cook Islands; Maori; New
Zealand
Mapuche: Penutian
Mapudungan: Chile; Penutian
Marathi: India; Indo-Aryan; Marathi
Marba: Chad
Mari: Finno-Ugric; Mari; Russia
Marquesan: French Polynesia
Marwari: Rajasthani
Marshallese: Marshall Islands
Masai: Masai; Nilo-Hamitic;
Nilo-Saharan
Masalit: Maban
Mataco: Argentina; Gê-Pano-Carib
Maya: Mayan; Mexico; Penutian
Mbai: Chad
Mbundu: Angola
Mende: Mande; Mende; Sierra Leone
Mennonite German: German,
Mennonite
Miao: China; Laos; Miao-Yao
Micmac: Algonkian
Mimi: Maban
Minchia: China
Mingrelian: Kartvelian
Min Nan: China; Chinese
Minoan: Linear A
Min Pei: China; Chinese; Taiwan;
Thailand

Mishnaic Hebrew: Hebrew
Mixteco: Mexico; Oto-Manguean
Moabite: Moabite
Mohawk: Macro-Siouan
Mohican: Algonkian
Moksha: Mordvin
Moldavian: Moldavian; Moldova
Molisano: Italy
Mon: Mon; Mon-Khmer
Mongo: Congo, Democratic Republic
of
Mongol: China; Kyrgyzstan; Mongol;
Mongolia; Mongolian
Mòòré: More
Mordvin: Finno-Ugric; Mordvin;
Russia
More: Burkina Faso; Ghana; More;
Voltaic
Morisyen: Mauritius
Mosi: Chad
Mossi: More
Motu: Motu
Mubi: Chadic
Mundari: Munda
Muong: Vietnam
Murmi: Nepal
Muskogee: Algonkian
Mycenaean Greek: Greek; syllabary
Myene: Gabon
Nahua: Nahuatl
Nahuatl: Aztec-Tanoan; Mexico
Nanai: Manchu-Tungus
Nandi: Nandi; Nilo-Hamitic;
Nilo-Saharan; Nilotic
Nauruan: Nauru
Navajo: Na-Dene
Ndebele: Ndebele; South Africa;
Zimbabwe
Neapolitan: Italy
Nenets: Nenets; Samoyedic
Nepali: Bhutan; Nepal; Nepali; Pahari
Newari: Nepal
Ngala: Congo, Democratic Republic of

Ngambai: Hausa
Nganasan: Samoyedic
Ngbaka: Adamawa-Ubangi
Ngbandi: Central African Republic;
  Sango
Nguni: Xhosa; Zulu
Nicobarese: Mon-Khmer; Nicobarese
Nigerian Pidgin English: Nigeria
Niuean: New Zealand; Niue
Nivkhi: Gilyak
Nkole: Uganda
Norn: Scandinavian
Norse, Old: Danish; Germanic;
  Norwegian; Scandinavian; Swedish
Norwegian: Germanic; Norway;
  Norwegian; Scandinavian
Novial: artificial language; Novial
Nuba: Sudan
Nubian: Egypt; Nubian
Nuer: Nilotic; Nuer; Sudan
Nung: Tai
Nupe: Benue-Congo
Nyamwezi: Tanzania
Nyanja: Malawi; Mozambique;
  Nyanja; Zambia
Nyankore: Uganda
Nynorsk: Norwegian
Occidental: Novial
Occitan: France; Italy; Occitan;
  Romance
Odul: Yukaghir
Ojibwa: Algonkian; Canada
Okanogan: Salish
Old Church Slavonic: Slavonic
Old English: English, Old
Old Norse: Scandinavian
Omok: Yukaghir
Oriya: India; Indo-Aryan; Oriya
Oromo: Ethiopia; Oromo
Oscan: Italic
Ossetic: Georgia; Iranian; Ossetic;
  Russia
Ostrogothic: Gothic

Ostyak: Khanty
Otomí: Mexico; Oto-Manguean
Páez: Macro-Chibchan
Pahlavi: Persian
Paiute: Aztec-Tanoan
Pakhto: Pashto
Palaic: Anatolian
Palauan: Austronesian; Belau
Pali: Pali
Panjabi: community language; India;
  Indo-Aryan; Pakistan; Panjabi;
  postposition; Singapore; United
  Kingdom
Papago-Pima: Aztec-Tanoan
Papiamentu: Netherlands, The;
  Netherlands Antilles; Papiamentu;
  US Virgin Islands
Parauk: Myanmar
Pashayi: Afghanistan
Pashto: Afghanistan; Iranian;
  Pakistan; Pashto; Persian;
  Tadzhikistan; United Arab Emirates
Patois: French Guinea; Patwa
Pattani Malay: Malay
Patwa: Dominica; Grenada;
  Guadeloupe; Jamaica; Martinique;
  Patwa; Saint Lucia
Paumotu: French Polynesia
Pennsylvanian Dutch: German
Pennsylvanian German: German
Persian: Caucasian; Iran; Iranian;
  Iraq; Oman; Persian; Urdu
Phoenician: alphabet; Phoenician
Phrygian: Anatolian
Pictish: ogham
Piemontese: Italy
Pijin: Solomon Islands
Pilipino: Philippines, The; Pilipino
Pitcairn-Norfolk: Norfolk Island
Polabian: Lekhitic
Police Motu: Motu
PoliceSpeak: Seaspeak
Polish: acute accent; alveo-palatal;

Sandawe: Khoisan

Sango: Adamawa-Ubangi; Central African Republic; Chad; Congo; Sango

Sanskrit: classical language; Devanagari; Grimm's law; India; Indo-Aryan; Indo-European; Pali; Panini; Sanskrit; Tamil

Santali: Bangladesh; Munda

Sara: Chad

Saramaccan: Suriname

Sardinian: Italian; Italy; Romance; Sardinian

Saxon, Low: Netherlands, The

Scottish Gaelic: Celtic; Scottish Gaelic; United Kingdom

Scouse: Scouse

Sea Islands Creole English: Sea Islands Creole English; United States of America

Selkup: Samoyedic

Senari: Voltaic

Senufo: Côte d'Ivoire; Mali

Serbian: Cyrillic; Serbian; Serbo-Croatian; Slavic; Yugoslavia

Serbo-Croat: Serbo-Croatian

Serbo-Croatian: accent; Austria; Bosnia and Herzegovina; Croatia; Croatian; Hungary; Macedonia; Serbo-Croatian; Slavic; Slovene; Slovenia; Yugoslavia

Serer: Senegal; West Atlantic

Sesotho: Lesotho; Sotho; South Africa

Sesotho sa Leboa: Sotho; South Africa

Setswana: South Africa; Tswana

Settla: Zambia

Shan: Myanmar; Tai

Shawnee: Algonkian

Sheldru: Sheldru

Shelta: Sheldru

Shluh: Berber

Shona: Botswana; Mozambique; Shona; Zimbabwe

Shoshone: Aztec-Tanoan

Siamese: Thai

Sicilian: Italy

Sindhi: India; Indo-Aryan; Pakistan; Sindhi

Singhalese: Sinhala

Sinhala: Sinhala; Sri Lanka; United Arab Emirates

Sinhalese: Indo-Aryan; Maldives; Sinhala

Sioux: Macro-Siouan

Slavonic, Old Church: Czech; Slavic

Slovak: Croatia; Czech; Polish; Slavic; Slovak; Yugoslavia

Slovene: Austria; Hungary; Italy; Slavic; Slovene; Slovenia

Slovenian: Slovene

Slovincian: Lekhitic

Solomon Islands Pidgin: Solomon Islands

Somali: Cushitic; Djibouti; Ethiopia; Somali; Somalia; United Arab Emirates; Yemen

Songai: Songhai

Songe: Congo, Democratic Republic of

Songhai: Mali; Nilo-Saharan; Songhai

Soninke: Mali; Senegal

Sorbian: Austria; Germany; Polish; Slavic; Sorbian

Sotho: Lesotho; Sotho

Spanglish: Spanish

Spanish: acute accent; alphabet; Andorra; Argentina; auxiliary language; Belgium; Belize; Bolivia; Canary Islands; Catalan; Chile; code mixing; cognate; Colombia; Costa Rica; Cuba; Dominican Republic; Ecuador; El Salvador; epenthesis; Equatorial Guinea; Gibraltar; Guaraní; Guatemala; Guinea; Honduras; international language;

ILLUSTRATIONS ACKNOWLEDGEMENTS

The author and publisher are grateful to the following for permission to include copyright material in this volume on the pages specified below.

Edward Arnold (Publishers) Ltd: from D. Crystal, *Introduction to Language Pathology* (1981). Used with permission: p 28.

Ray L. Birdwhistell: from *Kinesics and Context* (Allen Lane 1971). © R.L. Birdwhistell 1971. Used by permission of the author: p. 180.

Blackwell Publishers: from F. Coulmas, *The Writing Systems of the World*; from D. Crystal, *Dictionary of Linguistics & Phonetics*; and extract from Blackwell proof correction list. Used with permission: pp. 54, 70, 77, 86, 148, 177, 276.

Cambridge University Press: from D.B. Fry, *The Physics of Speech* (1979); from Chambers & Trudgill, *Dialectology* (1980). Used with permission: pp. 23, 81, 171.

The Commission of the European Communities: p. 337.

Croom Helm Ltd: from Sanderson, *Linguistic Atlas of England* (1978): p. 88.

Gerald Duckworth & Co Ltd: from Eric Singer, *A Manual of Graphology* (1969): p. 140.

Encyclopaedia Britannica International Ltd: p. 306.

International Phonetic Association: *International Phonetic Alphabet* (revised to 1989). Used with permission: p. 167.

Punch: cartoons reproduced by kind permission of *Punch*: pp. 6, 17, 39, 44, 63, 97, 122, 147, 164, 197, 213, 234, 243, 270, 280, 311, 338, 349, 364, 373.

Scientific American Inc: after N. Geschwind, 'Specializations of the human brain', September 1979, © 1979 Scientific American Inc. All rights reserved; from 'The Search for extraterrestrial intelligence' by Carl Sagan and F. Drake, May 1975, © 1975 Scientific American Inc. All rights reserved. Used with permission: pp. 186, 263.

Studentlitteratur: after A. Zettersten, *A Statistical Study of the Graphic System of Present-Day American English* (1969). Used with permission: p. 320.

EJDC (formerly *British Journal of Disorders of Communication*); from Hardcastle & Morgan, *BJDC*, 1982, p. 101.